PENGUIN BOOKS
Heroes

Stephen Fry is an award-winning comedian, actor, presenter and director. He rose to fame alongside Hugh Laurie in *A Bit of Fry and Laurie* (which he co-wrote with Laurie) and *Jeeves and Wooster*, and was unforgettable as General Melchett in *Blackadder*. He has hosted over 180 episodes of *QI*, and has narrated all seven of the Harry Potter novels for the audiobook recordings. He is the bestselling author of four novels – *The Stars' Tennis Balls*, *Making History*, *The Hippopotamus* and *The Liar* – as well as three volumes of autobiography – *Moab is My Washpot*, *The Fry Chronicles* and *More Fool Me*. *Mythos*, his retelling of the Greek myths, is a *Sunday Times* bestseller.

HEROES

Volume II of Mythos

STEPHEN FRY

PENGUIN BOOKS

PENGUIN BOOKS

UK | USA | Canada | Ireland | Australia
India | New Zealand | South Africa

Penguin Books is part of the Penguin Random House group of companies
whose addresses can be found at global.penguinrandomhouse.com

Penguin
Random House
UK

First published by Michael Joseph 2018
Published in Penguin Books 2019

016

Copyright © Stephen Fry, 2018

For picture credits see page 458

The moral right of the author has been asserted

Set in 12.15/14.42 pt Garamond MT Std
Typeset by Penguin Books
Printed and bound in Great Britain by Clays Ltd, Elcograf S.p.A.

A CIP catalogue record for this book is available from the British Library

ISBN: 978–1–405–94036–8

www.greenpenguin.co.uk

To all the heroes we have never heard of.

Perhaps you are one.

CONTENTS

FOREWORD

Heroes can be regarded as a continuation to my book *Mythos*, which told the story of the beginning of everything, the birth of the Titans and gods and the creation of mankind. You don't need to have read *Mythos* to follow – and I hope enjoy – this book, but plenty of footnotes will point you, by paperback page number, to stories, characters and mythical events that were covered in *Mythos* and which can be encountered there in fuller detail. Some people find footnotes a distraction, but I have been told that plenty of readers enjoyed them last time round, so I hope you will navigate them with pleasure as and when the mood takes you.

I know how off-putting for some Greek names can be – all those Ys, Ks and PHs. Where possible I have suggested the easiest way for our English-speaking mouths to form them. Modern Greeks will be astonished by what we do to their wonderful names, and German, French, American and other readers – who have their own ways with Ancient Greek – will wonder at some of my suggestions. But that is all they are, suggestions . . . whether you like to say Eddipus or Eedipus, Epi*daur*us or E*bee*thavros, Philo*c*tetes or Philo*cteet*ees, the characters and stories remain the same.

Stephen Fry

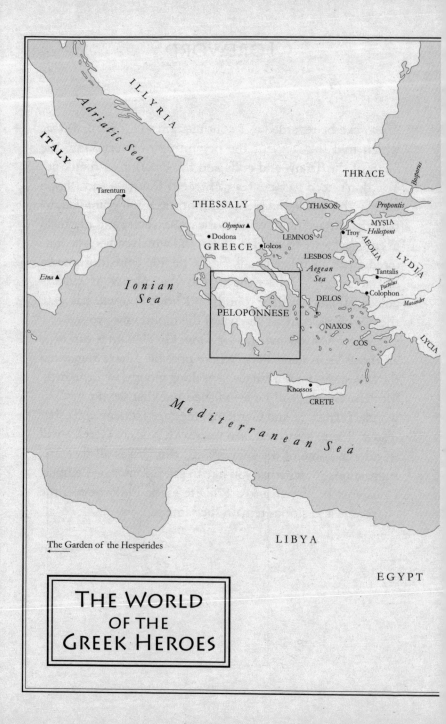

ILLYRIA

Adriatic Sea

ITALY

Tarentum

Etna ▲

THESSALY

Olympus ▲
● Dodona
GREECE ●Iolcos

Ionian
Sea

PELOPONNESE

THRACE

THASOS

Propontis

MYSIA
● Troy Hellespont
LEMNOS

LESBOS

Aegean
Sea

DELOS

NAXOS

COS

Bosporus

AEOLIA
LYDIA

Tantalis
●
Pactolus
●Colophon
Maeander

LYCIA

Mediterranean Sea

Knossos●
CRETE

LIBYA

The Garden of the Hesperides

EGYPT

THE WORLD
OF THE
GREEK HEROES

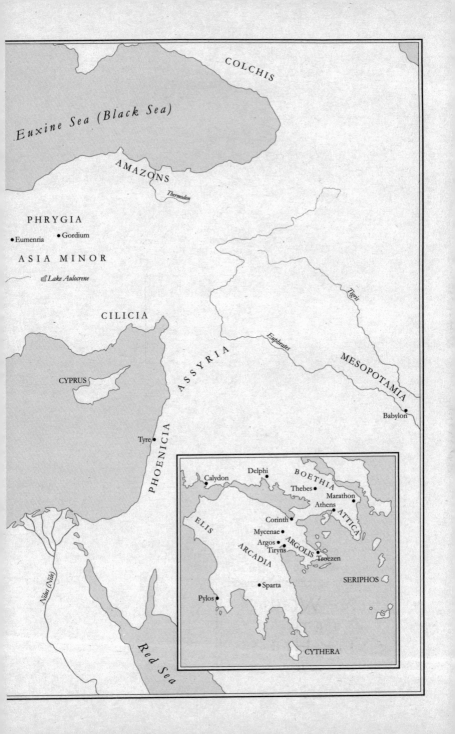

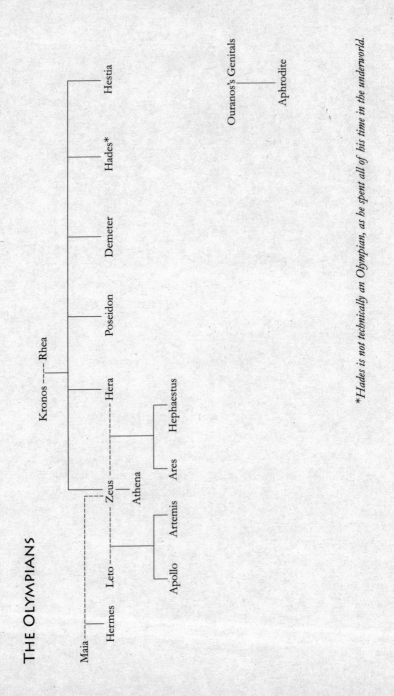

THE OLYMPIANS

Kronos ---- Rhea

Hestia
Hades*
Demeter
Poseidon
Hera
Zeus

Maia ---- Hermes

Leto

Apollo
Artemis

Athena

Ares
Hephaestus

Ouranos's Genitals

Aphrodite

*Hades is not technically an Olympian, as he spent all of his time in the underworld.

INTRODUCTION

ZEUS sits on his throne. He rules the sky and the world. His sister-wife HERA rules him. Duties and domains in the mortal sphere are parcelled out to his family, the other ten Olympian gods. In the early days of gods and men, the divine trod the earth with mortals, befriended them, ravished them, coupled with them, punished them, tormented them, transformed them into flowers, trees, birds and bugs and in all ways interacted, intersected, intertwined, interbred, interpenetrated and interfered with us. But over time, as age has succeeded age and humankind has grown and prospered, the intensity of these interrelations has slowly diminished.

In the age we have entered now, the gods are still very much around, favouring, disfavouring, directing and disturbing, but PROMETHEUS's gift of fire has given humankind the ability to run its own affairs, build up its distinct city states, kingdoms and dynasties. The fire is real and hot in the world and has given mankind the power to smelt, forge, fabricate and make, but it is an inner fire too; thanks to Prometheus we are now endowed with the divine spark, the creative fire, the consciousness that once belonged only to gods.

The Golden Age has become an Age of Heroes – men and women who grasp their destinies, use their human qualities of courage, cunning, ambition, speed and strength to perform astonishing deeds, vanquish terrible monsters and establish great cultures and lineages that change the world. The divine fire stolen from heaven by their champion

Prometheus burns within them. They fear, respect and worship their parental gods, but somewhere inside they know they are a match for them. Humanity has entered its teenage years.

Prometheus himself – the Titan who made us, befriended us and championed us – continues to endure his terrible punishment: shackled to the side of a mountain he is visited each day by a bird of prey that soars down out of the sun to tear open his side, pull out his liver and eat it before his very eyes. Since he is immortal the liver regenerates overnight, only for the torment to repeat the next day. And the next.

Prometheus, whose name means Forethought, has prophesied that now fire is in the world of man, the days of the gods are numbered. Zeus's rage at his friend's disobedience derives as much from a deep-buried but persistent fear that man will outgrow the gods as from his deep sense of hurt and betrayal.

Prometheus has also seen that the time will come when he will be released. A mortal human hero will arrive at the mountain, shatter his manacles and set the Titan free. Together they will save the Olympians.

But why should the gods need saving?

For hundreds of generations a deep resentment has smouldered beneath the earth. When KRONOS the Titan castrated his father, the primordial sky god OURANOS, and hurled his genitals across Greece, a race of giants sprang from where the drops of blood and seed fell. These 'chthonic' beings, these creatures sprung from the earth, believe that the time will come when they can wrest power from the arrogant upstart children of Kronos, the Olympian gods. The giants await the day when they can rise up to conquer Olympus and begin their own rule.

Prometheus squints into the sun and awaits his moment too.

Mankind, meanwhile, gets on with the mortal business of striving, toiling, living, loving and dying in a world still populated with more or less benevolent nymphs, fauns, satyrs and other spirits of the seas, rivers, mountains, meadows, forests and fields, but bristling too with its share of serpents and dragons – many of them the descendants of the primordial GAIA, the earth goddess and TARTARUS, god of the depths beneath the earth. Their offspring, the monstrous ECHIDNA and TYPHON, have spawned a multitude of venomous and mutant creatures that ravage the countryside and oceans that humans are trying to tame.

To survive in such a world, mortals have felt the need to supplicate and submit themselves to the gods, to sacrifice to them and flatter them with praise and prayer. But some men and women are beginning to rely on their own resources of fortitude and wit. These are the men and women who – either with or without the help of the gods – will dare to make the world safe for humans to flourish. These are the heroes.

HERA'S DREAM

Breakfast on Mount Olympus. Zeus sits at one end of a long stone table, sipping his nectar and considering the day ahead. One by one the other Olympian gods and goddesses drift in to take their seats. At last Hera enters and takes her place at the opposite end from her husband. Her face is flushed, her hair discomposed. Zeus glances up in some surprise.

'In all the years I have known you, you have never once been late for breakfast. Not once.'

'No, indeed,' says Hera. 'Accept my apologies, but I slept badly and feel unsettled. I had a disturbing dream last night. Most disturbing. Would you like to hear it?'

'Absolutely,' lies Zeus, who has, in common with us all, a horror of hearing the details of anyone else's dreams.

'I dreamt that we were under attack,' Hera says. 'Here on Olympus. The giants rose up, climbed the mountain and they assaulted us.'

'My, my . . .'

'But it was *serious*, Zeus. The whole race of them streamed up and attacked us. And your thunderbolts glanced as harmlessly off them as if they were pine needles. The giants' leader, the largest and strongest, came for me personally and tried to . . . to . . . impose himself.'

'Dear me, how very upsetting,' says Zeus. 'But it was after all only a dream.'

'Was it though? Was it? It was all so clear. It had more the feeling of a *vision*. A prophecy, perhaps. I have had them before. You know I have.'

This was true. Hera's role as goddess of matrimony, family, decorum and good order made it easy to forget that she was also powerfully endowed with insight.

'How did it all end?'

'Strangely. We were saved by your friend Prometheus and . . .'

'He is *not* my friend,' snaps Zeus. Any mention of Prometheus is barred on Olympus. To Zeus the sound of his once dear friend's name is like lemon juice on a cut.

'If you say so, my dear, I am merely telling you what I dreamed, what I saw. You know, the strange thing is that Prometheus had with him a mortal man. And it was this human that pulled the giant off me, threw him down from Olympus and saved us all.'

'A man, you say?'

'Yes. A human. A mortal hero. And in my dream it was clear to me, I am not sure how or why, but it was clear, so clear, that this man was descended from the line of Perseus.'

'Perseus, you say?'

'Perseus. There could be no doubt about it. The nectar is at your elbow, my dear . . .'

Zeus passes the jar down the table.

Perseus.

There's a name he hasn't heard for a while.

Perseus . . .

PERSEUS

The Shower of Gold

ACRISIUS, ruler of Argos*, having produced no male heir to his kingdom, sought advice from the oracle at Delphi as to how and when he might expect one. The priestess's reply was disturbing:

King Acrisius will have no sons, but his grandson will kill him.

Acrisius loved his daughter and only child DANAË,† but he loved life more. It was clear from the oracle that he should do everything in his power to prevent any male of breeding age from getting close to her. To this end he ordered the construction of a bronze chamber beneath the palace. Locked up in this gleaming, impregnable prison, Danaë was given as many creature comforts and as much feminine company as she asked for. After all, Acrisius told himself, he was not flint-hearted.‡

He had sealed the bronze chamber against all invaders, but he had reckoned without the lusts of the all-seeing, all-cunning Zeus, whose eye had fallen on Danaë and who was even now considering how he might penetrate this sealed

---

* One of the most important of all Greek city states. The name given to its people, the Argives, was often used by Homer simply to mean 'Greek'. Philip II and his son Alexander the Great, although Macedonian, were said to originate from Argos.
† Often rendered as Danaë, so it should, I suppose, be pronounced 'Danaye'.
‡ The Roman poet Horace, in his *Odes*, changed the bronze room to a bronze tower, and thenceforward it has often been portrayed as just such a fairytale Rapunzel-like minaret. The earlier sources insist, however, that it was a room, with slits in the roof to let in light and air.

chamber and take his pleasure. He liked a challenge. In his long, amorous career the King of the Gods had transformed himself into all kinds of exotic entities in his pursuit of desirable females and, from time to time, males. It was clear to him that to conquer Danaë he had to come up with something better than the usual bulls, bears, boars, stallions, eagles, stags and lions. Something a little more outré was required . . .

A shower of golden rain streamed down through the narrow slit of the skylight one night, poured itself into Danaë's lap and penetrated her.* It may have been an unorthodox form of coition, but Danaë became pregnant and in due time, with the help of her loyal female attendants, she gave birth to a healthy mortal boy, whom she named PERSEUS.

Along with the mortal healthiness of Perseus came a pair of very serviceable lungs, and try as they might neither Danaë nor her aides could stifle the wails and cries of the baby which made their way through the bronze walls of her prison all the way to the ears of her father two floors above.

His rage when confronted with the sight of his grandson was terrible to behold.

'Who dared break into your chamber? Tell me his name and I shall have him gelded, tortured and strangled with his own intestines.'

'Father, I believe it was the King of Heaven himself who came to me.'

'You are telling me – will someone please shut that baby up! – that it was Zeus?'

'Father, I cannot lie, it was.'

'A likely story. It was the brother of one of these damned maidservants of yours, wasn't it?'

---

* We do not know whether or not Danaë enjoyed the experience. There are those, it is said, for whom the prospect of a golden shower is actually rather . . . well . . . quite.

'No, father, it was as I said. Zeus.'

'If that brat doesn't stop screaming I'll smother him with this cushion.'

'He's just hungry,' said Danaë, putting Perseus to her breast.

Acrisius thought furiously. His threat with the cushion notwithstanding, he knew that there could be no greater crime than a blood killing. The murder of one's kin would provoke the Furies to rise up from the underworld and pursue him to the ends of the earth, scourging him with their iron whips until the very skin was flayed from his body. They wouldn't leave off until he was raving mad. Yet the oracle's prophecy meant that he could not suffer this grandson to live. Perhaps . . .

The next night, out of sight of gossiping townspeople, Acrisius had Danaë and the infant Perseus shut up in a wooden chest. His soldiers nailed down the lid and hurled the chest over the cliffs and into the sea.

'There,' said Acrisius, dusting off his hands as if to clear himself of all responsibility. 'If they perish, as perish they surely will, none can say that I was the direct cause. It will be the fault of the sea, the rocks and the sharks. It will be the fault of the gods. Nothing to do with me.'

With these weasel words of comfort, King Acrisius watched the chest bob out of sight.

THE WOODEN CHEST

Tossed in the wild waves of the sea, the wooden box bounced and buffeted its way from island to island and coast to coast, neither breaking up on the rocks, nor beaching safely on the soft sands.

Inside the darkness of the chest Danaë suckled her child and waited for the end to come. On the second day of their heaving, pitching voyage she felt a great lurch and then a terrible bang. After a few moments of stillness she heard the lid of the box creak and shift. All at once daylight poured in, accompanied by a strong smell of fish and the cry of gulls.

'Well, well,' said a friendly voice. 'Here's a catch!'

They had been caught in a fisherman's nets. The owner of the voice extended a strong hand to help Danaë out of the chest.

'Don't be frightened,' he said, though in truth he was the one who felt fear. What could all this portend? 'My name is Dictys* and these are my crewmen. We mean you no harm.'

The other fishermen crowded around, smiling shyly, but Dictys pushed them away. 'Let the lady breathe. Can't you see she's worn out? Some bread and wine.'

Two days later they landed on Dictys's home island of Seriphos. He took Danaë and Perseus to his small cottage behind the dunes.

'My wife died giving birth to a boy, so perhaps Poseidon has sent you to take their place – not that I mean . . .' he added in hasty confusion, 'I would not, of course, expect . . . I make no demands on you as a . . .'

Danaë laughed. The atmosphere of unaffected kindness and simplicity was just what she needed for rearing her child. Guileless amiability had been in short supply in her life. 'You are too kind,' she said. 'We accept your offer, don't we, Perseus?'

'Yes, mother, whatever you say.'

No, this is not the Miracle of the Talking Baby. Seventeen years have now passed on Seriphos. Perseus has grown into

---

* Which simply means 'net'.

a fine, strong young man. He is, thanks to his adopted father Dictys, a confident and skilled fisherman. Standing in a boat in swelling seas he can spear a darting swordfish, and he can flick up a trout from the fast waters of a stream with his fingers. He runs faster, throws further and jumps higher than any other young man on Seriphos. He wrestles, he rides wild asses, he can milk a cow and tame a bull. He is impulsive, perhaps a little boastful sometimes, but his mother Danaë is right to be proud of him and to believe him the best and bravest boy on the island.

The plainness of Dictys's home seemed all the more remarkable to Danaë when she discovered that this humble fisherman was the brother of Seriphos's king, POLYDECTES. The island's ruler was everything that Dictys was not: proud, cruel, dishonest, greedy, lascivious, extravagant and demanding. At first he had paid no particular attention to Dictys's houseguest. Over the last few years, however, his black heart had become more and more troubled with feelings of attraction for the beautiful mother of that boy, that impertinent boy.

Perseus had an instinctive way of interposing himself between his mother and the king that was most aggravating. Polydectes was in the habit of calling round when he knew that his brother would be out, but every time he did the pestilential Perseus would be there:

'Mum, mum, have you seen my running sandals?'

'Mum, mum! Come out to the rock pool and time me while I hold my breath underwater.'

It was too irritating.

At last Polydectes hit on a way of sending Perseus far away. He would exploit the youth's vanity, pride and bluster.

Messages were sent to all the young men of the island inviting them to the palace for a feast to celebrate Polydectes' resolution to seek the hand in marriage of HIPPODAMIA, daughter of King OENOMAUS of Pisa.* This was a bold and surprising move. Just as the oracle had prophesied that King Acrisius of Argos would be killed by a grandson, so it had told Oenomaus that he would be killed by a son-in-law. To prevent his daughter ever marrying, the king challenged every applicant for her hand to a chariot race, the loser to forfeit his life. Oenomaus was the finest charioteer in the land: so far, the heads of more than a dozen hopeful young men adorned the wooden stakes that fenced the racing field. Hippodamia was very beautiful, Pisa was very rich and the suitors kept coming.

Danaë was delighted to hear that Polydectes had thrown his hat into the ring. She had long felt uncomfortable in his presence and the surprising news that his heart was elsewhere came as a great relief. How gracious of him to invite her son to a feast and show that there were no hard feelings.

'It is an honour to be invited,' she told Perseus. 'Don't forget to thank him politely. Don't drink too much and try not to talk with your mouth full.'

Polydectes sat young Perseus in the seat of honour to his right, filling and refilling his cup with strong wine. He played the young man just as Perseus himself would have played a fish.

'Yes, this chariot race will certainly be a challenge,' he said. 'But the best families of Seriphos have each promised me a horse for my team. May I look to you and your mother to . . . ?'

Perseus flushed. His poverty had always been a source of

---

* Not the Italian Pisa of the Leaning Tower, but a city state in the northwestern Peloponnese. The quest for the hand of Hippodamia had repercussions that sounded down to the end of the mythic era and the aftermath of the Trojan War. But their details are for another time and place.

mortification. The young men with whom he played at sports, wrestled, hunted and chased girls all had servants and stables. He still lived in a stone fisherman's cottage behind the dunes. His friend Pyrrho had a slave to fan him in his bed when the nights were warm. Perseus slept out on the sand and was more likely to be awoken by a nip from a crab than by a serving girl with a cup of fresh milk.

'I don't really have a horse as such,' said Perseus.

'A horse as such? I'm not sure I know what "a horse as such" might be.'

'I don't really own anything much more than the clothes I wear. Oh, I do have a collection of sea shells that I've been told might be quite valuable one day.'

'Oh dear. Oh dear. I quite understand. Of course I do.' Polydectes's sympathetic smile cut Perseus deeper than any sneer. 'It was too much to expect you to help me.'

'But I want to help you!' Perseus said, a little too loudly. 'Anything I can do for you I will. Name it.'

'Really? Well, there is one thing but . . .'

'What?'

'No, no, it's too much to ask.'

'Tell me what it is . . .'

'I've always hoped that one day someone would bring me . . . but I can't ask you, you're just a boy.'

Perseus banged the table. 'Bring you what? Say the word. I'm strong. I'm brave. I'm resourceful, I'm . . .'

'. . . just a little bit drunk.'

'I know what I'm saying . . .' Perseus rose unsteadily to his feet and said in a voice everyone in the hall could hear. 'Tell me what you want brought to you, my king, and I will bring it. Name it.'

'Well,' said Polydectes with a rueful shrug of defeat, as one forced into a corner. 'Since our young hero insists, there is one thing I've always wanted. Could you bring me the head of MEDUSA, I wonder?'

'No problem,' said Perseus. 'The head of Medusa? It's yours.'

'Really? You mean that?'

'I swear it by the beard of Zeus.'

A little while later Perseus stumbled home across the sands to find his mother waiting up for him.

'You're late, darling.'

'Mum, what's a "Medusa"?'

'Perseus, have you been drinking?'

'Maybe. Just a cup or two.'

'A hiccup or two, by the sound of it.'

'No, but seriously, what's a Medusa?'

'Why do you want to know?'

'I heard the name and wondered, that's all.'

'If you'll stop pacing around like a caged lion and sit down, I'll tell you,' said Danaë. 'Medusa, so they say, was a beautiful young woman who was taken and ravished by the sea god Poseidon.'*

'Ravished?'

'Unfortunately for her this took place on the floor of a temple sacred to the goddess Athena. She was so angry at the sacrilege that she punished Medusa.'

'She didn't punish Poseidon?'

'The gods don't punish each other, at least not very often. They punish us.'

'And how did Athena punish Medusa?'

'She transformed her into a Gorgon.'

'Blimey,' said Perseus, 'and what's a "Gorgon"?'

'A Gorgon is ... Well, a Gorgon is a dreadful creature

---

* The description of the Gorgons in *Mythos* omits the idea of Medusa's separate creation as a mortal Gorgon. There are, of course, many different accounts. The story Danaë tells Perseus is perhaps the most popular.

with boar's tusks instead of teeth, razor-sharp claws of brass and venomous snakes for hair.'

'Get away!'

'That's the story.'

'And what does "ravished" mean, exactly?'

'Behave yourself,' said Danaë, slapping his arm. 'There are only two others like her in the world, Stheno and Euryale, but they were born as Gorgons. They are immortal daughters of the ancient divinities of the sea, Phorcys and Ceto.'

'Is this Medusa immortal as well?'

'I don't think so. She was once human, you see...'

'Right . . . and if . . . say, for example . . . someone was to go hunting for her?'

Danaë laughed. 'They'd be a fool. The three of them live together on an island somewhere. Medusa has one special weapon worse even than her serpent hair, her tusks and her talons.'

'What would that be?'

'One glance from her will turn you to stone.'

'What do you mean?'

'I mean that if you were to meet her eyes for just one second you would be petrified.'

'Scared?'

'No, petrified means turned into stone. You'd be frozen for all eternity. Like a statue.'

Perseus scratched his chin. 'Oh. So *that's* Medusa? I'd rather hoped she might turn out to be some sort of giant chicken, or a pig, maybe.'

'Why do you want to know?'

'Well, I sort of promised Polydectes that I'd bring him her head.'

'You *what*?'

'He wanted a horse, you see, and somehow this Medusa came up and I found myself saying I'd bring him her head . . .'

'You will go round to the palace first thing tomorrow morning and tell him that you will do no such thing.'

'But . . .'

'No buts. I absolutely forbid it. What was he thinking of? I've never heard of such a thing. Now, you go and sleep off that wine. In future you'll have no more than two cups in an evening, is that understood?'

'Yes, mum.'

Perseus sloped off to bed as commanded, but he awoke in a mutinous mood.

'I *will* leave the island and I *will* search for this Medusa,' he declared over breakfast and nothing Danaë said to him would make him change his mind. 'I made a promise in front of others. It's a matter of honour. I am of an age to travel. To have adventures. You know how swift and strong I am. How cunning and resourceful. There's nothing to be afraid of.'

'You speak to him, Dictys,' said Danaë, despairing.

Dictys and Perseus walked along the beach for most of the morning. Danaë was not pleased when they returned.

'It's like he says, Danaë. He's old enough to make his own decisions. He'll never find Medusa, of course. If she even exists. Let him go to the mainland and try out life for a while. He'll be back before long. He's well able to look after himself.'

The farewell between mother and son was all tears and distress on the one side and hand-patting and reassurance on the other.

'I'll be fine, mother. Ever seen anyone who can run faster? What harm can come to me?'

'I'll never forgive Polydectes, never.'

That at least, thought Dictys, was something.

He took Perseus by boat to the mainland. 'Don't trust anyone who offers you anything for free,' he warned. 'There'll be plenty who'll want to befriend you. They might be trust-worthy, they might not. Don't gaze around you as if it's the first time you've ever seen a busy port or a city. Look bored and confident. As if you know your way around. And don't be afraid to seek guidance from the oracles.'

How much of this excellent advice Perseus was likely to heed, Dictys could not tell. He was fond of the boy, and even fonder of his mother, and it grieved him to be complicit in so foolhardy an adventure. But, as he had told Danaë, Perseus was set on it and if they parted with hot words his absence would be all the harder to bear.

When they arrived on the mainland Perseus thought that Dictys' fishing boat looked very small and shabby beside the great ships moored at the harbour. The man he had called father since he had been able to speak suddenly looked very small and shabby, too. Perseus embraced him with fierce affection and accepted the silver coins slipped into his palm. He promised to try and send word to the island as soon as he had any news worth imparting and was patient enough to stand on the quayside and wave Dictys and his little boat goodbye, even though he was desperate to get going and explore the strange new world of mainland Greece.

THE TWO STRANGERS
IN THE OAK GROVE

Perseus was confounded and confused by the cosmopolitan clamour of the mainland. No one seemed to care who he was, unless it was to try and con him out of his few pieces of silver. It did not take him very long to see that Dictys was right:

if he was going to return to Polydectes with the head of Medusa he would need guidance. The oracle of Apollo at Delphi was a long way to walk, but at least it was free to all.*

He joined the long queue of petitioners and after two long days found himself at last standing before the priestess.†

'What does Perseus wish to know?'

Perseus gave a little gasp. She knew who he was!

'I, well, I . . . I want to know how I can find and kill Medusa, the Gorgon.'

'Perseus must travel to a land where people subsist not on Demeter's golden corn but on the fruit of the oak tree.'

He stayed there hoping for further information, but not a word more was forthcoming. A priest pulled him away.

'Come along, come along, the Pythia has spoken. You're holding up the others.'

'I don't suppose you know what she meant?'

'I've got better things to do than listen to every pronouncement that comes from her mouth. You can be sure that it was wise and truthful.'

'But where do people subsist on the fruit of the oak?'

'Fruit of the oak? There's no such thing. Now please, move along.'

'I know what she meant,' said an old lady, who was one of the many regulars who came daily to sit on the grass and watch the line of supplicants shuffling along to hear their fortune. 'It was her way of telling you to visit the oracle at Dodona.'

'Another oracle?' Perseus's heart sank.

'The people there make flour from acorns that drop from

---

* In later times a 'consultation tax' would have to be paid to the priestess, as well as the cost of the requisite sacrifices.

† The priestess, known as the PYTHIA, would hold on to a sacred tripod that connected her to the ground. She would receive her messages from clouds of sulphurous steam that rose (and still do) from under the earth at Delphi.

oaks sacred to Zeus. I've heard tell the trees can speak. Dodona is a long way north, my love,' she wheezed. 'A very long way!'

A long way it was. His small supply of coins had gone and Perseus slept under hedgerows and subsisted on little more than wild figs and nuts as he travelled north. He must have presented a forlorn figure by the time he arrived, for the women of Dodona were kind. They ruffled his hair and served him delicious acorn-flour bread spread thick with sharp goats' curd and sweetened with honey.

'Go early in the morning,' they advised. 'The oaks are more talkative in the cool hours before the noontide sun.'

A mist hung over the countryside like a veil when Perseus set out for the grove at dawn the next day.

'Er, hello?' he called out to the trees, feeling remarkably stupid. The oaks were tall, stately and impressive enough, but they did not have mouths or faces with recognisable expressions.

'Who calls?'

Perseus started. Unquestionably a voice. Calm, soft, female, but strong and deeply authoritative.

'Here to help.'

Another voice! This one seemed to contain a hint of scorn.

'My name is Perseus. I have come . . .'

'Oh, we know who you are,' said a young man stepping forward from the shadows.

He was young, startlingly handsome and most unusually dressed. Aside from the loincloth around his waist, a narrow-brimmed hat that circled his brow and winged sandals at his ankles, he was quite naked.* Perseus noticed that two live snakes writhed about the staff that he was carrying.

A woman holding a shield emerged behind him. She was

---

* By our standards at least. For a Greek he was more than usually clothed . . .

tall, grave and beautiful. When she raised her shining grey eyes to his, Perseus felt an extraordinary surge of something he could not quite define. He decided the quality was majesty and bowed his head accordingly.

'Don't be afraid, Perseus,' she said. 'Your father has sent us to help you.'

'My *father*?'

'He's our father too,' said the young man. 'The Cloud Gatherer and Bringer of Storms.'

'The Sky Father and King of Heaven,' said the shining woman.

'Z-Z-Zeus?'

'The same.'

'You mean it's really true, then? Zeus is my father?'

Perseus had never believed his mother's wild story about Zeus coming to her as a shower of golden rain. He had taken it for granted that his real father was some itinerant musician or tinker whose name she had never discovered.

'Quite true, brother Perseus,' said the tall woman.

'Brother?'

'I am Athena, daughter of Zeus and Metis.'

'Hermes, son of Zeus and Maia,' said the young man, bowing.

It was a lot for a youth of sheltered upbringing to take in. The two Olympians now told him that Zeus had been keeping an eye on him since his birth. He had guided the wooden chest into the net of Dictys. He had watched Perseus grow up into young manhood. He had seen him rise to Polydectes' challenge. He admired his boldness and had sent his two favourite children to assist their half-brother in his quest for the head of Medusa.

'You're going to help me?' said Perseus. This was so much more than he could have hoped for.

'We can't slay the Gorgon for you,' said Hermes, 'but we can help tilt the odds a little in your favour. You might find these useful.' He looked down and addressed the sandals at his feet. 'To my brother Perseus,' he commanded. The sandals unwrapped themselves from the god's ankles and flew to Perseus. 'Take your own off, first.'

Perseus did so and at once the sandals attached themselves to his feet.

'You'll have plenty of time to get used to them,' said Athena, watching in some amusement as Perseus leapt in the air like a dancer.

'You're confusing them,' said Hermes. 'You don't have to flap your feet to fly. Just think.'

Perseus closed his eyes and strained.

'Not like you're taking a crap. Just picture yourself in the air. That's it! You've got it now.'

Perseus opened his eyes to discover that he had risen up into the air. He dropped down again with a jarring bump.

'Practice. That's the key. Now here is a hood from our uncle HADES. Wear this and no one will be able to see you.'

Perseus took the hood in his hands.

'I have something for you too,' said Athena.

'Oh,' said Perseus, putting the hood down and taking the object she was offering to him. 'A satchel?'

'You might find it useful.'

After flying sandals and a cap of invisibility, a plain brown leather satchel seemed something of a disappointment, but Perseus tried not to show it. 'That's very kind of you, I'm sure it will come in useful.'

'It will,' said Athena, 'but I have more for you. Take this . . .'

She passed him a short-bladed weapon, curved like a scythe.

'Be very careful, the blade is very sharp.'

'You're not wrong!' said Perseus, sucking blood from his thumb.

'It is called a *harpe* and can cut through anything.'

'It is forged from adamantine,' Hermes added. 'A perfect replica of the great sickle Gaia made for Kronos.'

'And this shield is like no other,' said Athena. 'Its name is AEGIS. You must make sure its surface is always kept to a mirror shine like this.'

Perseus shaded his eyes from the flashing light of the rising sun that was reflecting from the polished bronze.

'Is the idea to dazzle Medusa with its glare?'

'You must work out for yourself how best to use it, but believe me, without this shield you will surely fail.'

'And die,' said Hermes. 'Which would be a pity.'

Perseus could hardly contain his excitement. The wings at his heels fluttered and he found himself rising up. He made some swishes with the *harpe*.

'This is all just amazing. So what do I do next?'

'There are limits to how much we can help. If you're to be a hero you must make your own moves and take your own –'

'I'm a hero?'

'You can be.'

Hermes and Athena were so fine. They shone. Everything they did was performed without any seeming effort. They made Perseus feel hot and clumsy.

As if reading his mind, Athena said, 'You will get used to Aegis, to the scythe, the sandals, the hood and the satchel. They are outwards things. If your mind and spirit are directed to your task, everything else will follow. Relax.'

'But focus,' said Hermes. 'Relaxation without focus leads to failure.'

'Focus without relaxation leads to failure just as surely,' said Athena.

'So concentrate . . .' said Perseus.

'Exactly.'

'. . . but calmly?'

'Concentrate calmly. You have it.'

Perseus stood for a while inhaling and exhaling in a manner that he hoped was relaxed, yet focussed, concentrated, yet calm.

Hermes nodded. 'I think this young man has an excellent chance of success.'

'But the one thing these – wonderful – gifts can't help me with is finding the Gorgons. I have asked all over but no one seems to agree where they live. On an island somewhere, far out to sea, that's all I have been told. Which island? Which sea?'

'We cannot tell you that,' said Hermes, 'but have you heard of the PHORCIDES?'

'Never.'

'They are sometimes called the GRAEAE, or Grey Ones,' said Athena. 'Like their sisters, the Gorgons Stheno and Euryale, they are daughters of Phorcys and Ceto.'

'They're old,' said Hermes. 'So old they have only one eye and one tooth between them.'

'Seek them out,' said Athena. 'They know everything but tell nothing.'

'If they don't say anything,' said Perseus, 'what use are they? Do I threaten them with the sickle?'

'Oh no, you'll have to think of something subtler than that.'

'Something much craftier,' said Hermes.

'But what?'

'I'm sure it'll come to you. They can be found in a cave on the wild shores of Kisthene, that much is common knowledge.'

'We wish you good fortune, brother Perseus,' said Athena.

'Relaxed but focussed, that's the key,' said Hermes.

'Goodbye . . .'

'Good luck . . .'

'Wait, wait!' cried Perseus, but the figures and forms of the gods had already begun to fade into the bright morning light and soon they had vanished entirely. Perseus stood alone in the grove of sacred oaks.

'This sickle is real at least,' said Perseus, looking at the cut on his thumb. 'This satchel is real, these sandals are real. Aegis is real . . .'

'Are you trying to blind me?'

Perseus swung round.

'Just watch how you flash that shield about,' came an irritated voice.

It seemed to be coming from the very heart of the oak tree closest to him.

'So you trees can talk after all,' said Perseus.

'Of course we can talk.'

'We usually choose not to.'

'There's so little worth saying.'

Voices came now from all parts of the wood.

'I understand,' said Perseus. 'But perhaps you wouldn't mind pointing me in the direction of Kisthene?'

'Kisthene? That's Aeolia.'

'More Phrygia, really,' another voice put in.

'I'd call it Lydia.'

'Well, it's certainly east.'

'North of Ionia but south of the Propontis.'

'Ignore them, young man,' boomed an older oak, rustling his leaves. 'They don't know what they're talking about. Fly over the isle of Lesbos and then up along the coast of Mysia. You can't miss the cave of the Grey Sisters. It's under a rock shaped like a weasel.'

'Like a stoat, you mean,' squeaked a young sapling.

'An otter, surely?'

'I'd've said a pine marten.'

'The rock resembles a polecat and nothing else.'

'I said weasel and I meant weasel,' said the old one, quivering all over so that his leaves shook.

'Thanks,' said Perseus. 'I really must be going.'

Throwing his satchel over his shoulder, attaching the scythe to his belt and settling the shield firmly in his grip, Perseus frowned in on himself to awaken the sandals and with a great shout of triumph shot up into the blue of the sky.

'Good luck,' cried the oaks.

'Look out for a rock in the shape of a marmoset . . .'

THE GRAEAE

By the time Perseus landed neatly, toes down, on the Mysian shore, outside a cave whose outer formation resembled, to his eyes at least, a squashed rat, the day was all but spent. Looking westwards he could see that HELIOS's sun-chariot was turning from copper to red as it neared the land of the HESPERIDES and the end of its daily round.

As Perseus approached the mouth of the cave he slipped on the cap that Hermes had given him, the Hood of Hades. The moment it was on his head, the long shadow that had been striding along the sand beside him disappeared. Everything was darker and a little misty with the hood over his eyes, but he could see well enough.

'I won't be needing these,' he said to himself, leaving the scythe, satchel and shield on the sand outside the cave.

He followed the murmur of voices and a glimmer of light

through a long, winding passageway. The light grew brighter and the voices louder.

'It's my turn to have the tooth!'

'I've only just put it in.'

'Then PEMPHREDO should let me have the eye at least.'

'Oh, stop moaning, ENYO . . .'

As Perseus entered the chamber he saw, held in the flickering light of a lamp that hung over them, three fantastically old women. Their ragged clothes, straggling hair and sagging flesh were as grey as the stones of the cave. In the bare lower gum of one of the sisters jutted up a single yellow tooth. In the eye socket of another sister a solitary eyeball darted back and forth and up and down in the most alarming manner. It was just as Hermes had said, one eye and one tooth between them.

A pile of bones lay heaped on the floor. The sister with the tooth was gnawing the side of one, stripping it of its rotten flesh. The sister with the eye had picked up another bone and was inspecting it closely and lovingly. The third sister, with no eye and no tooth, raised her head with a jerk and sniffed the air sharply.

'I smell a mortal,' she shrieked, stabbing a finger in the direction of Perseus. 'Look, Pemphredo. Use the eye!'

Pemphredo, the sister with the eye, cast wild glances in all directions. 'There's nothing there, Enyo.'

'I tell you there is. A mortal. I smell it!' cried Enyo. 'Bite it, DINO.* Use your tooth. Bite! Bite it to death!'

Perseus stole silently closer, taking great care not to step on any cast-off bones.

---

* The Graeae's names, as so often in Greek myth, have meanings. Pemphredo is 'she who guides the way', Enyo 'warlike' and Dino 'terrible' (as in *dinosaur*, which means 'terrible lizard'). Dino was sometimes called Persis 'the destroyer'. I've avoided that name on account of its similarity to Perseus. But it shows that Perseus and all the Pers- names carry 'destructive' meanings.

'Give me the eye, Pemphredo! I swear to you I smell mortal flesh.'

'Here, take it.' Pemphredo took the eye from her socket and the one called Enyo stretched out her hand greedily to receive it. Stepping forward Perseus snatched up the eye himself.

'What was that? Who? What?'

Perseus had brushed Dino, the sister with the tooth. Taking advantage of her open-mouthed astonishment he plucked the tooth from her mouth and stepped back with a loud laugh.

'Good evening, ladies.'

'The tooth! The tooth, someone has taken the tooth!'

'Where is the eye? Who has the eye?'

'I have your tooth, sisters, and I have your eye too.'

'Give them back!'

'You have no right.'

'All in good time,' said Perseus. 'I could return this cloudy old eye and this rotten old tooth. I've no use for them. Of course, I could just as easily throw them into the sea . . .'

'No! No! We beg of you!'

'Beg . . .'

'It all depends on you,' said Perseus, walking round and round them. As he passed they shot out their bony arms to try and grab him, but he was always too quick.

'What do you want?'

'Information. You are old. You know things.'

'What would you have us tell you?'

'How to find your sisters, the Gorgons.'

'What do you want with them?'

'I'd like to take Medusa home with me. Part of her at least.'

'Ha! You're a fool. She will petrify you.'

'That's turn you to stone.'

'I'm not ignorant. I know what "petrify" means,' said Perseus. 'You let me worry about all that, just tell me where to find the island where they live.'

'You mean our lovely sisters harm.'

'Tell me or I throw first the eye and then the tooth into the sea.'

'Libya!' cried the one called Enyo. 'The island is off the coast of Libya.'

'Are you satisfied?'

'They'll kill you and feast on your flesh and we shall hear of it and cheer,' screeched Dino.

'Now, give us our eye and our tooth.'

'Certainly,' said Perseus. These hags might be old, he told himself, but they have sharp claws and they are fierce and vengeful. I had better buy myself some time. 'Tell you what, let's make a game of it,' he said. 'Close your eyes and count to a hundred . . . Oh. Of course. No need to close your eyes. Just count to a hundred while I hide the tooth and eye. They'll be somewhere in this cave, I promise. No cheating. One, two, three, four . . .'

'Damn you, child of Prometheus!'

'May your flesh rot from your bones!'

Perseus moved swiftly round their chamber, counting with them. 'You should be thanking me . . . nineteen, twenty . . . not cursing me,' he said as they hurled fouler and filthier obscenities at him. 'Forty-five, forty-six . . . surely this is the most exciting thing to have happened to you for centuries . . . sixty-eight, sixty-nine . . . you will be talking about this day for ages and ages to come. Don't start looking till you reach a hundred, no cheating, now!'

As Perseus returned along the passageway towards the mouth of the cave and the open beach he heard the voices of the Graeae behind him squabbling, screaming and spitting.

'Out of the way, out of the way!'

'I have it, I have it!'

'That's just a chip of bone, you old fool.'

'The eye! I have the eye!'

'Let go of my tongue!'

GORGON ISLAND

Perseus smiled to himself as he buckled on the scythe and shield. He had hidden the tooth and eyeball well. The Grey Ones would be scrabbling for them for days. He felt sure that they would not think to break off their search to summon some bird or sea creature to warn their sisters of his approach. Even if they did, he had his marvellous armoury. The shield, Aegis, though . . . Why had Athena laid such stress on his keeping its surface polished to a high shine?

He rose above the surface of the sea and pointed himself in the direction of the Libyan coast.

The moon-chariot of SELENE was high in the sky as Perseus skimmed the sea searching for the Gorgon's home. He came upon it soon enough, more of a series of rocky outcrops than an island and entirely shrouded in fog. He descended low enough to pierce the mist. Scant moonlight penetrated here. He realised as he hovered over the island that what he had taken for rock formations were in fact lifelike statues: seals, seabirds – and men. Even some women and children. How extraordinary to find a sculpture garden in so remote and sombre a place.

Now he could see the Gorgons. The three lay in a circle fast asleep, arms clasped around each other in a tender sisterly embrace. It was not quite as his mother had described to him. All three had tusks for teeth and claws of bronze, just as she had said, but only one had living, writhing serpents for hair of a particularly bizarre beauty. This must be Medusa. She was smaller than the others. In the moonlight her face was smooth. The other two had scaly skin that drooped in pouches. Medusa's eyes were shut while she slept and Perseus could not resist looking at the closed lids, knowing that they only had to open for a second for his life to be ended. One single glance and –

Oh, fool that he was! The statues standing all around were not *art*, they were not the work of some gifted sculptor, they were the petrified forms of those who had met Medusa's gaze.

The sandals silently beat the air as he hovered. He unsheathed the curved blade of the harpe and held out the shield before him. What should he do next? Suddenly he understood why Athena had charged him to keep it polished. He could not look directly into the eyes of Medusa, but her reflection . . . that was another thing.

He held the shield out and tilted it down so that he could see the sleeping group reflected quite clearly in the surface of the shining bronze.

Anyone who has ever tried to snip a recalcitrant eyebrow in the bathroom mirror will know how difficult it is to perform so delicate a task accurately in the backwards world of reflection without stabbing oneself. Left is right and right is left, near is far and far is near. Perseus adjusted the mirror so that he could see himself swinging the scythe backwards and forwards.

But there was nothing to see! How could the mirror not work?

Of course! Cursing himself for his slowness of wits, he removed the Hood of Hades and tucked it into the satchel. This was no easy task. With a heavy sickle in one hand and the even heavier shield in the other, with his mind half on the danger of waking the Gorgons and half on keeping his sandals hovering at just the right altitude, he was sweating and panting hard by the time he had tucked the hood away and was ready to concentrate on practising his moves. His reflection now clearly visible in the shield, he taught himself how to swing his sword arm in the mirror image.

Without knowing it he had dropped a little lower. The swishing of the blade awoke the vipers on Medusa's head and they began to spit and rear. Changing the angle of the shield, Perseus saw they were looking directly at him and hissing. At any moment Medusa would wake – and perhaps her indestructible sisters too. He closed in on Medusa's sleeping form, weapon at the ready. In the shield he saw her stir and her eyelids flutter.

Her eyes opened.

He didn't know what he had expected, ugliness and horror, perhaps, certainly not beauty. But Medusa's eyes, for all their blaze and fury, had a quality that made him want to turn from the reflected image and look deep into them for real. He pushed the feeling down and raised his blade higher.

Medusa was staring into the shield. She lifted her head to look at Perseus directly, giving him a clear sight of her throat. The harpe swept through the air and he felt the blade slice through the flesh of her neck. He lunged down to snatch away the head and pushed it into his satchel before the thrashing, dying snakes could fix their fangs into him.

He tried to fly up and away, but something was tugging at his ankles. The other Gorgons, Stheno and Euryale, awake and screaming, were pulling him down. With a mighty effort he kicked and kicked, urging the sandals up. The screeches of the outraged sisters rang in his ears as he rocketed through the ceiling of fog and into the clear moonlit air, with never a backward glance.

Perhaps he should have looked back. A most remarkable sight would have met his eyes. Since the day Poseidon violated her in Athena's temple, Medusa had held in her womb twins from that union. With her head removed, they had at last a place from which they could be born. The first to rise out of the gaping wound was a young man bearing a weapon of shining gold. His name was to be CHRYSAOR, which means 'Golden Sword'.

Another form now emerged from the open throat of the dead Medusa. Not since the lovely APHRODITE arose from the frothing seed and blood of Ouranos's severed testicles was something so transcendentally beautiful born of something so appallingly foul. Chrysaor's twin was a shimmering white, winged horse. It pawed the air and flew up into the sky leaving its brother and the two shrieking sisters behind.

The name of the horse was PEGASUS.

ANDROMEDA AND CASSIOPEIA

'I did it! I did it! I did it!' Perseus shouted to the moon.

Indeed he had. With Medusa's head safely stored inside the satchel he had originally dismissed as so uninteresting, he flew on in a state of intoxicated excitement. Indeed, so excited was he, so high on the thrill of his achievement, that he took a wrong turn. Instead of turning left he turned right, and soon found himself flying along a strange coastline.

Mile after mile he flew, not tiring, but growing increasingly bewildered by the unfamiliar shore. And suddenly, in the first light of dawn, the most extraordinary sight met his eyes. A beautiful girl, naked and chained to a rock.

He flew up to her.

'What are you doing here?'

'What does it look like I'm doing? And I'll thank you to keep your eyes up on my face, if you don't mind.'

'I'm sorry . . . I couldn't help wondering . . . is there any way I can help you? . . . My name is Perseus.'

'ANDROMEDA, pleased to meet you.'

'How are you staying up in the air?'

'It's a long story, but more to the point, why are you chained to this rock?'

'Well . . .' Andromeda sighed. 'It was my mother, really. It's a long story too, but I've nothing better to do so I might as well tell you. My parents, CEPHEUS and CASSIOPEIA, are the king and queen.'

'Where are we exactly?'

'Ethiopia, where did you think we were?'

'Sorry, go on . . .'

'It was all mother's fault. She remarked out loud one day that I was more beautiful than all the NEREIDS and OCEANIDS in the world.'*

'Well, you are,' said Perseus.

'Oh shush. Poseidon heard this boast and he was so out-raged he sent a monstrous sea dragon called CETUS to ravage the shoreline.† No shipping could get through and the people began to starve. We rely on trade, you see. The priests and priestesses were consulted and they told my parents that the only way to appease the god and call off Cetus was to have

---

* The two main (and multitudinous) families of sea nymphs, the Oceanids and Nereids were daughters and grand-daughters respectively of the sea Titans OCEANUS and TETHYS. As such they were cousins of Poseidon. See the first volume of *Mythos* (page 10).
† Not to be confused with Ceto, mother of the two immortal Gorgons. Although the sea goddess does lend her name to all such sea monsters and, through them, our *cetaceans*.

35

me chained naked to the rocks. Cetus would devour me, but the kingdom would be saved. Oh no – there he is now – look, look!'

Perseus looked round and saw a great sea beast arching through the waves towards them. Without a moment's thought he dived into the water to confront it.

Andromeda looked on with feelings of admiration and relief that slowly turned to despair when, as the minutes passed, Perseus failed to surface. She could not know that he held the Seriphos underwater breath-holding record. Nor could she know that he was in possession of a blade so keen it could cut through even Cetus's hard horny scales. She let out a great cry of relief when Perseus's cheerful and triumphant face finally burst up through the waves, surrounded by a boiling mess of blubber and blood. He waved shyly before flying up to Andromeda once more.

'I can't believe it,' she said. 'I just can't believe it! How did you do that?'

'Oh, well,' said Perseus, breaking her shackles with two swift strokes of the *harpe*. 'I've always been at home in the water. Just swam underneath him with my blade up to slice through his belly. Fancy a lift?'

By the time they landed at the royal palace Andromeda was as hopelessly in love with him as he was with her.

Cassiopeia was overjoyed to see her daughter alive and thrilled to think of the handsome young hero becoming her son-in-law.

Cepheus the king said meekly. 'Don't forget, my dear, that Andromeda is already promised to my brother PHINEUS.'

'Oh poo,' said Cassiopeia, 'a loose agreement, no kind of a binding engagement. He'll understand.'

Phineus did *not* understand. As a brother of AEGYPTUS

and descendant of NILUS*, he believed that an alliance with Andromeda would allow him to unite the most powerful kingdoms of the Nile. He was not about to let some puppy with a scythe take that away from him. The rumours of the puppy being able to fly he discounted.

So it was that the music and laughter of the betrothal banquet in the great hall of the Ethiopian palace was silenced by Phineus and a large body of men storming in, armed to the teeth.

'Where is he?' roared Phineus. 'Where is the boy who dares come between me and Andromeda?'

Up on the top table where the royal party was feasting, Cassiopeia and Cepheus looked on in some embarrassment as Perseus rose uncertainly to his feet. 'I think there may have been some mistake,' he said.

'You're damned right there has,' said Phineus. 'And you made it. That girl was promised to me months ago.'

Perseus turned to Andromeda. 'Is this true?'

'It is true,' she said. 'But I was never consulted. He's my uncle, for heaven's sake.'†

'What's that got to do with it? You're mine and that's an end to it. And you,' snarled Phineus, pointing his sword at Perseus, 'you have two minutes to leave the palace and the kingdom, unless you want your head to decorate the gatepost.'

Perseus looked down across the hall towards Phineus. There must have been sixty armed men behind him. But talk of heads decorating gateposts gave Perseus an idea that made

---

* Nilus was one of the more important of the river gods, the *potamoi* – his descendants bred with Aegyptus, Libya and Ethiopia. As with Asia and Europa, the names of these deities, demigods and mortals can still be found on our maps today.

† Andromeda, like many mortals now, seems to show a distaste for incest. The gods are never so fussy.

his head spin. 'No,' he said. 'I'll give *you* two minutes to leave the palace – unless you want you and your men to decorate this hall.'

Phineus blew out his lips in amused contempt. 'You've got a nerve, I'll give you that. A purse of gold to the first to fire an arrow through this brat's insolent neck.'

The armed men roared in delight and started to draw their bows.

'Those with me, get behind me!' shouted Perseus, opening his satchel and bringing out the head of Medusa.

Andromeda, Cassiopeia, Cepheus and the wedding guests on the top table shrieked in astonishment as Phineus and his sixty men instantly froze.

'Why aren't they moving?'

'Oh, my lord – they're *stone*!'

Perseus put the head back into the satchel and turned to his parents-in-law to be. 'I hope you didn't like him too much.'

'My hero . . .' breathed Andromeda.

'How did you do that?' shrieked Cassiopeia. 'They're statues. Stone statues! How is this possible?'

'Oh, you know,' said Perseus with a modest shrug. 'I just happened to meet Medusa the Gorgon last night. Came away with her head. Thought it might come in useful.'

Perseus hid the extremity of his relief. He had by no means been certain that the gaze from the Gorgon's dead eyes would have retained the power to petrify, but an inner voice had told him that it was worth trying. Whether the inner voice was his own inspiration or the whispered advice of Athena, he would never know.

Cepheus put a hand on Perseus's shoulder. 'Always hated Phineus. Done me a great service. Don't know how to thank you.'

'The hand of your daughter in marriage is all the thanks I

need. I hope you will allow me to fly her to my home island of Seriphos to meet my mother? *No!*' Perseus slapped Queen Cassiopeia's hand which had inched forward to lift the flap of the satchel. 'Not a good idea.'

'Oh, mother,' sighed Andromeda. 'Will you never learn?'

THE RETURN TO SERIPHOS

'It's not a palace,' Perseus warned Andromeda as they flashed across the sea towards Seriphos. 'Just a simple cottage.'

'If it's where you grew up, I know I'll adore it.'

'I love you.'

'Of course you do.'

But when they landed on the beach, they found that Dictys's cottage had been burned to the ground.

'What can have happened? Where is everyone? What can have happened?'

Perseus found a group of fishermen mending nets not far off. They shook their heads sadly. Danaë and Dictys had been taken prisoner by Polydectes.

'They say the king is holding a great feast at the palace.'

'Aye. Even now.'

'Some announcement to make, they say.'

Perseus grabbed Andromeda's hand and flew with her to the palace. They arrived at the back of the throne room in time to see Danaë and Dictys, bound with ropes and being dragged before the seated Polydectes.

'How dare you? How dare you marry each other without my permission?'

'It was all my doing,' said Dictys.

'It was our doing,' said Danaë.

'But I offered you *my* hand. You could have been my

queen!' screamed Polydectes. 'For this insult, you will both die.'

Perseus stepped forward and walked towards the throne. Polydectes looked over the shoulders of Danaë and Dictys and saw him coming. He smiled broadly.

'Well, well, well. If it isn't brave young Perseus. You told me you wouldn't return without the head of the Medusa.'

'You told me you were going to challenge Oenomaus to a chariot race for the hand of Hippodamia.'

'I changed my mind.'

'Why have you arrested my mother?'

'She and Dictys are due to die. You can be hanged along-side them if you like.'

Danaë and Dictys turned.

'Run, Perseus, run!'

'Mother, Dictys, if you love me, turn and look at Poly-dectes. I beg you! All who love me, look on the king now!'

The smile on Polydectes' face was a little less certain. 'What nonsense is this?'

'You asked for the head of Medusa. Here she is!'

'Surely you don't expect me to —' Polydectes got no further.

'You can turn and look at me now,' said Perseus, putting Medusa's head back in the satchel. 'It's safe now.'

The statue of Polydectes on his throne, flanked by stone men-at-arms, became a popular attraction on Seriphos. Visitors paid to see and touch them, and the money was spent on the construction of a temple to Athena and the installation of a hundred herms around the island.*

---

* Herms or *hermai* were square columns used as good-luck boundary markers and signposts. They had a carved head, typically of the god Hermes (though usually uncharacteristically bearded) on top and male genitals lower down, which were thought to bring good luck when stroked in . . . a certain way.

Andromeda and Perseus left King Dictys and Queen Danaë on Seriphos and moved on. Perseus and Andromeda could have stayed and inherited the throne. They could have returned to Andromeda's homeland and ruled the combined kingdoms of Ethiopia and Egypt. But they were young, spirited and minded to travel, and Perseus was keen to visit the land of his birth. As a baby he had been there for less than a week. His grandfather King Acrisius had done everything to prevent his existence and shorten his life, but he was curious to see what Argos, the famous kingdom of his birth, was like.

When Perseus and Andromeda arrived, they discovered that Acrisius, after casting his daughter and grandson onto the waters in their chest all those years ago, had turned dark, cruel and despotic. Never a popular ruler, he had soon been toppled from his throne. Nobody knew where he was now. The people of Argos, having heard of Perseus's astonishing feats, invited him to fill the vacant throne. Uncertain what to do or where to settle, the young couple thanked the Argives and asked for time to consider.

They wandered about mainland Greece, Perseus funding their travels with prize money from athletic meetings that he entered and invariably won. They heard news that the King of Larissa was holding the richest games of the year and made their way north to Thessaly to compete. The finest athletes in Greece were taking part and great would be the honours awarded the competitor who won the most events. One by one, Perseus prevailed in every race and every competition. It came at last to the discus. Perseus threw his so far it shot over the longest mark, cleared the stadium and landed amongst the spectators. The great roar of delight that met this astounding feat swiftly turned to a groan of horror. The discus had struck someone in the crowd.

Perseus ran to the place. An old man was lying on the

ground, blood streaming from his gashed head. Perseus cradled him in his arms.

'I'm so sorry,' he said. 'So terribly sorry. I don't know my own strength. May the gods forgive me.'

To Perseus's astonishment the old man smiled and even managed to cough out a laugh.

'Don't worry,' he said. 'It's funny really. I defeated the oracle. How many can say that? It said I would be killed by my grandson, and here I am instead, felled by some clumsy oaf of an athlete.'

The old man's attendant pushed Perseus away. 'Give his majesty air.'

'His majesty?'

'Don't you know this is King Acrisius of Argos?'

Accident or not, preordained or not, it was a blood crime. Perseus and Andromeda made a sad pilgrimage to Mount Cyllene in Arcadia and the temple of Hermes that stood near the cave where the god was born. On the altar stone they laid the hood of invisibility and the *talaria*, the winged sandals. As they left the temple precincts, after a brief prayer to the god, they turned to look back at the altar. The hood and sandals had disappeared.

'We did the right thing,' said Andromeda.

Now they made their way to Athens, and in the deepest recesses of the temple of Athena they hid the sickle, the shield and the satchel that held the head of Medusa.

Athena herself appeared before them and blessed them.

'You did well, Perseus. Our father is pleased with you.'

She raised the shield and they saw that the face of Medusa, startled, dismayed, sad and somehow beautiful stared out, forever trapped within the shining surface of the bronze. From that time on the shield was the Aegis of Athena – her sign, her standard and her warning to the world.

It can be said of Perseus and Andromeda, and of no other great heroes I can think of, that they lived happily ever after. After their wanderings they returned to the Peloponnese – the large southwestern peninsula connected to the mainland of Greece by the land bridge of the Isthmus of Corinth* – and founded Mycenae, a great kingdom that in time, under the name of Argolis or the Argolid, absorbed neighbouring Arcadia and Corinth as well as Perseus's birth kingdom of Argos to the south.

Through their son Perses, their bloodline founded the Persian nation and people.

After their long lives, Perseus and Andromeda were awarded the greatest prize that Zeus can bestow on mortals. Along with Cassiopeia and Cepheus, they were taken up into the heavens as constellations. Together Perseus and Andromeda look over their unruly shower of meteor children, the PERSEIDS, whom we can still watch showing off in the night sky once a year.

---

* Strictly speaking the Peloponnese hadn't yet earned its name, which was taken from that of King PELOPS, whom we shall encounter later on.

HERACLES

THE LINE OF PERSEUS

Zeus sat alone at the breakfast table, musing on Hera's dream long into the morning. Someone would rise up to save the immortals. Someone from the line of Perseus. It was probable, he told himself, that it was nothing but an impertinent fantasy sent by MORPHEUS to delude and confound. But there was a chance, a slim one, perhaps, but a chance nonetheless, that the dream was indeed a warning – a prophecy. There would be no harm in making preparations. Besides, a little fun could be had along the way.

So. The line of Perseus. Where were we . . . ?

Zeus looked down on Tiryns, the capital of Mycenae. The royal pair of Perseus and Andromeda themselves had been catasterized, raised to the firmament as constellations; but were there, Zeus wondered, any direct descendants who might give birth to a hero whose bloodline would accord with the conditions of Hera's dream?

There seemed to be three obvious candidates. One son of Perseus and Andromeda was STHENELUS, the current King of Mycenae. He was married to a young woman called NICIPPE.* The couple was as yet childless.

The second was AMPHITRYON, who had fallen in love with and married his cousin, *another* grandchild of Perseus

---

* A daughter of Pelops and Hippodamia. It was Pelops who won the chariot race and the hand of Hippodamia that Polydectes had pretended he was going to try for. That story has to be told, but not just yet.

47

and Andromeda, the beautiful ALCMENE. They too were without issue.

It was possible, then, that one of these couples might produce a great hero. Now Alcmene, Zeus could not help noticing, happened to be very, very, *very* beautiful. Suppose she were to bear *my* son, not Amphitryon's, he asked himself. Since Alcmene was herself a grandchild of Perseus, such a child would be of his line, all right and tight, and thus satisfy the demands of Hera's prophetic vision. But it would also be a son of Zeus and therefore naturally constructed out of strong heroic stuff.

The more Zeus thought about it, the more he liked the idea. It would provide a hero that fitted the requirements of Hera's dream *and* give him pleasure along the way. But how to impregnate Alcmene? She and Amphitryon did not live in Tiryns, but all the way over in Thebes. The reason for this was complicated, but interesting.

While hunting, Amphitryon had accidentally killed Alcmene's father ELECTRYON (who was, of course, his uncle as well as his father-in-law). The killing of blood relations, I need not remind you, whether accidental or not, was held by the Greek mind to be the darkest and most unforgivable of all crimes. Amphitryon and Alcmene fled to Thebes where the ruler CREON expiated him for this blood crime. Cleansed and purified, Amphitryon left his wife behind in Thebes to return to Mycenae and settle a complex series of dynastic difficulties which Alcmene herself had demanded he do.

At the moment, therefore, Alcmene was alone in the grand villa in Thebes that Creon had lent the couple. She was a loyal, loving wife, so rather than manifest himself to her as an eagle, a goat, a shower of golden rain, a bear, a bull or any of the other animals or phenomena he had impersonated in the course of his lustful adventuring, Zeus elected to appear to her in the form of her beloved husband Amphitryon himself.*

Suitably armed and dusty from the road, Zeus-Amphitryon arrived one evening at the villa and told the delighted Alcmene that he had prevailed in Mycenae. Entranced by the details of how cleverly he had settled the difficulties she had sent him to solve, and thrilled to have him safely home, she welcomed him to her bed. Zeus stretched out the one night into the length of three, the better to enjoy himself. When morning finally came, he left.

Amphitryon – the real Amphitryon – returned that morning from Mycenae and was astonished to discover that Alcmene already knew every detail of his triumphant campaign.

'But you told me last night, you dear, silly goose of a husband,' she said. 'And then we made love – and oh, how wonderfully we did so! We made love time and time again and with such fire and force. Let's do it again.'

Amphitryon had been on the dusty road between Tiryns and Thebes for some days and had been so looking forward to just such amatory excitements that he put the oddity of her comments aside and leapt gratefully onto the bed.

When they had finished, Alcmene could not help remarking on the difference between Amphitryon's love-making that morning and the previous night.

'You're joking,' said Amphitryon. 'Last night I was still on the road. Ask my troops.'

'But . . .'

They had a long conversation between themselves and decided that only TIRESIAS was wise and insightful enough to be able to shed light on the mystery. Tiresias saw nothing

---

* Similar to a well-known episode in Arthurian legend. Merlin disguises Uther Pendragon as Gorlois, husband of Igraine, and in that form he sleeps with her and fathers Arthur . . .

with his eyes but everything with his prophetic mind.

The blind Theban seer listened to their separate accounts of the events of the last day. 'The first visitor to your bed was the Sky Father, Zeus,' he told Alcmene. 'And now something remarkable is happening inside you.'

He was quite right. Having slept with Zeus and Amphitryon in rapid succession, she had been made pregnant by each of them. Twins were forming in her womb, two sons – one fathered by Zeus and the other by Amphitryon. This phenomenon of polyspermy is common enough in littering mammals like cats, dogs and pigs, but is rare in humans. Rare, but not unknown. It rejoices in the name *heteropaternal superfecundation*.*

Up on Mount Olympus none of this was lost on Hera. Never had the Queen of Heaven been so infuriated by one of her husband's dalliances. In her mind his affairs with SEMELE, GANYMEDE, IO, CALLISTO, Danaë, LEDA and EUROPA were as nothing to this monstrous, humiliating betrayal. Maybe it was one infidelity too many, the amorous straw that broke the camel's back, maybe she felt Zeus's real affections had been engaged, maybe she felt most especially mortified because it had all come about on account of the dream she had shared with him. For whatever reason, an implacably vengeful Hera watched Alcmene grow closer and closer to term and resolved to do anything and everything she could to destroy the fruit of so insulting a union.

Hera could rely – of course she could – on her husband's vanity to provide the first opportunity for revenge. It came the night before Alcmene was due to give birth, when the King of the Gods was in his cups on Mount Olympus. Zeus, being Zeus, could not help himself.

---

* 'Even though the sound of it produces consternation,' as Mary Poppins and Bert the chimney-sweep might sing.

'The next child born of the house of Perseus will rule all Argolis,' he blurted out.

'You mean that, husband?' said Hera quickly.

'Certainly I mean it.'

'Swear it before all.'

'Really?'

'If you mean it, swear it.'

'Very well,' said Zeus, puzzled by this earnestness, but confident that nothing could go wrong. Alcmene was ready to give birth at any moment, after all. 'I proclaim before you,' he said in a loud, clear voice, 'that the next child to be born in the line of Perseus shall rule the Argolid.'

You will remember Perseus's other son in Mycenae, Sthenelus? Hera knew that his wife Nicippe had also become pregnant, although she was only seven months on. That circumstance would have been enough to stymie most people, but Hera was not most people. She was the goddess of marital fidelity, the Queen of Heaven and, more than that, a wronged wife. While she had a will – and no one ever had a keener one – she would find a way.

She summoned her daughter EILEITHYIA, goddess of childbirth * and commanded her to go at once to Thebes, sit herself on a chair outside Alcmene's bedchamber with her legs firmly crossed, and to remain in that position until further notice. This posture, in such close proximity to the pregnant woman, would prevent Alcmene from opening her own legs to give birth, which Hera knew must in time suffocate and kill the children trapped in her womb. Meanwhile,

---

* Also 'Ilithyia'. I pronounce her name, probably wrongly, like 'Alicia' said with a lisp. Eileithyia was depicted as a woman wielding a torch, representing the burning pains of childbirth, or with her arms raised in the air to bring the child to the light. The Romans called her Lucina or Natio.

she went to Tiryns with a potion to induce Nicippe to give birth to her son by Sthenelus prematurely.

A complicated, cruel and distasteful scheme, but clever and effective. Such were the powers of Eileithyia that Alcmene, writhing in pain, was indeed unable to open her legs. In Tiryns, Nicippe was successfully delivered of a healthy boy, whom she and Sthenelus called EURYSTHEUS.*

Hera returned to Olympus in triumph. 'My dear husband,' she trilled. 'Prepare to be overjoyed. A boy has been born, a direct descendant of Perseus, no less!'

Zeus smiled broadly. 'Ah, yes. I rather thought that might be the case.'

'Such delightful news,' trilled Hera. 'I'm so happy for the couple. Sthenelus is a grandson of Perseus, of course, but Nicippe's lineage is exemplary too. Quite a pedigree. Descended not only from Pelops but also – '

'Wait, wait, wait . . . *Nicippe*? *Sthenelus*? What in hell's name have they got to do with anything?'

'Why, didn't I say?' Hera looked surprised. 'It is Nicippe and Sthenelus who have given the world a son.'

'B-but . . .'

'Was there ever such splendid news? And now, just as you have sworn, this boy – Eurystheus, by name – son of Sthenelus and a grandson of Perseus will grow up to rule the Argolid.'

'But . . .'

'*Just as you have sworn,*' Hera repeated in her sweetest tones. 'In front of everyone. And I *know* you will ensure that no harm will *ever* come to the boy. For your word is law and mighty Cosmos would cry out and Olympus would crack

---

* Eurystheus means 'broad-shouldered', which might suggest that his delivery gave Nicippe a twinge of pain as he emerged.

and the gods fall should you be so foolish as to go against your own word.'

'I . . . I . . .'

'Mouth is open, darling, and there's a string of drool dribbling from your beard right into your lap. It's most unappealing. Would you like Ganymede to find you a napkin?'

Zeus had been outmanoeuvred in masterly fashion. Hera knew, and he knew, that he would be forced to honour his oath and allow this wholly unlooked-for grandson of Perseus, this Eurystheus, to rule over the Argolid – the united lands of Mycenae, Corinth, Arcadia and Argos. All the plans Zeus had formed for his son by Alcmene now threatened to come to nothing. The wretched boy would be stillborn and Hera would win. No warring husband and wife ever let the other win in a battle of wills if they could help it, but Zeus could not think what to do next. He sat on his throne and brooded darkly.

Fortunately for Zeus, and for history, Alcmene was as lovely in manner as she was in looks. Good people attract loyal, loving friends and none were more loyal nor more loving than the two women who attended her, GALANTHIS and HISTORIS. For seven days and seven nights they had watched their poor friend and mistress writhing in pain at the growing burden inside her. At last Historis, who was a daughter of Tiresias and highly intelligent, conceived a plan.

Outside the door Eileithyia sat as stiff as a statue, legs tightly crossed, wondering how long it would be before she could safely assume that the baby inside Alcmene had died and she would be able stand up and let the circulation flow back into her thighs.

Suddenly, there came from inside the bedchamber the sound of screams. Could this be the news she was waiting for? The doors to Alcmene's room were flung open and

Galanthis burst out, clapping her hands and shouting, not with despair but with *joy*.

'Spread the news, spread the news!' she exclaimed. 'Our mistress has given birth! Oh happy day, happy day!'

Dumbfounded, Eileithyia jumped up. 'This cannot be!' she cried. 'Show me!'

Too late did she realise that she had been tricked into standing and uncrossing her legs. Through the open door she saw Alcmene, attended by Historis, now open her legs and push. First one, then another baby boy emerged and filled the air with healthy wailing cries. Wrapping her garments tight about her, Eileithyia fled the scene. She knew well how great Hera's wrath would be.

Wild indeed was Hera's rage when she found out what had happened. With a fierce flick of her hand she turned the impudent scheming Galanthis into a weasel.*

She had never felt so cheated and humiliated. From that moment on she swore eternal enmity against Alcmene's son by Zeus.

But which of the twins was Zeus's and which Amphitryon's? They were both fine-looking babies, vigorous, strong and – as you might expect, being eight days overdue – hefty. The doting parents named the twin first from the womb Alcides, in honour of his grandfather Alcaeus, son of Perseus, the other they called IPHICLES.† They could not tell by looking which was the son of a mortal and which the son of a god.

They would discover which of the two was the son of Zeus soon enough.

---

* Historis somehow escaped her wrath. Perhaps she was smart enough to hide.
† 'Iphi-' means 'strong' or 'mighty' (cf. Iphigenia, the 'strong-born') and 'cles' means 'pride' or 'glory'. Apparently an 'iphi' is also a smallish Egyptian unit of dry measurement, familiar to the Greeks, and corresponding roughly to 1–1½ gallons. Perhaps he was dubbed 'the Glorious Half-Pint'.

The villa which King Creon had given over to Amphitryon and Alcmene for their use while resident in Thebes stood quietly in the moonlight. Only the most attentive sentry, and one with the most finely tuned senses, would have observed a slight parting of the tall grass of the outer perimeter as two turquoise snakes slid across the lawn in the direction of the terrace.

Hera wished to lose no time in unleashing her vengeance on the insolent mortal baby that had dared to commit the crime of allowing itself to be born. Not concerned with which of the twins was her husband's baseborn progeny, she had sent the two venomous serpents to kill them both.

A concerned weasel watched powerlessly as they slithered along the terrace and towards the room with the sleeping infants. There was nothing that Galanthis could do but hope and pray.

Amphitryon and Alcmene were awoken early the next morning by the hysterical shrieks of Historis.

'Oh come, come!' she urged them, pulling the sheets from their bed.

Alarmed, they followed the squealing girl to the twins' nursery, where the most extraordinary sight met their eyes. The two babies lay in their cot. The face of one was screwed up with fear and it was purple from screaming.

The other lay on his back, kicking his legs in the air. In each dimpled fist he clutched a strangled viper. He looked up at his parents as they peered down and waved the dead snakes at them like toys, gurgling with delight.*

---

* It would be pleasing to think that they were rattlesnakes and that this remarkable incident initiated the custom of giving newborn babies rattles to wave, but sadly there is no evidence that the species ever existed outside the Americas.

'Well,' said Amphitryon, looking from one infant to the other. 'I think we can safely say now which is the son of Zeus.'

'Alcides.'

'Exactly.'

'This is the work of Hera,' said Alcmene, picking up Iphicles and quieting his frightened sobs. 'She sent those snakes. She will stop at nothing to destroy my boys.'

'It isn't fair on Iphicles,' raged Amphitryon, chucking his true son under the chin. 'We must consult Tiresias again.'

They made their way that night to seek his advice. While they were gone, the god Hermes stole silently into the nursery, took Alcides from his cot, flew with him up to Olympus and gave him to the waiting Athena.

The two gods crept round to where Hera was sleeping. Athena gently dropped the baby Alcides on her breast. At once he began to gorge himself. But he guzzled at her teat with such vigour that Hera woke up with a cry of pain. She looked down, plucked Alcides from her nipple and threw him disgustedly from her. Milk sprayed from her nipple in a great arc across the night sky, imprinting it with stars. Stars which, from that moment, would be known as the Milky Way.*

Hermes had deftly caught the baby when Hera cast him aside and he now sped off back to Thebes to replace Alcides in his cot before anyone noticed he was gone.

The whole botched affair had been Zeus's idea. He wanted his son Alcides to feed on Hera's milk, which would make him immortal. His favourite son and daughter, Hermes and Athena, had done their best, but Alcides had ingested little

---

* Sounds silly, but it is true. The Milky Way is a galaxy and the word galaxy is derived from the ancient Greek word *gala,* meaning 'milk'. Hence galactic and, perhaps, Galaxy milk chocolate.

more than a mouthful and none of them wanted to try that trick again.*

In Tiresias's temple, meanwhile, Alcmene and Amphitryon listened to the seer's advice.

'I have seen that Alcides will do marvellous things,' he was saying. 'Slay terrible monsters. Topple tyrants and found great dynasties. He will achieve fame such as no mortal has ever known. The other gods will help him, but Hera will harry and hound him without mercy.'

'Is there nothing we can do to placate her?' asked Alcmene.

Tiresias thought for a moment. 'Well, there is one thing. Perhaps you could change the child's name.'

'Change his name?' said Amphitryon. 'How would that help?'

'If you were to call him "Hera's glory" for instance? "Hera's pride".'

And so it was decided. From now on Alcides would be called *Heracles*.†

YOUTH AND UPBRINGING OF A HERO

Young Heracles grew up with his twin half-brother Iphicles. Amphitryon and Alcmene raised them as equals, but the speed with which Heracles put on height, weight and muscle separated the two boys very early in the minds of all who encountered them.

The twins received the kind of education usual for children of a royal house in those days. Chariot driving, javelin

---

* Hera, who was herself a mother, would have had breast milk; Athena, a virgin goddess, would not have been able to feed the baby.
† While he was *Hercules* to the Romans and to many of us in everyday speech today, it has become the convention these days to render him *Heracles*.

and discus throwing, track jumping and running were taught by Amphitryon. EURYTUS, King of Oechalia, the most famed bowman in Greece and a grandson of the archer god Apollo himself, taught the young Heracles to string a bow and shoot arrows with speed and accuracy. By the time he was ten, Heracles had already acquired a reputation as a fearsome runner, jumper, horseman, driver, thrower and archer. It was noticed, though, that despite the boy's amiable and friendly nature, he also possessed a fiery and furious temper. When the red mist descended, he was ungovernable by all but his father.

As well as fostering physical prowess, rhetoric, mathematics and music were of the first importance in the education of noble young Greeks and it was a matter of pride amongst the better families to secure the finest teachers. LINUS, the brother of ORPHEUS and a fine musician himself, taught Heracles and Iphicles how to tune and play a lyre, how to compose and sing, how to tap out precise rhythms and how to dance. None of these graceful accomplishments came easily to the young Heracles, who hated how self-conscious, clumsy and uncoordinated he felt when he tried to sing in tune or move in time. The day came when Linus, infuriated by Heracles' refusal to attend to his instructions, lifted a stick and brought it down on the boy's back. A storm broke in Heracles' mind: he grabbed the cane with a savage roar and jerked it towards him, bringing Linus's face directly in front of his. He nodded down, cracking the tutor's brow, and then picked him up and flung him across the room. Linus fell dead to the floor, the bones of his arms, legs and back all shattered.

The scandal was too great to be hushed up, but in the end Heracles was forgiven. Iphicles had been in the schoolroom too and told anyone who would listen that his brother had been sorely provoked. EUMOLPUS, a son of AUTOLYCUS*, took over the music tuition. At the same time CASTOR himself, the twin of POLYDEUCES, and like Heracles the offspring of a divine heteropaternal superfecundation†, offered to complete the youth's training in weaponry and the manly arts.

The killing of Linus revealed that Heracles had a very short fuse, something that was to cause distress to him and many victims of his outbursts of temper in the years to come. The rest of his schooling revealed that . . . how shall we put it kindly? . . . It revealed that while nature and fate‡ may have gifted Heracles with many fine attributes, wit and wisdom, craft and cunning were not foremost amongst them. He was, as we might say today, far from the brightest pixel on the screen. He was not stupid, not a brainless oaf by any means, but his real strength was . . . his real strength.

For what could be said with confidence and admiration, was that by the time he grew into his later teens Heracles was the tallest, broadest, strongest and fastest young man in the world. Those gods who championed him came forward now with signs of their favour, to equip him for a life of warfare, trials and endurance. Athena presented him with a robe, Poseidon gave him fine horses, Hermes a sword, Apollo a bow and arrows, HEPHAESTUS a most wondrous breastplate of pure gold.

The young man's growing reputation was cemented by the slaying of a fierce lion on Mount Cithaeron when he was still only eighteen years old.§ For forty-nine days he tracked the terrible creature; while each night the King of Thespiae,

---

* See *Mythos*, Vol. I, for further information about Autolycus, rascally son of Hermes.
† We will find out more of these twins, known as the Dioscuri, a little later on.
‡ For nature and fate, the Greeks might have said *physis* and *moira*.
§ Variously an individual mountain and a mountain range. Sacred to Dionysus, it was here that Pentheus was torn to pieces by his mother and aunts, and Actaeon by his own hounds (see *Mythos*, Vol. I). Cithaeron will go on to play a vital role, as we shall see, in the life and tragic destiny of Oedipus.

the grateful Thespis*, whose realm had suffered most from this dreadful scourge, rewarded Heracles for his heroic efforts by sending him each night one of his fifty daughters.

When at last the fiftieth day dawned, the lion was cornered and killed. That night, after enjoying the fiftieth bout of passion with the fiftieth daughter of the king, Heracles went home. Each daughter went on to give birth to a male child, the eldest and youngest girls bearing twins. A son for every week of the year. Heracles was as virile and potent in his love-making as in his killing.

On Heracles' return, he single-handedly defended Thebes against an attack from King ERGINOS of Orchomenos. The people of Thebes had been proud enough of Heracles, but pride now turned to veneration. They revered him as the greatest Theban since their founder hero Cadmus. If they had their way, Heracles would rule over them as king. Thebes already had a king, Creon, who was smart and politic enough to offer Heracles the hand of his daughter Megara.†

All seemed so sweet in the life of the young Heracles. His fame increased and spread and happy years passed, during which he fathered a son and daughter by Megara and grew to full manhood as a devoted husband and father, very likely the heir to the Theban throne.

CRIME AND PUNISHMENT

Heracles' life in Thebes was almost modern in its rhythms. Each day he would kiss goodbye to his wife Megara and children and go off to work, killing monsters and toppling

---

* Not to be confused with the historical Thespis, Greece's first actor.

† We will meet Creon again when we tell the story of Oedipus.

tyrants. Today's commuter finds less drastic ways to defeat competitors and bestial colleagues perhaps – the dragons we slay may be more metaphorical than real – but the manner and routine is not so very different.

One fateful evening Heracles returned to the family villa to be met by two small but fierce and burning-eyed demons in the doorway. He charged them at once, grappled them to the ground, broke their backs and stamped on their screeching heads until they lay crushed and dead at his feet. Suddenly, a great dragon came screaming out of the house towards him, fire streaming from its mouth and nostrils. He rushed at it, closed his hands around its scaly neck and squeezed with all his strength. Only as the life went of the monster and it slipped dead to the floor did Hera lift the mist of delusion she had visited on him. Looking down, he now saw with appalling clarity that the dragon he had killed was his wife Megara and the two demons were his beloved children.

It was one of Hera's cruellest interventions, and evidence of the unfathomable depth of her hatred. She had been growing ever more frustrated at the sight of her loathed enemy living so happy and fulfilled a life. She chose to strip Heracles down to a state of absolute nothingness, to take in one swift and irreversible moment everything that mattered to him. Not just those he loved most, but his reputation too. When news broke of what he had done, no one would speak to, or come near to, him. He was polluted. From hero to zero is a tired phrase today, but nobody before had so swiftly gone from universal love and admiration to loathing and contempt.

Heracles' grief was overpowering. He wanted to die. But he knew that he must punish himself by undergoing an unrelenting penance. Only then would he feel fit to meet the souls of Megara and his children in the underworld. Without purification from a king, oracle, priest or priestess, those responsible for blood crimes had to attempt to cleanse themselves by a life of exile and atonement. If they failed to expiate their crimes, the Erinyes, the wild Furies, would rise up from Erebus and chase them down, flailing them with iron whips until they went mad.

Heracles exiled himself from Thebes, and went on his knees* to Delphi to seek guidance.

'To atone for his abominable crimes, Heracles must take himself to Tiryns and supplicate himself before the throne,' the Pythia chanted.

Heracles could not know this, but the priestess had been entranced by Hera and the words were hers.

'For ten years he must serve without question,' the priestess continued. 'Whatever he is told to do, Heracles must do. Whatever tasks he is set to perform, these must Heracles willingly undertake. Only then can he be free.'

Hera's spirit left the priestess and the voices of Apollo and Athena now enthused† her.

'Do all that you are asked without stint, without complaint, and immortality will be yours. Your father has promised it.'

Heracles did not want immortality, but he knew he must obey in any case. He turned his feet towards the road leading to Tiryns, capital of Mycenae. Its king was the now fully-grown Eurystheus, Heracles' relative, the one whose premature birth had been induced by Hera all those years ago to ruin Zeus's plan to secure the throne for Heracles.

---

* A practice of self-mortification that still goes on. I have seen with my own eyes penitents arriving on their knees at the shrine of Our Lady of Guadalupe in Mexico. Some of them have kneel-walked hundreds of miles to get there. Far from being Herculean, they are usually ancient and diminutive old ladies.

† *Enthusiasm* meant, originally, possession by a god. The verb 'enthuse' was a later American English back-formation.

Eurystheus had none of Heracles' heroic attributes, none of his strength, spirit, generosity or air of command. He had grown up all too aware of the reputation of his stronger, finer and more popular relative, and he had long smouldered with hatred, envy and resentment.

What self-control it took for Heracles to kneel in front of Eurystheus's throne and beg for expiation we can only guess.

'The filth of your unnatural crimes has revolted all people of feeling,' said the king, savouring every moment. 'You will not be worthy to live in the world of men until you have paid the full price. Ten tasks you will perform for me over ten years without assistance or payment. When you have completed the last of them I may be disposed to forgive you, embrace you as my relative and allow you your freedom. Until then you are bound to me as my slave. The Queen of Heaven herself has ordained it. Is this understood?'

Hera had instructed her instrument well.

Heracles bowed his head.

THE LABOURS* OF HERACLES

1. THE NEMEAN LION

Eurystheus rubbed his chin and thought hard. If he were to command his unruly relative and set him to useful work, he might as well begin at home. Eurystheus ruled not just Mycenae, but – thanks to Zeus's rash promise – all of Argolis, much of which was afflicted by terrifying wild beasts.†

The most obviously terrifying was a lion that preyed on the people of Nemea in the northeast of the kingdom, not far from the Isthmus of Corinth. Fear of this terrible animal was deterring mainland travellers and merchants from trading with the Argolid and the rest of the Peloponnese. Offspring of the monstrous CHIMERA‡, this was no ordinary lion. Its golden hide was so thick that spears and arrows bounced off it as though they were straws. Its claws were razor sharp and could tear through armour as though it were paper. Its powerful jaws could crunch rock as though it were celery. Many warriors had already perished trying to subdue it.

---

* In Greek they were variously called the *erga* or more commonly the *athloi* of Heracles. The word *ergon* simply means 'work' while *athlos* means more than labour, it carries a sense of 'test'. Our words athlete and athletic derive from it.

† At the risk of sending you mad by going over the family tree again, his father was Sthenelus, making Eurystheus a relative of Perseus. As was Heracles, whose parents Alcmene and Amphityron were cousins and each a grandchild of Perseus. But of course Zeus was really Heracles' father, as he was Perseus's. Therefore Perseus was both Heracles' great-grandfather and half-brother. Those Greeks, eh?

‡ For more about this beast, see the chapter devoted to the adventures of Bellerophon.

'Go to Nemea,' Eurystheus said to Heracles, 'and kill the lion that is laying waste the countryside.'

Shame really, Eurystheus thought to himself with a giggle. I shan't get ten years out of him. This first task will kill him. Oh well.

'Just kill it?' said Heracles. 'You don't want it brought back?'

'No, I don't want it brought back. What would I do with a lion?'

To gales of obedient laughter from his courtiers, Eurystheus tapped the side of his head as Heracles straightened, bowed and left the throne-room.

'Arms the size of an oak tree, brain the size of an acorn,' said the king with a snort.

Heracles spent months stalking the creature, as he had done years before with the Thespian Lion. He knew that his weapons, of formidable and divine providence as they were, would be of no use against the animal's impregnable pelt. He would have to rely on his bare hands, and so he spent these months in training. He took to uprooting trees and raising boulders above his head until his raw strength, mighty as it had always been, was now greater than ever.

When he knew that he was ready, Heracles tracked the lion to its lair. He fell on the immense monster and threw it to the ground. Never had anyone dared to attack the beast in this way. Grappling tight, Heracles gave it no chance to pull back and strike with claws or jaws. What use was its impenetrable hide against the iron grip of Heracles' hands around its throat? For hours they rolled in the dust until the life was at last throttled from it and the great Nemean Lion breathed no more.

Heracles stood by its body and bowed his head. 'It was a fair fight,' he said. 'And I hope you didn't suffer. I hope you will forgive me if I now flay the hide from you.'

Such respect for an enemy, even a dumb brute, was typical of Heracles. When an adversary was alive he knew no mercy, but the moment they were gone he did his best, where possible, to send them to the next world with honour and ceremony. He could not be sure that animals had souls or the expectation of an afterlife, even those descended from primordial entities like Echidna and Typhon, but he behaved as if they did. The greater the fight they put up, the deeper and more reverent his funeral prayers.

He had been stung by Eurystheus's contemptuous dismissal of him. He wanted to skin his kill and take the pelt in triumph back to Mycenae, which is why he asked permission of the lion's corpse. But Heracles found his sharpest knives and swords could not make so much as a scratch on that impenetrable hide. He hit, at last, on the idea of pulling out the lion's razor-like claws. These were sharp enough, and Heracles skinned off one great piece, snarling head included. He strung the deadly claws into a necklace and in an excess of frenzied joy he pulled up the greatest oak tree he could find and stripped it of its branches to form a mighty club.

With the necklace of claws around his neck, the indestructible pelt over his shoulders, the open jaws and glaring eyes of the lion on top of his head, and the mighty club swinging by his side, Heracles had found his look.

2. THE LERNAEAN HYDRA

Eurystheus had not expected Heracles to come back alive at all, certainly not dressed like some wild, untamed brigand of the mountains. The king, however, was crafty enough to hide his dismay.

'Yes . . . that was to be expected,' he said, stifling a yawn.

'An aged lion is no test. Now, for your next task. Do you know Lake Lerna, not that far from here? It is terrorised by the Hydra, which guards the gate there to the underworld. I wouldn't dream of interfering were it not that the creature has taken to attacking and killing innocent men, women and children who venture near. I am too busy to deal with it myself, so I send you, Heracles, to rid us of this nuisance.'

'As you wish,' said Heracles, nodding a bow of assent which caused the head of the Nemean Lion to snap its jaws violently shut. Eurystheus could not help but leap in alarm. With an ill-concealed grin of contempt, Heracles turned and left.

The goddess Hera had prepared Lake Lerna with malicious relish. Not only were its waters infested by the Hydra, a huge water serpent with nine heads (one of which was immortal), each capable of spraying jets of the deadliest poison known in the world, but she had hidden in the lake's depths a ferocious giant crab too.

The Hydra reared up at Heracles' approach, every one of its vicious heads spitting venom.* Confidently enough he lunged forward and sliced one of the heads clean off. Instantly two new heads grew up out of the stump.

This was going to be difficult. Every time Heracles sliced or clubbed a head two more sprang up in its place. To make matters worse the crab was now jumping up out of the water and making a frenzied attack. Its giant pincers came at him again and again, trying to slice him open and gut him. Leaping to one side, Heracles brought his club down with all his might and shattered the shell into thousands of fragments. The squelched creature inside reared its slimy body in the

---

* Greek ceramic representations of the Hydra tend to show a kind of upside-down octopus: a round, sometimes doughnut shaped body out of which extend nine snakes. Popular comic book art makes the creature more like a nine-headed dragon.

air, quivered and fell back dead. Hera placed her favourite crustacean in the stars where it shines today as the constellation Cancer, the Crab. But she was content. Her beloved Hydra was wreaking her revenge. Already it had twenty-four heads, each spraying a lethal poison.

Heracles made a tactical withdrawal. As he sat at a safe distance, pondering what to do next, his nephew IOLAUS, son of Heracles' twin brother Iphicles, came out from behind some trees.

'Uncle,' he said, 'I've watched the whole thing. If Eurystheus is allowed to encumber you with an extra trial, then I should be allowed to assist you. Let me be your squire.'

In truth, the intrusion of the crab had annoyed Heracles greatly. One quest at a time, that was what he had agreed to. The addition of a second, unannounced danger struck him as unfair. He accepted his nephew's offer and between them they came up with a new plan of attack. I am inclined to believe that the scheme was more likely to have emerged from the mind of Iolaus than that of Heracles, who was a man of action, a man of passions and a man of limitless courage, but not a man of ideas.

The plan was to approach the Hydra systematically: Heracles would advance and lop off a head, then Iolaus would step smartly in with a burning torch and sear the fresh stump, preventing any new heads from erupting in its place. Slice, cauterise, slice, that was the system they came up with – and it worked.

After hours of exhausting and disgusting effort there was only one head left, the immortal head, the head that could not die. At last Heracles hacked this off too and buried it far underground. To this day the Hydra's poisonous vapours breathe up their sulphurous gas in the drained malarial swamp where Lake Lerna once stood.

'Thank you,' said Heracles to Iolaus. 'Now you get home.

And not a word to your father.' Heracles knew that his twin would be angered if he heard that his son had been in such danger.

Heracles felt no need to pay his respects to the Hydra. After all, the immortal head was still alive and belching hate underground. He knelt beside the twitching body not in reverence, but to coat the tips of his arrows with its congealing blood. The envenomed arrows would prove to be immeasurably useful – and immeasurably tragic.

Their use would change the world.

3. The Ceryneian Hind

Eurystheus now turned cunning. A water serpent was one thing, but not even Heracles could match an Olympian.

'Bring me the golden hind of Ceryneia*,' he said.

He felt confident that this Third Labour must surely be Heracles' last, for success would mean certain death, or at the very least eternal torment.

The golden-horned, brass-footed Ceryneian Hind could do no harm to anyone. A deer fleeter than any hound or arrow, she presented a challenge to huntsmen, but not a danger. But the hind was sacred to Artemis, and *this* was where the threat lay. The savagery with which the goddess protected her own and punished any sacrilege against her or those who followed her was well known. She would never allow harm to befall her beloved hind.† Heracles would either fail in his task or be struck down by Artemis for

---

* Pronounced 'Serry-nay-uh' I think. Ceryneia, or Keryneia, today lies in the north west of the Peloponnese in the region known as Achaea. 'Achaean' is the name Homer most commonly gave the Greek forces in the Trojan War.

† What's the difference between a hind and a doe? Your guess is as good as mine.

presumption. Either way, Eurystheus was confident that his pestilential cousin would not return.

For almost a year Heracles pursued his quarry over hill and – one supposes – dale. Finally he succeeded in netting and subduing the animal.

He had no wish to harm so shy and beautiful a creature. He slung the hind gently over his shoulders and whispered to her as he walked back to Mycenae.

As he passed through a wood, Artemis emerged from the shadows.

'You dare?' she hissed, raising her silver bow.

'Goddess, goddess, I throw myself on your mercy.' Heracles, went down on one knee.

'Mercy? I do not know the word. Prepare to die.'

As Artemis took aim her twin Apollo stepped out of the wood and pushed the bow down. 'Now, sister,' he said. 'Don't you know this is Heracles?'

'If it was our father, the Storm Bringer himself, I would shoot him for daring to take my hind.'

'I understand,' said Heracles in his meekest voice. 'It is a terrible sacrilege, but I am bound to King Eurystheus and it was he who commanded me to take the animal. It is Hera's will that I obey him.'

'Hera's will?'

Apollo and Artemis conferred. The Queen of Heaven had at best a stiff and formal relationship with Zeus's children by other women* and had never made the twins' lives easy. It amused them to assist her enemy.

Artemis turned to Heracles. 'You may continue on your way,' she said. 'But when you have shown my hind to the court in Mycenae you must return her to the wild.'

---

* For the fraught circumstances of their birth see *Mythos*, Vol. I.

'You are as wise as you are beautiful,' said Heracles.

'Dear me,' said Apollo. 'That sort of flattery is not the way to my sister's heart. On your way.'

Eurystheus was astonished to see Heracles return with the glorious creature, which he announced he would make the prize exhibit in his private menagerie. Mindful of his promise to Artemis, however, Heracles replied:

'Certainly, my king. Come forward, she is yours to claim.'

Just as Eurystheus approached, Heracles, under the cover of his lion-skin cloak, gave the hind a sharp pinch on the rump. Eurystheus leapt to catch her as she reared up, but she galloped away with a bark, her bronze hooves setting up sparks from the palace flagstones.

'You failed in your task!' snarled Eurystheus.

'Majesty, I brought you the hind as agreed,' said Heracles. 'It's a pity you weren't quick enough to hold her and keep her, but I cannot be held responsible for that.' He turned to the court. 'Surely I did everything that was asked of me?'

A murmur of sympathetic agreement from his courtiers held Eurystheus back from venting his true feelings.

Sometimes, Heracles could display something approaching real cunning.

4. THE ERYMANTHIAN BOAR

Heracles' next task was to bring back alive a giant boar that was ravaging the area around Mount Erymanthus, in Arcadia.

The Labour itself was not the greatest challenge Heracles faced and would hardly be worth retelling were it not for one episode. It not only reveals our hero at his clumsiest and least appealing but might also be considered to have set in motion the circumstances that were to lead to his terrible death.

Heracles went to seek advice about the boar's habits from a friend of his who lived nearby, a centaur named PHOLUS. The offspring of IXION and the cloud goddess NEPHELE,* centaurs were a hybrid breed. From the head to the waist they were human, but the rest was pure horse. Expert archers, they made fierce and brave warriors, but often became ill-natured, violent and licentious when in drink. The great exceptions were CHIRON, master of the healing arts and the wise tutor of ASCLEPIUS† and, later, of JASON and Achilles, and Heracles' friend Pholus. Chiron was the immortal offspring of Kronos and the oceanid PHILYRA, while the mortal Pholus was sired by SILENUS, the pot-bellied companion of Dionysus and one of the Meliae, the nymphs of the ash-tree. His advice to Heracles was not to think of capturing the Erymanthian Boar until winter came.

'Trap him in a snow drift, that's the best way,' he said. 'Otherwise he'll run you ragged. Meanwhile, why don't you stay with me here in my cave?'

Heracles was only too happy to avail himself of the invitation. One night after dinner, he helped himself to a stone jar of wine. He had no reason to know that it was the common property of the whole centaur tribe. The smell of the wine attracted the other centaurs and they trotted up to demand their share. Heracles' short temper was piqued by this (perhaps his own inebriation didn't help) and an ill-mannered argument broke out. The row became a fight and the fight soon degenerated into slaughter as Heracles unloosed a volley of arrows, which were tipped, you will recall, with fatally

---

* See *Mythos*, Vol. I, for the story of Ixion. There is more to come on Nephele and Chiron in Jason's story, and we will meet the centaurs again with Theseus.
† See *Mythos*, Vol. I.

venomous Hydra blood.* Even poor Pholus died when he dropped an arrow on his foot, piercing the skin above the hoof and sending enough of the Hydra's venom into his bloodstream to kill him. A few of the Arcadian centaurs did survive. Amongst them was one called NESSUS, who would in time – as we shall see – revenge these deaths in the most terrible manner.

Meanwhile, a mortified and remorseful Heracles helped bury the dead before turning his mind to the business in hand, the capture of the boar. With snow now blanketing the higher slopes of the mountain, he easily tracked and trapped the animal in a deep drift, hoisted it over his shoulders and trudged back to Mycenae.

When Heracles returned with a boar that was still very much alive, Eurystheus was so terrified by the enormous beast that he leapt into a great stone jar and cowered there.

'What do you want me to do with it?'

'Take it away.'

'Don't you want to examine it? It's got lovely bristles.'

'Take it away *now*!'

Eurystheus's voice echoed around the interior of the jar.

This scene was a favourite amongst Greek pot painters who loved to depict the frightened Eurystheus cringing in his pithos while Heracles threatens to drop an enormous squirming pig down on top of him.

---

* In some versions of this episode, Chiron himself was accidentally scratched by one of Heracles' arrows and suffered the most appalling agony. He alone amongst his race, being a son of Kronos, was immortal. The prospect of living eternally in such pain was insupportable to him. He begged the gods to be released into death and Zeus granted his wish, casting him into the heavens as the constellation Sagittarius, the man-horse archer. This is an egregious example of timeline inconsistency since Chiron was later tutor to ACHILLES who was yet to be born.

5. THE AUGEAN STABLES

Halfway through – or so Heracles *thought*, we will cross that painful bridge when we come to it – and Eurystheus really believed that this time, *this time*, he had set Heracles a problem that he could never solve. Even if the task didn't kill him it would, the king told himself with malicious glee, deprive him of everlasting life. After all, the oracle had told Heracles that the *completion* of the tasks would guarantee Heracles immortality, merely attempting them was not good enough. As Yoda had expressed it a long time ago in a galaxy far, far away: 'Do. Or do not. There is no try.'

King AUGEAS of Elis, a son of Helios the sun god, was possessed of a herd of three thousand cattle. The animals were immortal and had consequently produced, over the years, a far greater than ordinary quantity of dung.* The stables in which they were quartered had not been cleaned for thirty years.

'You will go to Elis,' Eurystheus told Heracles, 'and thoroughly clean out the stables of King Augeas *in one day*.'

Arriving in Elis, Heracles sought an audience with the king and struck a deal: if he did manage to clean the stables between sun up and sun down the next day, Augeas would give him one tenth of his herd.

If I have given the impression that Heracles was a brainless lummox, a boneheaded oaf, a he-man of minimal intelligence, I have slightly misled you. He was *direct* – that is the quality I would associate most with him. We are perhaps too used to thinking that indirect, subtle, contrived tactics

---

* Was this Greek satire against the gods? A way of suggesting that the immortals were more full of shit than mortals?

are more intelligent and effective than uncomplicated assaults, but sometimes that is not so. I do not imagine that either the clever Theseus or the cunning Odysseus would ever have come up with so simple and splendid a plan as the diverting of the two local rivers, the Peneus and the Alpheus. Of course, enormous strength was required to hammer openings into the stable walls and gouge out the rivers' courses, but the idea was beautiful in its simplicity. Just as Heracles had planned, the waters poured through the stables and sluiced out the accumulated muck of thirty years. The manure-rich torrents swept down into the plains and fields of Elis and fertilised the land for miles around.

A triumphant Heracles applied to Augeas for his reward of three hundred head of cattle, but the king, who loved his herd more than anything in the world, refused to pay up.

'Eurystheus had sent you to cleanse my stables as his slave,' he said, 'so any reward would be unnecessary and wrong. Besides, I never struck such a bargain in the first place.'

'Oh, but you did!' cried Augeas's son, PHYLEUS, who admired Heracles and was shocked to see his father behave so meanly to his hero. 'I heard you distinctly.'

The king angrily banished both from his kingdom. Phyleus was exiled to Dulichium, an island in the Ionian Sea*, while Heracles made his way back to Mycenae, simmering with rage. He swore that one day he would return and have his revenge on Augeas.

The people of Elis, however, cheered Heracles as he passed through their kingdom on his way back to Tiryns. The newly fertilised fields, enriched with all that manure,

---

* The southern Adriatic. Confusing because the name 'Ionia' refers to parts of Asia Minor, today's Turkey, far to the other side of Greece.

would bring prosperity to their whole region. He had made Nemea safe, and Lernea and Mount Erymanthia too. Heracles was no longer just a hero for kings and warriors. He was a people's champion.

6. THE STYMPHALIAN BIRDS

Heracles presented himself at the palace of Tiryns to hear what Eurystheus had in store for him next. Without speaking, the king sat on his throne and stroked his beard.

'Very well,' he said at last. 'Your next task is to rid Lake Stymphalia of its infestation of birds.'

When it comes to the Stymphalian Birds, there is disagreement amongst the sources we usually rely upon for details of Heracles and his Labours. It is generally accepted now that these were fearsome man-eating creatures the size of cranes with beaks of iron, talons of brass and foul, toxic droppings. Sacred to ARES, the god of war, they infested the tree-lined shores of Lake Stymphalia, causing havoc and distress to the farmers and villages of northeastern Arcadia and rendering the countryside for miles around entirely uninhabitable.

The ground beneath the trees in which the birds nested was fetid swampland. When Heracles tried to approach, he sank up to his shoulders in the miasmic filth. Observing his plight Athena provided him with a great bronze rattle, manufactured in Hephaestus's forge. Its ear-splitting rapid-fire clacking flushed the birds from their roosts in panic and fright and Heracles was able to shoot them down in enough numbers to cause the remainder to fly away – we will encounter their deadly menace once again on another occasion.

7. THE CRETAN BULL

'The Cretan Bull?' repeated Heracles.

'Yes,' said Eurystheus testily. 'Do I have to tell you everything twice? The Cretan Bull. Ox. Steer. Male Cow. Crete. Island. Fetch.'

Many years ago, a great white bull had charged out of the sea onto the shores of Crete. It had been sent by the god Poseidon in answer to the prayers of King MINOS, who wished to awe his subjects with a sign that his rule was divinely sanctioned. The idea had been to sacrifice the bull to Poseidon once his brothers accepted this proof, but both Minos and his wife PASIPHAE were so enchanted by the creature's beauty that they hadn't the heart to slaughter it. Indeed, Pasiphae went so far as to mate with it. She bore it a son ASTERION, half man half bull, known as the Minotaur, who lived trapped in a cunning labyrinth built to house it by Minos's architect, inventor and designer, the great DAEDALUS.

The bull, meanwhile, rampaged around Crete, savage, untameable and terrifying. As a favour to Minos, Eurystheus sent Heracles there to subdue it and bring it to Tiryns – alive.

Heracles, so different in approach, as we shall see, from his younger cousin Theseus, had no technique other than confidence in his own strength and inexhaustible stamina. He found the bull, shouted at it, maddened it and planted himself in its way. When it charged, he simply grabbed its horns* and wrenched. The bull resisted with all its strength. Gradually Heracles pulled it to the ground, rolling around with it, much as he had the Nemean Lion and the

---

* Perhaps inspiring the phrase 'to take the bull by the horns'.

Erymanthian Boar. Never letting go of the horns he roared in the bull's ear, slapped it, punched it, tweaked it, thwacked it and bit it. Finally, the battered and exhausted beast lay down in the dust beneath him and submitted its will to his. Mounting the creature, Heracles rode it over the waves from which it had been born all the way back to the Peloponnese. He led it into the palace of Eurystheus, who once more sought refuge in his stone jar.

'All right, damn you, just get rid of it, will you?'

'Are you sure you don't want to tickle its ear?'

'Get rid of the damned thing!'

If Eurystheus had called out from the jar 'Sacrifice it to the gods', the whole history of the world might be different. As it was, Heracles obediently released the bull into the countryside. Once free of its master, it bucked and galloped for miles and miles, finally making its home all the way over on the east of mainland Greece, on the Plain of Marathon, where it tormented and harassed the local people until another great hero, as we shall see, finally came to face it down and end its extraordinary life.

8. THE MARES OF DIOMEDES
(INCORPORATING THE STORY OF ALCESTIS AND ADMETUS)

'So you've dealt with the bull,' said Eurystheus, pulling at his beard. 'Very clever, I'm sure. But one bull is hardly a test, is it?'

Heracles said nothing. He stood awaiting his instructions.

'Right. I'd like you to bring me the four mares of DIOMEDES.'

'Diomedes?'

'Do you know nothing? He's the King of Thrace. Mares

are female horses. Horses are quadrupeds with manes and hoofs. There are four of them. Four is a number between three and five. Now go – and don't come back without them, understood?'

On his way north to Thrace, Heracles dropped in at Pherae to stay with his friends King ADMETUS of Pherae and his queen ALCESTIS, a couple whose story is well worth hearing.

Many years earlier Zeus had been forced to kill Apollo's son Asclepius, the master of medicine and the healing arts.* Ares and Hades had complained about Asclepius's habit of bringing mortals back to life, making a nonsense of war and death. Zeus had accepted their arguments and struck Asclepius down with a thunderbolt. Apollo stormed up to Hephaestus's forge in a fit of rage and confronted the three CYCLOPES, who were responsible for the manufacture of Zeus's thunderbolts. Apollo couldn't punish the king of the gods for the death of Asclepius, but he could punish the Cyclopes: ARGES, STEROPES and BRONTES. He shot all three with arrows. Such insurrection was not to be tolerated and Zeus banished Apollo from Olympus, sentencing him to labour in bondage to a mortal. Being famed for his hospitality (always a sure way to Zeus's heart), the Thessalian king Admetus was the mortal Zeus selected, sending Apollo to serve as his herdsman for a year and a day.

The punishment turned out to be anything but a penance for Apollo. From the first he and Admetus got along wonderfully. Admetus, who had just inherited his throne and was not yet married, was charming, hospitable, warm-hearted and physically attractive. Far from being Apollo's master, the young king became his lover. Apollo enjoyed being a

---

* See *Mythos*, Vol. I, *Twice Born*.

herdsman and made sure that all of Admetus's cows gave birth to twins, greatly increasing the value of the royal herd. Ownership of cattle in those times – as it is around much of the world today – was a great marker of wealth and status. Admetus prospered and Apollo's period of servitude passed in a flash. The two remained friends and the god even helped his favourite win Alcestis, one of the nine daughters of King PELIAS of Iolcos*. Alcestis was so beautiful that princes and nobles from all over Greece were clamouring for her hand. Her father ruled that he would give her in marriage to the first suitor who proved able to harness a boar and a lion to a chariot. Yoking together two such incompatible wild beasts had proved impossible for all comers thus far, but with Apollo's help Admetus managed it. He drove the chariot up to Pelias and won his bride.

The god came to his friend's aid again when, what with the excitements of wooing and winning Alcestis, Admetus fell short in his devotions to Apollo's twin Artemis, who was perhaps more sensitive to slights real and imaginary than any other Olympian. She punished Admetus for this neglect by sending snakes into the bridal chamber, putting something of a damper on the couple's first night together. Apollo, however, helped Admetus by instructing him in which prayers and sacrifices would best mollify his prickly sister. The snakes vanished and the honeymoon proceeded. The ecstasy of the bridal chamber translated into perfect marital bliss and the marriage of Admetus and Alcestis proved to be as happy as any in Greece.

So fond of Admetus was Apollo that he could not bear the idea of his beloved friend dying. Rather than begging

---

* We will see more of Pelias in the story of Jason, where he is an important figure. Alcestis was one of the daughters who would make that unfortunate mistake with their father and the cooking pot.

Zeus to bestow immortality upon his favourite, as Selene and Eos had each done for a mortal lover,* Apollo approached the problem differently. He invited the MOIRAI – the three Fates, CLOTHO, LACHESIS and ATROPOS – up to Olympus and got them very drunk.

'Darling Moirai,' he said to them, staggering slightly and slurring his speech to give the impression that he was as intoxicated as they were, 'I love you.'

'Bloody love you too,' said Atropos.

'You're the . . . hup . . . best,' hiccupped Clotho.

'Always said so,' gulped Lachesis, wiping a tear from her eye.

'I'll take out anyone who says different and I'll do them.'

'Damn right.'

'They're dead.'

'So if I were to ask you ladies a favour . . .' said Apollo.

'Name it.'

'Condunder it sid – consider it done.'

'Only got to ask.'

'My friend Admetus. Lovely man. A prince.'

'I thought he was a king?'

'Well yes, he is a king,' admitted Apollo. 'But he's a prince of a man.'

'Sort of makes sense,' conceded Atropos. 'Prince of a king.'

'But not king of a prince?'

'The point is,' said Apollo, not wishing to be sidetracked, 'I'd like to ask your help in ensuring that his life doesn't get cut off.'

'The cutting off, that's my job,' said Atropos.

'I know,' said Apollo.

'You want me *not* to cut the thread of his life?'

---

* See *Mythos*, Vol. I, pages 309 and 315.

'I'd esteem it the greatest of favours.'

'You want him to live for ever?'

'If it could be managed.'

'Ooh, that's quite an ask. Cutting the thread of life is what I do. *Not* cutting it . . . well, that's a whole other thing. What say you, sisters?'

Apollo refilled their cups. 'Have another drink while you think about it.'

The Moirai put their heads together.

'Because we love you,' said Clotho at last.

'Lots . . .' added Lachesis.

'Because we love you lots, we will allow it. Just this one time. If your friend . . . What was his name?'

'Admetus. Admetus, King of Pherae.'

'If Admetus, King of Pherae, can find someone else willing to die in his place . . .'

'. . . then we don't see any reason why we need to thread his cut . . .'

'Cut his thread . . .'

'What she said.'

This then was the bargain Apollo explained to Admetus.

'You will never be taken down to the underworld so long as you can find someone, anyone, who'll agree to take your place.'

Admetus went to his parents. They've already seen the best of life, he reasoned, and one of them will surely agree to be taken early if it means my immortality.

'You begot me,' he said to his father PHERES, 'it must be your duty then to ensure that I keep living.'

To Admetus's surprise and mortification, Pheres was entirely unwilling to cooperate.

'Yes, I begot you, and I raised you to rule over this land, but I don't see that I'm bound to die for you. There's no law of our ancestors and no Greek law that says fathers should die for their children. You were born to live your own life, whether it's a happy one or a wretched one. I have given you all I need give you. I don't expect you to die for me, and you shouldn't expect me to die for you. So, you love the light of day. What makes you think your father hates it? Know this: we are a long time dead. Life may be short, but it is sweet.'*

'Yes, but you've lived your life and I . . .'

'I have lived my life when my life comes naturally to its end, not when you say so.'

Rebuffed by his own flesh and blood, Admetus cast the net wider. He had never considered immortality before, but once Apollo had told him how it was possible, the idea became an obsession with him. He now believed it was his right. He had thought that it would be a simple matter to find someone, anyone, to do this simple thing for him and die. It turned out that everybody seemed, like his father, unreasonably anxious to hang on to their lives. Eventually it was his loyal and loving wife Alcestis who came to his rescue. She announced that she would be content to die in her husband's place.

'You mean it?'

'Yes, my darling,' she said, calmly patting his hand.

'You're honestly happy to do this for me?'

'Quite happy, if it makes you happy.'

A fine marble tomb was constructed and Alcestis prepared herself for the allotted time of Admetus's decease, which would now mark her own. But when the day came, Admetus had a radical change of heart. He realised how

---

* Loosely taken from the fifth-century Athenian dramatist Euripides' version of this story, *Alcestis*.

much he loved Alcestis and how much less of a life he would have without her. In fact, he now saw that a long and endless existence alone would be worse than death. He begged her not to go. But her declaration of intent to take his place had been heard and recorded by the Fates. Die she must – and die she did.

It was at exactly this moment, with a devastated Admetus trying to come to terms with what he had done, that Heracles called in at the palace.

So mindful of his obligations as a host was Admetus that he could not countenance turning a guest away. He did his best to hide his sorrow and entertain his guest with all the warmth and generosity for which he was famous. Nonetheless, Heracles couldn't but notice that his old friend was dressed in black.

'Well, as a matter of fact, we have had a death in the palace.'

'I'll leave you then. I can always come another time.'

'No, no. Please, come in. I insist.'

Heracles was still unsure. Hosts have obligations, but so do guests. 'Who died? No one close to you?'

Admetus had no wish to burden his friend with his woes. 'No blood relation, I promise . . .' which was technically true. 'A woman of the household, that's all.'

'Oh well, in that case . . .' Heracles came through into the great hall. His eyes fell greedily on the table where the funeral banquet had been laid out. 'Always said you served the best wine and cakes,' he said, helping himself to lavish quantities of both.

'You are too kind,' said Admetus. 'I'll leave you for a moment but please, make yourself entirely at home.'

Heracles tucked cheerfully in. He finished all the wine on the table and yelled out for more. The chief steward of the household came, grim faced. He was a servant of the old school. Not even the risk of igniting the notorious temper of the strongest man in the world would make him swerve from his duty.

'Have you no shame?' he hissed. 'How can you eat and drink like this with the house in such bitter mourning?'

'Why the hell shouldn't I? Who's dead? Only some serving woman or other.'

'Listen to him, gods! Our dear queen has been taken from us and you dare call her "some serving woman"?'

'Alcestis? But Admetus told me . . .'

'His majesty is even now in the garden sobbing his noble heart out.'

'Oh, what a fool I am!'

Heracles now succumbed to one of his periodic bouts of guilt and violent self-abasement. He beat his breast and called himself the most insensitive buffoon that ever lived, unworthy to be a guest in any man's house, an arse, a clown an oaf and the lowest of the low. Then he came to his senses and realised what he had to do.

'I shall go down to the underworld,' he said to himself, 'and I shall fight anyone who stops me from bringing Alcestis back up. I swear I shall.'

As luck would have it, such a drastic course was not necessary. Before setting off, Heracles went to pay his respects at Alcestis's brand-new tomb. There he found THANATOS, the god of death, just as he was taking her soul.

'Let go!' bellowed Heracles.

'You have no business here,' said Thanatos. 'I command you to –'

With a roar Heracles was on him, wrestling the helpless Thanatos to the ground and pounding him with his fists.

Some time later Admetus left off his weeping in the garden

and went back into the palace. 'Where's Heracles?' he asked.

'Oh, him,' sniffed the steward. 'He left as soon as he found out that the queen was dead. Good riddance, I say.'

Just then Heracles burst in. 'I'm back,' he said, slapping Admetus on the shoulder, 'and I've brought a friend.' He turned to the doorway and called. 'You can come in now.'

Alcestis entered the room and stood before her disbelieving husband, a shy smile on her lips.

'I wrestled Death himself to the ground to bring her back to you,' said Heracles, 'so make sure you bloody well keep her this time.'

Admetus did not seem to hear him. He had eyes only for his wife.

'Yes. Well. I'll leave you to it, then. Due in Thrace. Got to fetch some horses.'

In sending Heracles for the four mares of Diomedes, Eurystheus had neglected to furnish him with any further details. However, the horses' names are known to us. They were PODARGOS, the 'flashing-footed'; XANTHUS, the 'yellow horse';* LAMPON, the 'shining one'; and DINOS, the 'terrible'.† More pertinently, Heracles was unaware that, due to the depraved king's habit of feeding them human flesh, all four had turned quite untameably mad and were kept chained with iron shackles to bronze mangers, a danger to all who approached.‡

When Heracles arrived at Diomedes' palace in Thrace, he was accompanied by his young friend and lover ABDERUS, a

---

* Also the name of the philosopher SOCRATES' legendarily shrewish wife. Really *Xanthos* is yellow with a tinge of red, so perhaps it means 'bay' in the equine sense. Strange that although they are mares, all the sources give names with *male* endings. It should really be Podarge, not Podargos.

† Cf. *dinosaur*, the 'terrible lizard', as mentioned in realtion to the Graeae.

‡ Some sources claim they breathed fire, too.

son of Hermes.* Leaving Abderus to watch over the horses, Heracles set off to negotiate with the king.

His curiosity getting the better of him, the boy drew too close to the mares. One of them caught his hand between her teeth dragged him into the stalls. He was torn apart and devoured in minutes.

Heracles buried the mangled remains and founded a city around the tomb, which he called Abdera in honour of his lost beloved.† The distraught and maddened hero now turned the full force of his wrath on Diomedes, slaughtering his palace guard, snatching up the king and throwing him to his own horses. The unpleasant taste of their one-time master caused the mares to lose their appetite for human flesh so that Heracles was able safely to harness them to a chariot and drive them all the way back to Mycenae. Eurystheus, who must surely have been getting used to the disappointment of seeing Heracles return unscathed by now, dedicated the mares to Hera and bred them for his own thoroughbreds. Later Greeks believed that it was from this line that Alexander the Great's famous mount, Bucephalus, was descended.

---

* Heracles, like most classical Greeks, was as happy to dine at the man-trough as at the lady-buffet. Iolaus his nephew and Hylas, his page during the quest for the Golden Fleece, were another two male lovers or *eromenoi*.

† Abdera still stands and was notable in the great age of Greek philosophy for producing Democritus, whom some regard as the founder of the scientific method (I recommend the Italian physicist Carlo Rovelli's thoughts on him in his excellent book *Reality Is Not What It Seems*). The sophist Protagoras, famous for his dialogue with Socrates as recorded by Plato, was also born there. Earlier, in the sixth century BC, the lyric poet Anacreon found sanctuary there from the Persians. His life and work inspired the creation in eighteenth-century England of the Anacreontic Society of gentleman amateur musicians. The tune of the club's song, 'To Anacreon in Heaven', was poached by the Americans in 1814 to fit the words of the poem 'The Star Spangled Banner', now their national anthem. Would that tune be heard at the start of every major sporting occasion in the United States if Abderus hadn't been eaten by horses? Such speculations might well drive a person mad.

9. THE GIRDLE OF HIPPOLYTA

'Far to the east, along the banks of the Thermodon, lives the race of Amazons!' said ADMETE, breathless with excitement.

Heracles bowed. Eurystheus's daughter was being 'given' a Labour of Heracles as a coming of age present.

'Set him to do anything you want, my darling,' Eurystheus had told her. 'The more difficult and dangerous, the better. Heracles has had it too easy.'

Admete had known straight away what she would demand of the hero. Like many young Greek girls, she worshipped this band of strong, independent and fiercely unapologetic women and had long dreamed of being an Amazon.

'The daughters of Ares and the nymph HARMONIA,' she told Heracles, 'the Amazons dedicate themselves to fighting and to each other.'

'So I have heard,' said Heracles.

'Their queen ...' Admete was flushed with excitement now, 'is HIPPOLYTA. Hippolyta the brave, Hippolyta, the beautiful, Hippolyta the entirely fierce. No man can conquer her.'

'That too have I heard.'

'She wears a belt, a most marvellous jewelled girdle, given her by her father Ares. I want it.'

'Excuse me?'

'You are to bring me the girdle of Hippolyta.'

'And if she would rather keep it?'

'Don't toy with my daughter, Heracles. Obey her.'

So it was that Heracles found himself sailing east towards the land of the Amazons. The fame of these proud female warriors had spread throughout the ancient world.* Riding on horseback – the first warriors in the world to do so – the Amazons had defeated all the tribes they had encountered in battle. When they conquered and subdued a people they took home the males that they judged would father the best daughters and bred with them. When the men had done their duty by them they were killed, like the males of many species of spider, mantis and fish. They put to death any male babies they bore, raising only girls to join their band. If they were accused of cruelty, they pointed out how many girl-children around the 'civilised' world were left exposed on mountainsides to die† and how many women were used as childbearing livestock and given no other purpose in life than to serve, please and obey.

By no means did Heracles underestimate the magnitude of the task facing him. But when his ship reached Pontus, on the southern coast of the Black Sea, he was surprised to be met by a friendly welcoming party including Queen Hippolyta herself. The Amazons and their queen were not the only heroic fighters to have achieved a reputation across the ancient world. For more than eight years Heracles had uncomplainingly achieved the impossible, and the news of his strength, courage and fortitude against such stacked and unjust odds had travelled far and wide. He had rid the world of much menace and terror. He had met magic and monstrosity with valour and dignity. Only the churlish or envious could fail to admire him. The Amazons' admiration for valour, dignity and strength

---

* The name *Amazon* means or may mean 'breastless', and while later artists and sculptors often depicted the women as being either without breasts or single-breasted, it is now thought that the name derived from their matchless skill at archery. In that to draw back a bow to its full extent, the breast has to be tucked out of the way . . .

† See under Atalanta, page 271.

had overcome their instinctive distrust and dislike of men enough for them to welcome him and his crew with warmth and respect.

Heracles and his crew were garlanded with flowers and feasted on the banks of the Thermodon.*

Heracles was deeply attracted by Hippolyta. She had poise, wit and a natural air of command that was rare in the world. She never raised her voice or seemed to expect attention or adoration, and yet Heracles found himself attending to no one else and felt closer to veneration for her than for any other woman, or indeed man, he had known.

She seemed to like him equally. If there was a trace of a smile on her face when she saw that her hands together were nowhere near meeting around the muscles of his upper arm, it was a smile not so much of mockery as of amusement at the freakish wonder of such a specimen living in the world.

'This will do it,' she said, unbuckling her belt.

She was right, her waist and Heracles' biceps had the same dimensions. Fixing the clasp, she announced that it improved his appearance greatly.

'That horrible lion's head and pelt, the ugly club . . . no doubt they're useful for frightening fools and cowards, but a man should be never be afraid to show a little colour and sparkle.'

She smiled again as Heracles examined the jewelled belt around his arm. She noticed that his face was clouded with a frown.

'Don't tell me that you are afraid that such a bangle does not consort with your great masculinity? I thought better of you than that.'

'No, no,' said Heracles. 'It isn't that . . .'

---

* Now the River Terme in northern Turkey.

'What then?'

'You say that you have heard of the tasks my cousin Eurystheus has set me?'

'All the world knows of the Labours of Heracles.'

'Is that what they call them?'

'Even if we allow for some natural exaggeration of your feats as the tales are passed mouth to ear, it seems you have done miraculous things.'

'I'm sure most of the stories are nonsense.'

'Well, is it true that when you carried the Erymanthian Boar into Eurystheus's throne room he was so frightened that he dived headfirst into a stone jar?'

'That, yes, that is true,' Heracles conceded.

'And that you fed Diomedes to his own horses?'

Again Heracles nodded.

'So tell me, great hero, what it is that can trouble you now?'

'Well, you see, I'm on the ninth of these tasks, these "Labours" as you call them. That is the reason I am here.'

Hippolyta stiffened. 'I hope it is not to drag Hippolyta in chains before that vile tyrant?'

'No, no . . . not that. It's this girdle . . .' He looked down at the belt circling his arm. 'His daughter, Admete, sent me to fetch it. But now that I have met you I cannot find it in my heart to . . .'

'Is that all? It is yours, Heracles. Accept it gladly as my gift to you. One warrior to another.'

'But it was a gift from your father, Ares the god.'

'And now it is a gift from your lover Hippolyta the woman.'

'They say that its wearer is invincible in battle. Can this be true?'

'I have worn it since I was fourteen and I have never been defeated.'

'Then I have no right . . .'

'Please. I insist. Now, let me see if all your dimensions are in proportion . . .'

We will leave Heracles and Hippolyta locked together in a fierce embrace in her royal tent on the banks of the Thermodon.

You might be thinking that this Ninth Labour had come all too easily to Heracles. Certainly the goddess Hera believed just that. The hatred she bore him had not diminished over the years. If anything it grew more intense each time he triumphed over yet another adversity. His popularity enraged her. She had set out to humiliate and destroy him. Instead there were children and even towns being named after him and songs being composed about him praising his strength, courage and lack of self-pity. She would show the world they had chosen the wrong man to celebrate.

In the form of an Amazon warrior Hera walked the riverbank sowing confusion, doubt and distrust.

'Heracles cannot be trusted . . . he is here to kidnap our queen . . . I have heard that even now his men are preparing to take us prisoner, rape us and sell us as slaves in the markets of Argolis . . . We should kill him before he gets a chance to destroy us all . . .'

In the tent Heracles sat up, suddenly alert.

'What is that noise?'

'Just my women celebrating with your crew, no doubt,' said Hippolyta sleepily.

'I can hear horses.'

Heracles leaned across Hippolyta's prone form and lifted a flap of canvas. Amazons on horseback were firing arrows at his men! A party of them was galloping towards the tent. At once the blood throbbed in his temples and a red mist closed all around him. The smiles and hospitality had been a trap. Hippolyta had tried to make a fool of him.

'Traitor! he cried. 'You . . . deceitful . . . *witch*!'

He took her head in his hands and with the last raging word he twisted her neck round so that it snapped like the dry branch of a tree.

He snatched up his club and ran out of the tent. He swung and dismounted three of the Amazons riding towards him with one sweeping blow. The others saw Hippolyta's belt around his arm, the symbol of her authority and her invincibility. The fight went out of them. Heracles' men, heartened by the sight of their leader with his blood up and roaring like a lion, rallied. In a short time the banks of the river were littered with the bodies of dead Amazons.

Heracles and his men broke the long return journey back to Mycenae by putting in at Troy. It was ruled at this time by LAOMEDON, grandson of the king TROS who gave Troy and Trojans their names, and the son of King ILOS, who gave the city its other name, Ilium, as in Homer's great epic, the *Iliad*.

Troy was a fine city, the construction of its walls had recently been completed by the gods Apollo and Poseidon. But the greedy, duplicitous and foolish Laomedon refused to pay them for their work. In revenge Apollo fired plague arrows into the city, while Poseidon flooded the plain of Ilium and sent a sea monster there to harry and devour such Trojans as tried to escape their disease-ridden city.

The priests and oracles of Troy told Laomedon that the only way to save Troy from disease, famine and disaster was to chain his daughter HESIONE naked to a rock in the floodplain, for the sea monster to feast upon*.

---

* An identical indignity to that suffered by Andromeda. The image of the helpless damsel tied to a rock awaiting her fate at the hands of a dragon is a pervasive one, not just in Greek myth and art. We can all, I dare say, offer interpretations according to our adherence to varying schools of psychology, gender politics and so on.

This was the situation when Heracles arrived. He promised to free Hesione if he could have the horses that had been bred from Zeus's gift to Tros.* Laomedon agreed and Heracles promptly killed the monster and rescued Hesione. Once more Laomedon reneged on a deal. He refused to honour the agreement and give up his horses.

There wasn't time for Heracles to put this right. His year was nearly up and he needed to get to Eurystheus and be sent on his Tenth Labour. Vowing to return and have his revenge on Laomedon, he made his way back to Mycenae.

10. THE CATTLE OF GERYON

'There!' Heracles flung the belt at Admete's feet. 'I hope it brings you luck.† Now, mighty king, my tenth and final quest, if you please.'

Eurystheus shifted uncomfortably on his throne. He was sure a number of courtiers had tittered at the epithet 'mighty king'.

'Very well, Heracles,' he said. 'You will go to Erytheia and bring me back GERYON's cattle. The entire herd.'‡

---

* Two generations earlier Zeus had Ganymede, the beautiful Trojan prince, to be his lover and cupbearer. He sent magical horses to Tros by way of compensation.

† The girdle of Hippolyta was successfully excavated from the ruins of the Temple of Hera at Mycenae by Dr Henry Walton 'Indiana' Jones Jnr., but currently languishes in a crate hidden in a vast US government warehouse along with the Ark of the Covenant and a copy of the board game Jumanji.

‡ The frequent appearances of bulls, cows, boars, sows, rams, ewes, stags, hinds and horses that feature in the heroic adventures are of course a reflection of the importance of these animals in ancient Greek economic, social and agricultural life. Their place in farming, commerce and civilisation contrasts with the threat to these elements of life posed by dragons, centaurs and other monsters. The class of mutant or savage boars and bulls might be said to represent a medial state between the tame and the monstrous. Snakes, sacred to Athena and Hera especially, might be said to exist in a class of their own. They can be lethal, they can be prophetic but they cannot be tame.

You will remember that, when Perseus sliced off the head of the Gorgon, Medusa, two unborn children from her liaison with Poseidon flew from the gaping wound. One was the flying horse PEGASUS, the other Chrysaor, the young man with the golden sword. Chrysaor (by his union with CALLIRRHOË, the 'sweet-flowing' daughter of the sea Titans Oceanus and Tethys) had fathered the three-headed Geryon, a most terrible monster who fiercely protected an enormous herd of red cattle in the western island of Erytheia.* To help him guard this rare and valuable breed, he had the giant EURYTION, a son of Ares, and a ferocious two-headed dog, brother to CERBERUS, called ORTHRUS.

Erytheia lay so deep into the unexplored western reaches of the world that to reach it Heracles had to go further than he had ever travelled before. He became so hot and bothered while toiling across the Libyan desert that he shouted up in rage at the glaring sun and threatened to shoot Helios down from his chariot with his arrows. Helios may have been of the immortal Titan race but he still feared the terrible damage Heracles' arrows could do him.

'Don't shoot, Heracles, son of Zeus,' he yelled, in some panic.

'Then help me!' Heracles shouted back.

Helios agreed not to fly so close to the land if only the hero promised not to shoot. What's more, to help make the journey westwards easier he offered to lend Heracles his

---

* Erytheia's name means 'red', or 'reddish', because by the time the sun had travelled that far west it was close to its red, sunset colouring. Some Greek and later Roman writers placed Erytheia in the Balearics. Maybe it was Ibiza. Others located it further west; the volcanic island of Madeira is a possibility. Given the presence of the fabled dog Orthrus, perhaps it was one of the Canary Islands – the word 'canary' deriving, of course, not from a bird but from the Latin *canus*, meaning 'dog'. Lanzarote would be the best candidate, since the 'rote' in its name means 'red'; though dull, factually obsessed historians will tell you that this is a coincidence.

great Cup. Each day Helios would ride his sun-chariot from the lands of the distant east* across the sky until he settled in the far kingdom of Oceanus†. There he would spend the night reposing in his western palace, before setting out eastwards again in an enormous cup or bowl borne along Oceanus' fast flowing current. This 'River of Ocean' circling the earth returned Helios to his eastern palace where he could prepare his horses and set out for another day.

Heracles gratefully accepted the loan of the Cup, a seaworthy bowl‡ in which he sat, knees up, in perfect comfort zooming towards Erytheia. At one point, the waters on which he was carried grew choppy and he threatened to turn his arrows on Oceanus. I think it is not that Heracles was arrogant in assuming he could best a god, more that he regarded all living things, divine or mortal, as his equals. In any case the threat alarmed Oceanus who, as frightened of those terrible arrows as his nephew Helios had been, quelled the waters. Heracles arrived on the island of Erytheia safe and dry in no time at all.

He was welcomed on shore by the savage barking of Orthrus, the two-headed dog.

'Orthrus!' cried Heracles. 'You, like so many of the world's ugliest creatures, are a son of Typhon and Echidna. Don't you know that the time is up for your kind? I have already killed your sister, the Lernaean Hydra, and your son, the Nemean Lion. Now it is *your* turn to be cleansed from the earth.'

With a roar from each throat the creature hurled itself at Heracles, who raised his club and smashed it down on one of the heads. The other turned with a startled yelp to look at its

---

* India, most sources are agreed.

† Ireland? Britain? Portugal? There are many theories.

‡ Perhaps Helios's western palace was in Wales and the bowl-shaped coracles that Welsh fisherman use are descendants of the Cup of Helios.

ruined companion, now dangling lifeless from the common neck. Before the second head had time to mourn, the club crashed down, ending the dog's life.

The herdsman Eurytion heard the commotion and approached, brandishing his own mighty club.

'You will pay,' he snarled. 'I loved that dog.'

'Then join him!' cried Heracles loosing an arrow into his throat. The Hydra's venom did its work and Eurytion was dead before his body hit the ground.

Heracles now set about trying to herd the cattle. Before long Geryon himself lumbered into view.

So few mortals ever saw Geryon and lived to tell the tale that reports of his physical appearance are varied. All concurred that this son of Chrysaor and Callirrhoë had three heads. Most described him as having three distinct torsos too, although one source maintains the three heads sprang from a single neck and single torso. Where the disagreement is strongest is in how those torsos were connected to the ground. Some asserted that they tapered into one waist and that the giant therefore had one pair of legs; others, however, were sure that he had three sets. I tend to the two legs but three torsos and heads variant. What is beyond doubt is that Geryon was huge, tricephalous and possessed a vicious temper.

'Who dares steal my cattle?' roared the left head.

'Heracles dares.'

'Then Heracles dies,' said the middle head.

'Slowly and in agony,' said the right head.

'When you die,' Heracles replied, 'it will be three times more painful than any death that has gone before.'

So saying he loosed an arrow right into Geryon's navel. The Hydra poison made its way up each torso, up through the three necks and into the three heads, scalding and corroding as it went.

'It burns!'

'It burns!'

'It burns!'

The screams were terrible.

Quite how Heracles got the cattle across the sea is not recorded. We must assume he ferried as many as would fit with him in the Cup of Helios, shuttling back and forth until the whole herd stood on the North African shore. As a memorial of his great trip, he erected two vast pillars of stone, one on the northern, Iberian, side of the straits that open from the Mediterranean into the Atlantic, the other on the southern, Moroccan, side. To this day the Pillars of Hercules greet travellers who pass through the straits. The African pillar is called Ceuta, the Iberian is known as the Rock of Gibraltar.

It took Heracles an inordinately long time to get the cattle back to Eurystheus. He drove them up through Spain, and the Basque Country, across southern France and northern Italy and down the Dalmatian coast before the welcome mountains and valleys of Greece told him that he was nearing home. But Hera in her spite sent down clouds of gadflies whose painful stings caused the herd to buck, stampede and scatter all over mainland Greece.* Heracles managed to retrieve most of them, but it was a weary and travel-stained Heracles who led the herd through the gates of Tiryns and into the palace courtyard of King Eurystheus.

'Oh, dear me,' said Eurystheus, stroking his beard. 'Is this all? I had understood that Geryon's herd numbered more than a thousand, and yet even to my untrained eye there seem to be no more than five or six hundred here.'

'It is all that remain,' said Heracles. 'And now, my service

---

* A favourite torment. She had done the same to Zeus's lover Io. The moon goddess Selene also sent one down to sting Ampelos, the beloved of Dionysus (see *Mythos*, Vol. I, for both stories).

to you is over. I have accomplished all that you have asked of me, and more. It is time for you to release me from my bondage and allow me to go home a free man, expiated of my crime.'

Eurystheus gave a vicious crack of laughter. 'Oh no. I don't think so,' he said. 'No, no. You still owe me two more tasks.'

'You said ten tasks, and ten tasks have I performed.'

'Ah, but the Second Labour,' said Eurystheus. 'Your nephew Iolaus helped you defeat the Hydra. Without his searing the wounds of each severed head you would never have succeeded. The agreement was that you would complete each task alone and unaided. So we cannot count the Hydra.'

'That is outrageous!'

'Tsk tsk, hold that famous temper of yours, Heracles. You know what happened to Megara and your children.'

Eurystheus was enjoying this. He licked his lips as Heracles relapsed into a shamed silence. 'Then there is the matter of those stables in Elis. You accepted a reward from King Augeas, did you not?'

'Well, yes, but . . .'

'That means you did not perform the duty as a part of your penance to me, but as a hired hand. It cannot possibly count.'

'He never paid me!'

'That is beside the point. By demanding payment you violated the terms of our agreement. Your Ten Labours have now become Twelve.'

Of course it had been Hera, through one of her priestesses, who had whispered these cruel technicalities into Eurystheus's ear.

Heracles dropped his head. He knew that if he lost his

temper and lashed out or stalked away in a sulk, then all the effort and pain of the last ten years would have been for nothing. The immortality promised him by the Delphic oracle could only be his if he was cleansed of his guilt and only his coward relative Eurystheus, this grinning despot, this cruel vessel of Hera, could do it. Immortality as such did not interest him, but as an immortal he could surely go down to the underworld and bring up Megara and his children.

'Given the feeble number of cattle you've managed to bring me today, you're lucky I don't make it *three* more,' said Eurystheus. 'In reality I should, but luckily for you I'm triskaidekaphobic. So, if you've finished whining and complaining, I shall name your eleventh task. Bring me the Golden Apples of the Hesperides.'

11. THE GOLDEN APPLES OF THE HESPERIDES

The Hesperides, nymphs of the evening, were the three beautiful daughters of NYX, the goddess of Night and EREBUS, the god of darkness, who first sprang from formless Chaos. It was known that the Hesperides tended a garden in which grew an appletree whose golden apples conferred immortality on whomever might be lucky enough to eat one. Gaia herself, the earth goddess and mother of all, had presented some of the fruit to Zeus and Hera for their wedding feast, and now Hera had set another ghastly child of Typhon and Echidna, the hundred-headed dragon LADON, to guard the tree.

The overwhelming problem that confronted Heracles was not the dragon coiled round the tree – such obstacles were incidental to him – it was that no one had the least idea where the Garden of the Hesperides was. Some said far north of the Mediterranean, in the icy realm of the Hyperboreans, others maintained that it lay to the west of Libya.

In northern Europe Heracles encountered the nymphs of the river Eridanus.* They urged him to seek the advice of NEREUS, one of the Old Men of the Sea.†

'If you can hold onto him, he will tell you all he knows,' they chorused.

As with most divinities of water, Nereus was capable of changing his shape at will. His knowledge was immense and, like all those blessed with the gift of prophecy, he always told the truth . . . But seldom the whole truth, and even more rarely a clear, uncomplicated and unvarnished truth.

I don't know how long it took Heracles to track Nereus down, but he did locate him at last on some remote shore, curled up asleep on the sand. The moment Heracles laid a hand on his shoulder Nereus transformed himself into a fat walrus. Heracles hugged him tight. Now Nereus was an otter. Heracles fell to the sand but still managed to clutch on to him. In rapid succession he found himself grappling a horseshoe crab, a manatee, a sea cucumber and a tunny fish. No matter what shape Nereus shifted into, Heracles held fast and refused to let go. At last Nereus gave up and turned himself into a bearded old fisherman – perhaps the closest to his real shape he ever came.

'You must circle the mother sea,' Nereus said, 'until you

---

* Perhaps the Rhine, possibly the Danube. Some even maintain that the river flowed in the legendary Cassiterides, the 'Tin Islands', which probably refer to the British Isles . . . If Heracles did visit Britain it is likely that in Cornwall he invented the sport of Tug of War.

† A title also given to the minor sea deity Proteus, who shared with Nereus the gifts of prophecy and shapeshifting. Hence 'protean'. NEREUS is perhaps most familiar as the progenitor – along with his wife, the Oceanid DORIS – of the numerous friendly sea nymphs named Nereids in his honour.

find the one who calls out your name from a high place. You will help them and they will help you in return.'

Not a word more could Heracles get from Nereus, so he relaxed his grip and watched him soar away into the sky as a gliding seagull.

Beginning with the coast of Africa, Heracles roamed the outer fringes of the known world, seeking clues. Along the way, being Heracles, he despatched a number of nuisances. In the lands between today's Morocco and Libya* he encountered the half-giant ANTAEUS, a son of Gaia and Poseidon whose major amusement in life was to challenge passers-by to wrestling matches. Whoever lost the bout had to die, and Antaeus had raised a temple to his father on the seashore constructed entirely from the skulls and bones of his innumerable victims. News had reached Heracles that his younger cousin Theseus had defeated King CERCYON on the road to Athens by using the new art of *pankration*, which combined the traditional close grappling, chopping, kicking and throwing with feinting, dodging and the use of the opponent's weight and strength against himself. Heracles was used to sheer muscle being the only weapon he needed in weaponless fighting, but he had nonetheless trained himself in Theseus's art and felt that a lumbering bully like Antaeus could present no threat, however fine a fighter he might be. Heracles made his way to the temple and called out his challenge.

'Ho!' cried Antaeus, with a roar of delight. 'So I am to be the great one who lives on in history as the champion who defeated and killed the people's hero Heracles? Let it be so!'

They stripped down in accordance with custom and faced each other, feet pawing the sand like bulls squaring up to charge. Heracles was the first to move in, bodychecking Antaeus,

---

* Tunisia and Algeria, we must suppose.

putting him in a choking headlock, then pivoting him over his hips and slamming him down with such force that the ground shook. The force of the throw would have killed or certainly incapacitated most of the opponents Heracles had ever fought. But to Heracles' surprise, Antaeus leapt up and rushed at him as if nothing had happened. This was strange.

For the Greeks the aim in wrestling was to throw your opponent and pin him to the ground until he submitted. Heracles managed easily to pin Antaeus down again and again, but instead of weakening and submitting he seemed to grow stronger and stronger each time. Heracles realised that *he* was the one tiring. He could not understand it. He had the full measure of his opponent. He swept his legs from under him and slammed him to the ground time and time again. Yet when he did, Antaeus merely sprang with renewed vigour as if nothing had happened. It was almost as if – *of course*!

The truth dawned on Heracles. Antaeus was a son of Gaia. Every time he made contact with the ground he was able to draw strength from his mother Earth.

Heracles knew what he must do. With a final grunt of effort he wrapped his arms around Antaeus in a bear hug and, squatting down to let his legs do the final push, lifted him bodily off the ground. He held him high over his head until he felt the strength start to drain from the giant's frame. With a final heave he snapped his spine and threw him dead on the ground. Gaia's touch could not bring her son back to life. His broad skull, Heracles found, made a fine centrepiece to the pediment of Poseidon's temple.

Resuming his journey eastwards, Heracles now encountered BUSIRIS, one of the fifty sons of Aegyptus*. The Greeks felt

---

* Aegyptus, you will recall, was the grandson of Poseidon and Libya, and the uncle of Andromeda. Heracles' descent from Perseus and Andromeda made Busiris a distant relative.

distaste for the human sacrifices performed by the priests of OSIRIS, from whom Busiris got his name. In order to put a stop to the vile practice, Heracles allowed himself to be captured and chained up as the next sacrificial victim. As the knife was descending on his chest, he burst his manacles and killed Busiris, along with all the priests of his order. Heracles renamed the town of Busiris in honour of the city of his birth, Thebes – which is why, from that moment on, geographers and historians have always needed to distinguish between Thebes, Greece and Thebes, Egypt.*

Despite the distraction of such incidental adventures, Heracles never lost sight of his need to locate the Garden of the Hesperides.

Obeying the Old Man of the Sea's injunction to 'circle the mother sea' (which he correctly took to mean circumnavigate the Mediterranean†), Heracles arrived at last in the lands between the Black and Caspian seas. It was here, when he reached the Caucasus Mountains that, just as Nereus had prophesied, he was hailed by a voice from high above.

'Welcome, Heracles. I have been expecting you.'

Heracles looked up and shaded his eyes against the sun. A figure was chained to the rock.

'Prometheus?'

Who else could it be? Zeus had shackled the Titan to the side of a vast mountain and daily sent an eagle‡ to tear out and devour the Titan's liver. Each night, Prometheus being immortal, the liver grew back and the following day the torture began anew. Countless generations of the race of men and women had risen, fallen and risen since their creator and

---

* The ruins of Thebes, Egypt, are contained within the cities of Luxor and Karnak.

† The Greeks usually called the Mediterranean just The Sea, or sometimes The Great Sea or Our Sea.

‡ Or a vulture. See *Mythos*, Vol. I, page 147.

champion had been made to endure these agonies.

Heracles knew who this figure chained to the rocks was, of course. Everybody did. But only Heracles dared to raise his bow and shoot down Zeus's avenging eagle as it soared out of the sun towards them.

'I can't pretend that I am sorry to see him go,' said Prometheus watching it plunge to its death. 'He was only doing the Sky Father's bidding, but I have to confess I had learned to hate that bird.'

It did not take Heracles long to shatter Prometheus's manacles with a blow of his club.

'Thank you, Heracles,' said the Titan rubbing his shins. 'You have no idea how much I have been looking forward to this moment.'

'I am not sure that my father will be so grateful.'

'Zeus? Don't be so sure. You are his vessel in the race of men. I have heard of your feats. The voices of birds inform me of the goings on in the world and visions come to me in my dreams. I know that you, as your cousin Theseus is doing, are ridding the world of its foulest beasts, its dragons, serpents and many-headed monsters. Through the work of heroes like you the gods are clearing the world of the old order of beings.'

'Why would Zeus want to do that?'

'He is as subject to the laws of Ananke* as the rest of us. He knows that it is necessary for the world to be made safe for humankind to flourish. The day will come when even benign creatures will vanish from mortal sight – the nymphs, fauns and spirits of the woods, waters, mountains and seas;

---

* Ananke is the Greek personification of Necessity. Like Moros (Doom) and Dike (Justice) the laws of these gods are more powerful than the will of the gods. To call them personifications is perhaps stretching it a bit. They can be talked about as if they are deities, but in reality they are treated as ineluctable elements of fate.

they will become no more than rumours. Yes, us Titans too. Even the gods on high Olympus will fade from man's memory. I see it, yes, but it is yet a distant future. There is more to be done in the meantime. Soon you will be called upon to rescue Zeus and the gods from a great and urgent threat, the threat of the giants, who even now are preparing to rise up and conquer Olympus. It is why you were born.'

Heracles frowned. 'Are you telling me that I am nothing but an instrument of the gods' will? Have I no say myself?'

'Fate, Doom, Necessity, Destiny. These are real. But so are your mind, will and spirit, Heracles. You can walk away from it all. Find a beautiful companion with whom to spend the rest of your life in peace, tending your flocks, raising children and living a life of tranquil contemplation, love and ease. Forget Zeus's plans for you. Forget Hera and Eurystheus. Forget their cruel exploitation of your remorse. You have more than paid. Do it. Go. You are free.'

'I would . . . I would like such a life. Oh, how I would . . .' said Heracles. 'Yet I know that is not what I was put on this earth to do or be. Not because you or the oracles have told me, but because I *feel* it. I know what I am capable of. To deny it would be a betrayal. I would end my days hating myself.'

'You see?' said Prometheus. 'It is your *fate* to be Heracles the hero, burdened with labours, yet it is also your *choice*. You choose to submit to it. Such is the paradox of living. We willingly accept that we have no will.'

This was all a touch too profound for Heracles. He saw, but did not see. In this he shared the same bemusement on the subject of free will and destiny that befuddles us all. 'Yes, well, never mind all that, I have a job to do.'

'Ah yes. The eleventh of these tests that your cousin is setting you. The Golden Apples. You will not be able to pick them from the tree, no mortal can. My brother Atlas holds up the sky there. That was his punishment for his part in the war of the Titans against the Olympians.* You must persuade Atlas to help you. The Garden of the Hesperides lies in the far west. You have a long journey ahead of you. Plenty of time to dream up a plan of action. Now . . .' The Titan stood and stretched his legs. 'I think I should go and find Zeus. I shall bow my head and beg his forgiveness. I am confident that he has softened in his anger against me. He may even realise that he needs me.'

'But you see the future, you *know* what happens next.'

'I think ahead. I consider and I imagine. It is not entirely the same thing. Go well, Heracles, and accept my blessing.'

As Heracles was making his way to the Hesperides, Prometheus turned his feet towards Olympus and Zeus's throne.

'Remind me,' said Zeus. 'Prothemus? Promedes? It's Prosomething, I'm sure of it.'

'Funny,' said Prometheus. 'Very, very funny.'

'Your betrayal tore my heart out every day. A liver grows back more easily than a heart. I never loved a friend as much as I loved you. '

'I know that,' said Prometheus, 'and I'm sorry. Necessity is a hard . . .'

'Oh yes. Hide behind Necessity.'

'I'm not hiding behind anything, Zeus. I'm standing before your throne and offering my services.'

'Your services? I already have a cupbearer.'

Athena had been listening and came forward from behind a rock. 'Come on, father. Let's get this over with. Embrace him.'

There was a silence. Zeus stood up with a sigh.

---

* See *Mythos*, Vol. I.

The pair edged towards each other. Prometheus opened his arms.

'You've lost weight,' said Zeus.

'I wonder why. Is that a flash of white I see in that beard of yours?'

'The cares of office.'

'Oh, for heaven's sake,' said Athena, 'get on with it.'

'Athena, as ever, is wise,' said Prometheus as the two extricated themselves from an unbearably awkward, unbearably male hug. 'Never was the phrase "for heaven's sake" more apt. The Giants are coming. You know they are coming?'

Zeus nodded.

Some say Heracles, as he crossed the Black Sea and Mediterranean, once again sailed in the Cup of Helios. Whichever means of travel he chose, he did at last find the Garden of the Hesperides.

Peering over the wall, he saw the tree with its gleaming crop of golden apples. Around its trunk was coiled the great serpent dragon Ladon. At the sight of a mortal peeping over the wall it raised its head and hissed.

Heracles fired his arrow, the dragon screamed in pain and the coils slid slowly down the trunk. Another child of Echidna and Typhon lay dead.

Heracles climbed over the wall and went to the trees. He found, as Prometheus had warned him, that being mortal he could not pick the apples. It was not that he lacked the strength, it was that every time he reached out to touch one it would vanish.

After an hour of trying and failing, he left the garden and made towards the coast in search of Atlas.

'The attempt,' said Heracles to himself, with a rare stab at wit, 'was fruitless.'

He found Atlas hunched, bunched and straining in the heat of the noonday sun.

'Go away, sir. Go away. I hate being stared at.'

The sight of that great figure carrying such a burden on his shoulders was worth looking at. You will have seen versions of it in early maps of the world, which took the name of 'atlas' from him. The sea to the west of him, too, is still known as the 'Atlantic' Ocean in his honour.

'I do apologise,' said Heracles. 'I send greetings from your brother Prometheus.'

'Ha!' grunted Atlas. 'That fool. He has learned the bitter lesson that to be a friend of Zeus is even more dangerous than to be his enemy.'

'He has told me that you could secure for me the golden apples that grow in the Garden of the Hesperides.'

'Go and fetch them yourselves, see where it gets you.'

'There was a dragon, but I killed it.'

'My, aren't you clever? So why haven't you got the apples?'

'Every time I tried to pick one, it disappeared.'

'Ha! That was the Hesperides. They are only visible in the evenings. They are my friends. They come and talk to me. They bathe my brow in the heat of the afternoon. Why should I help you steal from them? What would you do for me in return?'

Heracles explained the nature of his quest. 'See, if I don't return to Tiryns with those apples for my relative Eurystheus, I will never be washed clean of my terrible crime. So your assistance would be of the greatest possible value to me. But I can do something for you too. For generations you have groaned under the weight of the heavens. I could relieve you of that burden while you fetch me the apples. I would have what I need and you would experience a blessed interlude without the sky bearing down upon you.'

'You? Carry the sky? But you're a *mortal*. A well-muscled

one, I grant you,' he added, looking Heracles up and down.

'Oh, I'm strong enough, I'm sure of it.'

Atlas considered. 'Very well. If you think that you can hold up the heavens without being crushed, come alongside me and let's give it a try.'

Heracles had performed many feats of superhuman strength in his time, but nothing to match this. When Atlas transferred the sky to his shoulders he staggered and fought for balance.

'For heaven's sake, man, do you want to cripple yourself? Your *legs* should take the weight, not your back. Don't you know anything about lifting?'

Heracles did as he was told and let his thighs take the incredible strain.

'I've got it,' he gasped, 'I've got it!'

'Not bad,' said Atlas. He straightened himself up and arched his back. 'Never thought I'd stand upright ever again. All the apples?'

'Bring me the Apples of the . . . Hesperides' . . . that is what . . . I was . . . told . . .' said Heracles. 'So . . . yes, I suppose . . . all . . .'

'And the dragon is dead?'

'Couldn't be deader.'

'Right. Well. Back in a tick.'

Atlas departed and Heracles concentrated on his breathing. Whatever happens, he told himself, I will be able to tell my children that I once carried the sky on my back. When he thought of his children, it was not the scores of sons and daughters he had fathered all round the world over many years which came to mind, but only the two that he had killed when under Hera's spell. Having the weight of the heavens on your back, he thought, is nothing like so terrible a burden as having the blood of your children on your hands.

What a long time Atlas was taking.

Helios passed low overhead, dipping down into the redness of his western palace.

Finally Atlas arrived carrying a basket crammed with golden apples.

'Thank you, Atlas! Thank you. You are good and kind to do this.'

'Not at all,' said Atlas, a crafty look coming into his eye. 'It's a pleasure to be of assistance. In fact, I can help you further by going to Tiryns and giving these to your relative Eurystheus for you myself. Wouldn't be any trouble at all . . .'

Heracles knew exactly what was in the Titan's mind. But Heracles, as we have discovered, while not the subtlest man in the world, was far from a fool. He preferred to be direct and uncomplicated in his dealings but had learned over the years the hard lesson that simulation and deceit can be greater weapons than honest strength and raw courage.

'Really?' he said, in a tone of grateful excitement. 'That would be most marvellously kind. But you will come back?'

'Of course, of course,' Atlas assured him. 'I'll deliver the apples to Eurystheus and return directly – without so much as staying a single night at his palace. How's that?'

'I can't thank you enough! But before you go, I really need some padding for my neck . . . If you just take the weight for a second time, I can fold up my cloak and put it across my shoulders.'

'Yes, really can chafe around the upper back, can't it?' said Atlas, cheerfully relieving Heracles of the burden. 'Even my calluses have got calluses . . . Wait! Where are you going? Come back! You traitor! Cheat! Liar! I'll kill you! I'll grind you into a thousand pieces! I'll . . . I'll . . .'

It was a full night and day before Heracles no longer heard the roaring, howling and cursing Titan. Many years later, when the days of the gods were coming to an end, Zeus relented and turned Atlas into the mountains that still bear his name. They shoulder the sky in Morocco to this day.

Eurystheus knew that he could not keep the apples. The priestesses of Hera and of Athena all insisted they be returned. They were left in Athena's temple overnight and in the morning they were gone. Athena herself restored them to the Garden of the Hesperides.

But desirable golden apples had not yet finished with human history.

Meanwhile, an unpleasant smile was curling on Eurystheus's lips as he considered what the twelfth and final task should be. The twelfth and *very* final task.

'Bring me . . . now, let me see . . . yes. Bring me . . .'

Eurystheus relished the tense silence that fell over the court as he stretched out his dramatic pause.

'Bring me . . .' he said, inspecting his fingernails, 'bring me Cerberus.'

The gasp from his courtiers exceeded his expectations.

Trust Heracles to ruin the moment. 'Oh, Cerberus?' he said, and if he had added 'Is that all?' he could hardly have punctured the drama of Eurystheus's big reveal more completely. 'Very well. Loose, or on a leash?'

'Either will suffice!' snapped Eurystheus. Then, with a curt flick of the hand, 'Now, out of my sight.'

12. CERBERUS

In truth Heracles' insouciance had been a show of bravado. When he heard what Eurystheus was demanding of him, his heart leapt and banged against his ribs like a polecat trapped in a cage. Cerberus, the hound of hell, was yet another of the grotesque abominations bred from the union of Typhon and Echidna. Heracles had killed Cerberus's sister the Hydra and brothers, Orthrus and Ladon. Perhaps Cerberus did not know this. Perhaps these monsters felt no affection for their siblings. Heracles did not doubt that he could subdue the savage three-headed dog, but getting him out of Hades' realm was another matter. The King of the Dead would place insuperable obstacles before him.

As he trudged away from Eurystheus's palace a nebulous plan formed in Heracles' mind. If he were safely to leave the underworld with Cerberus, he had better placate Hades. The nearest way to what counted as Hades' heart was through his wife PERSEPHONE. For six months of the year she ruled by his side as Queen of the Underworld. In the world above, her mother Demeter, the goddess of fertility, mourned the loss of her beloved daughter and all the growth and life that were Demeter's responsibility and gift to the world slowly withered into the dry death of autumn and the barren chill of winter. When, after six months below, Persephone ascended from the realm of the dead, the new life and buds of spring broke out, followed by full fertile fecund fruitful summer, until it was time for Persephone to return to the underworld and for the whole cycle to begin again.

Over the years the Greeks had learned to celebrate this annual rhythm of death and renewal in the ritual known as the Eleusinian Mysteries, a dramatic and ceremonial playing out of the seizing of Persephone by Hades and her descent into his kingdom, the desperate search by Demeter for her daughter and finally her return to the upper world. Heracles believed that if he were initiated into this ritual it would endear him to the Queen of the Underworld and that through her he might win Hades' permission to lead his favourite pet out into the light of day.

The priests, priestesses and hierophants of Eleusis, led by Eumolpus, the founding celebrant of the order, granted Heracles' request and duly inducted him into the mysteries of their cult of growth, death and regrowth.*

Heracles now journeyed to Cape Tainaron in the Peloponnese, the southernmost point of all Greece,† where could be found a cave that formed one of the entrances to the underworld. Here he was met by the arch-psychopomp, the chief conductor of dead souls, Hermes himself, who offered to accompany him. No one knew their way about the caverns, passageways, galleries and halls of Hades better than he.

It was on his way to the throne room of Hades and Persephone that Heracles happened upon his cousin Theseus locked in the Chair of Forgetfulness next to his friend PIRITHOUS. Unlike the other spectral shapes that flitted around they were not spirits, not incorporeal ghosts, but living men. Muted by the enchantment of Persephone and bound fast by two giant snakes that coiled around them, they held out their hands in a silent plea. Heracles extricated Theseus, who scrambled up to the daylight above, babbling thanks; but when he tried to do the same for Pirithous, the earth beneath them shook. His crime, after all, the attempted abduction of Persephone herself, was too great to allow forgiveness.‡

As he progressed deeper into hell's interior, Heracles saw the shade of Medusa. Revolted by her hideous appearance and the writhing of the snakes on her head, he drew his

---

* Another version says he went to Attica for the ceremony and that he needed to be made a citizen of Athens to undergo the ritual. This may be the people of Athens wishing to claim the greatest of all heroes, greater even than their beloved Theseus, as one of their own.

† Perhaps more familiar nowadays under its other name of Cape Matapan.

‡ The disgraceful adventures of Pirithous and Theseus are coming soon.

sword. Hermes stayed his hand. 'She's just a shade, a phantom and can do no harm to anyone now.'

Further along he saw the shade of his old friend MELEAGER, the prince who had led the Calydonian Hunt. Heracles had been one of the few heroes not to take part in that epic adventure, so Mealeager told him the tale – how it had resulted in his sad and agonizing end. How his mother, driven mad with rage at his actions, had cast onto the fire the log whose burning through meant his own death.*

'But *your* feats of heroism have reached even these sad caverns,' said Meleager. 'It does my heart good to know that there is one such as you in the world of the living. If I were alive I would invite you to join your bloodline to my own.'

'Why not?' said Heracles, greatly moved. 'Do you have a sister or daughter I could marry?'

'My sister DEIANIRA is a great beauty.'

'Then, when I am freed of the burden of these Labours, I shall take her as my wife,' promised Heracles. Meleager smiled a ghostly smile of thanks and floated away.

At last Hermes opened the gates to the throne room and announced to the King and Queen of the Underworld that they had a visitor.

Persephone, flattered by Heracles' pious submission to the Eleusinian Mysteries, welcomed her half-brother cordially. Her husband Hades was more grudging.

'Why should I give you my dog?'

Heracles spread his hands. 'Eurystheus has sent me for him, mighty PLOUTON†.'

---

* The disturbing fate of Meleager will be revealed when we reach the story of Atalanta.

† Most accounts of the Twelfth Labour use this, later, name for Hades. Plouton became fused with the Roman PLUTO, the god of wealth. Precious metals and precious crops come from under the ground, so it was a natural elision.

'You'll bring him back?'

'Once I am freed from my servitude, I will undertake to do so. You have my solemn oath.'

'I don't like it. I don't like it one bit.'

'No, I can understand that,' said Heracles. 'Hera feels the same.'

'What's that?' said Hades, sharply.

'It is Hera who has set me these tasks. She wants me to fail.'

'Are you saying that if I let you borrow my dog, Hera will be upset?'

'Upset? She'll be furious,' said Heracles.

'Take him, he's yours.'

'You mean that?'

'So long as you promise to bring him back. You'll have to subdue him, of course. You can't use any weapons. Not down here. No sword, no club, none of your famed poison arrows. Is that understood?'

Heracles bowed his assent.

'Hermes here will take your arms from you, accompany you and ensure that you do not play foul. You are dismissed.'

On his way out Hermes nudged him. 'And they say you're an idiot. How did you know the way to get Hades to do something is to tell him Hera would hate it?'

'Who says I'm an idiot?'

'Never mind that, hand over your weapons and follow me. "Hera will be furious!" – you wait till I tell Zeus. He'll love it.'

The fight with Cerberus was marvellous to behold. Hermes clapped his hands like an enchanted child and rose up in the air on fluttering heels, so entertained was he by the spectacle of Heracles, his Nemean Lion skin tightly wound about him, groping for a choke-hold around the three necks of the savagely furious hound, while all the time its serpent tail reared, spat and struck, trying to find open skin to pierce with its razor fangs.

In the end Heracles' sheer persistence paid off and the great hound fell back, exhausted. Heracles, who like many Greek heroes knew and loved dogs, knelt by his side and whispered in his ear. 'You're coming with me, Cerberus. All the children of Echidna and Typhon are gone now, save you, for you have a purpose and a role to play in the great mystery of death. But first I need your help in the world above.'

Cerberus put out his tongues and pulled a paw across Heracles' arm.

'You're ready to come, then? You're tired. I'll carry you.'

Hermes' amusement turned to astonished admiration when he saw Heracles pick Cerberus up and place him across his shoulders.

'With no more effort than if he were a woollen scarf,' Hermes said to nobody in particular.

When Heracles strode into the throne room with Cerberus padding beside him, Eurystheus had occasion once more to jump into the stone *pithos*.

'Take him back down, take him back down!' his terrified voice echoed inside the jar.

'Really?' said Heracles. 'You don't want to say hello? See him do his tricks?'

'Go away!'

'Am I free of you? Have I done enough?'

'Yes'

'Louder, so the whole court can hear.'

'YES, damn you. You're free. You have done all that was asked. I release you.'

Bestowing a kick to the jar which must have set Eurystheus's ears ringing for a week, Heracles departed with Cerberus. They said farewell at the gates of hell.*

'Goodbye, you terrible brute,' said Heracles affectionately. 'The gods alone know what I shall do now.'

'No they don't,' said Hermes, stepping forward from the shadows with Heracles' weapons. 'It is for you to decide. All our father Zeus knows is that you will do many great things, perhaps even save Olympus.'

AFTER THE LABOURS: CRIMES AND GRUDGES

The first thing Heracles did, freed of his servitude to Eurystheus, was search for a wife.† Word reached him that King Eurytus of Oechalia‡ was holding an archery competition, the winner to claim the hand of his beautiful daughter IOLE in marriage. Heracles couldn't have been more pleased. Eurytus was the very man who had taught him how to string a bow and shoot when he was a child and would make a delightful father-in-law.

He entered the competition and (not using his Hydra-venom-tipped arrows, for once) he easily set about putting up the best scores. When Eurytus saw this, he disbarred Heracles from the competition.

'But why?' Heracles was downcast. 'I thought you'd be proud of your pupil and happy to have me as a son-in-law.'

'After what you did to Megara and your own children?'

---

* They say that where Cerberus's drool fell aconite grew, the deadly poison sometimes called wolf's bane.
† He seems to have forgotten his plan to bring his own wife back and, for the moment, his promise to seek out Meleager's sister Deianira as a bride.
‡ Pronounced 'Eekaylia'.

said Eurytus. 'My beloved daughter Iole married to a wife-murderer? An infanticide? Never.'

Eurytus's son IPHITUS admired Heracles and pleaded with his father on his behalf, but the king would have none of it. Heracles stormed off, promising to wreak a terrible revenge. He may, or may not, have taken some of Eurytus's prize cattle with him. Certainly twelve of the herd went missing around that time. Iphitus came to Tiryns to stay with Heracles and negotiate for their return, but under the influence of another of his horrible fits, Heracles hurled the young man to his death from the city walls.*

The gods punished this crime against *xenia*, or 'guest friend-ship', by infecting Heracles with a disease.† Once again in search of purification and atonement, Heracles visited king NELEUS of Pylos and asked him to perform the necessary rites, as anointed kings had the power to do.‡ But Neleus was an old friend of Eurytus. Iphitus had been like a second son to him, and he pointblank refused to cleanse Heracles of the murder. Our hero left Pylos vowing revenge on Neleus, too.

Heracles had marked up two new grudges. They were added to his old beef (literally) with Augeas, who had refused the promised payment of cattle for sluicing out his filthy stables; nor had Heracles forgotten how Laomedon of Troy had failed to stump up when he had rescued his daughter Hesione from the sea monster sent by Poseidon.

'Eurytus, Neleus, Augeas and Laomedon,' he muttered to himself as he made his way to Delphi. 'They will all pay.'

He knelt before the oracle. 'I need to be cleansed. Tell me what I must do.'

---

* See the 'Rages of Heracles' afterword for thoughts on this.

† We don't know which gods. It seems a bit direct for Hera, so perhaps it was Zeus, for whom *xenia* was sacred.

‡ Neleus was the brother of King Pelias of Iolcos, and so the father of Alcestis.

'You are impure,' said the priestess, whose name was XENOCLEA.* 'You murdered a guest. We can say nothing to you until you are purified.'

'That's why I've come to you. To tell me how I can be purified.'

Not a word more would Xenoclea say.

At this point Heracles lost his famous temper and snatched the sacred tripod from her hands.

'Damn you,' he yelled. 'I'll go and set up my own oracle.'

Apollo came down from Olympus to restore order to his shrine. But before long Heracles was snarling at the god and spoiling for a fight. Only Heracles would have dared.

Zeus split the pair apart with a thunderbolt. Reluctantly the half-brothers shook hands. Heracles returned the tripod and Xenoclea, at Apollo's command, gave Heracles the advice he sought.

'The only way you may be cleansed of Iphitus's murder is by entering into slavery,' she said. 'For three years you must serve another without question. The wages you would have earned will go to Eurytus in compensation for the loss of his son.'

Would this never end? Twelve years he had been in bondage to Eurystheus and now he was sentenced to another three? One might say Heracles brought it all upon himself by killing Megara and his children and hurling the harmless Iphitus over a wall. Equally one might reply, in his defence, that he acted under the influence of delusions sent to him by the spiteful Hera. Or one might suggest that he was a man born with an illness of some kind that made him susceptible to fits and hallucinations. One could add that his remorse always drove him to seek honourable expiation. But however disposed one might

---

* An especially apt name, given Heracles' crime against *xenia* or guest friendship. Xenoclea is a name that glorifies the stranger or guest.

be to forgive Heracles, one also has to accept that, fits or no fits, delusions or no delusions, remorse or no remorse, he was still capable of nursing the most implacable grudges. This new punishment only strengthened his vengeful resolve. Eurytus, Neleus, Augeas and Laomedon would all pay.

But first Heracles had to submit to this fresh period of subjugation. Xenoclea's arrangement was that he would become the property of Queen OMPHALE of Lydia,* who had ruled her kingdom alone since the death of her husband, the mountain king TMOLUS.† She seemed to take a perverse delight in humiliating her new slave. Above all, she enjoyed sporting both the great club and the pelt and head of the Nemean Lion that had long been Heracles' signature costume. What's more, she commanded that Heracles was to dress himself only in female attire while in her service. Despite this humiliation or – who knows? because of it – Heracles fell in love with Omphale, obediently wore women's clothes, protected the kingdom of Lydia from such brigands and monsters as threatened its peace and even fathered a son by her.‡

When the three years were up Omphale took the wages Heracles would otherwise have earned for his services and offered them, as instructed by Xenoclea, to Eurytus. He refused them with scorn. 'I have lost a son and twelve cattle and you offer me three year's wages?'

Free at last to pursue his vendettas, Heracles gathered an

---

* Omphale's name might be considered to be related to omphalos, meaning 'navel', it also can mean 'button' which plays into the cross-dressing narrative. It also means 'boss' which is apt enough – but the name had no such double meaning to the Greeks, of course.

† One of the judges in the musical competition between Pan and Apollo in which Midas made such an ass of himself. See *Mythos*, Vol. I, page 390.

‡ According to Herodotus, the 'Father of History', who lived in the fifth century BC, the descendants of this son (the name is variously given as AGELAUS or LAMAS), ruled Lydia for twenty-two generations. The most famous monarch of this dynasty was the sixth-century King CROESUS, who was as rich as . . . as rich as himself.

army and sailed off to exact his vengeance on the enemy who was nearest at hand: King Laomedon of Troy. He was accompanied by his old friends the brothers TELAMON and PELEUS, who had been present when Laomedon had refused to honour his debt to Heracles. They sacked the city and slaughtered the king and all the royal household save Hesione, who was given to Telamon as a bride.* Heracles also spared the youngest of Laomedon's sons, Prince PRIAM, who was left in charge of the smouldering ruins of a once fine city.†

Heracles now sailed back to Greece and gathered more allies for the invasion of Augeas's kingdom of Elis. Augeas got wind of this and mustered his own force under the command of the conjoined twins, EURYTUS ‡ and CTEATUS.§. Fused together at the hip they might have been, but their combined strength and divine paternity made them a formidable enemy. They killed Heracles' own brother Iphicles, the beloved twin with whom he had shared the cot to which Hera sent the snakes when they were newborns. This fully roused Heracles into one of the raging furies that turned him into a cyclone of unrelenting savagery. He split Eurytus and Cteatus apart with his sword and stamped on their dying bodies. Next he killed Augeas and all his children save one, the son Phyleus who had spoken up

---

* Fine heroes in their own right, Peleus and Telamon also joined Heracles in the quest for the Golden Fleece, as we shall see. But they are now most remembered as the fathers of the two mightiest Greek heroes of the Trojan War: AJAX, son of Telamon, and Achilles, son of Peleus. The son of Telamon and Hesione was the legendary bowman TEUCER, who fought beside his half-brother Ajax at Troy.

† Some say it was in revenge for the abduction of his sister Hesione that, many years later, Priam sent his son PARIS to carry off Helen of Sparta, thus sparking the cataclysmic conflict which brought ruin upon both Greeks and Trojans. But that dreadful tale is for another day.

‡ Confusing, but not the same Eurytus whose son, Iphitus, Heracles threw from the walls of Tiryns.

§ Not many words or names begin with 'Ct-', do they? The twins were sons of Poseidon and MOLIONE (hence their joint name of the MOLIONIDES). Molione was married to Augeas's brother ACTOR, hence their loyalty to him.

for Heracles when he had claimed payment for cleansing the stables and who had paid for his filial disobedience with banishment on the island of Dulichium. Heracles summoned him back from his exile to rule in his dead father's place.

It was here, in Elis, that Heracles now established athletic competitions to be held every four years, in honour of his father Zeus. He called them, after the name of his father's mountaintop abode, the Olympic Games.

Heracles next turned his attentions to Neleus of Pylos, who had refused to conduct his propitiation for the murder of Iphitus. He attacked the kingdom* and once again he found and slaughtered all the members of an entire royal house. Except one. As in the case of Augeas, there was a single surviving son to take over the throne. Young Prince NESTOR had had the good fortune to be away at the time of Heracles' onslaught. He returned to a devastated Pylos that, in time, he built into a peaceful and prosperous kingdom,† earning himself a reputation as one of the wisest kings in the history of the Greek world. Nestor was famed not only for his sound judgement but also, in his later years, for his distinguished service during the quest for the Golden Fleece and as the valued counsellor and brave ally of AGAMEMNON in the Trojan War.

Nestor's father Neleus had been aided in his defence of Pylos by his ally HIPPOCOÖN, the King of Sparta. The unrelenting Heracles now attacked this king, too. Although such an assault may seem nothing more than a mean-spirited and vindictive temper tantrum, the attack on Sparta

---

* Presumably at the head of some sort of force or army: the mythographers aren't very clear on this. Though such was his strength and temper that he certainly could do the work of one hundred armed men.
† Known to this day as Pylos-Nestoras (Navorino to the Italians across the Adriatic Sea).

was to have consequences that would sound down through history.

Heracles killed the king and his sons, installing on the throne his older brother TYNDAREUS, the rightful King of Sparta, whom Hippocoön had ousted years earlier. This detail is worth mentioning since Tyndareus and his wife Leda were to have such a vital part to play in the story of the Trojan War. Without Heracles placing Tyndareus on the throne of Sparta, it is doubtful there ever would have *been* a Trojan War.

It may seem that all Heracles did was go about the place slaying and deposing, but in truth – as I have noted before – he was instrumental not only in clearing the natural world of ancient and savage threats but also in establishing new regimes and dynasties in the political sphere that were to be play crucial roles in Hellenic history. If Cadmus was the founder hero of Thebes and Theseus the founder hero of Athens, Heracles has a claim to be considered the founder hero of Greece.

THE GIANTS: A PROPHECY FULFILLED

It began, like many Greek stories, with some cattle rustling.* The sun god Helios was jealous of his fine herd of cattle.† Their theft by the giant ALCYONEUS proved the final provocation, the spark that lit the fuse in what the Greeks were to call the Gigantomachy – the War of the Giants.

The giants, you might recall, sprang out of the earth in the earliest times from the blood that poured from the severed

---

* Consider, for instance, the stories told of Hermes and of his son Autolycus in *Mythos*, Vol. I, pages 101 and 268. Or, more recently, the quarrel of Eurytus and Heracles that we have just heard.

† As Odysseus and his men would discover to their cost one day.

genitals of the primordial sky god Ouranos.* This made them the generation of Gaia, the 'Gaia-gen', which over time became GIGANTES and, in our language, 'giants'.†

Gaia had heard of Hera's dream, the prophetic vision which forecast the rise of her gigantic children against the Olympian gods and their defeat at the hands of a mortal man. She tirelessly watched the exploits of the human heroes for a sign that the fatal individual had been born and the moment of the prophecy was nigh.

Realising that the theft of Helios's cattle heralded war, Gaia began to search for a rare medicinal herb‡ that would protect her giants from any harm this human hero might do them. Zeus, however, was ahead of her: he told Selene and Helios not to drive their chariots of the moon and sun by night or day, and while the world was plunged into darkness he gathered the entire store of the herb for himself.

The first manoeuvre over, Zeus summoned the twelve Olympians and Prometheus, with whom he had now been reconciled, for a council of war.

'We must prepare ourselves for imminent attack,' said Zeus. 'Hera dreamt of this moment. Athena, go down and bring Heracles to us. We need him now.'

The violence started when the cattle thief Alcyoneus scaled Olympus, pushed the gods aside and forced himself on Hera. Heracles arrived in time to pull him off her and shoot him with one of his poisoned arrows. Alcyoneus fell, but raised himself up and rejoined the fray as if nothing had happened. No matter what Heracles did, Alcyoneus seemed

---

* See *Mythos*, Vol. I, page 22.
† Thus 'giant' and 'gigantic' really mean 'earthborn' and have nothing to do with size, despite the way the words are now used and how the 'giga-' was taken from 'gigantic' to mean 'huge'.
‡ The Greek word is *pharmakon*, as in 'pharmacy' and 'pharmaceutical'.

always able to recover. Athena pulled Heracles aside.

'Alcyoneus draws strength from his native soil. You can never kill him while he is in contact with it.'

'Ah, I fought someone like that once before,' said Heracles, remembering his encounter with the wrestler Antaeus. He hurled Alcyoneus one more time to the ground and dragged him from Greece to Italy. There, at last, the power drained from him and Heracles buried him under Vesuvius, where he lies grumbling to this day, waiting to burst back up and spew his hot rage over the world of men.

Now the other giants began to assail Olympus. How many fought isn't agreed upon – from the large quantity of ceramics, sculptures, relief carvings and other representations it seems safe to suggest that there was a more or less equal number of gods and giants in the struggle. The earth all around the Mediterranean shook as Heracles, Prometheus and the gods fought long and hard to protect Olympus and especially Hera, whom the Giants forced themselves upon one after the other. After Alcyoneus, first EURYMEDON, the King of the Giants, tried to assault her, then PORPHYRION, the 'purple one'. The giants seemed to believe that if they got her with child the offspring would be their great champion. Or perhaps they more brutishly hoped that her rape would so disgrace the gods that they would surrender in shame.

At all events Heracles saved Hera from wave after wave of attacks. Never for a moment did he think of all the pain and suffering she had visited on him throughout his life.

Zeus's thunderbolts, as Hera had foretold, could not blast the giants, but they could at least stun them. As the battle raged, Zeus smote them one by one and Heracles took advantage of their dazed state to finish them off with his poisoned arrows.

When it was all over, the most powerful giant of all, ENCE-LADUS, still steaming and smoking with fury, was imprisoned by Athena under Etna. His brothers lay dead. The giants would never rise again.

Hera's dream had seen it all. A mortal hero from the line of Perseus would arise to save the gods. Her hatred turned to grateful love and her enmity to amity. No more would she visit monstrous fits or delusions upon him. Heracles could live the rest of his life free from her curse.

THE SHIRT OF NESSUS

Exactly as he did at the end of his Labours, Heracles now turned his thoughts to marriage. This time he called to mind his encounter in the kingdom of Hades with the shade of Meleager and the promise he had made to wed his old friend's sister Deianira.*

Accordingly, he made his way to Deianira's home of Calydon to win her hand, only to discover that she was being wooed, against her will, by the river god ACHELOUS. He had presented himself to her in three different guises:† a bull, a snake and a creature that was half bull and half man. Achelous might have thought this a seductive courting ritual and one guaranteed to win a girl's heart, but it filled Deianira with dread and disgust.‡ Next to this shape-shifting river monster Heracles seemed a sweet, normal and eligible candidate for marriage

---

* Pronounced 'Die-an-era'.

† Like most water divinities he could change his shape at will – witness those Old Men of the Sea, Nereus, Proteus and later Thetis.

‡ At least so says Sophocles, the Athenian tragedian of the fifth century BC in his play *Women of Trachis*, which tells the story of Deianira and of the later life and death of Heracles.

and she welcomed his suit with relief. But to win her Heracles had first to defeat his rival.

Achelous was immortal, of course, so Heracles couldn't kill him, but he easily wrestled him into submission, breaking off one of the god's horns in the process. To get it back, the defeated Achelous offered in exchange the fabled Horn of Plenty, which the Romans called the CORNUCOPIA. The young Zeus had accidentally snapped this off the head of his beloved AMALTHEA, the nanny-goat who suckled him during his infancy and childhood on Crete. * To compensate, Zeus had magically filled it with food and drink. No matter how many times it was emptied, it always replenished itself. From then on Heracles carried it in his belt and never went hungry.

Marriage to Deianira suited him. He hadn't been happier or calmer since his life with Megara all those years ago in Thebes. They lived together in Calydon and had four sons, HYLLUS, GLENUS, CTESIPPUS† and ONITES, and a daughter, MACARIA. All would have been harmony and bliss had not Heracles once again lost his temper with fatal results. One night, at a feast, the cupbearer of his father-in-law OENEUS accidentally spilled wine all down Heracles and he lashed out at the unfortunate youth, knocking him dead to the ground with one blow of his fist.

Despairing at his own clumsiness Heracles decided to leave Calydon for a spell. Along with Deianira he headed for Trachis, which was ruled over by his friend CEYX and his wife ALCYONE.‡

It was while they were on their way there that something

---

* See *Mythos*, Vol. I, page 32.

† You meet one person whose name begins with 'Ct' and then another pops up ten minutes later.

‡ Pronunciation? Your guess is as good as mine. Kay-uhx perhaps, or maybe Cakes. I assume Alcyone is pronounced to rhyme with Hermione.

happened which would, in the end, cause Heracles to die a terrible death.

To reach Trachis, Heracles and Deianira had to cross the fast-flowing waters of the River Euinos. As they approached, they saw a centaur in a bright purple shirt standing on the near bank who kindly offered to ferry Deianira across. Heracles did not recognise him, but he recognised Heracles. For the centaur was Nessus, one of the herd Heracles had attacked while staying in the cave of Pholus on his way to hunt the Erymanthian Boar.

Nessus and Deianira were halfway over when he attempted to molest her. Heracles heard her cries, saw what was happening and fired one of his arrows into the centaur's back. It staggered through the water to the riverbank and deposited Deianira on the grass.

Nessus had evaded the lethal arrows before, but now their poison was spreading through him. Even in his mortal agony, the outlines of a diabolical plan of revenge came to him. He did not admit to Deianira that he knew Heracles. Tender-hearted and compassionate, she was horrified that her husband had reacted so violently. She knelt by Nessus's side, stroking his flanks and begging forgiveness.

'No, no . . .' he panted. 'It was all my fault . . . I was just so captivated by your beauty. Your husband was right to punish me . . . Now listen . . . if I were married to you I would never leave your side, but you know what men are like. Take my shirt from me; it is charmed. Keep it with you always. Should the day come when you feel your husband has started to grow weary of you, make him wear it . . . You will find that his love for you will come flooding back . . .'

'Oh, you sweet thing!' cried Deianira, filled with sympathy and very touched by his compliments.

'So . . . little . . . time . . . Quick, take the shirt . . .'

She tenderly removed it from Nessus's back, sodden with blood as it was, folded it up and was just tucking it into her satchel when Heracles came splashing across the river to join her. He aimed a kick at the dying centaur.

'Damned brute. Laying hands on you like that.'

Deianira and Heracles settled at the court of King Ceyx, but after a year or so Heracles marched out to Oechalia to settle his final grudge. Despite his happy marriage to Deianira he had still not forgiven his old archery tutor Eurytus for denying him the right to compete for the hand of his daughter Iole. An insult was an insult and had to be paid for. He laid waste to Oechalia, slaughtered Eurytus and all his family save Iole, whom he decided to keep as a slave. He dragged her off home in triumph to Trachis along with the rest of his booty. When Deianira caught sight of her she was overcome with fear and jealousy.

'This is the girl he always wanted to wed. She is so much younger and more beautiful than me. What chance do I have?'

She thought of the enchanted shirt that Nessus had given her. That was the way to win back Heracles' affection.

'Welcome home, my darling,' she cried embracing him fondly. 'You won another great battle, I hear?'

'Oh, you know. It was nothing really.'

'I have a present for you. A reward for your famous victory.'

'Really? What is it?' Heracles loved presents.

'Something for you to wear this evening. A shirt.'

'A shirt? Oh. A shirt. Thank you.' Heracles tried to keep the disappointment out of his voice.

'I'll send Lichas to your room with it. You promise to come down to dinner wearing it?'

'If it pleases you,' said Heracles, tickling her under the

chin. Women were so funny. The smallest things upset them and the littlest things gave them pleasure.

Half an hour later, Heracles' servant Lichas came to his room carrying the shirt and helped him into it. For perhaps five or six seconds Heracles felt nothing. Then the skin on his back started to tingle and he idly scratched it. The tingling turned to fire and he leapt, twisting and bucking, as he tried to pull the shirt off. But the Hydra poison in the dried blood had been reactivated by his body heat and was already beginning to eat into his flesh and bones, burning and corroding as it went.

No one had ever heard Heracles scream before. No one who heard him now would ever forget the sound. He lashed out in fury at Lichas, killing him instantly. His son Hyllus ran in.

'Deianira . . . her shirt . . .' yelled Heracles, tears streaming from his eyes as he stamped and threw himself around the room before staggering out into the garden and running around like a wild animal.

Hyllus watched in horror as his father, all the while yelling in mortal pain, now started to uproot trees. Heracles' nephew Iolaus and dozens of other friends and followers dashed outside, drawn by the appalling shrieks. They had all seen Heracles lose his temper before, they had witnessed his fits and foaming tantrums, but this was something new. Deianira too now rushed from the house and added her own screams. What had she done?

The uprooting of the trees seemed to everyone to be a sign of madness, but even in his death agony Heracles was undertaking a labour. It became apparent that he was constructing a funeral pyre.

He clambered on top of it and lay back. 'Light it!' he screamed. 'Light it!'

No one moved. No one wanted to be remembered by history as the one who set fire to Heracles.

'I'm begging you!'

Finally Philoctetes, trusted friend and comrade on many adventures, took a torch from its bracket on the wall of the house and stepped forward.

'Do it, old friend,' gasped Heracles.

Philoctetes was weeping.

'If you love me, do it for me.'

'But . . .'

'It's my time. I know it.'

Philoctetes touched the flames of the torch to the pyre.

'Now quickly,' said Heracles, 'take my bow and my arrows.'

Philoctetes took them and bowed his head.

'They are . . . powerful' panted Heracles. 'Guard them with your life.'*

He arched his back as another spasm of pain went through him. The flames rose up.

'The fire . . .' he whispered, as they all came forward to make their farewells, 'is not as painful as the poison . . . In fact . . . it is a blessed relief . . .'

'Oh, my friend . . .'

'Oh, my uncle . . .'

'Oh, my father . . .'

'Oh, my husband . . .'

With a shudder and a sigh the soul fled from Heracles. The great hero was finally at peace, freed from his life of almost unendurable torment and toil.

Hyllus turned on his mother with a snarl. 'You killed him. How could you do it? How?'

Deianira ran wailing back into the house and stabbed herself to death.

---

* In Philoctetes' possession, the arrows of Heracles would play a crucial part in the climax of the Trojan War. The gods move in mysterious ways to achieve their ends.

APOTHEOSIS

Zeus remembered his promise and drew the soul of Heracles up to Olympus.* In a touching ceremony it was clothed in flesh formed from the robes of Hera – once his bitterest enemy, now his loving friend and stepmother – and reborn.

Here, amongst gods and goddesses with whom he shared Zeus as a father, Heracles himself achieved immortality and divine status. As a mark of her deep affection, Hera bestowed the hand of her cupbearer, the goddess Hebe, on him as his final and eternal wife.†

And, at the last, Zeus raised his favourite human son into the firmament as the constellation Hercules, the fifth largest in our night sky.

Back down on earth, the sons of Heracles – the HERACLIDES – eventually raised an army that defeated the tyrannical Eurystheus, who still ruled in Tiryns; Hyllus himself hunted down the fleeing king and beheaded him. They seized control of the Argolid, before installing ATREUS, son of Pelops, on the throne of Mycenae. For a while, a time of

---

* In *The Odyssey,* Homer places Heracles in Hades, a discrepancy that caused later mythographers to offer confusing and rather unconvincing explanations. His mortal shade went to the Underworld, they suggested, while the immortal one rose up to Olympus. There hadn't been a suggestion before this, so far as I know, that anyone could be endowed with two souls, whether they had a divine parent or not. The Greeks, if the truth be told, were far too wise to have a consistent eschatology that presumed infallible knowledge of an afterlife. They had noted that no one ever returned from death and took the sane and sensible view that those who claimed to know what happened to a person after they died were either fools or liars. Thus there was no 'system' to Elysium, Tartarus, Erebus, the Fields of Asphodel and the Underworld. Nor is there any such consistent law of the afterlife in either testament of the Bible, come to that. All the threats of hell and punishment and promises of heaven and reward came much, much later in our history.

† Hebe would be Heracles' half-sister of course, but that's nothing. Perseus was simultaneously his great-grandfather and half-brother.

peace and prosperity descended upon the Peloponnese.

For most Greeks and others across the Mediterranean world, Heracles was the greatest of the heroes, the *ne plus ultra*, the nonpareil, the paradigm, model and pattern of what a hero should be. The Athenians would come to prefer his kinsman Theseus, who, as we shall see, exhibited not just the strength and valour expected of a great hero, but intelligence, wit, insight and wisdom too – qualities that the Athenians (much to the contempt of their neighbours) believed uniquely exemplified their character and culture.*

Yet Heracles was the strongest man who ever lived. No human, and almost no immortal creature, ever subdued him physically. With uncomplaining patience he bore the trials and catastrophes that were heaped upon him in his turbulent lifetime. With his strength came, as we have seen, a clumsiness which, allied to his apocalyptic bursts of temper, could cause death or injury to anyone who got in the way. Where others were cunning and clever, he was direct and simple. Where they planned ahead he blundered in, swinging his club and roaring like a bull. Mostly these shortcomings were more endearing than alienating. He was not, as the duping of Atlas and the manipulation of Hades showed, entirely without that quality of sense, gumption and practical imagination that the Greeks called *nous*. He possessed saving graces that more than made up for his exasperating faults. His sympathy for others and willingness to help those in distress was bottomless, as were the sorrow and shame that overcame him when he made mistakes and people got hurt. He proved himself prepared to sacrifice his own happiness for years at a stretch in order to make amends for the (usually unintentional) harm

---

* Athenian exceptionalism at the height of the classical era was as unpopular with the rest of the world as British exceptionalism in the days of the Raj or American and Russian exceptionalism are today.

he caused. His childishness, therefore, was offset by a child-like lack of guile or pretence as well as a quality that is often overlooked when we catalogue the virtues: *fortitude* – the capacity to endure without complaint. For all his life he was persecuted, plagued and tormented by a cruel, malicious and remorseless deity pursuing a vendetta which punished him for a crime for which he could be in no way held responsible – his birth. No labour was more Heraclean than the labour of being Heracles. In his uncomplaining life of pain and persistence, in his compassion and desire to do the right thing, he showed, as the American classicist and mythographer Edith Hamilton put it, 'greatness of soul'.

Heracles may not have possessed the pert agility and charm of Perseus and Bellerophon, the intellect of Oedipus, the talent for leadership of Jason or the wit and imagination of Theseus, but he had a feeling heart that was stronger and warmer than any of theirs.

BELLEROPHON

THE WINGED ONE

The hero Bellerophon* was either the son of GLAUCUS, King of Corinth, or of Poseidon, god of the sea.† It is certain that Bellerophon's mother was EURYNOME, a special favourite of Athena who taught her wisdom, wit and all the arts over which the goddess had dominion.‡

The story of Bellerophon suggests that while he was fit, strong, brave, accomplished and attractive, he might perhaps have been just a tiny bit spoilt by his doting mother and by Glaucus, who – whether or not Poseidon really was the father – raised the boy as his own son and a true prince of Corinth.

Bellerophon grew up aware of the common gossip that whispered how Poseidon had slipped into his mother's bed and begotten him, but he set little store by it. He had never been drawn to the sea and, in his own estimation, seemed painfully lacking in divine powers. On the other hand, he had a brother, DELIADES, and the two were as unlike in character or physical appearance as it was possible to be, which certainly might suggest different paternity. And on

---

* Usually pronounced with the emphasis on the second 'e' – 'Bell-*er*-ophon'. The early Greeks tended to call him *Bellerophontes*.

† As we shall discover in due course, Theseus had a similarly problematic paternity.

‡ The poet Hesiod says of Eurynome, in a fragment from the eighth century BC: 'A marvellous scent rose from her silvern raiment as she moved, and beauty was wafted from her eyes.' No one has ever said anything as wonderful as that about me.

the *other* other hand, Bellerophon had always had a way with horses. Horses were very much the province of the god of the sea. At school Bellerophon had been taught that in the earliest times of the gods Poseidon created the very first horse as a gift for his sister Demeter. The god had fashioned all kinds of different animals, which he had thrown away before he managed to hit on the perfect creation. The discarded animals – the failures – had been the hippopotamus, the giraffe, the camel, the donkey and the zebra, each one getting closer to the perfect dimensions, beauty and balance of the horse. But this, Bellerophon felt as he grew into his teenage years, was a fairy tale for children. As were all the other stories of gods, demigods, nymphs, fauns and magical beasts with which his head had been filled ever since he had been old enough to walk and talk. All he knew was that Corinth was a big, bustling city and kingdom filled with very real and very mortal men and women; and while there were plenty of priests and priestesses around, he had never witnessed a hint of anything immortal or divine. No gods had ever manifested themselves to him, none of his friends had ever been turned into flowers or blasted with thunderbolts.

Around the time of his fourteenth birthday, stories began to circulate about a winged white horse called Pegasus that had emerged from the throat of the decapitated Medusa and flown to mainland Greece. Sightings of this marvellous creature were reported everywhere, but Bellerophon dismissed them as yet more superstitious fantasies for children. Then some Corinthian citizens began excitedly to claim that Pegasus was actually amongst them! Not in the city itself, but just outside. He had been seen by sober witnesses drinking from the fountain at Pirene (which was not an ornamental feature, but a natural spring bubbling from the ground).

Some had even tried to steal up on him and climb on his back, but he was always too alert.*

'No harm in going to Pirene and looking,' Bellerophon said to himself. 'I mean, it's sure to be some wild pony of the hills, but even so it might be fun to tame it. I could even make some wings for him and ride him into town. That would stir things up a bit.'

When he arrived at the fountain of Pirene he saw a couple of men hanging about there, but no horse, winged or otherwise.

'We frightened it off,' said one of the men. 'Probably won't be back for a while. Shy as anything. Skitters away at the slightest sound.'

They left Bellerophon to himself. He hunkered down behind a laurel bush and waited. 'It's not that I believe there are such things as flying horses. It's just that I'm interested in how these rumours start. There's sure to be an explanation.'

The sun beat down and before long Bellerophon had fallen asleep. He was awoken by a soft snorting sound. Not quite daring to hope, he raised his head and peeped over the bush.

Standing with legs slightly splayed, neck down to the water, a white horse stood, plain as day. A *winged* white horse. There could be no doubt about it. The wings grew smoothly out from the animal's sides – there was no join where a

---

* Poseidon was a god not just of the wide oceans, but of springs and fountains too. His offspring Pegasus, after flying free from the severed neck of Medusa, made landfall first on Mount Helicon. He struck his hoof on the ground and water bubbled up to become the famous Hippocrene, which means horse fountain. Helicon, like Parnassus, was one of the places where the nine MUSES liked to live (see *Mythos*, Vol. I, page 46). To drink from the Hippocrene became a metaphor for poetic inspiration (as in Keats's longing for 'the true, the blushful Hippocrene' in his *Ode to a Nightingale*). But Pegasus did not linger there, he flew on to Corinthian Pirene, another place sacred to the Muses.

trickster might have glued or tied them. If Bellerophon could just get close enough to nuzzle him and win his confidence. He tiptoed round in a wide circle. Horses have eyes at the sides of their heads which makes it very difficult to steal up on them unawares. They have ears that twitch backwards and forwards and can pick up the slightest sound. And when they stoop down to drink, both these senses are on the highest alert. Bellerophon hadn't moved three paces towards Pegasus before the horse raised his head, shook his mane with a startled whinny and galloped away. Bellerophon watched open-mouthed as the front hoofs pawed at the air, the wings spread out and in an instant Pegasus was flying through the air and out of sight.

From that moment on, the winged horse became Bellerophon's waking, sleeping and dreaming obsession. Every spare hour of the day and through many long nights he watched him from all kinds of different vantage points and hiding places. He climbed trees in the hope of dropping down on his back, but the horse always smelled him out. He left apples and carrots and hay in little heaps all around the fountain, and in a trail leading to one of his hiding places, but Pegasus was too wily for that. Bellerophon once got close enough to touch him, but he bucked and bolted into the air and was darting into the clouds before Bellerophon could leap up and fling himself on his back. All he could do was hope that the shy, nervous creature would in time become accustomed enough to his scent, voice and presence to learn to trust him. Meanwhile, he determined to stake him out night and day. He would never give up.

Bellerophon's mother Eurynome noticed the dark rings around his eyes, the yawning and irritability, and took it to mean that her beloved son was pining with unrequited love. She knew better than to tease or quiz a sensitive adolescent on so delicate a subject, so she sent for the priest and seer POLYIDUS and asked him to have a word, man to man.

'It's none of her business,' snapped Bellerophon when Polyidus explained his mission. 'She wouldn't understand.'

'No indeed,' said Polyidus. 'I, however, do understand.'

'Of course you do. You're a prophet so I'm sure you already know everything that's going to happen and everything I'm thinking.'

'There's no need to be rude. Yes, I see much. Sometimes just the shape of things, their outline. I look into your eyes and I see . . . yes, I see something like love. It is not a girl, however. Nor a boy. No, I see a horse.'

Bellerophon flushed. 'Don't be disgusting. I'm not in love with a horse.'

'"Something like love", I said. Is it the horse everyone is talking about? The horse called Pegasus?'

Bellerophon's reserve broke down at the sound of the name. 'Oh, Polyidus, if only I could tame him! I feel we're made for each other. But he won't let me close enough to tell him that I mean him no harm.'

'Well now, if you really feel the need to ride this horse so keenly . . .'

'I do, I do!'

'Then go to the temple of Athena. Lie down full length on the floor, close your eyes and ask the goddess for help. Ha! I see the disappointment in your eyes. I know you think I'm a charlatan . . . Oh yes, there's no use denying it, you do . . . But consider this: if I am wrong, what will you have lost by it? You will be able to tell all your friends that Polyidus is an old fraud through and through, just as you suspected. And if I am right . . . well . . .'

Muttering to himself for being such a credulous fool Bellerophon slouched his way to the temple. He waited until late evening, when the last of the worshippers had left, before going through to the cella, which he found lit by a single flame flickering in a copper bowl and unoccupied save for the presence of an ancient, toothless but clawingly friendly priestess. He pressed silver into her palm and fell to his knees, stretching himself out on the hard stone floor just as Polyidus had instructed.

The thick cloud of incense that the priestess sent billowing through the close confines of the temple stung his throat and nostrils; as he tried to concentrate on his prayer, he found himself choking and coughing. The priestess cackled and sang and his mind began to swirl like the smoke from the censer as strange images and sounds filled his head.

'Bellerophon, Bellerophon,' came a grave female voice. 'Do you really dare ride the son of Poseidon?'

'I thought *I* was the son of Poseidon,' Bellerophon said, whether out loud or not he could not tell. Was that the shining figure of Athena shimmering before him?

'You *are* my son,' came a deeper voice. Now the great bearded face of Poseidon seemed to rise up, dripping with seawater. 'And so is winged Pegasus.'

Bellerophon, in the fog of his memory, recalled being told that Poseidon had coupled with Medusa before Athena turned her into a Gorgon. If that was true, then Pegasus would indeed be the offspring of the god.

'He is shyer than any horse you have ever handled,' said Athena. 'Take with you the golden bridle and he will submit to you.'

Bellerophon wanted to ask 'What golden bridle?' but he couldn't form the words.

'Ride him gently. After all, he is your half-brother,' said Poseidon. The god bubbled with laughter as he dropped from sight.

'And use your wits,' said Athena. 'You can't expect to defeat him with strength alone.' She laughed too, but the laughter of the gods was really just the screeching cackle of an old woman and Bellerophon felt himself being shaken roughly awake.

'You were drooling, dear. Drooling and talking nonsense.'

He rose to his feet. Unable to think what else to do, he offered the priestess another silver coin.

'Bless you, child. Don't forget your bag.'

He looked down to where she was pointing and saw a sack on the floor. 'That's not mine . . .'

'Oh, I think it is, dear.'

As he bent to pick up the sack, he saw a flash of gold inside. He opened it wider. A bridle. A golden bridle.

Bellerophon made his way unsteadily past the smiling priestess, out of the temple and into the street. The moon was riding high in the night sky as he made his way to Pirene.

It was true, all true! The gods *existed*. He, Bellerophon of Corinth, was a son of Poseidon! He would have thought the whole experience in the temple a fantastic hallucination were it not for the jangling and chinking of the golden bridle in the bag that swung by his side as he ran to the hillside.

Perhaps the priestess had drugged him? On the orders of Polyidus perhaps. Could it all have been a trick? It was possible . . . Yet Bellerophon knew in his heart that this had been real – no fake show, but a genuine theophany, a real manifestation of divinity.

And there he was, his white coat silver in the moonlight, cropping the grass. Pegasus!

The newfound confidence that possession of the bridle gave Bellerophon seemed immediately to transmit itself to the horse. Skirting around the fountain he closed softly in, giving a low whistle. Pegasus raised his head, his sides gave a shivering twitch, he scraped the ground with a hoof, but he did not dart away.

'I'm here, brother. Just me. Just me . . .' breathed Bellerophon, edging closer and closer until he was able to lay a hand on Pegasus' back. The horse stood patiently as he stroked and then gently pushed the muzzle and the rest of his head into the bridle. It fitted easily and without protest. Bellerophon stayed there a long while without moving, just caressing, patting, clicking his tongue and letting the creature get used to the feel of the bridle.

When he felt the time was right he swung himself gently onto the horse's back and took up the reins.

'Shall we?'

Pegasus dipped his head and broke into a trot. The trot became a gallop. Bellerophon leaned forward until he was almost lying on the mane as the great white wings opened and began to beat the air.

Half an hour later they landed with a clatter of hoofs in the courtyard of the royal palace. Bellerophon calmed Pegasus, who became immediately alarmed by the shouts of the guards and then by the cries of his father Glaucus, his mother Eurynome and his brother Deliades, who all rushed out with the others to see what the fuss was about.

The crowds that came every day to watch Bellerophon ride the white horse through the sky were enormous. When he wasn't riding, Bellerophon kept the bridle with him at all times. No one else could approach Pegasus; he flinched and bolted when anyone but Bellerophon came near.

People can accustom themselves to almost anything, and in time the crowds thinned. Everyone but visitors from other provinces soon became used to the sight of the boy, the youth and now the young man astride his flying horse.

One day a messenger arrived from King PITTHEUS of Troezen, a small city state tucked away in the southeastern corner of the Peloponnese. Bellerophon was cordially invited to stay in the palace to meet the king's daughter, AETHRA, with a view to betrothal. Bellerophon flew down on Pegasus and before long he and the princess had fallen in love. Their engagement delighted King Pittheus, who had long wanted to strengthen Troezen by uniting it with Corinth.

It would be easy to envy Bellerophon. He was a handsome prince engaged to a beautiful princess. His parents doted on him. Women swooned at his lithe athleticism and insolent charm. He had a flying horse that he, and he alone, could ride. How much more in life could anyone want?

But the Fates delight in preparing nasty surprises for those who ride on top of the world. Bellerophon was no more exempt from their malice and caprice than the rest of us.

BEARING FALSE WITNESS

It began as a day like any other. Two weeks before the wedding in Troezen, Glaucus, Deliades and Bellerophon went hunting for wild boar in a forest outside Corinth. It was a hunt on foot, so there had been no call for Pegasus. No one quite remembered how disaster struck. Without mentioning it to his brother or father, Deliades had slipped away to relieve himself behind some bushes. Bellerophon heard what sounded to him like the unmistakable sounds of a charging boar (his brother straining at stool, it is to be supposed) and hurled his spear in the direction of the bellowing and snorting noises. A terrible cry was heard and Deliades staggered out from the bushes, transfixed and mortally wounded by the spear. He died before they could get him home.

We must not tire of reminding ourselves that to the Greeks blood crime, the killing of a relative, was the most serious of all transgressions. Purification could only be performed by oracles and the priestly caste, or by an anointed king. To go without such a purification was to invite pursuit by the Furies.

The first consequence of the killing of Deliades was the immediate cancellation of Bellerophon's engagement to Aethra. Next, he was sent from Corinth to Tiryns, in the neighbouring kingdom of Mycenae, to serve out his period of penitence and purification. The ruler PROETUS was a friend of the family and by virtue of his mystical kingly powers was able to cleanse Bellerophon of his crime.

Proetus had a wife called Stheneboea*, who was so excited by the proximity of such a desirable young man that she knocked on his bedroom door one night. He opened the door and he saw her standing there, rushlight in hand, an alluring smile on her face. She was dressed in a sheer silk nightdress that revealed more than it hid.

'Aren't you going to invite me in?' she cooed.

'I . . . I . . . no! No. It would be most improper.'

'But impropriety is such fun, Bellerophon,' she said, pushing him aside and making for the bed. 'Narrow, but plenty of room if one of us is on top of the other, don't you think?' She laid herself down and traced coy little circles on the counterpane.

Bellerophon was in agony. 'No! No, no, *no*! Madam, I am a guest in this palace. Proetus has shown me nothing but kindness. To betray him would be the act of a swine.'

---

* Pronounced Sthen-a-*bee*-a or perhaps Sthen*ee*bia. Up to you. The name means 'strong cow' – or, if one is feeling kinder, 'one made strong through their possession of cows'. Earlier sources, like Homer, called her ANTEIA.

'Ride me like you ride that horse of yours. You want to, don't you? I can sense that you do.'

Bellerophon now made a terrible mistake. Of course he would very much have liked to lie down and do lustful things with Stheneboea. She was immensely appealing and he was a young man filled with sap and juice, but to defy the laws of hospitality while still in the process of being cleansed for a blood crime would be unthinkable. He should have said so. Instead, believing that this would solve his predicament, he said, 'No. As a matter of fact I wouldn't like to. I'm not in the least attracted to you and I'll thank you to leave.'

At this Stheneboea rose with a hiss and stalked from the room, her cheeks aflame. Never had she been so affronted. Well, she would show that pious little prick. Oh yes. All night she tossed and turned in an agony of mortification and wounded pride.

Proetus was in the habit of snoring terribly and the royal couple had long enjoyed separate sleeping arrangements, but it was not uncommon for Stheneboea to visit her husband in the mornings and talk through their plans for the day. This morning she came in with a bowl of warm goat's milk stirred with honey.

'Ah, bless you, my dear,' said Proetus, sitting up and taking a grateful sip. 'Fine morning by the looks of it . . . I thought I might go hunting with young Bellerophon later on. He's a . . . good heavens! How red your eyes are!'

As well they ought to have been after being rubbed vigorously with raw onion for a full quarter of an hour.

'It's nothing, nothing . . .' sniffed Stheneboea.

'Darling, tell me what it is.'

'Oh, it's only . . . No, I can't. I know how much you like him.'

'Like him? Who?'

'Bellerophon.'

'Has he done something to upset you?'

And so it all came tumbling out. Last night he had hammered on her bedroom door, barged his way in and tried to force himself upon her. It was all Stheneboea could do to keep the wild beast off and push him from the room. She was so scared. Felt so ashamed, so horribly polluted.*

Proetus leapt from his bed and paced the room. He was in a quandary. After blood murder, perhaps the second most serious sin in the Greek world was an infraction of *xenia*, those laws of hospitality or guest-friendship that were especially sacred to the King of the Gods himself, *Zeus Xenios*, protector of guests. Naturally, the young man's repulsive attempt to ravish Stheneboea was itself a crime against *xenia*, but this did not give Proetus the right to transgress in return. No, he must find another way to avenge the family honour.

A few more turns about the room and he had hit upon the answer. 'Of course!' he cried. 'Darling, I shall send Bellerophon to your father, with a sealed letter. That will fit the case perfectly.'

'What will you say?' Stheneboea's eyes shone with malice.

'I shall tell him the truth,' said Proetus. 'Now, let me sit down and write it.'

Bellerophon awoke later that morning from an uneasy sleep. He could not be sure if it was his duty to report Stheneboea's appalling behaviour to her husband, or whether it was best to be tactful and spare their marriage the trouble

---

* A not uncommon mythic trope or 'mytheme'. You may remember in the Bible (or the musical) that Potiphar's wife made the same false accusation against Joseph after failing to seduce him. Achilles' father Peleus was to suffer similarly at the hands of ASTYDAMEIA, wife of King ACASTUS, who – in just the same way that Proetus was purifying Bellerophon – was cleansing Peleus of the crime of accidental fratricide at the time. Make of these repetitions what you will.

such a revelation would be certain to stir up. He had settled on the latter course when a page arrived to tell him that the king awaited his pleasure.

'Ah, Bellerophon, come in, come in, my boy . . .' Proetus was later to congratulate himself on the warmth and friendliness with which he conducted this meeting. Inwardly he was seething with rage at the vile effrontery of the monster of debauchery who dared to stand gazing at him with such round and innocent eyes. 'It's been a delight having you here. That unfortunate accident in which your brother died . . . you are, you know, almost wholly cleansed of that now. Any other crimes for which you may feel a twinge of guilt are none of my business, of course.' He fixed Bellerophon with a skewering glance and was not surprised to see the young man's cheeks flush red.

Bellerophon for his part was writhing inside. Perhaps not telling Proetus about his wife's infidelity was a sin. Perhaps now was the time to speak up . . . He cleared his throat. 'There's something you should know . . .'

'Tush tush. Enough talk. I sent for you to say that I have a message I need delivered to my father-in-law in Lycia. Thing is, it's rather urgent. Family matter. Needs to be settled.'

'Lycia?'

'Yes, my father-in-law IOBATES is King of Lycia.* It's a fair way, but with that flying horse of yours you can cover the distance in no time. Besides, you've completed your period of piacular penance, what? Young men of noble birth should visit Ionia and Asia Minor, don't you think? Here's the letter. It also introduces you to Iobates and begs him to treat you with all the hospitality that you deserve.' Proetus was pleased

---

* Often given the rather more handsome name Amphianax (pronounced 'Amph-*eye*-an-ax').

with that last remark. It was exactly what the letter did require of Iobates.

'Sir, you are more than kind . . .' Bellerophon felt a great surge of relief. This was for the best. Any more nights under the same roof as Stheneboea would be awkward. He could leave by chariot at once for Pirene, bridle Pegasus and be in Lycia by tomorrow.

Proetus and Stheneboea waved from the doorway as Bellerophon drove away. 'Vile pervert,' muttered Proetus. 'Good riddance to him.'

What a pity, thought Stheneboea to herself. A slim, golden body with a sweet and lovely face to go with it. Such a lovely, firm round behind, too. Like a peach. Oh well, can't be helped . . .

IN LYCIA

Bellerophon landed Pegasus in a sheltered meadow some distance from the city of Xanthus, where the royal palace of Lycia stood.

'You must stay there until I return for you,' he whispered, hitching him to a tree. 'Sorry to tie you up, but it's a long rope. There's a stream if you're thirsty, and plenty of grass to graze on.'

Neither of them enjoyed the clamour, excitement and hysteria that the sight of Pegasus engendered. If he got to know and trust Iobates, Bellerophon would introduce them, but long experience of boys who thought it was funny to fire at Pegasus' rump with catapults and even bows and arrows, and thieves who tried to capture him with nets and snares, had taught him that it was best to be cautious.

Bellerophon walked by himself in to Xanthus, announced

himself at the palace gates and was shown to the king's private chamber.

'Bellerophon, eh?' said Iobates, taking the letter. 'My son-in-law Proetus has written to me about you before. Says you're a fine fellow. That sad business with your brother was clearly an accident. Could have happened to anyone. You're welcome, young man. Very welcome.'

Iobates put the unopened letter down on his desk. He summoned his palace staff, called for wine, and arranged for a feast to welcome the Corinthian prince. 'You do my house honour,' Iobates said, raising a cup to his guest.

'Sir, you are most kind.'

'You haven't brought that famous flying horse with you, I don't suppose?'

Bellerophon laughed.

'No. Never believed that story myself. The nonsense people will swallow, eh? So, tell me,' he said with a nudge. 'Like to ride mortal horses on solid ground do you?'

Nine days and nights passed in which Iobates and Bellerophon rode, hunted, drank and feasted. The king treated the younger man as the son he had never had. He was blessed with two daughters: aside from the fearsome Stheneboea safely married off to Proetus in Mycenae, there was a younger unmarried daughter, PHILONOË, who still lived in the palace. She very quickly developed a crush on the handsome visitor. Bellerophon's experience with her sister made him very wary of being alone in a room with Philonoë, which Iobates took as the sign of a decent and honourable nature.

It was on the tenth day that Iobates, nursing a hangover, decided he really should clear the backlog on his desk. He found the letter from Proetus and unsealed it. He read the one line, centred on the single page, with gaping disbelief.

*'The bearer of this letter tried to rape my wife, your daughter. Kill him.'**

Iobates stared at the words for some time. He was now in precisely the same quandary that Proetus had been in. Bellerophon was a guest: he had stayed nine nights under the king's roof. Iobates couldn't contemplate killing a guest. What to do? What to do? Oh, why hadn't he opened that damned letter straight away?

An hour or so later Bellerophon came into the king's chamber, rubbing his face. 'Goodness me,' he said. 'You really are the most incredible host. I can't imagine how much we drank last night. But forgive me, sir, you look distracted.'

'Yes, yes,' Iobates tapped the letter on the desk and thought frantically. 'Cares of state, you know. We have concerns in the kingdom. Great concerns . . .'

'Anything I can help with? You've only to say the word.'

'Well, now that you mention it . . .' *Yes!* Of course. The very thing. Iobates cleared his throat. 'Did you ever, I wonder,' he said casually, 'hear tell of the *Chimera*†?'

'No, sir. What is it?'

'*She* is a beast. A two-headed monster. Progeny, it is said, of Typhon and Echidna. She ravages the countryside around Methian, near the border with Caria and Pamphylia. Few who see her live to tell the tale, but word has it that she has the body and head of a lion. A second head, that of a goat,

---

* When Homer has Bellerophon's grandson GLAUCUS tell this story in the *Iliad*, the letter is actually not written but composed of 'symbols' or 'murderous signs' enclosed, not in a letter, but a 'folding tablet' . . . Homer pre-dated paper and alphabets (or at the most coincided with the very beginning of the Phoenician alphabet), but he would have been aware of the Linear B syllabary and other early scripts. The tablets would have been of clay.

† Usually pronounced 'kai-meera', though the Greeks say something closer to 'heemera', with a hissy opening 'h'.

rises from her back. Her tail, some have claimed, is a venomous lashing serpent . . .'

'Surely not!'

'Well, you know what country people are like. Probably exaggerated, but it's certain that the land all about is littered with dead and savaged livestock. Who knows what to think?'

'And you'd like me to find this creature and kill it?'

'It's too much to ask, too much. You're my guest. Besides, you're just a young man . . . No, no, no.'

'Sir, I *insist* that you let me do this for you.'

Nothing that Iobates could say would dissuade Bellerophon.

'But only the bravest hero could even get near. You're far too young.'

'With respect, sir, that's nonsense.'

'Besides, forgive me, but I haven't told you the worst part yet. They say . . .' Iobates lowered his voice to a hoarse whisper, 'they say the Chimera *breathes fire*! Yes! I've heard it sworn as fact. To go against her would be suicide. Anyone would understand if you backed out . . .'

Strangely, these desperate bids to offer the young man a way out seemed only to strengthen his resolve. Outwardly Iobates shook his head and clicked his tongue in distress. Inwardly he hugged himself. How cleverly he had played on the young hothead's vanity and pride. There was no possibility that Bellerophon could subdue or slay the Chimera, whose immortal bloodlines made her one of the most terrible monsters ever to have risen from the earth. Bellerophon would most certainly die in the great jets of searing, roasting, devouring flame that the creature belched. Justice for daring to lay hands on Stheneboea and no stain on me, Iobates told himself, for harming a guest. Altogether a perfect solution.

The King of Lycia helped himself to a fig and smiled.

CHIMERICAL REACTION

Iobates waved Bellerophon goodbye, his left arm around the weeping Philonoë.

'Try to put him out of your mind, my dear,' he said. 'There'll be other men in your life, just you wait and see.'

'But none as wonderful as my Bellerophon,' sobbed Philonoë.

Bellerophon himself set out cheerfully enough. He would slay this Chimera, bring its heads and pelt to Iobates, stay a few more weeks in Lycia and finally return to Corinth to resume his life there as prince and heir. Now that he was cleansed of his accidental fratricide he would be able to marry Aethra. Life was good. But first he needed to find a competent smith. He had had an idea about how best to tackle the Chimera.

A short time later, Bellerophon marched into the meadow where he had left Pegasus, a fine new lance forged to his special instructions canted over one shoulder. The horse came trotting forward to greet him.

'What happened to your tether?' Bellerophon asked in surprise.

Pegasus shook his mane and stamped a hoof. The rope lay mangled under his hoofs, chewed in pieces.

'You're a cunning one,' said Bellerophon, cupping the soft muzzle. 'Now, before we fly off, we need to be sure of ourselves. A two-headed fire-breathing monster with a venomous snake for a tail. Think you're up to it?'

Pegasus tossed his head.

'I'll take that as a "yes".' Bellerophon set the lance in its sheath. 'Come on then. Up, up and away.'

Looking down at the landscape around Methian,

Bellerophon could see that much of the land was badly scorched. Deserted villages, fields empty of livestock and the burnt-out shells of barns and farmhouses all bore witness to catastrophe. Of his monstrous quarry herself he could see no sign.

'Up, up!'

He had never ridden Pegasus so high. It was a cloudless day, but he shivered in the rush of cold air. The land below now took on an intricate, ordered pattern that reminded Bellerophon of barbarian carpets from the east. The jagged coastline came into view and the green lands of Caria, Phrygia and Lydia lay beneath him, picked out by a network of glinting threads meandering down from the mountains towards the sea.* He searched the landscape for anything that might betray the presence of the Chimera. He saw a mountain from which rose a thin wisp of smoke. He tried to recall his lessons in geography. Mount Taurus? He leaned forward and urged Pegasus down. The fire could be anything, of course, but he was low enough now to see that what had looked like a thin wisp was really a thick cloud. The forest in the foothills was ablaze. A wave of warm air came up as they descended.

Men, goats and deer were running from the flames down to a lake. Wildfires were not uncommon. Bellerophon did not see what he could do to help and was just about to drive Pegasus back up to resume their high search when a great stag burst out from the trees below. It was being chased by a lion and . . . a lion and a . . .

It was just as Iobates had said. A lion's body with a goat's head sprouting out of the middle of its back.

---

* Almost certainly a *literal* meandering. He was over Caria, through which the River Maeander, eponym of all wandering streams, still winds its lazy course.

'Down, Pegasus, down!'

Pegasus dived down until Bellerophon could see every detail. The Chimera leapt onto the stag and a flailing ball of antlers, goat horns, lion and serpent rolled down the hill. The savage horns on the goat's head tore at the stag's flanks. The snake tail darted and jabbed at the underside. The lion's jaws opened and roared fire into the face of the stag which screamed and fell back, instantly blinded. The claws of the lion ripped the belly open and its heads dived gorging into the mess of guts that came tumbling out.

Pegasus circled lower and the shadow of horse and rider fell over the scene. The Chimera raised a head to look at them. The stag shuddered and jerked as it tried to rise and – the lion's blood-mottled head still staring up into the sun and sky – the snake tail extended her fangs and stabbed down into its hindquarters to finish it.

A jet of flame shot up towards them. Bellerophon yelled at the intense heat and kicked Pegasus upwards. Again the Chimera bellowed fire at them, but this time it fell short.

'Are you all right?' Bellerophon smelled burnt hair. His own or Pegasus's, he could not tell.

As they circled higher, he took his bow and notched an arrow.

'Steady now, steady . . .' He looked down, took aim and fired. His arrow struck the neck of the goat, just where it grew out from the lion's back. The yellow goat eyes widened and she let out a shriek of pain. The goat head shook herself and the arrow dropped free. Bellerophon shot again, and kept shooting. Some arrows glanced off and some pierced the lion flanks of the Chimera, who had now worked herself into a bellowing fury.

'I'm sorry, but I have to get closer,' shouted Bellerophon, pulling out the lance from its sheath.

Pegasus circled and swooped till the sun was behind him and then hurtled down.

If the smith had been surprised by Bellerophon's commission, he had not shown it.

'A "lance", you say, sir?'

'That's right. Half as long as I am high.'

'But the tip made of lead?'

'Lead.'

'Very soft, is lead. You won't be piercing no armour nor no hide with a spearpoint of lead.'

'Nonetheless, that is what I require.'

'Your money,' said the smith. 'Makes no difference to me if it's tin or tissue.'

The Chimera saw Pegasus diving out of the sun and reared up, claws thrashing. Bellerophon leaned out as far as he could. The jaws of the monster opened wide to blast one last great ball of fire and Bellerophon hurled the lance deep into the open mouth and down the tunnel of its throat. A tidal wave of heat burst over them as Pegasus pulled out of the dive at the last minute. He rocketed upwards, almost crashing into the tops of the trees, before steadying himself.

Bellerophon looked down and saw the monster screaming and bucking – the leaden tip of the lance had instantly melted in the fierce fury of the fire, and molten lead was pouring into her interior. Fatally wounded, she floundered and fell. The goat's head exploded in steam, flame and blood, the lion's fur was ablaze and with one last ear-splitting shriek and twitch, the Chimera died.

Bellerophon landed and dismounted. A foul stench arose from the smoking carcass. Bellerophon cut off the snake tail and the lion's head, mangled and charred as they were. Grisly mementos, but proof of his victory.

When he went to mount Pegasus, he saw that the under-side of the horse's neck was burned and the mane singed.

'You poor fellow,' said Bellerophon. 'We'll find you a healer. Think you can make it to Mount Pelion?'*

FLYING TOO HIGH

Iobates hid his fury well when a cheerful Bellerophon strode into his chamber and dropped a stinking, scorched lion's head and suppurating snake carcass on his desk. Philonoë gasped.

'You killed her! Oh, you're *so* brave!'

Bellerophon winked and her cheeks flared red.

Iobates was thinking hard. 'That's . . . good lord . . . my, my . . . I wouldn't have believed it if I hadn't seen it with my own eyes. Come, share a cup of wine with me. You killed her!'

'Her death should bring peace and prosperity back to your kingdom,' said Bellerophon, downing his wine with the casual modesty that only arrogance can produce.

'Yes indeed . . .' mused Iobates. 'Only . . . that is . . . well, it's nothing.'

'Don't tell me there's another monster rampaging about?'

'No, no, not a monster. We do have a problem with the men of Pisidia. They're descended from SOLYMUS. Heard of him? No? Well, Solymus married his sister MILYE, and you know what the offspring of incestuous couplings are like. His descendants – the Solymi, they call themselves – they pay no taxes, they raid neighbouring towns and villages, and word has it they are even now rising up to revolt against my

---

* Home of the wise centaur Chiron, master of the healing arts. See the story of Jason (pages 192, 229).

rule. I've sent platoons and even large companies of soldiers against them, but they've always been ambushed and either kidnapped for ransom or slaughtered.'

'So you'd like them brought into line?' said Bellerophon with an infuriatingly cocky grin and another wink at the round-eyed Philonoë.

'It's too much to ask . . . too much . . .'

A few days later a column of Solymi trooped into the palace to bow low and swear allegiance to Iobates for ever. They had lost seventy of their finest when Bellerophon and Pegasus descended on their town, and that was enough.

Now Iobates urged Bellerophon *not* to go to war with the Amazons, who were in the habit of raiding Lycia from their fastness in the northeast. Mounted on Pegasus, Bellerophon dropped great boulders on these fierce female warriors until they too pledged themselves by treaty to leave Iobates and his kingdom alone.

Next Bellerophon defeated the pirate CHEIMARRHUS, having ignored Iobates' entreaties about leaving such a fearsome foe *well alone.** News of this latest exploit reached Iobates ahead of Bellerophon. Desperate to finish off the arrogant youth once and for all, the king now ordered his own citizens to take up arms and kill the pestilential youth as soon as he returned to Xanthus.

Arriving at the gates of the palace to see the troops lined up against him and barring entrance to the city, Bellerophon at last understood: all this time Iobates had meant him harm. Without Pegasus, whom he had left behind in his meadow,

---

* Cheimarrhus was said to sail in a ship with a lion's figurehead for the prow and a serpent for the sternpost which, taken with the similarity of his name to that of the Chimera (both derive from a Greek word for 'goat'), makes one wonder if he wasn't just another version of the monster's story. See the Afterword for a discussion of this kind of 'Euhemerism', or historical interpretation.

he was all but defenceless against such numbers. All he could do was pray to his father Poseidon.

Behind Bellerophon, the River Xanthus began to overflow its banks, flooding its plain with water which swept towards the city. Iobates, watching in horror from the tower of his palace, sent men to plead with the hero, but the iron had entered Bellerophon's soul and he marched grimly on, the waters surging behind him.

Finally the women of Xanthus, desperate to save their homes and families, hoisted their dresses right up and ran towards him. Bellerophon, so bold and self-assured in other ways, was modest, shy and awkward when it came to sexual matters. At the sight of the women's buttocks, breasts and bushes he turned and ran, shocked and hot with shame and embarrassment. The floodwaters receded with him and the city was saved.

It was time for Iobates to understand the obvious truth: this hero was protected by the gods. The letter of his son-in-law Proetus made no sense. If Bellerophon had truly tried to rape Stheneboea, surely the gods would have abandoned him? Now Iobates came to think of it, his daughter Stheneboea had always been trouble. Perhaps he had misjudged the boy? A sudden clamour drew him to look down into the courtyard. Bellerophon and Pegasus had landed; the young man dismounted and was now striding towards the king's apartments, sword in hand.

When he burst into the chamber, he found Iobates waving a letter at him.

'Read this, read this!' cried the king.

Bellerophon snatched the letter and read it. 'B-but it was the other way round,' he said. 'It was *she* who tried to seduce *me*!'

Iobates nodded. 'I see that now. Of course I do. Forgive me, my boy. I owe you everything.'

*

In the end it turned out that Bellerophon didn't want to go back to Corinth and marry Aethra, the princess of Troezen. Over the weeks and months he stayed in Xanthus, he had begun to notice how beautiful and sweet-natured young Philonoë was.

When the news reached Stheneboea that her sister was to marry Bellerophon, she knew the story of the botched seduction and spiteful, duplicitous revenge would come out. Proetus would hear of it. The whole of the Peloponnese would whisper of it. Unable to bear the shame, Stheneboea hanged herself.*

Like the Chimera herself, Bellerophon's story begins with a glorious and majestic roar but ends with a sharp serpent's bite. It gives me no pleasure to relate that his youthful cockiness soured over the years into a very unappealing arrogance and vanity. He believed that his divine parentage, his relationship with Pegasus and the heroic feats he undertook with that magical horse had all raised him to a level greater than that of a mere mortal.

One day he mounted Pegasus and rode the winged horse up to Mount Olympus.

'The gods will welcome me,' he told himself. 'I am of their blood. I have always been marked out for greatness.'

Such hubris was a blasphemy that could not go unpunished. When Zeus saw Bellerophon flying towards the summit, he sent a gadfly to torment Pegasus. The insect's vicious sting maddened the horse, who bucked and reared, throwing Bellerophon. The hero plummeted down through the thin air, smashing his hip on the rocks far below. Pegasus landed on the top of Olympus and Zeus kept him there as his

---

* Another version says that Bellerophon returned to Tiryns, made a show of forgiving Stheneboea and offered her a ride on Pegasus. Once they were far out at sea he pushed her off.

glamorous pack animal, charged with carrying his thunder-bolts.

Bellerophon dragged out the rest of his days shunned by society for his sacrilege, until he died a crippled, embittered and lonely old man.

Few heroes die peacefully in their beds after long lives filled with happiness. But few have had sadder ends than the once glorious Bellerophon.

ORPHEUS

THE POWER TO SOOTHE
THE SAVAGE BEAST

Orpheus was the Mozart of the ancient world. He was more than that. Orpheus was the Cole Porter, the Shakespeare, the Lennon and McCartney, the Adele, Prince, Luciano Pavarotti, Lady Gaga and Kendrick Lamar of the ancient world, the acknowledged sweet-singing master of words and music. During his lifetime his fame spread around the Mediterranean and beyond. It was said that his pure voice and matchless playing could charm the beasts of the field, the fishes of the sea, the birds of the air and even the insensate rocks and waters. Rivers themselves diverted their courses to hear him. Hermes invented the lyre, Apollo improved upon it, but Orpheus perfected it.

It is agreed who his mother was, but there is less certainty about his father. Here we come to a theme that repeats in many variations in this Age of Heroes. That of double parenthood. CALLIOPE, Beautiful Voice, the Muse of Epic Poetry, was Orpheus's mother by a mortal, the Thracian king OEAGRUS.* But Apollo was believed to be Orpheus's father too, and Orpheus was quite a favourite of the god. In any case, young Orpheus romped with his mother and eight Muse aunts on Mount Parnassus and it was there that the

---

* Who would certainly have been father of Heracles' unfortunate music teacher, Orpheus's brother or half-brother Linus.

doting Apollo presented his son with a golden lyre, which he personally taught him to play.

Soon the prodigy's skill at the instrument exceeded even that of his father, the god of music. Unlike MARSYAS, who may have been his stepbrother, Orpheus did not boast about his prowess, nor did he make the mistake of challenging his divine father to a competition.* Instead he spent his days mastering his craft, charming the birds of the air and beasts of the field, causing the branches of the trees to bend down and listen to his lyre and the fishes to jump and bubble with joy at his soft, seductive strains.

His character matched the sweetness of his playing and singing. He played for the love of music and his songs celebrated the beauty of the world and the glory of love.

ORPHEUS AND EURYDICE

So great was his fame that when Jason gathered a crew for the *Argo* and his quest for the Golden Fleece, he knew he had to have Orpheus on board. But more of Jason later. For now, all we need to know is that the gods rewarded Orpheus for his bravery and loyalty in this adventure with the gift of love, in the shape of the beautiful EURYDICE.

As might be imagined, the wedding was quite an affair. All the Muses attended. THALIA entertained with comedy sketches; TERPSICHORE led the dances. Each of the other sisters also delighted the guests with examples of their own particular art. But a strange and uncomfortable incident clouded the happy event in the minds of many who witnessed it.

---

* See *Mythos*, Vol. I.

Among the guests was Orpheus's half-brother HYMEN, a son of Apollo and the Muse URANIA. A minor deity of song (he gave us the word 'hymn') Hymen served as one of the Erotes (the young men in the love god Eros's retinue), with a special responsibility for weddings and the marriage bed. Our words 'hymen' and 'hymenal' also derive from him. His presence at his half-brother's wedding was natural and a great compliment, but for some reason – jealousy perhaps – Hymen failed to bless the union. The torch he bore spluttered and smoked, causing everyone to cough. The atmosphere was so acrid that even Orpheus was unable to sing with his accustomed sweetness of tone. Hymen soon departed the feast, but the cold unfriendliness of his presence left a taste in the mouth quite as unpleasant as that of the black smoke from his torch.

Orpheus and Eurydice, this dark note quite banished from their minds, set up a happy house together in Pimpleia, a small town that nestled in the valley below Olympus, close to the Pierian Spring, sacred to the Muses.

It was Eurydice's misfortune, though, to catch the eye of ARISTAEUS, a minor god of bee-keeping, agriculture and other country crafts. One afternoon, on her way home from the market, she took a shortcut through a water meadow. In the distance she could just hear her beloved Orpheus strumming his lyre as he tried out a new and lovely song. Suddenly Aristaeus burst out from behind a poplar tree and bore down upon her. Frightened, she dropped the bread and fruit she was carrying and fled wildly, zigzagging across the fields. Aristaeus pursued her, laughing.

'Orpheus! Orpheus!' Eurydice cried.

Orpheus put down his lyre. Was that his wife's voice?

'Help me, help me!' screamed the voice.

Orpheus ran towards the sound.

Eurydice wove this way and that, trying to escape the remorseless Aristaeus, whose hot breath she could feel on her neck. In her blind panic she stumbled and fell into a ditch. Aristaeus closed in, but by now Orpheus had appeared and was running towards them, shouting. Aristaeus knew an angry husband when he saw one and turned away, disappointed.

As Orpheus reached the scene he heard Eurydice cry out again. The ditch into which she had stumbled was the home of an adder which struck out angrily, sinking its fangs into her heel. Orpheus reached her side in time to see her sink back in mortal agony.

He took her in his arms. He breathed into her, sang softly into her ear, begging her to return to him, but the venom of the viper had done its work. Her soul left her body.

The cry that escaped from Orpheus struck horror and fear into the whole valley. The Muses heard it, the gods on Olympus heard it. It was the last sound they were to hear from Orpheus for some time.

His mourning was as absolute and unwavering as could be. He put his lyre aside. He would never sing again. He would never smile again, compose a lyric again, so much as hum again. What life was left to him would be spent in pain and anguished silence.

The town of Pimpleia was given over to lamentation, grieving more over the loss of Orpheus's music than the life of Eurydice, well-loved as she had been. The nymphs of the woods, waters and mountains fell into mourning too. Even the gods of Olympus pined and fretted at the drying up of the music.

Apollo went to visit his son. He found him sitting in the porch, gazing out across the very fields where Eurydice had met her end.

'Come now,' said Apollo. 'It's been more than a year. You can't mope like this for ever.'

'Watch me.'

'What would persuade you to pick up your lyre again?'

'Only the living presence of my beloved wife.'

'Well . . .' a thoughtful frown appeared on the golden god's smooth brow. 'Eurydice is in the underworld. The gates are guarded by Cerberus, the three-headed hound of hell. No one but Heracles has ever penetrated the underworld and returned, and even he didn't come back up with a dead soul. But if anyone can do it, you can.'

'What are you saying?'

'Why not go and get her?'

'You just said, "No one has ever penetrated the underworld and returned."'

'Ah, but no one has ever had the power you have, Orpheus.'

'What power?'

'The power of music. If anyone could tame Cerberus and charm CHARON the ferryman, it is you. If anyone could melt the hearts of Hades and Persephone, it is you.'

'You really think . . . ?'

'Have faith in what music can do.'

Orpheus went into the house and retrieved his lyre from the dusty cupboard into which he had thrust it.

'String it with these,' said Apollo plucking from his head twenty-four golden hairs.

Orpheus restrung the lyre and tuned it. Never had it sounded more beautiful.

'Now go, and come back with Eurydice.'

ORPHEUS IN THE UNDERWORLD

Orpheus travelled all the way from Pimpleia to Cape Tainaron in the Peloponnese, the southernmost point of all Greece,* where could be found a cave that formed one of the entrances to the underworld.

The path from the cape sloped down, after many mazy turns, to the main gate guarded by Cerberus – the slavering, shuddering, slobbering three-headed dog, offspring of the primordial monsters Echidna and Typhon.

At the sight of a living mortal daring to enter the halls of hell, Cerberus wagged his serpent tail and drooled in anticipation. Only the dead could pass him, and in order to dwell in peace in the Meadow of Asphodel† they would know to bring with them a piece of food with which to placate him. Orpheus had no sop for Cerberus other than his art. Inwardly quaking but outwardly assured, he brushed the strings of the golden lyre with his fingers and began to sing.

At the sound of the song, Cerberus – who had bunched himself up ready to bound forward and savage this presumptuous mortal – gave a whining gulp and froze in his tracks. His huge eyes rounded and he began to pant with pleasure and an inner joy that was entirely new to him. He dropped down on his haunches and curled himself on the cold stone of the gateway, like a huntsman's favourite hound dreaming by the fire

---

* Now Cape Matapan.

† The Asphodel Meadow was sometimes given as the place where ordinary, non-heroic mortals resided in the underworld. As I mentioned in a footnote on the death of Heracles, there is little consistency across the sources and poets as to what happened to the dead. An asphodel, incidentally, is a white heathland flowering plant. Homer's *Odyssey* seems to have the first mention of such a flower carpeting the Elysian Fields of Hades, but it later entered the poetic language across Europe and wider. William Carlos Williams' poem 'Asphodel, That Greeny Flower' is a notable example.

after a long day in the field. Orpheus's song slowed into a gentle lullaby. Cerberus's six ears flopped down, his six eyes closed, his three tongues passed across his chops with a great slap and his three massive heads dropped into a deep and happy sleep. Even the snake of his tail drooped in peaceful slumber.

Orpheus climbed over the snoring form and, still humming his lullaby, he headed along the cold dark passageway until his progress was blocked by the black waters of the River Styx. Charon the ferryman poled his way towards him from the further bank where he had just deposited a new soul. He stretched out his hand for payment but quickly withdrew it when he saw that the young man standing before him was alive.

'Hence! Avaunt!' cried Charon in a hoarse whisper.*

In reply Orpheus strummed his lyre and began a new song, a song praising the overlooked profession of ferryman, glorifying the unrecognised diligence and industry of one ferryman in particular – Charon, the great Charon, whose central role in the vast mystery of life and death should be celebrated the world over.

Never had Charon's ferry skimmed the cold waters of the Styx with such alacrity. Never before had Charon, his skiff now beached, put an arm round a fare and helped them gently to disembark. And for sure, never, not in all eternity, had such a stupid, fatuous smile played over the ferryman's habitually gaunt and unrelenting features. He stood supporting himself on his pole, his adoring gaze fixed on the person of Orpheus who, with a final wave and strum of the lyre, was soon swallowed up by the darkness of the passageways that led to the palace of Hades and Persephone.

---

* Charon liked to use old-fashioned words like 'Avaunt', 'Nay' and 'Forsooth'. He believed they enhanced his dignity.

On entering the palace's great hall, Orpheus found himself facing the three Judges of the Underworld, MINOS, RHADAMANTHUS and AEACUS, enthroned in a grim semicircle.* The light of Orpheus's living spirit dazzled their eyes.

'Sacrilege! Sacrilege!'

'How dare the living invade the realm of the dead?'

'Summon Thanatos, lord of death, to suck the insolent soul from his body!'

Orpheus took up his lyre and before the last command could be obeyed, the three judges were smiling, nodding their heads and tapping their sandaled toes in time to the intoxicating strains.

Their retinue of ghoulish servants, sentries and attendants had not heard music for so long that they could not remember how to respond to it. Some clutched at the air as if the sounds they heard were butterflies that could be caught in their hands. Some clapped, clumsily at first, but soon in time to the beat of the lyre's chords. An awkward shuffle turned into a rhythmic stamp that became a frenzied dance. Within minutes the whole chamber was alive and echoing with singing, dancing and cries of joy and laughter.

'What is the meaning of this?'

At the sight of Hades, King of the Underworld himself, and his pale consort Persephone, the hall fell into an instant and guilty silence. As in a game of musical chairs, they froze to a halt with thuds and skids. Only Orpheus appeared unmoved.

Hades curled a beckoning finger. 'If you wish to avoid an eternal punishment more excruciating than those of IXION,

---

* The three judges were sons of Zeus, mortal kings famed for the righteousness of their rule, who determined on behalf of Hades the fates of the dead in the underworld. Heracles sensibly avoided them during his visit. See the first volume of *Mythos* (page 143).

1. The Olympians, triumphant on Mount Olympus.

2. Prometheus continues to endure his terrible punishment.

3. The shower
of gold.

4. Danaë and Perseus, rescued from the wooden box.

5. Perseus holds the head of Medusa, whose body lies on the ground.

6. The Head of Medusa.

7. Perseus rescues Andromeda from the sea dragon Cetus.

8. The infant Heracles
choking a snake.

9. The creation of
the Milky Way.

10. Heracles' First Labour, the great Nemean Lion.

11. Heracles holds the Erymanthian boar over Eurystheus, cowering in his stone jar.

12. An Amazon defending herself from one of Heracles' men.

13. Heracles, with his lion skin, club and bow, navigates while standing inside the Cup of Helios.

14. The Garden of the Hesperides.

15. The Gigantomachy, or the Fall of the Giants.

16. Pegasus and Bellerophon.

17. Orpheus plays for love, before Hades and Persephone.

18. Orpheus turns too quickly.

SISYPHUS and TANTALUS combined, you had better explain yourself, mortal. What possible excuse could you have for this indecent display?'

'Not an excuse, sir, but a reason. The best and only reason.'

'A pert reply. And what is this reason?'

'Love.'

Hades replied with the barrage of bleak barks that was the closest he came to laughing.

'My wife Eurydice is here. I must have her back.'

'Must?' Persephone stared at him in disbelief. 'You dare use such a word?'

'My father Apollo –'

'We do no favours for Olympians,' said Hades. 'You are mortal and you have trespassed into the realm of the dead. That is all we need to know.'

'Perhaps my music may change your mind.'

'Music! We are immune to its charms here.'

'I tamed Cerberus. I charmed Charon. I bewitched the Judges of the Underworld and their retinue. Are you perhaps afraid that my songs might enchant you also?'

Queen Persephone whispered briefly in her husband's ear.

Hades nodded. 'Fetch Eurydice!' he commanded. 'One song,' he said to Orpheus. 'You may sing one song. If it fails to delight, the relentless agony of your torture will be the talk and terror of the cosmos till the end of time. If your music moves us, well – we will allow you and your woman to return to the world above.'

When Eurydice's spirit floated into the hall and saw Orpheus standing so boldly before the King and Queen of the Dead, she let out a great cry of joy and wonder. Orpheus saw the shimmering form of her shade and called out to her.

'Yes, yes!' said Hades, testily. 'Most affecting. Now. Your song.'

Orpheus took up his lyre and gave a deep breath. Never had an artist asked more of their art.

The moment his hands touched the strings everyone present knew that they were going to hear something entirely new. Nimbly, Orpheus's fingertips flew up and down the strings, causing a cascade of trilling notes so quick and pure that everyone caught their breath. And now, out of the golden ripple emerged the voice. It asked everyone to think of love. Surely, even here, in the dark caverns of death, love still sat in their souls? Could they remember the first time they felt the sweeping rush of love? Love came to peasants, kings and even gods. Love made all equal. Love deified, yet love levelled.

Persephone's hand tightened around Hades' wrist as she recalled the day his chariot erupted into the meadow where she had been gathering flowers. Hades found himself thinking of the bargain he had struck with Demeter, Persephone's mother, allowing him access to his beloved for six whole months in every year.

Persephone turned to look at her husband, the man who had taken her by force but kept her by his steadfast love. Only she understood his dark moods and the honest passions that boiled within. He returned her gaze. Could that be a tear she saw welling up in his eye?

Orpheus reached the climax of his song to Eros. It wound its way along the passageways and through the chambers, galleries and hallways of hell, binding all who heard it – the servants of Hades, the emissaries of death and the souls of the departed – in a spell that took them, for as long as the music played in their ears, far away from the remorseless miseries of their endless captivity and into a kingdom of light and love.

'Your wish is granted,' boomed Hades huskily as the last notes faded away. 'Your wife may depart.'

At his words Eurydice's shade took on the substance and form of quick and breathing life. She ran into her husband's arms and they held each other tight. But a frown was forming on Hades' brow. The loss of just one dead soul tormented him. When it came to the spirits doomed to spend eternity in his kingdom, he was a hoarder, a miser of the meanest kind.

'Wait!'

The moment Eurydice had returned to flesh and blood, Orpheus had stopped playing and singing and the powerful spell of the music began to weaken its hold. It was a memory, a keen and a beautiful one, but the transcendent mood it engendered, like all the keenest pleasures, vanished like steam the moment the closing notes died away. Hades now regretted bitterly that while imprisoned in the bewitching coils of Orpheus's song he could have been so weak as to agree to Eurydice's release. How foolish he had been to give his word in front of so many witnesses. He leaned across for a whispered consultation with Persephone. Nodding, with a small smile of triumph, he kissed her cheek and pointed a finger at Orpheus.

'Let go of the woman. Turn and leave us.'

'But you said . . .'

'She will follow. As you make your way to the upper world, she will remain ten paces behind. But if you turn round to look at her, if you cast so much as the briefest backward glance in her direction, you will lose her. Trust, Orpheus the musician. You must show that you honour us and have faith in our word. Now go.'

Orpheus took Eurydice's face in his hands, kissed her cheek and turned to leave.

'Remember!' Persephone called after him. 'Look back for just one instant and she will be ours. No matter how many times you return, and how many songs you sing, you will have lost her for ever.'

'I won't be far behind. Have faith!' said Eurydice.

Orpheus reached the door that led to life and freedom.

'Faith!' replied Orpheus, his eyes fixed resolutely ahead of him.

And so he began to make his way along the slowly rising stone corridors and passageways. Hundreds of flitting souls acknowledged him and breathed messages of good luck as he passed. Some alarmed him by begging to be taken to the upper world with him, but Orpheus waved them away and kept resolutely to his course, upwards and ever upwards. Gates and doors opened mysteriously before him as he went.

To encourage Eurydice, but mostly to reassure himself, he called out continually.

'Still there, my darling?'

'Still there.'

'Not tiring?'

'Always ten paces behind. Trust me.'

'So close now.'

Indeed, over the last two hundred or so paces Orpheus had become aware of a cool breeze fanning his face and fresh air filling his nostrils. Now he saw light ahead. Not the underworld's light of rush torches, pitch lamps and burning oil, but the pure light of living day. He quickened his step and pressed forward. So close, so fantastically close! In just fifteen, fourteen, thirteen, twelve steps they would be free, free to live their lives again as husband and wife. Free to have children, to travel the world together. Oh, the places they would visit. The wonders they would see. The songs and poetry and music he would compose.

The mouth of the cave opened wide as Orpheus strode on

with joy and triumph in his heart. One more step – out of the shadows and into the light.

He had done it! He was out in the world, the sun was warming his face and its light was dazzling his eyes. Ten more steps forward to be sure, and now he could turn and take his beloved in his arms.

But no! No, no, no and *no*!

Orpheus had not known it, but his last twenty or so steps had accelerated into a run. Eurydice had quickened her own pace to try to match his, but when he turned round she was still too far behind, still in shadow, still in the realm of the dead.

Her eyes, filled with horror and fear, caught his for a second before the light inside her seemed to die and she was pulled back into the darkness.

With a cry of anguish Orpheus ran into the cave but she was flying away from him at tremendous speed, no longer flesh and blood but an immaterial spirit once more. Her unhappy cries echoed as Orpheus ran blindly into the black-ness after her. The doors and gateways that had opened to let them leave now slammed shut in his face. He beat his fists against them until they bled, but to no avail. He could no longer hear her cries of despair, only his own.

If he had waited just two blinks of an eye before turning, they would have been united and free. Just two heartbeats.

THE DEATH OF ORPHEUS

Orpheus's later life was a sad one. After a long second mourn-ing period, he picked up his lyre again and continued to compose, play and sing for the rest of his life, but he never found a woman to match his Eurydice. Indeed, it is reported in several sources that he turned away from women altogether and lavished what affection he had left on the male youths of Thrace.

The Thracian women, the Ciconians, followers of Dionysus, were so enraged at being overlooked that they threw sticks and stones at Orpheus. However, the sticks and stones were so charmed by his music they just hung in mid-air, refusing to hurt him.

At last the Ciconian women could bear the degradation and insult of being ignored no longer and, in a Bacchic frenzy, they tore Orpheus to pieces, pulling off his limbs and wrenching the head from his shoulders.* The golden harmonies of Apollo were always an affront to the dark Dionysian dances and dithyrambs.

Orpheus's head, still singing, was cast into the River Hebrus where it floated out into the Aegean. Eventually it found its way onto the beach at Lesbos; it was taken up by the inhabitants of the island and placed in a cave. For many years people came from all over to the cave to ask the head of Orpheus questions, and it always sang the most melodious prophecies in reply.

At last Orpheus's father Apollo, perhaps jealous that the shrine was threatening the supremacy of his own oracle at Delphi, silenced him. His mother Calliope found his golden lyre and carried it heavenwards, where it was placed amongst the stars as the constellation Lyra, which contains Vega, the fifth brightest star in the firmament. His aunts, the eight other Muses, gathered up the fragments of his body and buried them at Libethra, below Mount Olympus, where nightingales still sing over his grave.

---

* The Greeks even had a word for this Dionysian tearing apart, this frenzied dismemberment – they called it *sparagmos*.

Finally at peace, Orpheus's spirit descended once more into the underworld where he was at last reunited with his beloved Eurydice. Thanks to Offenbach, they still perform a joyful cancan together in the realm of the dead every single day.

JASON

Ixion, a king of the Lapiths, had once dared to attempt to

THE RAM

The voyage of Jason's ship *Argo* in the quest for the Golden Fleece involves backstory, backstory and more backstory. But it's good, juicy backstory, so I hope you will dive in. A lot of names will come at you now like quills shot from a porcupine; but don't worry, the important ones will stick.*

We can start with BISALTES, a founder hero of the Bisaltae peoples of Thrace. His mother was the primordial earth goddess Gaia and his father the sun Titan Helios†. Bisaltes' beautiful daughter THEOPHANE caught the eye of the sea god Poseidon, who snatched her up and took her to the island of Crinissa, where he turned himself into a ram and Theophane into a ewe. In the course of time she gave birth to a beautiful golden ram.

Point One – there now existed in the world a beautiful golden ram, of immortal lineage.

Ixion, a king of the Lapiths, had once dared to attempt to seduce Hera, the Queen of Heaven, at a banquet on Mount Olympus‡. To expose his depravity Zeus entrapped Ixion by sending to him a living cloud in the exact likeness and form of Hera. The brutish Ixion had leapt all over this cloud,

---

* And are capitalised.

† Helios was also Gaia's son, so she stood as both mother and grandmother to Bisaltes. This is nothing compared to the far more bizarre double and triple relationships of some.

‡ See *Mythos*, Vol. I, page 257.

thinking it was the goddess herself. As a punishment for such blasphemous intent, Ixion was bound to a revolving wheel of fire and sent spinning across the heavens, and latterly down into the underworld to remain there for ever. The cloud took on the name NEPHELE and went on to marry King ATHAMAS of Boeotia* by whom she had twins, a boy, PHRIXUS, and a girl, HELLE.

Point Two – the twins Phrixus and Helle are born to Athamas of Boeotia.

In time Nephele took her place back in the sky as a cloud and as a minor goddess of *xenia*, the highly prized principle of hospitality. Athamas looked to take a new wife and chose INO, one of the daughters of CADMUS, the founding King of Thebes.† Ino installed herself in Athamas's palace and, as second wives will, instituted a new regime to banish all memories of her predecessor. Ino came with a reputation as the most caring and nurturing of women – it was she who had suckled her sister Semele's child by Zeus, the infant Dionysus. Her other sisters, AGAVE and AUTONOË, had rejected Semele and paid a terrible price when a grown Dionysus visited Thebes and sent them mad to tragic effect.‡ But Ino had survived with her life and good name intact, and the world loved her for it.

Inside, however, Ino was ambitious, relentless and cruel. She had taken an instant dislike to her stepchildren Phrixus and Helle and decided to get them out of the way. By Athamas she had her own sons, LEARCHUS and MELICERTES, and

---

* Usually pronounced 'Bee-*oh*-shuh'.

† Although often called 'the First Hero', Cadmus more properly belongs in the first volume of *Mythos*, where you will find his story (page 210).

‡ The tragic effect that Euripides dramatised in his play *The Bacchae*, and the best known example of Dionysian *sparagmos*.

was determined they should rule Boeotia when Athamas died, not Phrixus and Helle. An archetype of the wicked stepmother that was to dominate myth, legend and fairy tale for ages to come, Ino hatched a formidably malicious and elaborate plan to destroy the twins.

First she persuaded the women of Boeotia to ruin the seedcorn in the barns and silos by charring it, so that when their husbands went out to sow in the fields it would be unable to sprout. As she had hoped, the next year's harvest failed and famine threatened the kingdom.

'Let us send messengers to Delphi, dear husband,' said Ino to Athamas, 'and find out why this disaster has been visited on us and what we can do to set it right.'

'How wise you are, dear wife,' said the besotted Athamas.

But the messengers sent to Delphi were paid agents of Ino and the words they claimed now to bring back from the oracle were hers and hers alone.

'My lord king,' said the chief messenger, unfurling a roll of parchment, 'hearken unto the words of Delphic Apollo. "To placate the gods for the sins of the city and the vanities of its citizens, your son Phrixus must be sacrificed."'

On hearing this Athamas let out a howl of anguish. He was too distressed to consider how uncharacteristically direct and unambiguous this pronouncement was from an oracle notorious for its equivocations and double meanings.

Young Prince Phrixus stepped up. 'If my life will save the lives of others, Father,' he said in a clear, steady voice, 'then I go happily to the sacrificial altar.'

His mother Nephele, high in her palace of clouds, heard this and made ready to intervene.

Phrixus, head held aloft, was led to the great sacrificial stone that had stood in the town square for generations.

Human sacrifice, especially involving the young, was now looked on as barbaric, an unwanted legacy from the days when gods and men were crueller. But gods and men never lose their cruelty and the stone remained, just in case.

A royal guard stood high on a roof and began to pound his drum. If the youth was to die, better to make a good show of it. The women of Boeotia put scraps of linen to their eyes and made a great display of weeping. Children who had never known the privilege of witnessing a ritualistic killing of this kind pressed forward to get a better view.

Athamas howled and beat his breast, but the townspeople had all had a surfeit of famine. The words of the oracle were clear and the sacrifice was required.

The high priest, dressed all in white, stepped forward, a ceremonial knife of shining silver in his hand.

'Who gives this child to the Lord Zeus?'

'No one, no one!' wailed Athamas.

'I give myself!' said Phrixus stoutly.

Young Helle, who had not let go of her brother's hand from the moment he had volunteered himself for the sacrifice, now added her voice. 'I die with my brother!'

Ino almost hugged herself. 'Really, this is better than I dared hope!' she thought.

'No!' cried Athamas.

Strong hands took both children and laid them on the sacrificial slab.

As the priest raised his knife and held it poised for the strike, a voice called down from the sky.

'On his back, Phrixus! Quick, Helle! Hold tight!'

Down from the clouds flew a golden ram. It landed on the stone in front of Phrixus and Helle who, obeying the command of their mother, clutched at the thick fleece and fell forward onto the animal's back. They were taken up into the air before the priest, their guards, Ino or anyone else had time to react.*

Phrixus and Helle gripped the golden fleece as the ram flew east over the narrow straits that separate Europe from Asia. Here a gust of wind and a sudden swift turn from the ram caused Helle to fall from the ram's back. Phrixus cried out in vain for it to stop. He looked down in horror and saw his sister plummet to her death in the water of the straits, which the Greeks were to call in her honour 'the Hellespont' or Sea of Helle.† A distraught Phrixus wept bitter tears into the fleece as the golden ram flew further east, towards the Propontis, or Sea of Marmara, and over the Bosporus until they saw the glittering waters of the great inland sea that we call today the Black Sea, but which for the Greeks presaged the outer limits of what was civilised and Grecian. Beyond its shores lay strangers, barbarians and the deranged denizens of the eastern edge of the world, so it was known to them as the Unfriendly Sea, the Hostile Sea, the Sea of Enmity.‡ As they passed the Caucasus Mountains, Phrixus could make out the naked, sunburnt form of Prometheus manacled and spread out on the rock. The shadow of an

---

* In the Book of Genesis, you may remember, the patriarch Abraham was tested by God and told to sacrifice his son Isaac. Just as Abraham's knife was descending God showed him a ram caught in a nearby thicket and told him to kill the animal in place of his son. One version of the story of Iphigenia and Agamemnon, which helped set in motion both the Trojan War and its tragic aftermath, is another example of this mytheme – but it is not yet time to hear that particular tale.

† Today the straits are known as the Dardanelles, which is another name derived from a figure of Greek myth – in this case DARDANUS, son of Zeus and ELECTRA (one of the seven heavenly sisters known as the PLEIADES). Dardanus was the father of Tros, the founder of Troy; it is because of him that Homer sometimes refers to the Trojans as 'Dardanians'.

‡ *Axeinos* in Greek. Latterly, the Greeks gave it the wistfully optimistic name *Euxinos* – the 'Euxine Sea' – which means 'hospitable'. In the same way the 'Cape of Torments' had its name changed to the 'Cape of Good Hope' by Portuguese navigators in the late fifteenth century.

eagle passed over it. Phrixus knew it was on its way to feast on Prometheus's liver, a torture the Titan endured every day.*

On the far eastern shores of the Black Sea lay a kingdom of some wealth and size. This kingdom, which we would call today a province of the Republic of Georgia, was known in those days as Colchis. Its king was AEËTES, a son of Helios the sun Titan and an Oceanid called PERSEIS. He ruled from the capital, Aia.

If Aeëtes was astonished to see a golden ram land in front of his palace and a youth step down off its back, he was too cautious and politic to say so. Mindful of the rules of hospitality, he invited Phrixus to dine with him. Phrixus, grateful for the honour, sacrificed the ram to Zeus and presented Aeëtes with its golden fleece. It seems hard on so amiable and obliging an animal, but with death came the ultimate compliment: Zeus, pleased with the sacrifice, raised the noble creature to the stars as Aries, the Ram.

The GOLDEN FLEECE was a most precious gift. Aeëtes hung it on the branches of an oak that stood in a grove sacred to Ares, the god of war. Aeëtes had somewhere about the palace grounds a huge serpent,† terrible to look at and endowed with the special gift of never closing its eyes. This was set to guard the oak and its valuable burden. At some point Phrixus married CHALCIOPE, one of Aeëtes' daughters, and all was well in Colchis.

Meanwhile, back in Boeotia, we left Athamas and Ino staring up at the sky as a golden ram, with Phrixus and Helle on board, disappeared into the clouds.

It was not long before Athamas came to understand that the whole crop-failure/famine/oracle/human-sacrifice affair

---

* This backstory takes place before Heracles frees Prometheus of course.
† Yet another child of Typhon and Echidna, or (according to Apollonius Rhodus) of Gaia and Typhon.

had been a ruse devised in the evil mind of his wife. In a frenzy, he lashed out and killed his son by her, Learchus.* Ino fled with their other boy, Melicertes. But Athamas cornered them and, in her despair, Ino threw herself and Melicertes over the cliffs and into the sea. Dionysus, ever mindful of his foster mother's kindness to him, did not let her drown, but instead transformed her into the immortal LEUCOTHEA, the 'white goddess' of the sea.† Melicertes became PALAEMON, a dolphin-riding deity and guardian of ships.

Athamas's life had not been a happy one‡, but we can see how it led indirectly, through Nephele's intercession to save their twins, to the hanging of the Golden Fleece on the oak in the Grove of Ares in Colchis on the far shores of the Black, Unfriendly Sea, also called the Euxine Sea.

I should say that all of the above is really backstory to the *main* backstory – whose narrative strands I will now try to separate here.

Even setting aside the marriages of Athamas, his family was notorious. He had three quarrelsome and villainous brothers. One brother, Sisyphus, was soon to be doomed to push his boulder uphill for eternity as punishment for his many crimes and blasphemies§. Another brother, SALMONEUS, tried to pass himself off as a god of thunder and storms and was blasted to atoms by Zeus for his impertinence. Just to make matters even more complicated, Salmoneus's daughter

---

* Some say that the madness that overtook him was sent by Hera, who never tired of punishing anyone who had anything to do with the raising, succouring and support of Dionysus, born of one of Zeus's most brazen and outrageous affairs. It was enough for Hera that Athamas was married to Ino, and Ino had nursed the young Dionysus.

† Ino/Leucothea plays a key role generations later in the adventures of Odysseus.

‡ Athamas did have time to marry again: Themisto, his third wife, bore him four children, one of whom was Schoeneus, who went on to father (and abandon) Atalanta, whose story is told soon.

§ See *Mythos*, Vol. I.

TYRO married and had children by each of her uncles: with Athamas himself, with Sisyphus and with CRETHEUS, the third brother. Tyro's eldest son by Cretheus was AESON, but she also had two sons by Poseidon – Pelias and Neleus.* I pause to remind you that I am aware of how complicated and forgettable such divagations into the family tree may be, but they are relevant to the main line of our story. You mustn't feel obliged to memorise these names and relationships. It is enough to get a sense of what all this portends.

Cretheus ruled over IOLCOS, a city in Aeolia, the north-eastern region of mainland Greece that included Larissa and Pherae. Therefore Aeson, his son by his niece Tyro, was the rightful heir and would succeed to the throne when Cretheus died. But Aeson's half-brothers, Pelias and Neleus, believed that they, as sons of Tyro and the great Olympian god Poseidon, had a claim not just to Iolcos but to all of greater Aeolia. Accordingly, the moment Cretheus died they besieged Iolcos. Aeson and his wife ALCIMEDE†, fearing that the city was lost, managed to smuggle out their firstborn child, JASON.

Alcimede was friendly with the centaur CHIRON, and it was he who received and raised the boy.

Shortly after, Pelias broke into the city and slaughtered every man, woman or child connected by blood to the throne, all but Aeson and Alcimede whom he threw in prison. While in captivity the couple had another son, PROMACHUS.

It is worth mentioning too that Pelias's and Neleus's mother Tyro had been mistreated by SIDERO, Cretheus's second wife. Pelias and Neleus ran Sidero down to a temple, in whose precincts they killed her. This proved to be a disastrous mistake, for the temple was dedicated to Hera. The Queen of Heaven,

---

* We have already encountered both brothers, at a later stage in their careers, in the story of Heracles (pages 80 and 119).

† Sometimes she is called Polymede.

outraged at such desecration, swore instant enmity against these two sons of Poseidon. Of all the gods to make an enemy of, Hera was the most dangerous and implacable.

So there we have it. A GOLDEN FLEECE far to the east. IOLCOS and Aeolia in the grip of the tyrannical and murderous Pelias, who rules the region cruelly but with a resolute grip that no rebel can hope to loosen. In fact, as we find today, rebellions from the outside nearly always fail: familial quarrelling, dynastic feuding, party disunity, the palace coup and the stab in the back . . . these are what dislodge regimes and topple tyrants.

Pelias knows this and is haunted by just enough suspicion and despotic paranoia to consult an oracle on the security of his throne.

'One of your own blood will end the life of Pelias. Beware the man who comes from the country wearing but one sandal.'

Was that two people or one? If a man of his own blood would kill him, who could this single-sandaled rustic be? Did they know each other? Were they *both* blood relations? Were they one and the same? Why couldn't oracles ever be straight? It really was too tiresome.

Meanwhile, on the slopes of Mount Pelion, towering over Iolcos, the rightful heir to the city – Jason – is being tutored by the wise and clever Chiron.

RETURN TO IOLCOS

Some years earlier, when Apollo's son Asclepius had been his pupil, Chiron had detected in him preternatural skill in science and the healing arts, which led to the mortal, under Chiron's tutelage, rising to become the foremost practitioner and theorist of medicine in the Greek world – and would later bring about his elevation to divine status.* Although Chiron perceived little of such potential in Jason, he gave him a thorough grounding in medical and herbal theory, knowledge and practice, nonetheless. Mostly he saw in the child, and the young man he became, boundless courage, athleticism, intelligence and ambition. He saw too lots of words beginning with 'self', which gave him pause. Self-belief, self-possession, self-righteousness, self-confidence, self-love. Perhaps these characteristics are as necessary to a hero as courage.

So Jason began to grow up. He knew the story of his father's imprisonment at the hands of the usurper Pelias, but he was prepared to bide his time before setting out to avenge the injustice and claim the throne of Iolcos. One of the many virtues he learnt at the feet of the noble Chiron was patience.

It might have been that any inward ambition to become a great hero was kindled by an unexpected visit from the hero Bellerophon, who landed one day outside Chiron's cave on the back of a flying horse.

'Chiron, you are famed around the world for your mastery of the healing arts. You are half-horse yourself – who better to help my poor friend?'

Pegasus, immortal but not immune from harm, had been badly burned around the neck and mane during Bellerophon's fight with the Chimera. While Chiron set about smearing a medicinal paste on the wounds, Bellerophon related his adventures to a spellbound young Jason.

Chiron was amused by Jason's round-eyed wonder; but before Bellerophon left with a restored Pegasus, the centaur could not resist a lecture. 'You are pleased with what you have done, Master Bellerophon,' he said. 'Certainly you have been brave and resourceful. But I hope you understand

---

* See *Mythos*, Vol. I, page 251.

enough of the ways of the Fates and of the gods to know that only darkness and despair awaits those who believe that their achievements are theirs and theirs alone. Pay proper homage to the gods who helped you and the immortal horse without whom you would be just another insignificant little prince.'

Bellerophon laughed and exchanged an eye-rolling shrug with Jason, who giggled.

Chiron shook his head as they waved Bellerophon and Pegasus off on their way back to King Iobates and the resumption of their adventures.

'It is the fate of the young never to learn,' the centaur sighed. 'I suppose it is arrogance and unwavering self-belief that propels them to their triumphs, just as surely as it is arrogance and unwavering self-belief that unseats them and sends them plummeting to their ends.'

Jason hadn't heard. He was watching Bellerophon and Pegasus disappear into a small dot in the distant sky. Chiron clapped his hands in front of the boy's eyes.

'You are in a trance. Wake up and tell me. Which herbs did I use in the poultice I applied to Pegasus? What was the juice I added to make the paste heat up, foment and fizz?'

And so the years passed, with Jason learning as much as he could while dreaming all the time of a heroic future. It would be too much to expect that he could ever be in possession of a flying horse, but he would find something – some symbol, some animal, some object – which would grant him everlasting fame.

Soon, too soon in Chiron's view, Jason had grown to be a fit, strong, tall and handsome young man, ready to leave Chiron's cave on Mount Pelion and make his way down to Iolcos.

'Remember,' cautioned the centaur. 'Modesty. Observance of the gods. In a fight, do not do what you want to do, but what you judge your enemy least wants you to. You cannot control others if you cannot control yourself. Those who most understand their own limitations have the fewest. A leader is one who . . .' and on and on, precept after precept, warning after warning.

Jason nodded and pretended to take in every word. For psychological effect, to draw attention to and accentuate the physique he had built up over years of training, he had dressed himself in a leopard skin. With his long golden hair, tanned musculature and burning eyes he would present a fierce and fascinating figure to the strangers he encountered on the way.

'Don't worry, old friend,' he said, embracing Chiron. 'I'll make you proud.'

'You'll make me proud,' Chiron called after him, tears running down his cheeks, 'if you don't make yourself proud.'

Not long on his journey, Jason came to a fast-flowing river, the Anaurus. On its banks stood a frail old woman, bent double by age, uncertain how to cross without being swept away.

'Hello there. Let me carry you across and don't you worry about a thing, dear mother,' said Jason, not meaning to sound patronising, but managing to, nonetheless.

'Too kind, too kind,' wheezed the old woman, who leapt with surprising agility onto Jason's back, her fingernails digging hard into his flesh.

Jason waded into the torrent, the old lady chatting into his ear and pinching his skin as she held on. The sharp pain of her grip at one point caused Jason to stumble. He caught a foot between two stones and nearly fell over. When he reached the other side and was able to deposit his garrulous burden, he realised that he was missing one of his sandals. He looked back and saw it wedged in the rocks where his foot had been stuck. He made to retrieve it, but the old lady was pawing at him.

'Thank you, young man, thank you. How kind. I bless you. I bless you.'

Jason watched the sandal loosen itself and float away on the strong current.

But when he glanced down to acknowledge the woman's gratitude, he was surprised to see that she had disappeared. Extraordinarily fleet of foot for such a frail little thing, he thought to himself.

We should have guessed straight away that this was no frail little thing, but Hera, in one of her favourite disguises. The Queen of Heaven knew very well that Jason was journeying to Iolcos to wrest the kingdom from his uncle, the same Pelias who had so outrageously and unforgivably desecrated one of her temples. Hera wanted to be sure that the enemy of her enemy was worthy of her support and protection. His uncomplaining courtesy at the river confirmed that he was. From now on she would do all that she could to help him. The same Hera that strove every step of the way to hamper and torment Heracles would strive every step of the way to guide and favour Jason. The motive, so typically of Hera, was not love of Jason but hatred of Pelias.

When the people of Iolcos saw the mesmerising figure of Jason with his leopard skin, rippling hair and bulging muscles stride into the marketplace they knew at once that here was somebody who should be paid attention to. Palace messengers ran to find their lord and king Pelias, who never took kindly to being anything other than the very first to hear important news.

He was seated at a map table in his great hall, planning games to be held in honour of his father Poseidon.

'Stranger?' he said. 'What kind of stranger? Describe him.'

'Come in from the country, he has,' said one herald.

'His hair is gold, my lord king,' said another.

'And long. Right down his back,' sighed a third.

'He wears the skin of a lion.'

'Er, actually it's leopard, not lion.'

'No, pretty sure it's lion.'

'You can see the spots . . .'

'Markings, yes, but I wouldn't call them "spots". Lions have . . .'

'Thank you!' Pelias cut in. 'This stranger is wearing the pelt of some large cat. Good. Is there anything else?'

'Could just as easily be lynx.'

'Or bobcat, maybe.'

'A bobcat *is* a lynx.'

'Really? I thought they were different?'

'Enough!' Pelias smashed a fist down on the table. 'Is he tall, short, dark, fair? What?'

'Fair.'

'Tall, very tall.'

'And he walks with a limp.'

'Well, I wouldn't call it a limp, exactly,' said the second herald.

'He's lame, man!' countered the first.

'Yes, but that's because, if you noticed, he's only got one sandal, so naturally he's going to list to the side a bit . . .'

'What did you say?'

'Well, my lord, just that it's more of a list to one side than a full-blown limp . . .'

'Yes, your majesty. I'd call it maybe a mild hobble.'

Pelias grabbed the second herald by the throat. 'Did you just say that he was wearing one sandal?'

'Yes, sire,' gasped the herald, going purple in the face.

Pelias let go of him and looked at the others. 'You all saw this?'

They nodded.

Fear gripped Pelias's heart. The stranger from the country

with one sandal! What could he do? To attack or imprison a visitor would be to defy the laws of hospitality sacred to Zeus and Nephele . . .

Nephele! The mention of her name awoke an idea in Pelias's mind.

He strode out to the marketplace where he found Jason drinking at a fountain surrounded by a crowd of admiring children. Yes, there could be no doubt. The man's left foot was unshod, naked. As bare as truth.

'Welcome, stranger!' Pelias managed to say, in what he hoped was an amiable, yet suitably grand, manner. 'What brings you to our kingdom?'

'It is indeed "our kingdom", uncle,' was Jason's bold reply. He had decided to be forthright from the first in his approach to Pelias.

'*Uncle*?' Pelias had many brothers, sisters, nephews, nieces and cousins, thanks to his mother Tyro's multiple marriages. But the use of the word from this single-sandalled stranger struck dread into his heart. The oracle had warned him to beware not just of a man with one sandal, but also of a kinsman, a man of his own blood.

'Yes, Pelias, son of Tyro,' said Jason. 'I am Jason. My father is Aeson, son of Tyro and of Cretheus, the former King of Iolcos. Aeson, the rightful ruler of this kingdom. I have come to claim our inheritance. What you have gained from your years of usurpation you may keep. All the cattle, treasure, buildings and land are yours. But from now on the kingdom is mine and you must release my parents from their imprisonment.'

'Ah,' said Pelias, grasping Jason by the shoulders. 'Welcome, nephew. You come at just the right time.'

'I do?'

'This land is yours by right, Jason, of course it is. I have been ruling in your place, but will happily step aside now that you are here, only –' He broke off in some confusion.

'Only what?' demanded Jason.

'Only this land is . . . *cursed*!'

'Cursed?'

'Oh yes, quite cursed. Isn't that so, people?'

Those citizens of Iolcos who had crowded around to see more of the impressive and strikingly dressed stranger knew very well how to interpret the wishes of Pelias. If he wanted them to agree with what he was saying, they had better agree. And wholeheartedly. Neither by word nor sign did they betray their complete ignorance of any such curse. Instead they nodded their heads decisively and threw in vigorous words of agreement.

'Oh yes, cursed . . .'

'Terrible curse.'

'Curse on the land.'

'A blight, a curse . . .'

'On the land.'

'*On* the land? All over it, more like . . .'

'But what kind of curse?' asked Jason.

'Ah, well.' Pelias had never felt so inspired. A perfect plan was forming in his mind. 'You know of my nephew – your cousin – Phrixus, son of your uncle Athamas and the cloud goddess Nephele?'

'Who has not heard of Phrixus?'

'He died not long ago in far Colchis. Since that moment a curse has descended upon us.'

'Upon our land!' said one citizen.

'Blighting and cursing and blighting our land,' muttered another.

'But why?' Jason asked.

'I wanted to know the answer to that same question,' said Pelias, 'and so I consulted the oracle. Didn't I, people?'

'Certainly you did, my lord.'

'Who says you didn't? They're a liar!'

'How well we remember. Consulted the oracle, he did.'

'It had never been so consulted.'

'Yes, yes. The point is,' continued Pelias, 'that the oracle made plain that this kingdom could never know peace or prosperity unless its king went to Colchis and brought back the Golden Fleece here to Iolcos, where it should find its new home for eternity. That is what the oracle proclaimed. Did it not, people?'

'Aye, aye!'

'Exactly that. Word for word.'

'And since you are, as you say, the rightful King of Iolcos, you, Jason, must be the one to . . . fetch the Fleece and raise the curse. Am I not right?'

'Aye, majesty, aye!' cried the people. They were not sure what they were celebrating or assenting to, but they could see triumph and satisfaction in the eyes of Pelias, and that was enough to make them cheer and cheer.

Pelias was congratulating himself on devising a scheme that had in fact been all the work of Hera, who saw in Jason the heroic instrument to fulfil – with a little divine assistance, where needed – two of her desires simultaneously. He could unseat the brutish Pelias, who had so flagrantly dishonoured her temple. And he could bring the Golden Fleece home to mainland Greece where it could form the centrepiece of a magnificent new shrine sacred to Hera and Hera alone. The golden ram, it must be remembered, belonged to Nephele who, as a proxy in Hera's likeness, had been the instrument of saving her from violation at the licentious hands of Ixion. The Fleece therefore was holy to the Queen of Heaven, and she did not like the idea of it being trapped in a Grove of Ares on the far eastern edge of the civilised world.

Hera chose her champions well. It is doubtful that many other mortals would have considered so dangerous and groundbreaking a quest as this. The Golden Fleece was known to be guarded by a fierce serpent that never slept or closed its eyes. King Aeëtes and his soldiers would undoubtedly have added further protection over the years. The journey would have to be made by sea, and such a lengthy voyage through such dangerous waters had never yet been undertaken.

But Jason was blithe, fearless and possessed of that supreme self-confidence which Chiron had recognised in the makeup of his pupil as both an attractive virtue and a less-appealing flaw. And ever since Bellerophon and Pegasus had visited Chiron's cave when he was a boy, Jason had dreamed of an adventure, a quest that would prove his mettle and prove him worthy of the word Hero.

'The Golden Fleece, eh?' He smiled broadly. 'What a splendid idea, uncle. It shall be done.'

THE ARGO

A map can show you how far it is by sea from Iolcos in Aeolia to Colchis on the shores of the Black Sea. It cannot show in detail the natural and unnatural obstacles that made such a voyage so uniquely hazardous.

Jason's first requirement was a suitably hardy and well-equipped vessel for the journey. He chose as his shipwright ARGUS*, and the unique vessel that he built became known as the *Argo* in honour of her creator. It is said the goddess

---

* Not the same ARGUS PANOPTES whom Hera once turned into a peacock (see the first volume of *Mythos*, page 191), but Argus the Argive from Argos. His father Danaus was king of Argos and (according to Apollodorus) the possessor of the first ship ever to set sail on the seas.

Athena, who like Hera smiled favourably on Jason's quest, assisted Argus in the ship's construction. The *Argo* was equipped with a rowing deck, much like an ordinary galley, but no seagoing vessel before her had been fitted with more than one mast and such complicated and clever arrangements of sailcloth and rigging. Athena brought oak from the sacred grove at Dodona (those that had spoken to Perseus and helped him on his way to the Graeae). This timber formed the prow, or beak, of the ship; carved into it was the representation of a female head – some said of Hera herself – endowed with the power of prophecy and speech. A mortal seer was appointed a member of crew too: IDMON, a son of Apollo, agreed to come along despite having foreseen that the quest for the Golden Fleece would bring him fame but also death early in the venture.*

Argus appointed as his helmsman TIPHYS, who brought on board his kinsman Augeas (later to become famous for the filthy condition of his stables) and ANCAEUS, King of Samos, himself a skilled helmsman. Athena instructed Tiphys and Ancaeus in the use of the sails that were to give such speed to the *Argo*. Whether Athena taught them by inward whispered inspiration or a direct manifestation is not quite known. Tiphys also came up with the idea of leather cushions for the rowing seats, not for comfort but to allow the oarsmen to slide backwards and forwards on their benches; this added to the rowing stroke the strength of their legs as well as the strength of their backs. Although no one knew it yet, this innovation was to prove of vital importance to the expedition.

Meanwhile Jason had been spreading the news. The word

---

* Idmon did die, as we shall see. But he also achieved his prophesied fame – for here I am, thousands of years later, writing about him.

went out around Greece and its islands that a new kind of voyage was being organised, a quest of unprecedented ambition. A party of heroes was required to crew the ship and help win eternal glory. Being sailors on the *Argo* they would be known as ARGONAUTS and their mission was to sail to Colchis under Jason's command and bring the Golden Fleece home to the Greek mainland.

The trickle of applicants travelling to Iolcos soon became a torrent. A handful, then dozens, then scores of candidates arrived in the city, all eager to take part in an adventure that would be sure to bring lustre to their names and assure the prosperity of their houses. If Pelias felt put out or sidelined by the obvious admiration demonstrated by the people for Jason's courage and confidence, not to mention the general assumption that his young nephew was *already* King of Iolcos, he was wise enough to conceal it. Indeed, Pelias made a great show of offering support to the venture and lavished the most openhanded hospitality on all who came to Iolcos clamouring for a place on board the *Argo*. All the time he remained happily convinced that the mission must be suicidal and that Jason would never return to claim his throne.

Aside from many whose names are remembered for nothing other than their appearance in the lists of Argonauts handed down to posterity,* some of the best-known figures of the Greek world were enlisted, heroes whose fame already preceded them or was to grow great after their involvement in the voyage. Heroes such as NESTOR of Pylos, for example.

---

* It is generally held that, in historical ancient Greece, many grand families from Athens, Sparta, Corinth, Thebes and all over the Greek world laid claim to Argonaut ancestors. Over the generations, poets and historians were paid to include such ancestors in 'definitive' accounts of the voyage in order to lend prestige to the pedigrees of the rich and powerful. For this reason there is no single, authoritative, universally recognised crew list or manifest for the *Argo*.

He would survive to become an invaluable advisor to the Greek leadership in the Trojan War, where his name would be forever associated with wise counsel.

PELEUS of Aegina (not to be confused with Pelias of Iolcos, Jason's wicked uncle) volunteered for the quest along with his brother TELAMON. They would each go on to father heroes. Telamon's sons were Teucer, the legendary bowman, and Ajax (the Great), both of whom would play key roles in the siege of Troy. The only surviving offspring of Peleus by his marriage to the sea nymph Thetis was to be Achilles, perhaps the most glorious and perfect of all the heroes.*

In the prime of their young manhood, and unaware of the destinies of their children, Peleus and Telamon came for adventure. They brought with them the strongest man of the age, HERACLES, who was between Labours and had with him his beloved young page HYLAS. The adoring pair were joined by Heracles' brother-in-law, POLYPHEMUS.†

MELEAGER, son of Oeneus, was present too. He was to be one of the principals in the hunt for the Calydonian Boar, in which many of the Argonauts would participate.‡ Meleager's cousins, CASTOR and POLYDEUCES – the Dioscuri – are usually included in the manifest too, as were yet another pair of brothers, CALAIS and ZETES§. As sons of Boreas, the North Wind, they were often referred to as the BOREADS. Their paternity endowed them with the ability to take to the air and fly.

---

* Although all heroes are, of course, imperfect.

† Not to be confused with the Cyclops of the same name whom Odysseus encountered on his way home from the Trojan War. This Polyphemus was married to Heracles' half-sister Laomene. He was a Lapith, and helped Theseus and Pirithous defeat the centaurs: see the story of Theseus (page 215).

‡ See the story of Atalanta (page 271).

§ Pronounced 'Calayiss' and 'Zee-tees'.

It is said that the far-famed hunter ATALANTA – whose story would later be so tightly intertwined with that of Meleager – applied to join the quest but was turned down by Jason, who thought the presence of a woman on board ship would bring ill-luck.* If such blatant discrimination sounds harsh to our ears, it is at least more pleasingly typical of a true Greek hero that Jason should reserve a place for music in his crew list. ORPHEUS, greatest of all singers, poets and composers was welcomed into the ship's company. The enchanting power of his lyre would prove invaluable.

PIRITHOUS, King of the Lapiths was there too†. He had a special reason to join the crew perhaps, for he was descended from Ixion, whose inappropriately libidinous handsiness with Hera, you will recall, was the primary cause of the creation of Nephele, the summoning of the golden ram and its flight to Colchis with Phrixus and Helle in the first place. Two other Argonauts are worth mentioning here: PHILOCTETES, who was to play crucial parts in the story of Heracles and in the Trojan War; and EUPHEMUS, a son of Poseidon who could walk on water. All in all the ship's complement amounted to around fifty souls . . . the conventional crew for a 'penteconter'.

Phew! It's all rather a lot to take in. All those heroes, all those figures descended from so many kings and queens and so many gods, goddesses and minor deities. In many ways the voyage of the *Argo* might be regarded as a kind of dress rehearsal for the epic siege of Troy and, even more so, its

---

* Other versions of or references to the quest for the Golden Fleece have Atalanta playing an enthusiastic role in the voyage and its subsidiary adventures, but the main source on which I and most mythographers rely (the *Argonautica* of Apollonius Rhodius) tells that she was turned away.

† In some tellings he was accompanied by Theseus, but this messes too much with chronology, as the end of Jason's story will show.

aftermath, the Odyssey and the fall of the house of Atreus.*
The interference, protection and enmity of the Olympians;
the treachery of some heroes and the selfless sacrifice of others; the wit and cunning, the horrible cruelty, the endurance,
patience, faith and determination of the warriors in the teeth
of what wind, weather, malice, chance and betrayal threw at
them – all these were as much a feature of the voyage of the
Argo as the legendary expedition to and from Troy.

THE ISLE OF LEMNOS

Pelias and the citizens of Iolcos gathered at the harbour to
join in the praising and blessing of the *Argo*'s voyage. Goats
screamed under the knives of priests, smoke from their burnt
flesh rose up to the gods. Flowers were strewn and grains
were sown on the water; flocks of released doves rocketed
into the sky; choirs of children sang; dogs barked, fought
and mated. On board the *Argo* laughing stowaway youths
were pulled from their hiding places and thrown onto the
quayside, into the arms of their whooping, drunken friends.
Jason's mother and father, Aeson and Alcimede, now freed
from their imprisonment by the apparently repentant Pelias,
stood and waved up from the dockside, conflicted by alter-
nating feelings of pride and consternation. Their young son
Promachus was there, stamping his feet and sobbing because
he had been deemed too young to join the crew.

'I'll be thirteen soon! That's old enough to go on a
voyage.'

Jason had ruffled his hair. 'When I come back, I'll let you sail

---

* At the inception and conclusion of which the sisters of the Dioscuri – Helen of
Sparta and CLYTEMNESTRA, wife of Agamemnon – were to play such crucial roles.

with me on my next voyage. Until then your job is to look after our mother and father. I want you all safe here in Iolcos.'

Those words would haunt Jason one day.

A reverential silence fell as Orpheus stood on the prow and struck up a hymn upon his lyre. The brothers Calais and Zetes called on their father Boreas, the North Wind, and on AEOLUS, keeper of all the winds.

On the foredeck, Jason, the bright rays of the morning sun seeming to set his hair ablaze, stood hand on hip calling out orders to cast off and set sail. Three girls in the crowd swooned and fainted dead away. Deckhands heaved on the rigging and the people gasped to see the *Argo*'s sails unroll from their twin masts and stretch to catch the wind. They cheered as Jason sprang down and cried to Tiphys to raise the anchor stone and let slip the mooring ropes.

The *Argo* plunged a little, as if ducking to wet her beak, then came upright and surged serenely forward, the surf streaming from the painted figurehead on her prow. Never had such a ship been seen. Not a roll, not a yaw and not a creak from her timbers. So stable and so sturdy, so swift, straight, trim and true.

The citizens of Iolcos stayed to gaze after her until she was no more than a speck on the horizon. Pelias climbed into his litter, glancing back at Aeson and Alcimede who now stood alone on the quay, arm in arm. 'They can wait till they rot of old age,' he said to himself, 'their precious son won't be coming back.'

Pelias was well aware of the dangers that awaited the Argonauts. He stroked his beard. 'I wonder where they will first put in? Lemnos would be about right. Oh, I do hope it is Lemnos.'

His malicious hope was to be fulfilled. Myrina, on the isle of Lemnos, was indeed the first port of call planned by Jason. The

Argo had sailed eastwards from Iolcos without incident. Jason found the ship everything he had hoped for and more. Never had so well-built or so well-provisioned a vessel put to sea. Morale was high; dolphins leapt in the bow waves, auspicious sea eagles mewed high above them. They had the music of Orpheus to raise their spirits and the knowledge that they were all members of the finest crew of men ever to set out on a quest.

'Lemnos in an hour, sir,' Tiphys said to Jason, squinting up at the sun and making his calculations.

'Gather round, everyone,' commanded Jason. 'For those who do not know, let me tell you about Lemnos.' He was grateful now that he had, for the most part, paid attention during those long lessons when his tutor Chiron patiently took him through the history and practices of the tribes, peoples, provinces, islands and kingdoms of the known world. 'As I'm sure most of you learned at your mothers' knees, Lemnos is where the infant Hephaestus was brought up after being cast down from Olympus by his mother, the Queen of Heaven.' Jason touched the fingers of his right hand to his lips and raised them heavenwards in a salute to his divine protectress, Hera. 'But since then Lemnos has had a heavy history. There are no men on the island, only women.'

Cheers, laughter and crude expressions of delight from the crew.

'Yes, yes. But listen. Generations ago, the women of the island began to neglect Aphrodite. We all know how the goddess treats those who insult her, but what she did to the Lemnian women was extreme, even for the Lady of Cyprus. She made the women smell so rancid, disgusting, so foul that the island's male population couldn't bear to go near them. So the men took to sailing off to the mainland and bringing back Thracian women and girls instead. The Lemnian wives wouldn't stand for that so they murdered the men in their beds one after the other, leaving an island of women only. Their queen is HYPSIPYLE * and when we put in you must give me a chance to call on her and make sure we will be welcomed.'

'Do they still stink then, these women?'

'Well?' said Jason, directing the question to the figurehead on the prow. Though carved into a likeness of Hera, her voice and manner more resembled those of the talking oaks of Dodona, of whose timbers she was composed.

'Are you talking to me?'

'The women of Lemnos. Are they still cursed with the foul stench?'

'You'll just have to find out, won't you?'

When they put in at the small harbour, Jason and the crew were met by a knot of stern-looking women from whom no discernible odour arose. Nor did Queen Hypsipyle, who received Jason with warmth and respect, give off anything but an air of friendly welcome. It seemed to all the Argonauts that the curse of Aphrodite must have been lifted, for the women soon showed nothing but delight in the company of men.

'Let's stay,' said Tiphys, who already had his arm round two smiling and blushing Lemnians.

Jason, entirely smitten by the beauty of Hypsipyle, willingly assented.

The Argonauts stayed long enough for the queen to bear Jason twin sons, EUNEUS and THOAS, the latter named after Hypsipyle's father, whom she had secretly spared from the general massacre of Lemnian menfolk.

'I hid my father in a wooden chest and sent him out to sea,' she confided to Jason. 'I have since heard word that he

---

* Pronounced 'Hip-sipperly'.

survived and is well.* Don't tell the other women – they'll never forgive me.'

'Such mercy is so like you,' said Jason lovingly. Mercy was a strange word to use, perhaps. Hypsipyle had willingly allowed every other man on the island to be slaughtered in their sleep, but Jason did not let that spoil the perfect image of Hypsipyle that he carried in his lovestruck mind. He had sworn eternal fidelity and meant it. First love is like that.

Another year passed. Then one day Heracles – who had taken no part in the general frolicking and fornicating – paid Jason a visit.†

'We're supposed to be searching for a Golden Fleece,' he grumbled. 'Not rutting like bloody stags.'

'Yes,' said Jason. 'Yes. You're right.'

The goodbyes were fraught.

'Take me with you,' begged Hypsipyle.

'My darling, you know we have a "strictly no women" rule on board.'

'Then take the twins. This is no place for them to grow up. They need men to learn from.'

'We do have a strict "no children" rule too . . .'

It was all very sticky, but he and the Argonauts managed to extricate themselves and Lemnos was barely out of sight before Jason was thinking only of what lay ahead. Hypsipyle and their twin sons vanished from his mind as quickly as they vanished from view.

On the island, meanwhile, word came to Hypsipyle that

---

* Hypsipyle's father THOAS found his way to Tauris on the Crimean peninsula, where he was to play a part in the aftermath of the Trojan War and the fraught destiny of Agamemnon's family.

† Unusual for Heracles, who was capable of spreading his seed far and wide, as the huge number of his descendants, the Heracleides, testifies. Perhaps it was because at this period in his life he had eyes only for Hylas.

rebellion and revenge were in the air. Jason *might* have let slip to some of his fellow crew members that she had spared her father from slaughter. One or two of those fellow crew members *might* have let slip that fact to the women on the island with whom they were consorting. Now that Hypispyle's protector had left, the women were ready to tear their queen to pieces for such treachery. She took her twin boys Euneus and Thoas and fled the island. They were soon captured by pirates and sold as slaves to king LYCURGUS of Nemea.* Euneus was later to return and rule Lemnos. During his reign the island played a small but pivotal role in the outcome of the Trojan War. Some time later it served as a springboard for the Great War's ill-fated Gallipoli campaign.

THE DOLIONIANS

On ploughed the *Argo*, through the Dardanelles and on to the Propontis, the Sea of Marmara as we call it today. On the Asian side the Argonauts came to the coastal kingdom of the Doliones, or Dolionians, ruled over by the young King CYZICUS† and Queen CLITE, who welcomed them with lavish hospitality.

It was while they were recovering from a night's feasting that the *Argo* was attacked by a neighbouring tribe of giants‡,

---

* The kingdom which Heracles rid of its monstrous lion for his First Labour.

† A top score in Scrabble. He is pronounced 'Sizzy-kuhss' (while his wife Clite rhymes with 'high tea' rather than 'bite').

‡ The tribe who attacked them are often called the *Gegeneis*, but that is just another way of saying giants. The word has same root as 'gigantic'. The *-geneis* means 'birth' or 'born' as in 'genes', 'genesis', 'generation', etc. The *Ge-* is like the *geo-* in 'geography' and 'geology' and derives from Gaia the earth. Thus 'giant', 'gigantic' and 'Gegeneis' really mean 'earthborn' or 'chthonic' and have nothing to do with size, despite the way the words are now used and how the 'giga' was taken from 'gigantic' to mean 'huge'.

great six-armed earthborn monsters. Heracles came splendidly into his own here and led the strongest of the Argonauts out to meet them. By the time he had finished, the giants all lay dead.

Cyzicus and Clite were immensely grateful to be rid of the marauding predators that had raided the kingdom for generations and urged Jason to stay for more feasting. Mindful of the time they had wasted on Lemnos, Jason thanked them but insisted that regretfully they had better get going.

The night after the Argonauts' departure a great storm caught the *Argo* and blew her back to the shore. But it was dark; neither the Argonauts nor the Dolionians recognised each other and fierce fighting broke out. With Heracles on their side it was unlikely that the Argonauts would lose, and before long most of the Doliones, friendly King Cyzicus included, lay dead on the ground. When morning broke, Queen Clite was the first to leave the palace. When she saw the body of her husband, whom Jason himself had unwittingly killed, she ran to her bedchamber and hanged herself. In the light of day the Argonauts discovered with horror what they had done. They helped bury the dead, made expiatory sacrifices to the gods and left the Dolionian coast in sombre mood.

'I do think,' Jason said to the figurehead and Idmon the Seer, 'that you might have warned us.'

'You never asked,' said Idmon.

'There was a storm howling about our heads. Waves higher than the ship were tossing us about like leaves in the wind. How could I have asked?'

'Could have raised your voice, couldn't you?' said the figurehead.

'Where are we sailing to now? You can at least tell me that.'

'Thrace,' said Tiphys, while Idmon and the figurehead ummed, ahhed and tutted.

The southern shores of Thrace, which we would call Bulgaria today, formed the northern coastline of the Propontis. The region was known for its fierce and warlike people, descended from THRAX, a son of Ares.

'Anything we should look out for, especially?' enquired Jason.

'All the aitches,' said the figurehead.

'Aitches?'

'Harpies, Hylas and Heracles,' explained Idmon.*

'What about them?'

Idmon and the figurehead would say no more.

HYLAS DISAPPEARS

Mostly they sailed, but sometimes, when the wind dropped, they rowed. Which is to say Heracles rowed. He could do the work of the whole crew. All he required was water to drink, fruit to eat and his beloved Hylas to mop his brow and say soothing things to him.

He was needed in the dead calm that followed the storm that had propelled them back to the Dolionians and the tragedy that had ensued there. Hugging the Mysian coast, Heracles rowed with long, powerful strokes; perhaps his temper or sorrow made him pull more violently than usual, for suddenly his oar broke. It could not be replaced on board: the other oars were like pencils next to his: a pine tree, with the branches stripped off and a great iron shovel fixed to it

---

* Of course strictly speaking the Greeks didn't have aitches, only the asper, or rough, 'breathing'.

for a blade. The shovel was undamaged but the shaft splintered beyond repair. It was agreed that the *Argo* should stop and Heracles and Hylas could find a new tree. They leapt down and waded ashore, followed by Heracles' friend and brother-in-law Polyphemus.

'You look that way, and I'll look this,' said Heracles to Hylas, pointing beyond the dunes. Hylas nodded and disappeared into the woods that lay beyond.

Heracles soon found the perfect tree. He hugged it and heaved. Up it came, roots and all. Leaning it on his shoulder like a sentry's spear, he whistled for Hylas.

He called again as he strode back towards the beach, 'It's all right, Hylas. I've found the perfect tree.'

He stood and waited for Hylas, but only Polyphemus emerged, a puzzled look on his face.

'Very odd,' he said. 'I heard a kind of cry.'

'Where from?'

Polyphemus pointed back towards the woods.

Heracles dropped the tree and they both ran into the woods, calling all the while.

Heracles uprooted bushes and trees, turned over boulders and cleared undergrowth, but he could find no sign of Hylas. Polyphemus followed, shouting and shouting his name.

They widened their search. Beyond the woods there were fields and ditches, but very little cover. No Hylas. He had vanished.

Heracles returned to the shore and began searching the rockpools and caves in desperation.

'Strange thing is, there's no wild animals for miles around,' said Heracles. 'I don't understand it. He would never leave me, never.'

'A shame,' said Polyphemus. 'A tragedy. Come, we will sacrifice a great bull for him when we arrive in Colchis.'

'I'm staying here,' said Heracles. 'Not going till I find him.'

'But we need to be on board. Tiphys said that the wind was beginning to get up. He'll want to catch it.'

'They can wait,' said Heracles, who was as strong-willed as he was strong-muscled.

That evening Tiphys hoisted the sails and the *Argo* left. It never occurred to Jason, nor any of the other Argonauts, that Heracles, Hylas and Polyphemus were still ashore.

Only when they were miles out to sea did they discover their absence. Jason and many of the others were all for turning back at once.

'No, no,' said Calais.

'Their lookout,' said Zetes.

'They knew we were leaving on the good wind our father sent.'

'We *must* return!' said Telamon, Heracles' closest friend amongst those still on board. 'How can we expect to win the Golden Fleece without him? He's worth ten of *them* . . .' he pointed scornfully at Calais and Zetes.

'Oh really?' said Zetes. 'Shall we ask our father to send another wind?'

'One that will smash this ship to splinters?'

'Then we'll see who's worth what.'

'Are you threatening the ship?' Telamon grabbed Calais by the throat. 'That's mutiny. I should throw you over board.'

'We'd only fly away,' said Zetes. 'Then you'd look bloody silly, wouldn't you?'

'Enough!' Jason interposed himself.

Just then the sea surged and rocked them all nearly off their feet. Up from the waves rose the sea god GLAUCUS. He had been born a mortal fisherman in Boeotia, but achieved divine status when he nibbled at a herb that he had observed to have the power to bring dead fish back to life. The herb conferred immortality on him, but caused him to grow fins and a fish's tail. He acted now as a guide, rescuer and friend to stricken sailors.

'The *Argo* must not turn back!' he commanded. 'It is Heracles' destiny to return to the court of Eurystheus and complete the tasks he was given. Nothing must interfere with this.* Polyphemus too has a future. He will found the city of Cius. These things are ordained.'

With a shake of his finny arms and a nod of his barnacled head, Glaucus disappeared beneath the waves.

'I'm sorry,' Jason said to Telamon with genuine regret. 'What must be, must be. We cannot turn back.'

Telamon nodded. For the sake of harmony on board he resisted the urge to wipe the smug, gloating grins from the faces of Calais and Zetes.†

Heracles never found his adored Hylas. After months of fruitless searching, he made his way sorrowfully home to mainland Greece to receive his next Labour from Eurystheus, but not before charging the local Mysian people to continue the search for Hylas. If they did not, he promised he would return and wreak vengeance upon them. To make sure they did keep searching, he took several sons of the noblest Mysian families back with him as hostages.

Polyphemus did, as Glaucus had foreseen, go on to found

---

* This is how Apollonius Rhodius, a Greek poet of the third century BC, describes it in his *Argonautica*, the fullest surviving ancient narrative of the voyage of the *Argo*. In other sources Heracles joins Jason's crew *after* the completion of his Labours.

† Telamon had his revenge though. On his return from the quest he told his friend Heracles of the twins' insistence that they sail on and not turn back to pick him and Polyphemus up. Heracles never forgot the insult, and when he came upon the twins on the island of Tenos he didn't think twice about killing them. He constructed two pillars to mark their graves, which were said to sway whenever their father the North Wind blew.

the city of Cius on the Bithynian coast, not far from where Hylas was lost.* He subsequently died trying to rejoin the Argonauts and was buried on the southern shores of the Black Sea, where a white poplar marked his grave.

But what had happened to Hylas? Well, a little while after he parted from Heracles and went into the wood, he came upon a pool of water and knelt down to drink from it. Unlike NARCISSUS, he did not fall in love with his own reflection.† Instead, it was the water nymphs of the pool who were smitten at the sight of the beautiful youth. They rose to the surface, sang to him, seduced him and eventually lured him in.‡

As the *Argo* sailed steadily on, the figurehead remarked smugly to Jason:

'Told you to watch out for the aitches. Harpies next.'

HARPIES

The Argonauts anchored off the coast of Thrace§ and made their way inland, searching for food with which to provision the ship. It was not long before their path was blocked by a blind and emaciated old man.

'Who's there?' he cried, waving a stick in their general direction. For all his pitiable state, his manner was sharp and imperious.

---

* The city of Cius became an important chain on the ancient Silk Road, but is now a ruin.
† See *Mythos*, Vol I, page 301.
‡ A scene beloved of artists ever since, most notably the post-Pre-Raphaelite (if that makes sense) J. W. Waterhouse.
§ In Apollonius Rhodius' version they first stopped off at the kingdom of the Bebryces, on the Asian shore, where Polydeuces defeated their king and champion AMYCUS in a boxing match.

'Jason of Iolcos and his crew. Out of our way, if you please.'

'Ah!' cried the old man eagerly. 'I knew you would come! Are the sons of the North Wind of your company?'

Calais and Zetes stepped forward. 'Who wants to know?'

'PHINEUS, the king.'*

'Of Thrace?'

'You are in Salmydessus, and I am its ruler.'

'I have heard of you,' said Jason. 'You put out your own sons' eyes and you were blinded as a punishment.'

'Not true, not true! That is a lie put about by my first wife. Zeus, the father of us all, granted me the gift of prophecy and it was he who took away my sight.'

'Why?'

'He thought I was too generous in revealing the future to anyone who cared to know. But that was not all he had in store for me. Look, can you see that?'

With trembling hands Phineus pointed his stick towards a stone table. There were pieces of bread, fruit and smoked meats on it, but they were all spattered with something that looked like mud.

'Pee-yew! It stinks!' cried Calais and Zetes who had gone close.

'Their droppings,' said Phineus. 'It is not enough that they seize everything they can before I can eat it, they shit on whatever is left.'

'They?' said Jason. 'Who are "they"?'

'The Harpies. Two monstrous flying women†. Women? They have the faces of women I am told, but the wings and talons of birds. Human vultures. Food is put out for me, but

---

* Not the Phineus of Egypt pertrified by Perseus, of course.

† Their names were Aello ('storm') and Ocypete ('swift of flight'). Homer mentions a third, Podarge, ('flashing foot' – the same name as one of the Mares of Diomedes. Harpy itself means 'snatcher'.

219

whenever I try to eat they fly down shrieking and shitting. They snatch the food from my very mouth and fly off screeching with laughter. It is enough to send a man mad. But I stayed sane because I knew salvation was coming. I knew that the Boreads with their gift of flight would come and deliver me from their curse.'

Calais and Zetes shifted uneasily. 'Whoa there, old man. Are you saying you want *us* to get rid of them?' said Calais.

'If Zeus sent them, he's not going to thank us for interfering,' said Zetes. 'We're sorry for you, really we are, but we're not going to offend the Cloud-Gatherer and Lord of Storms. Not for anything.'

'No, no!' said Phineus, thrusting out a quavering hand in his direction, as if the act of touching Zetes might change his mind. 'You will not be punished for aiding me. I assure you. I have seen. It is ordained that you will release me from the Harpies and so you will. And when you have done this,' he added with a smile of some cunning, 'I will tell you the only way you can safely proceed on your journey. A terrible obstacle lies ahead of you. Unless you overcome it, you will never reach Colchis. No, you will all perish.'

'What obstacle?' Jason demanded.

'It is enough to say that, without my help, it will destroy your ship and cause the death of everyone on board.'

Jason turned to Calais and Zetes. 'Well, boys? It's up to you.'

The twins exchanged glances and nodded. 'We'll do it.'

While Tiphys and two of the *Argo's* crewmen wiped down the stone table, two other sets of brothers, Telamon and Peleus, and the twins Castor and Polydeuces were sent to forage for food. They returned with basketfuls of figs, olives and apples, to which was added the remaining store of *Argo's* bread and smoked fish. The food was heaped up in appetising piles on the stone table. Jason guided Phineus into his seat at the feast and all the Argonauts withdrew to a high vantage point, save Calais and Zetes who concealed themselves behind a tree close to the table. When all was still and the trap set, Calais gave a low whistle. Phineus stretched out his hand and picked up a fig. It was barely halfway to his mouth when with a demented scream, the two harpies dived down from the clouds. One snatched the fig from Phineus's fingers and devoured it. The other seized a pile of the fruit in her enormous claws, defecating on the rest as she did. The first joined her in ransacking and fouling the food.*

Calais and Zetes, with their own blood-curdling cry, shot from their hiding place. Twisting their bodies round, they launched themselves spinning into the air to catch the fast-flowing gust sent from their father. The eyes of the harpies started from their unpardonably ugly human faces and they screamed in shock, scattering food and faeces everywhere.

The other Argonauts ran out into the open and watched as the Harpies were pursued across the sky and out of sight.

As the brothers told Jason afterwards, it had been a close run thing. The terrified Harpies flapped their wings as hard as they could, covering a huge distance as they flew westwards; but the twins, streaming after them on their swift current of air, eventually caught up with them near to the Floating Islands†. They were on the verge of seizing the seizers when their way was barred by the sudden appearance of

---

* Anyone who has observed the behaviour of seagulls in seaside towns will wonder if they were the inspiration for the story of the Harpies. They snatch ice-cream cones from children and their droppings cake the promenades and seafronts.
† Stamphani and Arpia, two islets of the Heptani archipelago, or Ionian Islands, west of mainland Greece. The Strophades remain important sites for birds to this day.

a brightly coloured arc in the sky, from whom the rainbow goddess IRIS herself spoke.*

'Leave them, Boreads, leave my sisters be. Zeus sent them and only he can choose their fate. Leave them and know that they will harass Phineus no more.'

So the twins turned back. In honour of this, the Floating Islands became known, as they still are today, as the Strophades, the Turning Islands.

When their father Boreas dropped them gently back on the ground in Salmydessus, next to the table, the twins saw that the befouled food had been cleared away and Phineus was enthusiastically gorging on a fresh supply.

'So,' said Jason, when he had heard about Iris and her promise that Phineus would be left alone. 'This "obstacle" you claim we must overcome to reach Colchis . . .'

'Yes, yes,' Phineus nodded, fig juice dripping from his chin. 'There is but one way from the Propontis into the Euxine Sea.† You must sail through the narrow strait they call the Symplegades, the Clashing Rocks.'

'We know about those,' said Jason, annoyed. 'Nestor, tell him your plan.'

'Any ship that dares to try the channel between the rocks will be smashed to pieces,' said Nestor. 'They sense its passage and clash together, crushing anything in their path. So, my plan is that Argus, Tiphys and his men dismantle the *Argo* into portable sections which we take overland from the eastern shore of the Propontis to the western

_____

* Like Hermes, Iris was a messenger of the gods. Her colourful qualities give us the name of the iris of the eye and all words that refer to the *iridescence* of the rainbow – petrol in water, that sort of thing. Like the Harpies, she was a daughter of the Titaness Electra.
† The Black Sea to us.

shore of the Euxine Sea, thus circumventing the Symplegades entirely.'

Phineus sprayed fruit and bread everywhere as he snorted
with derisive laughter. 'Circumventing, you say? Oh dear me,
that's a good one. Circumventing. The land between, your
'circumventing land' bristles with bandits, some of them
only half human. They hide in the bushes, shoot arrows and
wait for you to die of your wounds. You'll never see them.
For all your crew of musclebound heroes you'd be better
turning for home than trying such a foolish thing. Suppose
they only got ten of you – that would be ten pieces of your
ship you vitally need. Circumvent *that.*'

Nestor rubbed his chin. 'I fear there is much in what he
says, Jason. My stratagem is weak, very weak.'

'Very well then,' said Jason. 'You say you know how we
can get through. Tell us, all-seeing Phineus.'

They waited for the old man to finish his mouthful of
bread. Finally, he swallowed, wiped his sleeve across his
mouth and told them.

THE CLASHING ROCKS

By the time they had reprovisioned the *Argo*, Phineus had put
on weight and grown even more bumptious and impossible.

'I see what will happen to you,' he told each of the Argonauts in turn. 'Ooh. Goodness me, that's nasty. Dear, dear, I
only hope I'm wrong.'

'Don't know why Zeus took his eyes,' Castor said to Jason.
'Should have taken his tongue.'

'Either tell us our futures or be silent,' said Jason.

'Oh, I can't tell you. Don't want to risk the return of those nasty
Harpies. But it's grim,' he added with a cackle, 'oh yes, it's grim.'

The hour for embarkation and departure could not come quickly enough.

The *Argo* sailed east and soon came to the narrow strait that connected the Propontis to the Euxine Sea. It was over this waterway that Io flew after Zeus had turned her into a cow and Hera sent a gadfly to torment her.* For that reason the narrow passage had been given the name 'Cow-Crossing', or Bosporus. It was one thing to fly over it, quite another to sail through.

Two great rocks loomed up ahead. They faced each other like cliffs, massive and immobile. Jason saw that they were a marvellous blue in colour.† It seemed impossible that they could move an inch.

He stood on the foredeck and addressed the crew.

'Orpheus, you have the dove?'

'I have her.' Orpheus, his hands tenderly cupped, stepped past Jason until he stood at the very tip of the prow.

'The rest of you, take up your oars. Tiphys, bring us as near as you can without waking the rocks.'

Every Argonaut went to their appointed rowing stations and waited.

When they were as close as Tiphys dared take the *Argo*, Jason brought down his arm. Orpheus released the dove which shot from his hands, rose into the air and made for the channel.

A great grinding sound filled the air and Jason saw the

---

* See *Mythos*, Vol. I, page 189.

† For that reason they were sometimes called the Cyanean Rocks. Of course, few questions are more moot, vexed and thorny than whether or not the Greeks really saw blue, had a word for blue, or even knew what blue was. Famously, Homer often refers to the sea as *oinops pontos* 'the wine-looking sea', usually translated as 'wine dark'. William Gladstone, finding time while serving as Prime Minister of Great Britain, wrote a book on Homer which included the first serious study of Greeks and colour. It has recently re-emerged as an interesting element in the renewed Sapir-Whorf debate in academic linguistics. If you are interested, I recommend Guy Deutscher's *Through the Language Glass: Why the World Looks Different in Other Languages.*

rocks tremble and shift on their bases. Gulls rose with startled cries from their ledges and nests on the rock face. The dove was already a quarter of its way through to the other side when the rocks began to move together with surprising speed. Halfway, and the passage was narrowing fast. The dove flew gamely on. Jason had to shade his eyes to see it battling towards the light and the open sea beyond.

Phineus had told them that the speed of a dove over the distance of the strait matched the speed of a strongly rowed galley. If the bird was crushed therefore, the *Argo* would never be able to make it.

The gap between the rocks left a mere slit of light and Jason could no longer see the dove. With a thunderous clash that set the *Argo* pitching and rolling the rocks slammed together. It was all Jason could do to stay upright on the foredeck.

When it was quiet and stable enough, Orpheus took up his lyre and strummed. He sang as loudly as the crew had ever heard him, calling and calling to the dove he had been training ever since Phineus had told them the key to their safe passage through.

The Argonauts rested on their oars and scanned the sky. Of the dove they saw no sign.

The rocks had started to separate now, causing the water to suck back through the channel.

'Hold!' cried Tiphys. 'Back oars.'

They pushed hard with their oars against the current to keep the ship from being pulled towards the rocks, which had now returned to their original positions and stood tall, stately and still. It was hard to believe they had ever moved.

Still the strains of Orpheus's song filled the air.

'There!' shouted Pirithous stabbing a finger in the air.

The dove flew towards Orpheus and the whole crew cheered as she landed on Orpheus's outstretched palm and with rippling coos of triumph accepted her grains, strokes and congratulations.

'Look!' said Orpheus, holding the bird up, 'her tail is gone.'

It was true. Where there should have been a neat fan, Jason could see only a torn and ragged row of broken feathers. He turned to address the crew.

'This tells us that it will be close,' he said. 'Very close indeed. Every man must row as if his life depends on it. For his life does. Picture this in your minds. What you most desire lies on the other side. Love, fame, riches, peace, glory. Whatever you have dreamt of is there. If you're too slow, it will disappear for ever, but if you strain yourself you can reach it.' He leapt down to take up the one remaining rowing station.

'Oars!' he cried, gripping and twisting the handle of his own to present its blade to the water.

His fellow Argonauts followed suit.

'Are we ready?'

'Aye!'

'Are we ready?'

'Aye!'

'Are we ready?'

'Aye! Aye! Aye!'

'Then row, my friends, row!'

With a great cheer they engaged oars and the *Argo* lurched forward. Never had a galley flown through the water with such speed. Every man pulled hard, sliding backwards and forwards on their leather cushions. Every man save Orpheus. As an artist, his strengths lay elsewhere. He was the only man bar the steersman facing the direction of the *Argo's* travel and could urge the men on. He had two wooden chests either side of him and he began thumping them like drums to drive the beat of the oars.

'Heave!' he cried. 'And *heave*, and *heave*, and *heave*!'

They all heard the shuddering, grating roar of the rocks.

This is it, thought Jason. They're moving now. No turning back. Only hard rowing will get us through.

A quarter of the way through and Orpheus felt that they were going to make it. He could see the open waters of the great sea ahead and the rocks, though closing, looked as though they would lose the race.

'*Heave*, and *heave*, and *heave*!'

But the rocks seemed to be moving faster. Jason and the oarsmen could see the cliffs rising and growing higher and higher and closer and closer. The clear view he had had of the Propontis was beginning to be cut off.

Looking in their direction of travel, Orpheus was no longer so sure that they could make it. As they passed the halfway mark he increased the stroke of his pounding on the wooden chests until his fists felt they would catch fire.

"*Heave*-and-*heave*-and-*heave*-and-*heave*!'

The walls towered above them now. Were they going to be crushed like flies in the slapped hands of a child? All this effort. All this planning and praying. For nothing? Jason felt his lungs bursting, his back and thighs burning.

'Yes!' yelled Orpheus. 'Yes, yes, yes! We're going to make it! Faster, faster, faster. Put everything into it. Pull, pull, pull! Pull, you bastards, pull!'

The rocks were on them now. Jason could even make out the green weeds growing in crevices. A chill darkness was closing in until . . . daylight flashed across him and the whole ship. They were through! The rocks crashed and still the Argonauts rowed as the aftershock of waves tossed them up and forward, further out of reach.

Jason stood up and let out a barbaric hoot of triumph. All around him the others were doing the same. Euphemus pointed back at the rocks.

'Look!'

The left-hand rock was cracking. The crag opposite was sliding back to its original position as usual, but its neighbour – partner? lover? – crumbled and disintegrated, sending an avalanche of boulders into the water.

The Symplegades never clashed again. Separating Asia from Europe, the Bosporus is still narrow today; but ever since that moment it has lain open to all shipping.

The exhilaration of their triumph banished the crew's exhaustion.

'We did it!'

'And without Heracles!'

Meleager pointed to the rear of the ship. 'Look! We lost our tail feather too!'

It was true. The final clash of the rocks had sheared off *Argo's* sternpost as they pulled through. That is how close it had been.

While they paused to repair the stern timbers, the figure-head called back to them from the prow.

'Make sure you mend that sternpost well, Jason, or one day you will regret it. One day far, far ahead, you will regret it.'

Meleager and Pirithous approached Orpheus.

'*Pull, you bastards, pull?*'

Orpheus eyed the two warily. 'I had to motivate you . . . Those rocks were closing in fast.'

'*Bastards?* Let's show him, Pirithous.'

Meleager took his arms and Pirithous his legs.

'Let go, let go!'

'Heave and heave and *heave!*' Pirithous chanted, in a fair imitation of Orpheus's lyric tenor, as they swung him back and forth.

On the final 'heave' the protesting musician was hurled

into the sea. The crew leaned over and cheered as he splashed below them.

'You *are* bastards!' he gasped.

'Sing out for a dolphin, like Arion!'*

So began the tradition, which has lasted to the present day, of a victorious rowing crew throwing its cox into the water.

DEATHS, RAZOR-SHARP FEATHERS AND THE PHRIXIDES

Eastwards the *Argo* sailed. After the initial high, the exertions of the crew were beginning to catch up with them. The breakage of the sternpost had forced Argus to work hard to make a new steering blade.

Not for the first time Jason was grateful that Chiron had instructed him so well in the healing arts.† He prepared medicinal salves for the blistered hands and chafed buttocks of the crew, and even allowed them a little wine, albeit mixed with honey and water. Orpheus, a blanket over his shoulder, made a great show of sneezing.

The Euxine Sea was living up to its optimistic name. No pirates, sea monsters or unfavourable gales hindered their passage to Colchis. They made a few stops along the way however, which did have unhappy outcomes. The first occurred in the kingdom of Mariandynia, where Idmon the Seer met the end that he had always known was coming. As he walked through the woods, a wild boar burst from the undergrowth and gored him with its tusks. Peleus speared the beast, but the damage was done and Idmon died of his

---

* The story of 'Arion and the Dolphin' is recounted in the first volume of *Mythos* (page 363).

† The name Jason actually means 'healer'.

wounds. He was not the only casualty of that stopover. Tiphys succumbed to a fever and died too. He was replaced as helmsman of the *Argo* by Ancaeus of Samos. Funeral rites were observed for both and it was a far sadder crew that left Mariandynia behind.

They were at least fortunate that it was summer, their new helmsman Ancaeus told them, for the winters this far east could be cruel.* As they sailed on, passing the lands ruled over by the Amazons, they suddenly found themselves under attack from above. A flock of wild birds was dropping their feathers onto them. But these were no ordinary feathers, the crew soon discovered. Their quills were bronze and their vanes razor-sharp, so that they fell like arrows. The Argonauts had to take refuge under their shields for protection. For once Orpheus's singing was of no help; if anything, it seemed only to enrage the birds into further assaults.

'Let's just yell at them,' Philoctetes suggested. They hooted, screamed, and bashed their swords against their shields until at last the birds flew away.

'What the hell were they?'

'No idea,' said Jason.† 'But let's put in at this island and make sure their feathers haven't ripped the sail or cut the rigging.'

The island at which they now dropped anchor was called Areonesos, or 'the isle of Ares', because of a small temple where the Amazons sometimes came to worship their father, the war god. The avian arrows seemed to have done no serious harm to the *Argo*, and Jason and Nestor were debating whether to spend the night there or press on when four young men approached and introduced themselves. Their names were

---

* They were not so far, after all, from Sochi, where the 2014 Winter Olympics were held.

† According to some they were the birds who had flown from Lake Stymphalia when Heracles disturbed them with Athena's rattle during his Sixth Labour.

ARGOS,* CYTISORUS, PHRONTIS and MELAS, and they were the PHRIXIDES, or sons of Phrixus. Phrixus, you will recall, was the child of Nephele and Athamas who had been rescued along with his sister Helle by the golden ram, whose fleece Jason and the Argonauts had come all this way to bring back to Greece.

'But why are all four of you here?' Jason asked.

'We were shipwrecked,' said Melas. 'Our grandfather accused us of plotting against him.'

'Which was untrue!'

'So untrue . . .'

'We just simply weren't . . .'

'Whoa!' said Jason. 'Your grandfather?'

The brothers explained. When Phrixus had landed at Colchis, sacrificed the golden ram and given its fleece to King Aeëtes, he had then married Aeëtes' daughter Chalciope. She was the boys' mother, so Aeëtes was their grandfather.

'Your own grandfather expelled you?'

'Expelled us? He was going to *kill* us!'

'We escaped on a ship before he got the chance.'

'We wanted to get to Greece and maybe try our luck with our other grandfather, Athamas.'

'But we were shipwrecked . . .'

'And here we are . . .'

'Thought we'd die here . . .'

'But you arrived . . .'

'Who are you, by the way?'

When Jason explained that he and his men were on a quest for the very fleece their father had brought to Colchis, their eyes widened.

'It's the Fates,' said Phrontis.

---

* I've spelled his name this way to avoid confusion with Argus the shipwright.

'No question.'

'I detect their hand here too,' said Jason. 'Come with us back to Colchis. We'll protect you from Aeëtes. You can introduce us to your father Phrixus. The Fleece is his by right. Surely he would let us bring it back to Greece?'

'That would be a problem,' said Cytoros.

'Dad died last year.'

With these four new crewmen enlisted, the *Argo* sailed from the isle of Ares and finally reached the port of Phasis at the mouth of the river of the same name.* Somewhere upriver and inland, Jason knew, lay Aia†, the capital of Colchis. And somewhere in Colchis the Golden Fleece hung on its tree awaiting them.

'Do we have to leave the *Argo* here,' he asked the four grandsons of Aeëtes, 'or can we safely navigate up?'

'No problem,' they replied. 'Plenty of shipping gets to Aia.'

The shallow draft of the *Argo* and the shallow rise of the Phasis towards its distant source in the Caucasus Mountains did indeed allow them to travel far upstream.

As they made their way along the river, the four grandsons of Aeëtes told Jason a little of how things went in Colchis.

'Our grandfather is a tough man. Some say he killed our father Phrixus. We don't know about that.'

'He's the son of the sun, and he never lets anyone forget that.'

Jason had indeed heard the rumour that Helios the sun Titan was the father of Aeëtes by the Oceanid Perseis, herself a daughter of one of the original twelve Titans.‡

---

* In today's Republic of Georgia the river is now the Rioni and the port is Poti, headquarters of the Georgian navy.

† Now Kutaisi, Georgia's legislative capital.

‡ Should you so wish, you can be introduced to the twelve original Titans in the first volume of *Mythos* (page 7).

'His sisters,' said Melas, 'are our great-aunts Pasiphae, Queen of Crete, and the enchantress CIRCE. I'm sure you've heard of them.'*

Jason had indeed. 'There is magic in your family.'

'None that *we've* inherited, but yes.'

'And Aeëtes is still married?'

'Oh yes, to our grandmother, IDYIA.† They had two daughters, Aunt Medea and our mum Chalciope . . .'

'. . . and a very late son, Uncle ABSYRTUS.'

'. . . who's actually younger than us.'

'I believe that does happen,' said Jason. 'Uncles can be younger than their nephews and nieces. So your mother Chalciope married Phrixus?'‡

'Correct.'

'Whom you say Aeëtes may have killed?'

'It's a pretty fair bet.'

'And yet your mother stays at the palace in Aia?'

'She loves her father. Now, two more bends in the river and we will see that palace.'

'We'll stop here then,' commanded Jason.

The talk of Aeëtes' power and apparently murderous propensities put Jason on his guard. He ordered everyone to disembark from the *Argo* and lift her out of the river. They carried her across to a wooded area that he picked out as a sheltered hiding place. They covered her with some of the netting they used for catching fish on the voyage. Jason

---

* See under Theseus for the story of Pasiphae (page 363). Circe will feature in the story of Odysseus's journey home from the Trojan War.

† Pronounced 'ee-dee-ya' I would think. She was Aeëtes' aunt, being an Oceanid, and therefore a sister of his mother Perseis.

‡ If you're anything like me, you'll find all these relationships wildly confusing, although they are probably no more complicated than those in your own family. Save that you are less likely to be so incestuously connected to Titans, sea nymphs and enchantresses.

instructed them to twist saplings and leaves through the netting so that from a distance the ship was invisible in its woodland setting.

'Animals merge into their backgrounds to avoid danger,' he said. 'Why shouldn't we?'

Carrying gifts for the royal court they set out on foot over the short distance to Aia.

But before the Argonauts reached the city, the four sons of Phrixus took their leave, promising to meet up later. Aeëtes would not take kindly to seeing them amongst Jason's party.

THE EAGLE KING

If King Aeëtes* was surprised or alarmed by the band of renowned heroes that trooped into his court, he concealed it well. He accepted with dignified courtesy the gifts Jason offered, before introducing his family.

'My wife, Queen Idyia . . .'

Jason bowed towards an old lady, who inclined her head with markedly stiff and frosty disdain.

'My daughter, Medea . . .'

A pair of green eyes flashed towards him and turned away.

'My daughter Chalciope . . .'

Something approaching a smile here.

'And my son, Absyrtus . . .'

A boy of eleven or twelve gave a small wave, blushed and looked down at the ground.

'It is an honour, majesty,' said Jason with another bow.

'You have sailed all the way here without having to change ship, you say?'

---

* *Aeëtes* is thought to be a form of the Greek word for 'eagle'.

'Indeed.'

'Remarkable. You must tell me how you managed such a feat. I should have thought it was impossible. Meanwhile, you are all welcome here. Where are you bound after this? Even further east?'

'This is our final destination before we return home, my lord king.'

'Colchis? We are honoured. I wonder what you expect to find here.'

'We have come to claim the fleece of the golden ram that Phrixus, son of Athamas, left here.'

'Oh really?'

'My grandfather Cretheus was a brother of Athamas. Through him I am the rightful King of Iolcos and have come to take the Fleece back to its home.'

King Aeëtes stroked his beard. This young man was resourceful, he could see that. He had with him some of the most celebrated warriors and wonder-workers alive. If he really was the grand-nephew of Athamas, his claim to the Fleece was just. Aeëtes could hardly send him and his men back to Greece with a blank refusal. They had – how, he could not guess – sailed directly here. They must have a most remarkable vessel. They might return with a whole fleet of them. Even if he somehow managed to kill them all before they could get back home . . . a mass poisoning at a feast, for example . . . the scandal would reverberate around the civilised world. Orpheus alone was as famous as any man since Perseus. Others would come for revenge. No, he must be cleverer than that.

'So,' he said, 'you come for the Fleece, do you? I wondered if the day might dawn when someone would. I prayed to the gods for guidance many years ago on this very matter. They told me that the Fleece could only be taken by one prepared to undergo three tests.'

'Tests?' said Jason.

'If you agree to undertake them, the Fleece will be yours.'

'May I know what they are?'

'First you must agree. And your men must swear not to aid you in any way.'

Jason could see no other choice. 'Very well. Name them.'

'You swear before the gods to accept these trials as the only way to take the Fleece?'

'I swear before the gods.'

'And your men?'

Jason turned and indicated to the Argonauts that they too must assent. They went down on one knee, struck their breasts and pledged their oath.

Aeëtes concealed his delight very well. 'Now. The great god Hephaestus made a gift to me. A pair of bulls with mouths and hoofs of bronze – the fire-breathing Oxen of Colchis, the Khalkotauroi.'

'I have heard of them.'

'Doubtless you have. They are very famous. Your first task is to yoke these two great beasts together and plough a field with them.'

'Consider it done.'

'Good. I am a collector of antiquities and objects of curiosity and historical interest. I have in my possession some of the dragon's teeth that Cadmus used when he founded Thebes. You will sow the furrows you have ploughed with the oxen of Hephaestus with these teeth. When this is done, armed men will rise up from the earth. You must defeat them. That will be task number two.'

'Splendid,' said Jason picking an invisible thread from the sleeve of his tunic. 'A chance to get some exercise.'

'Thirdly, you will go to the Grove of Ares where the Fleece hangs on the branches of a sacred oak. A dragon that never sleeps is coiled around its trunk. Overpower the dragon and the Fleece will be yours.

'Phew,' said Jason. 'For a moment there I was worried that you were going to make it something difficult.'

Aeëtes smiled a thin smile. He knew bravado when he saw it. He knew he was safe.

Jason felt none of the confidence he had publicly shown.

In an ever-darkening mood he followed the servants that led him to his guest room. When he was alone he threw himself on the bed.

'Why, gods,' he groaned, 'why did you get me all the way here only to place such an insuperable barrier before me? First Pelias sends me on one impossible quest and now, when I am close, another king sets me more unachievable tasks. Am I a mouse, gods, to be batted back and forth in your cruel catlike claws?'

THREE GODDESSES

Jason's anguished complaints rose into the heavens where they reached the ears of Athena and Hera on Mount Olympus.

'He has a point,' said Athena.

'Until now I greatly admired his spirit,' said Hera. 'This whining self-pity is a disappointment. Comparing us to cats playing with mice. That is hardly proper.'

'He has some cause,' countered Athena. 'To have got so far and now be trapped into promising the impossible.'

Hera arched an eyebrow. 'Nothing is impossible.'

'You are suggesting we intervene? Go down and assist him?'

'That would hardly do. Zeus has made it clear that he frowns on too much of that sort of thing. And heaven knows

I have tried to make clear my views of *his* mortal entanglements. No, one rarely if ever makes appearances these days. We could send a plague to kill Aeëtes, perhaps?'

'But Jason has already sworn an oath to undergo the three trials. It makes no difference whether Aeëtes is alive or dead.'

'This is all most vexing,' said Hera. 'I am beginning to think my plan to use the young man as a means to punish Pelias for daring to violate my temple is too elaborate, too indirect. Perhaps Jason is not the right vessel. So young. So cocky and headstrong.'

Athena stroked the chest of the owl that sat on her shoulder. 'Ah, I think I have it. The daughter of Aeëtes . . .'

'Chalciope?'

'No, the other – Medea.'

'What of her?'

'It happens that she is a worshipper of HECATE and skilled in her arts.'*

'Is she now?'

'None more so, they say. She could help Jason.'

'But why should she?'

'What is it that drives mortals more than anything? More than power or gold?'

'Ah!' said Hera, nodding her head. 'How wise you are, Athena. Seek Aphrodite out.'

Athena found the goddess of love in Cyprus.

'How may I help you?' asked Aphrodite.

'Hera and I need a Princess of Colchis called Medea to fall in love with a Prince of Iolcos called Jason. You see, Hera intends this Jason to . . .'

---

* Hecate, goddess of witchcraft and potions, was a daughter of the second generation Titans Perses and Asteria. She features in Shakespeare's *Macbeth*.

'I really don't need the reason,' said Aphrodite. 'I know this Medea. It has long irritated me to see how she devotes herself to Hecate while neglecting me. I shall send my boy to her at once.'

MEDEA

Medea was sitting and reading a clay tablet on a window seat in the corridor of the palace when Eros arrived in the early morning. She did not see him, for the god of desire was invisible. He stood there, his quiverful of arrows over his shoulder and his silver bow strung and ready.

'What a beautiful young woman,' he thought to himself. 'No wonder mother is annoyed that she has remained single all her life. Lucky Jason.'

He turned his head towards the entrance to the palace's guest wing and blew.

Jason woke suddenly in his bed. He sat up and rubbed his eyes. Strange dream. Eros had whispered in his ear and commanded him to . . .

It was all nonsense. He had other things to think of than the sport of love. He must see if there was a way to defeat these oxen. No reason not to explore the palace; he might find something that could help.

Eros shot his arrow into Medea's chest and stepped back. She looked up from her tablet. The young prince Jason was walking along the corridor in her direction. Why had she not noticed how handsome he was? Oh my heavens, he was more than handsome, he was *beautiful*! That hair, that walk, those eyes, that slim but muscled frame. She stood.

'Jason!'

He saw her.

'Ah, Princess Medea, isn't it? I wonder if you can help me. I'm looking for –'

'I can help you. Come, come with me.'

She led him by the hand to the corner of the palace where she kept her shrine to Hecate. She turned to him, her green eyes alight.

'I am going to help you with your three trials.'

'That's wonderful. Why?'

'Why? Because I love you, Jason. I love you and will come with you when you return to Greece. I will be by your side, always.'

This could only be the work of Eros. That must be what his dream had meant. Jason knew that his prayers had been heard. And how wonderful a way to answer them. This Medea was very beautiful indeed.

'I am going to prepare a salve, an ointment,' she said. 'In the morning you must rub yourself all over with it. Every part of you, from the crown of your head to the soles of your feet.'

'Why?'

'It will protect you from the fire of the bulls. You will be invulnerable for the course of one day. As you anoint yourself, pray to Hecate. That is important. I'll teach you the right words. You must learn them.'

'I will.'

'I love you, Jason. I would do anything for you. Anything.'

Anything.

She meant it.

THE KHALKOTAUROI

At one side of a broad hedged field King Aeëtes and his court were gathered on a platform under a large canopy that shaded them from the heat and glare of the noonday sun. A crowd of excited spectators pressed in around the other three sides of the field.

'It's going to be rather bloody,' Aeëtes warned his wife.

'I enjoy a good spectacle,' said Idyia, stifling a yawn.

'What about you, my dear?' said Aeëtes, turning to his daughter Chalciope. 'Think you can take a bit of a gore?'

She nodded listlessly.

Still fretting herself about those sons of hers, thought Aeëtes. Good riddance to them. Phrixus was gone, those boys of his were gone and soon this Jason would be gone. All who threatened him would be gone.

Now his daughter Medea joined them.

'Ah, *you* don't mind some blood and guts, do you?'

Medea smiled. 'I am so looking forward to this, papa.'

Absyrtus clambered up onto the dais.

'No, my darling . . .' said Aeëtes firmly, but with a soft affection he reserved only for his youngest child, the 'consolation for my old age' as he called him.

'But papa!'

'You're too young. Tell him, Idyia.'

'Obey your father, child,' said Idyia without turning round.

'It's not something fit for a boy of your age to see,' said Aeëtes. I'll make it up to you, I promise. We'll go and see the dragon tomorrow. How's that?'

Absyrtus swung moodily round and clambered down.

Aeëtes clapped his hands and nodded to his steward who signalled to the musicians.

Trumpets sounded, the crowd of Colchians cheered and Jason stepped forward, holding a yoke and harness.

He presented the most magnificent sight. He was naked but for a shield and sword and his whole body gleamed.

'Ha! The fool's rubbed oil all over himself. That'll only

make matters much worse. One blast from the bulls and his skin will catch fire. Oh, this is going to be good!'

Another fanfare and gates at the far end of the field opened. Two enormous bulls trotted out. They stopped for a moment, pawing the ground with their bronze hoofs.

Medea gazed at Jason, trying to keep the look of love out of her eyes.

Aeëtes glanced across at her. She really is a bloodthirsty little thing, he thought to himself. Quite my favourite daughter.

In the centre of the field Jason dropped the yoke and harness and began to beat his sword against his shield. The crowd roared their approval. The bulls looked up and bellowed. With flames bursting from their mouths and smoke pouring from their nostrils, they charged.

Jason held his ground. 'By the gods, this ointment better work,' he muttered to himself, as the bulls galloped towards him.

The flames enveloped him as they approached, but he felt nothing. Leaping to one side he slammed his shield into the first bull, which stumbled. The other turned on him and directed a ball of fire directly into his face. Jason stabbed its side with his sword and its bellow turned to a shriek.

The bulls had never had to fight before. Their flames had always been weapon enough. On Jason they had no effect and it demoralised them. They circled him, puffing smoke and jetting out ever more feeble spears of fire.

The crowd stood to their feet as Jason picked up the yoke and attached it to the bulls who bowed their heads, humbly submissive to his touch.

The royal steward approached Jason with a wooden ploughshare. He skirted the yoked bulls with evident fear, which set the crowd jeering.

The ploughing itself was easy enough. The bulls were

subdued and obedient and the furrows they ploughed straight and deep.

Jason turned towards Aeëtes.

'One!' he shouted.

'One!' echoed the crowd.

Aeëtes swept his hand in a gesture that was supposed to combine impassive acceptance, a modicum of admiration and an air of regal graciousness. It succeeded only in looking petulant.

A trumpet sounded and the steward approached Jason again, bearing this time a silver box high above his head. Jason took it and gave it a shake. He heard the rattle of the dragon's teeth.

Aeëtes watched with a frown. How this conceited youth could have withstood the blast of the oxens' breath was more than he could understand. It was displeasing too that the crowd should be so loudly and unmistakably on his side. Well, it was one thing to tame the bulls, quite another to defeat the armed men that would spring from the soil.

Jason walked the furrows, sowing the long, sharp yellow dragon's teeth in the grooves. When he had finished he stood back and looked for a suitable stone. Medea had told him that the way to defeat the *Spartoi*, the 'sown men' that would rise up fully armed from the earth, would be to throw a large stone into their ranks.

He saw a jagged boulder that was big but not too heavy for him to lift and edged round to it. He looked across the field. The eyes of the king and the crowd were on the ploughed earth, from which the tips of spears were beginning to sprout. The green eyes of Medea were on him. He nodded and leaned down to pick up the boulder.

The spear tips were followed by helmets, then shoulders, trunks and legs. The field was now filled with row on row of rough, virile soldiers. They roared in unison, grunting out war cries and brandishing their weapons. The sight and sound of them was terrible.

Jason raised the boulder above his head and hurled it with all his might. It landed on two of the *Spartoi* in the middle of the field and bounced off onto the shoulder of another. Immediately they turned on each other with a snarl and started to fight. Others joined in, and soon they were all stabbing, roaring, thrusting and throttling each other.

One by one they fell, until only one was standing. The lone soldier staggered groggily about the field of his slain companions. Jason marched smartly up to him and with one sweep of his sword, cut off his head.

He held the head high as he turned to Aeëtes and shouted. 'Two!'

'Two!' yelled the crowd.

Aeëtes stood, turned his back on the field and left. The rest of the court went with him, but the crowd stayed to chant Jason's praises.

He knelt down and thanked Hecate, Hera, Athena, Aphrodite and all the gods he could think of for his deliverance.

'And thank you, Eros,' he added, 'for sending me Medea.'

THE GROVE OF ARES

Late that afternoon Aeëtes called a council of his leading warriors, chieftains and nobles.

'This kingdom will be humiliated in the eyes of the world if we let Jason leave Colchis with the Fleece. It cannot be allowed to happen.'

The council murmured assent.

'But how did he defeat the Khalkotauroi?' asked one of the noblemen.

'Yes, that's what I want to know.'

'Perhaps I can help,' came a female voice.

They all turned to see Idyia, Aeëtes' wife, standing in the doorway

'Really, my dear,' said Aeëtes, 'this is a royal council. We cannot have women walking in and –'

'Oh well, if you don't wish to know who is responsible for helping this Jason, it really makes no difference to me,' she said, turning away with a shrug of the shoulders.

'You *know*? Then you must tell us.'

'Our daughter Medea,' said Idyia. 'Who else is versed enough in witchcraft? Besides, I saw them together yesterday afternoon. She was kissing him.'

Aeëtes barked orders everywhere. 'Find her! Arrest her! Imprison her!'

'But what if Jason gets away with the Fleece?' said one of the generals of Aeëtes' army.

'I ordered that his ship be found. He won't get too far without that.'

'Yes, my lord, but we have scoured the countryside far and wide without success. One party searched all the way to Phasis. The vessel must be out to sea.'

'Well in that case they'll have to follow the river to join it. We can cut them to pieces if they try.'

We leave Aeëtes to his council and turn our attention back to Jason. We find him, having reunited with the four grandsons of Aeëtes, being led by them through the dusk of evening to the Grove of Ares. They were soon joined by Medea, who pulled up short at the sight of the nephews.

'You!'

'Yes, it's us, Aunt Medea! Jason has told us you're are on our side. We're with him too.'

'I'm glad to hear it.'

'Wasn't it fantastic, the way that he dealt with the Khalkotauroi!'

'We watched the whole thing with Absyrtus through a gap in the hedge, didn't we Absyrtus?'

Medea's young brother, who had been hiding behind his nephews, came forward and smiled up at his sister. 'Hey there, Medea.'

'You as well?'

'Let's face it,' said Melas. 'None of us ever liked the old man, did we? He's grown so cruel with age. And as for grandmother – she's a dead fish.'

'Yes, yes,' said Jason. 'This is all very charming, but you must go now. Round up the crew and accompany them to the *Argo*. If I don't join you tonight with the Fleece you are all to leave without me, you understand?'

'But –'

'This is not a subject for debate. Go!'

The four brothers and young Absyrtus left.

Medea fell into Jason's arms. 'They are searching for me. My father must have guessed at my part in your victory. Oh darling, you were so splendid!'

They kissed.

'We must hurry, my love,' she said. 'The grove is just there . . .'

Medea pulled Jason along with her and they hurried through a long avenue of trees. At the end stood a great oak. Moonlight streamed down upon it, illuminating the golden-scales of thick coils that wound around the trunk. As they approached, the head of a great dragon came round from the other side of the tree and opened its mouth with a hiss.

'Whatever I do,' Medea said quietly, 'you are not to inter-fere. You promise?'

Jason nodded. He was content to keep his distance. He had never seen a dragon before. Were they all as huge as this one? It raised its head high and gazed down at them.

Medea stepped forward. The dragon hissed. Medea threw up a hand and sang out some words that Jason could not quite hear. The dragon lowered its head so that it was level with Medea. She stared deep into the vertical slits of its yellow eyes, the eyes that could never close, chanting her incanta-tions all the while. The dragon froze, its mouth sagged open and great strings of drool dropped to the ground. The grass and moss below hissed and steamed as the venomous saliva hit them. Medea took dried herbs, roots and flowers from her satchel and rubbed them into a ball in the palms of her hands. The dragon was frozen and immobile, but Jason could hear the slow panting of its breath.

Medea pushed the ball into the dragon's open mouth. It fizzed on its tongue; with a sigh, the creature lurched and tottered to the ground.

'He's sleeping,' said Medea. 'Now let's take the Fleece and go.'

'But where is it?' said Jason, gazing up at the oak in confusion.

'The other side, you idiot.'

Jason moved round the trunk. The Fleece was hanging from the lower branches, but still too high for him to reach.

Medea leapt on his shoulders, reached up and threw it down.

It was a fleece of rough and ragged sheep's wool, of the kind you might see draped on the hedges of any field. But it was gold, so very gold. It shimmered when Jason stroked it. A million sparkles of light glittered as he ran his fingers through its shining fibres.

'Plenty of time to play with it when we are safely aboard your ship,' said Medea. 'Come!'

They stepped round the sleeping dragon and, hand in hand, ran laughing down the grove, the Golden Fleece slung across Medea's shoulders like a peasant's shawl.

ESCAPE FROM COLCHIS

The *Argo* floated down the Phasis, the river's current strong enough to speed them away from any pursuit.

The crew had found their ship securely hidden under her camouflage netting. When the Argonauts saw Jason and Medea coming through the dark and the Fleece gleaming and streaming they had let out a great cheer. Now, as they glided down the river, each Argonaut came up in turn to touch it.

When he had finished feeling it, Orpheus had tears in his eyes. 'Men will sing of this through the ages,' he said, 'but let me be the first.'

He tuned his lyre and softly sang as the other Argonauts approached one by one to admire the Fleece.

The grandsons of Aeëtes and young Absyrtus were open-mouthed with astonishment.

'Only seen it from a distance,' they said.

'Never thought this day would come.'

Nestor was as profoundly moved as Orpheus. 'Yet there is a long distance, and a long time, between here and now and Iolcos,' he warned. 'Aeëtes will surely pursue us. They say he has a navy second only to that of Minos of Crete.'

Jason had long grown accustomed to relying on Nestor's wisdom. When everyone had finished paying homage to the

Fleece, he took Nestor and Ancaeus the helmsman aside.

'I agree that Aeëtes will come after us with all the force he can muster,' Jason said. 'What do you advise we do about it?'

Nestor considered awhile before speaking, a habit of his that irked many but which guaranteed that nothing foolish ever came from his mouth. 'Aeëtes is certain to discover that the Symplegades are no longer blocking the Bosporus. News that the passage between the Propontis and the Euxine Sea lies open will have spread through all the ports and towns in the region. He will pursue us there. Therefore we should go another way.'

Jason stared. 'What do you mean "another way"? There *is* no other way. The Euxine is an inland sea. The Bosporus is the only connection with the Propontis and thence the Hellespont, the Mediterranean and home.'

'What about the Istros?' said Nestor.

'The Istros!' Jason leaned forward and kissed Nestor on the forehead. 'You are a genius, my friend.'

'Yes,' cried Ancaeus. 'Istros! Why didn't I think of that?'

The Istros was a long river that flowed through many strange kingdoms to the north of Greece. It rose somewhere in the barbarian west, but its great delta drained through the northwestern shore of the Euxine Sea. We call it the Danube today.

Nestor explained to the two helmsmen, Ancaeus and Euphemus, that they could sail up the Istros, across the top of Thrace and westwards along the river courses almost to Galatia; from here they could voyage south along the western coast of Italy, round Sicily and the Ionian islands, thence to the Peloponnese and north along the east coast of Greece for Thessaly and Iolcos. This would entirely fool Aeëtes, who would be certain to go the direct route – the route the *Argo* had taken on her outward voyage.*

They reached the port of Phasis without incident, stocked the *Argo* with as much food, water and other necessary provisions as they could barter or buy and, barely four days after Jason and Medea had passed Aeëtes' three tests and won the Fleece, they were sailing across the Euxine Sea heading northwest for the Istrian delta.

By the afternoon of the first day out from Phasis, it was apparent that a ship was in hot pursuit behind them. Keen to disguise their intentions, they changed course, as if heading to the Bosporus. Medea looked back and recognised the prize galley of the Colchian fleet.

'It is my father,' she said. 'His is the fastest ship in the world. It has three banks of oars.'

'He's gaining on us,' said Jason. 'Damn. We'll have to turn side on and fight.'

'He has a catapult on board. He will happily toss balls of flaming pitch onto our decks. He stops at nothing to get what he wants.'

'But he would burn the Fleece along with us.'

'That wouldn't worry him. He's fighting for pride, not the Fleece. But fear not, my darling Jason, I stop at nothing too.'

She took Jason's face in her hands and kissed him hard. 'Back in a moment.'

Jason turned back to watch the Colchian ship bearing relentlessly down upon them. It was close enough now for him to be able to make out the brightly coloured prow, dipping and rising in the waves. It was painted to look like the face of the guardian dragon of the Golden Fleece.

---

* Unless you are fortunate enough to possess the wisdom of Nestor, you might find his plan easier to understand after a look at the map on pages 252–253. I don't mind waiting.

Medea returned to the sternpost, arms around her young brother Absyrtus.

'Look, there's daddy's ship,' she said, pointing.

Absyrtus's eyes widened. 'He's going to be so cross when he sees me.'

'Upset rather than cross, I think,' said Medea, cutting open the boy's throat with one swift stroke of a curved knife.

Jason stared in horror as the blood gushed from the child. 'Medea!'

'The only way,' said Medea. 'Fetch me an axe, and hurry – they're gaining on us.'

The boy's head was the first to go overboard. It bobbed along in the *Argo's* wake. Jason and Medea watched as the ship of Aeëtes slowed down, raised its oars and came to a stop.

'He loved that boy,' said Medea, looking on with satisfaction. 'He will never allow his soul to go the underworld unless the body has been purified and all proper funeral rites observed.'

Jason said nothing. Medea was beautiful. She was devoted to him. But there were limits. Surely there were limits.

THE JOURNEY HOME

By the time the last pieces of Absyrtus had been dropped into the water at careful intervals, Aeëtes' ship was far behind, out of sight below the horizon. Night had fallen when Jason and Ancaeus felt confident in altering course back to their original destination.

A week later the *Argo* slipped safely and unobserved through the marshes that fringed the mouth of the Istros and entered into Thrace.

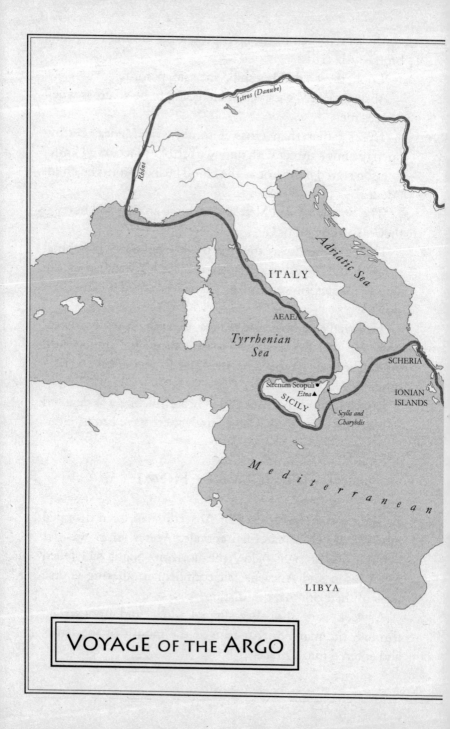

VOYAGE OF THE ARGO

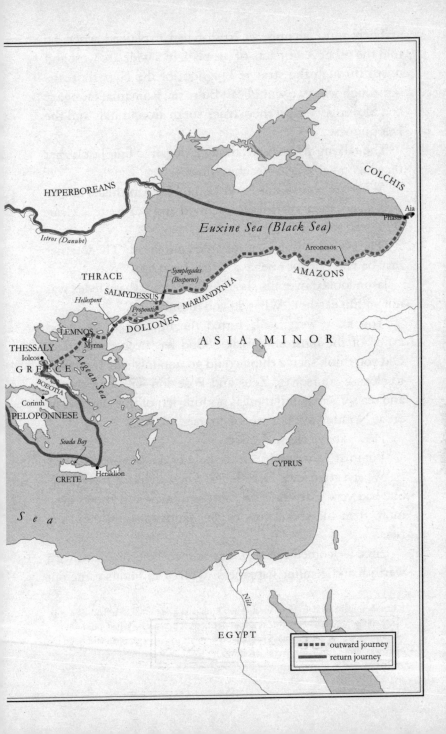

outward journey

return journey

Their route swung, as Nestor had explained when he told the other Argonauts of his plan, in a wide arc west and north through the strange kingdom of the Hyperboreans – through what we would call Bulgaria, Romania, Hungary and Slovenia* – until they struck south around Italy and the Peloponnese.

The talking figurehead, though, began telling Jason that they had no chance of reaching Iolcos.

'What are you saying?' said Jason. 'The Colchians lost us weeks ago, there's fair weather ahead and our route is clear. What can stop us?'

'The gods can stop you,' said the figurehead. 'The weather may be fair, but your behaviour has been foul.'

Jason looked over his shoulder to be sure that Medea was not within earshot. 'What do you mean?'

'You know very well,' tutted the figurehead. 'A blood crime of the most abominable kind has been committed. Did you think such a thing could go unpunished? If you fail to cleanse yourselves, Zeus and Poseidon will send storms and sea serpents until there is nothing left of this ship and its crew. Nothing left but me, of course . . .'

'How can we cleanse ourselves?'

'Put in at Aeaea and seek the help of the sorceress Circe.'

'What a good idea,' said Medea, who had heard everything. She had very sharp hearing. 'She is my aunt and knows even more than me about potions, enchantments and cleansing rites.'

Circe welcomed them on her home island of Aeaea with warmth and genuine happiness. Wolves and lions came out

---

* On their way through, Jason established Ljubljana, the capital of today's Slovenia. The people there celebrate him as a founder hero. They say he killed a dragon in a lake and saved the inhabitants. That dragon remains the city's emblem (although the story was later Christianized and Jason was replaced by St George).

with her to meet them, but they proved to be as tame as domestic dogs and cats, licking them and nuzzling around their ankles. She lived a lonely life, taking most of her pleasure in turning sailors unfortunate enough to land on Aeaea into domestic animals.*

Circe took great delight in performing the rituals, chanting the appropriate incantations and piacular prayers, for the purification of her niece and the proper propitiation of the gods.

Overnight, however, the truth of what Medea had done was revealed to Circe in a dream and the following morning she cursed them off her island with shrieks of disgust.

'In the name of all that is holy, he was your younger brother, my nephew! It is only because I fear committing a blood crime like yours that I let you leave unharmed!' she yelled after them. 'Go and never return!'

'I thought that went rather well,' said Medea sweetly as they sailed south, hugging Italy's western coast.

They were upon *Sirenum Scopuli*, the Siren Rock, before they knew it. The strains of sweet music were wafted into the ears of everyone on board as they approached. Members of the crew began to snatch at the air trying to catch the sound, like puppies snapping at butterflies. They stood at the gunwales of the *Argo* and leaned out, straining to get closer.

Jason was ready for his – 'Now!' he shouted to Orpheus, who stood high on the foredeck, picked up his lyre and began to sing his own song.

The two most enticing sounds in the world intermingled. Orpheus's music, being in closer proximity to the Argonauts, won the day. He had been saving a special song, his most perfect, for just this occasion. Jason and the others turned

---

* As Odysseus was to discover many years later, during his decade-long struggle to return home to Ithaca after the Trojan War.

away from the Sirens on their rock and let the rippling of Orpheus's lyre and the sublime tones of his voice enter their minds and hearts.

Only one member of the crew was immune to the competing sounds of Orpheus's lyre. A Sicilian king named BUTES had been recruited solely for his prodigious skill with bees. Each time the *Argo* had occasion to put in to shore he would go inland to hunt out honey, giving the crew a chance to sweeten their often unappetising rations. The song of the Sirens, no one later could explain why, maddened him more violently and uncontrollably than anyone else and, wresting himself free of the others, he threw himself overboard and started swimming towards their island.

The tender beauty of the Sirens' music was inversely proportional to the vicious cruelty of their purpose. They sang to entice sailors – birds and wildlife too – and draw them onto the rocky cliffs of their home. They would hop from their crags to the wrecked ships and feast on their transfixed crewmen. Orpheus's competing song had frustrated them, but when they saw Butes floundering on the waves they knew that they would at least have something to eat that day.

Even that small snack was to be denied them, however. Aphrodite swept down, whisked Butes from the waves and carried him to Lilybaeum in his home island of Sicily.*

As soon as the *Argo* sailed clear of the Siren Rock, Jason was faced with a difficult choice. To the west lay the channel that passed between the fearsome SCYLLA and CHARYBDIS.

---

* Lilybaeum is today's Marsala, famous for its honey-sweet wine. Butes and Aphrodite became lovers. Some say it was around the time of her affair with ADONIS (see *Mythos*, Vol. I, page 325), and that she only did this to make Adonis jealous. She bore Butes a son, ERYX, who grew up to be one of the finest boxers of his generation. Not fine enough to survive a bout with Heracles, however. Even in his later years the great hero was too much for Eryx. He knocked him dead with one punch. Doubtless, being Heracles, he was filled with remorse and tried to put him back together again.

Scylla was a dreadful six-headed monster who would lean down from a cliff to pluck up and eat six crew members of any ship that passed too close to her. But try to steer too far away from her cliff and a vessel would be pulled into the path of Charybdis, a fast churning whirlpool that could suck down an entire ship.

Instead, Jason ordered Ancaeus to veer away, avoiding Scylla and Charybdis altogether, but taking them towards another danger – the infamous Planctae, or Wandering Rocks.* These were turbulent waters close to Mount Etna, whose fury caused them violently to froth and churn between dangerous reefs, bubbling with flame and smoke.

Once the *Argo* was caught in their currents, there could be no turning back. Ancaeus fought to steer as they were flung towards streaming black volcanic boulders. The *Argo* was a large ship but now she was nothing more than a toy boat hurtling through foaming white rapids.† Above the roar of the torrent, Jason could hear the precise nagging tones of the figurehead. When he was finally able to make out what it was saying, he pulled Ancaeus round and yelled in his ear.

'Don't try to steer! Let go!'

'What?'

'Let go of the tiller bar. Just let go!'

'Are you mad?'

'Do as I say!'

Ancaeus obeyed. In truth controlling the tiller had been like trying to catch a tiger by the tail, and he was more than glad to let go and commend his spirit to heaven.

---

* Planets are 'wandering rocks' too – they get their name from the same Greek source word *planetai* meaning 'wanderers'. Early astronomers were alerted to their difference from other heavenly bodies when they observed them roaming apparently randomly across the sky and called them *planetes asteres,* wandering stars.

† Or like the *Millennium Falcon* trying to steer through an asteroid field.

They were all in the hands of the gods now – and that was just as the figurehead intended. Hurled this way and that, slammed sideways and spun round and round, plunging down and rearing up, the ship somehow threaded her way through without once touching a rock. When they were at last vomited out of the mad ferment into calm sea, the Argonauts fell to their knees and thanked the gods for their miraculous salvation.

All but one.

'That was fun,' said Medea, looking back at the smoke, steam and spray raising from the reefs. 'Can we have another go?'

'It was Hera, Queen of Heaven,' said Jason. 'She guided us through. When next we make landfall, we must sacrifice a great heifer to her.'

They made landfall a few days later, on the green and fertile island of Scheria, home of the Phaeacian people.* Their king and queen, ALCINOUS and ARETE, welcomed them, feasted them and provided them with the animals that allowed them to send up their grateful prayers and sacrifices to Hera for their deliverance from the Planctae.

They had been on Scheria a week when five strange ships dropped anchor in the harbour. Ships from Colchis. Aeëtes himself was not on board, but their leader presented himself before King Alcinous and insisted that Medea be handed over.

'She is the property of King Aeëtes, not of the pirate Jason. Aeëtes demands her return.'

'But my understanding is that Medea does not wish to go back to Colchis.'

'It is the wishes of the king her father that are paramount. She and this Jason are not man and wife. She is also in

---

* Today's Corfu.

possession of a valuable and sacred object belonging to our kingdom.'

'What object is that?'

The deputation conferred. 'We are not at liberty to state.'

In another part of the palace Medea was kneeling before Queen Arete.

'You do not understand how cruel my father is,' she wept. 'He is a monster.'

'But Jason sounds like a monster too,' said Arete. 'The Colchians tell us that he kidnapped your young brother and chopped him up, dropping pieces into the sea. Can you really want to live with a man like that?'

'That is a lie!' sobbed Medea, letting her hair fall over the queen's feet and waving it backwards and forwards as she wailed. 'My brother died of fever and Jason was the first to insist we lose valuable time to give him a proper funeral.'

Arete's heart was moved. 'I shall go to my husband immediately,' she said.

She arrived at the throne room in time to hear Alcinous delivering his judgement. 'If Medea is a virgin,' he ruled, 'she belongs to her father and must return with the Colchians. If she is not, she must stay with Jason. I have sent for a venerable and wise priestess who lives in the north of our island and who knows how to determine the . . . er . . . the state of female parts.'

Arete left and ran to Medea and Jason. 'There is no time to lose. I must ask you this. Have you slept together? By which I mean . . . have you coupled?'

Jason blushed. 'We have had no time . . . on board ship it has hardly been possible . . .'

Arete turned to Medea. 'My dear, are you still intact?'

Medea dropped her head. For once she had no need to lie. 'I am.'

'Then tonight you must put that right,' said Arete. 'Tomorrow morning a woman will arrive and inspect you. If she finds you are still intact, my husband will deliver you into the hands of the Colchian legation.'

It was a tableau of rare power and beauty. Jason and Medea spread out the Fleece and made love on its soft and golden wool.

The next morning the frustrated Colchians departed. Alcinous summoned Jason to his throne room.

'My ships will escort you until you can be sure of your way home,' said the king. Now that he had made his decision, he was not of a mind to let the Colchians ambush the *Argo* when they left Scheria.

The Argonauts sailed under the Phaeacian escort for three days and nights before saluting a grateful farewell and threading their way round the islands of the Ionian Sea.* They neared Crete having sighted no Colchian ships for days, only to be faced by the most extraordinary threat they had yet encountered.

As they approached Souda Bay great surging waves rocked them until the *Argo* nearly capsized. On the Cretan shore they saw a huge man . . . not a man . . . a machine made to look like a man and formed entirely of bronze. It stamped its great bronze feet up and down and sent waves crashing against the *Argo's* hull.

'Quick, turn the ship about! And row!' yelled Jason. 'Row like you rowed through the Clashing Rocks!'

Once they were safely out of range, they looked back. The huge automaton was striding round the corner of the island and out of sight.

'What the hell was that?' demanded the Argonauts.

---

* The Southern Adriatic. Confusing because the name 'Ionia' refers to parts of Asia Minor, today's Turkey far to the other side of Greece.

'TALOS,' said Nestor. 'That was Talos.'

'My tutor Chiron told me about him when I was a child,' said Jason, 'but I always thought it was just a stupid story made up to amuse me.'

'He's real enough as you have seen,' said Nestor. 'He walks around Crete three times every day to protect the island from pirates and invading fleets.'

'Is it true that Hephaestus constructed him in his Olympian forge at the command of Zeus?' asked Jason.

'I thought Daedalus built him for King Minos,' said Meleager.

'No, no. I believe I am right in saying that he is the last of the great race of Bronze Men,' Nestor said. 'They were born from the Meliae – you know, the nymphs of the ash tree who sprang from the earth when Kronos castrated his father Ouranos.'*

'If that is true,' said Medea, 'then he is not a machine, but a mortal; and as a mortal he can be killed.'

'But darling,' said Jason. 'He is made of solid bronze.'

'Not quite true,' said Nestor. 'Whether he is man or machine, it is certain that he has a single tube or pipe running down from his neck to his ankle like a great vein. This is where his ichor runs, the divine fluid necessary for his life and motion.† It is all held in by a brass nail in his heel. If that nail is dislodged, the liquid will run out and he will fall.'

'Why risk engaging with him?' Meleager asked. 'Let's just leave.'

'We need provisions,' said Euphemus. 'We're out of fresh water, bread, fruit . . . everything.'

'Besides,' said Ancaeus, 'he's here again!'

---

* See *Mythos*, Vol. I.

† Ichor, the silvery-gold blood that ran in the veins of the gods was deadly poison to mortals.

It was true, Talos had reemerged and was sloshing through the waves towards them.

'Let me,' said Medea, standing up high on the foredeck, calling out her incantations. 'Come Talos, come! Come to me, come to me!'

Talos stopped mid-stride and cocked his head. Medea stared deep into the blank eyes chanting all the while. As the dragon in the Grove of Ares had done, Talos froze.

'There,' said Medea. 'Now, someone go down and pull out that nail of his.'

Pirithous was only too happy to dive into the water and do the deed. He came up from the waves, a bronze pin between his teeth. Behind him the automaton creaked, tottered and crashed into the sea.

Jason hugged Medea. 'You're a miracle worker!'*

They crept east along the northern shore of the island and put in at Heraklion,† where the collapse of Talos had yet to be noticed.

Now provisioned for the final leg of their homeward voyage they sailed on to Iolcos.‡

---

* The word he used must have been 'thaumaturge'. A lifetime ago, when I was learning ancient Greek as an eight-year-old, the textbook the school used liked to remind one of the English words that derived from Greek: 'graph' and 'graphic' from *grapho*, 'telephone' from *phonos*, that sort of thing. I will never forget my puzzlement when, in a vocabulary list, it presented the verb *thaumazo*, offering this helpful thought: '*thaumazo*, I wonder, or marvel at. This is easily remembered by thinking of the English word "thaumaturge".' And I suppose that was true, since I've never forgotten it.

† Also known as Chandax.

‡ This is where the *Argonautica* of Apollonius Rhodius comes to an end (as does the *Argonautica Orphica*, a Byzantine Greek retelling of the fifth or sixth century AD ostensibly narrated by Orpheus). Whether Apollonius failed to finish, or whether he felt he had best remain true to his title and deal only with the voyage and not with the repercussions and aftermath, is not known.

THE MAGICAL DEATH OF PELIAS

Jason knelt before Pelias, the Fleece spread out before him.

The successful return of Jason and his crew complete with Golden Fleece was the last thing that Pelias had expected or hoped for. Wicked men who send heroes on their quests always believe that they are sending them to certain death. Wicked men never learn, for wicked men have no interest in myths, legends and stories. If they had they would learn from them and triumph, so we must be glad of their ignorance and dullness of wits.

'Sorry it took so long,' said Jason, 'but Colchis is a fair distance and there were one or two obstacles on the way.'

Pelias, under the curious gaze of his court, did his best to look pleased.

'I accept this Fleece. It certainly looks genuine. You may leave.'

They withdrew. It was clear at once that Pelias had no intention of giving up his throne. What is more, Jason now discovered that his father and mother, Aeson and Alcimede, were dead. Some said that, along with his young brother Promachus, they had been executed by Pelias; others that a distraught Aeson had poisoned his wife and son and fallen on his own sword after Pelias told him that it was certain the *Argo* had sunk with all lives lost.

'In either case,' said Jason bitterly, 'Pelias is responsible for their deaths.'

'Let me deal with that, darling,' said Medea. 'He's your kinsman and it wouldn't be right for you to be seen to end his life. You know how fussy gods and mortals are about such things.'

Medea befriended Pelias's nine daughters, the PELIADES:*
ALCESTIS†, ALCIMEDE, ‡, ANTINOË, ASTEROPEIA, EVADNE,§
HIPPOTHOË, MEDUSA (not the Gorgon), PELOPIA and PISIDICE.

'It is *so* sad that your father is growing old,' she said to them. 'My own father, Aeëtes, is twenty years Pelias's senior, but he looks – and acts – young enough to be his grandson.'

'How is that?' the daughters demanded.

'I expect you've heard of my powers,' said Medea.

'They say you're a *witch!*' said Pelopia.

'I always think that's such a terrible word. I prefer "enchantress". Yes, there are ways to make your father youthful, but I don't suppose you'd be interested?'

'Oh, we would, we would!' cried the girls, who loved their father very much.

Medea now prepared a gruesome conjuring trick. With the girls watching in open-mouthed stupefaction, she took an old ram and cut its throat before butchering it into small pieces which she threw into a great cauldron. Next she sprinkled magic herbs into the pot and made dramatic passes over it with her hands. Suddenly, a bleating sound was heard and a lamb leapt alive from the cauldron and gambolled away¶.

The girls gasped and clapped their hands.

'There you are,' said Medea, handing them a packet of herbs. 'Now you try it. Don't forget to move your hands

---

* Not to be confused with the Pleiades, the Seven Sisters, daughters of Atlas and Pleione. See the first volume of *Mythos* (page 100). Euripides wrote a tragedy called the *Peliades*, but it is lost.

† She was later won by Admetus, and offered to die in his place. Heracles wrestled Death for her soul if you recall.

‡ Same name as Jason's mother, which is confusing.

§ I know, that name rather stands out amongst the others, doesn't it? It's the only one the spell-checker didn't challenge. Evadne means 'very holy' which makes me think, wrongly, of Evander Holyfield.

¶ 'Looking for a ewe's teat to suckle from' as Ovid rather endearingly puts it.

exactly like this . . .' She repeated the mystical gestures she had made over the pot.

The girls ran to Pelias's chamber where he was taking his afternoon nap. With cries of joy and excitement they slit his throat and cut him up. They carried the bloody chunks of his flesh to the cauldron, dropped them in, sprinkled in the herbs and made the magical passes with their hands. They waited breathlessly for a rejuvenated Pelias to spring from the pot, but strangely he did not.

When they went sobbing to their brother Acastus and told him what they had done, he immediately knew that the girls had been tricked.

'She gave you the wrong herbs, you fools!'*

Acastus arranged not only a grand funeral for his father, but funeral games too. They were to become the most famous yet celebrated, surpassed only by those held a generation later by Achilles to honour the death of his beloved friend PATROCLUS, cut down by HECTOR before the walls of Troy.

Acastus was a far more likeable man than his father† and the people of Iolcos believed him when he apportioned as much blame to Jason as to Medea for the death of Pelias. From being the popular hero Jason became overnight a loathed criminal. Until he atoned for the blood killing – Pelias was, after all, his uncle‡ – he could not even stay in Iolcos, let alone claim its throne.

---

* It is far more likely to have been a magic trick than real witchcraft. I don't doubt my friends the magnificent Penn and Teller could reproduce the effect perfectly. It's very much in their wheelhouse – their frequently sordid and spectacularly sick wheelhouse. They are, in some respects, the Medeas of our time.

† Acastus is often listed as one of the Argonauts, which would mean that Pelias was either willing to sacrifice him – for he never believed the *Argo* would return – or perhaps that Acastus was there to ensure the Fleece, if found, would be returned to him.

‡ Half-uncle if my calculations are correct. Can there be such a thing as a half-uncle? At any rate, Pelias was a half-brother of Jason's father Aeson, sharing Tiro as a mother.

So Medea and Jason fled, leaving Acastus to rule the kingdom. The crew of the *Argo* dispersed, returning to their homes, lives and subsequent adventures. Many of them were to meet up again and join in the Calydonian boar hunt. Meanwhile, it is worth leaving Jason and Medea for a moment to relate the story of Ancaeus, the man who took over the duties of helmsman of the *Argo* following the death of Tiphys.

Once the *Argo* had put in at Iolcos, Ancaeus made for his home island of Samos, just north of Patmos. Before he left to join the Argonauts, he had planted out a vineyard, which he hoped would be bearing grapes by the time he came back* The island's seer told Ancaeus that, while he would certainly return to Samos safe and sound, he would never taste the vineyard's wine. On his return Ancaeus saw to his delight that the grapes had ripened beautifully and been turned into wine. He summoned the seer before him and raised a cup of the wine to his lips.

'So much for your false prophecies,' he said, waving the cup in the seer's face. 'I should sack you for incompetence.'

'There's many a slip 'twixt cup and lip,' said the seer.†

Just as Ancaeus was about to take a drink, a clamour rose up outside. A wild boar was ravaging the vineyard. Ancaeus put down the cup and ran out to inspect the damage. The boar charged out, tossed him on his tusks and gored him to death.

The seer, fully aware that he had coined a new proverb that would be repeated for generations, picked up the cup of wine and drained it.

---

* Samos was famous for the quality of its wine. It is celebrated by Byron in the glorious 'Isles of Greece' section of his epic poem *Don Juan*. 'Fill high the bowl with Samian wine!'

† His words were Πολλὰ μεταξὺ πέλει κύλικος καὶ χείλεος ἄκρου (*Polla metaxu pelei kulikos kai cheileos akrou*) according to Jenny March in her excellent *Dictionary of Classical Mythology*. If you put that into Google Translate however, it comes out as 'A lot of people are screaming and screaming' – go figure.

The boar was later sent by Artemis to Calydon, as we shall find out when we follow the adventures of Atalanta.

MEDEA RISES UP

The story of Jason and Medea now moves to Corinth where they found refuge from the wrath of Acastus and the people of Iolcos.*

King CREON† offered them sanctuary, and they soon settled in comfortably enough to life in his palace. Medea bore Jason three sons‡ and all was well until Jason's eye fell upon Creon's daughter CREUSA.

Eros's arrow, when it struck Medea, had never pierced a heart more ready for utter devotion. Her love for Jason was animal, obsessive and terrifyingly passionate. Her fury when she discovered his betrayal no less volcanic.

To herself she swore revenge, yet she had enough inner strength somehow to conceal her rage, her hurt and her drastic intentions.

'Can it be true,' she asked Jason, 'that you have decided to leave me?'

'It's political,' he replied. 'If I marry into Creon's family then one day our children might rule Corinth *and* Iolcos. You can see the value in that, surely?'

'After all I've done for you?' Medea kept her voice steady.

---

* What follows is based on Euripides' version of the story in his tragedy *Medea*.

† No relation to the Theban royal of the same name in the stories of Heracles and Oedipus. This Creon was a descendant of Sisyphus which suggests some kind of family tie to Jason, which may explain his offer of sanctuary.

‡ Euripides doesn't give them names, but according to Apollodorus they were Thessalus, Mermerus and Pheres.

'Who was it who helped you defeat the fire-breathing oxen and the great serpent of the Grove of Ares? Who was it who overcame Talos of Crete . . .'

'Yes, yes, yes. But it was Aphrodite when you come to think of it. Idmon told me the whole thing before he died. Aphrodite sent Eros to make you fall in love with me. On the orders of my protectress Hera. It was all her doing really, *she* was the one who helped me. You were merely her vessel.'

Merely – her – vessel. In the days to come Medea would repeat those words to herself many times. But what came out of her mouth now was:

'Of course, my love. You are right. I know that. I am happy for you, and happy for Creusa and her family. And to prove it, I shall send her the finest wedding gifts I can procure.'

'You're an angel,' Jason kissed her on both cheeks. 'Knew you'd understand.'

Slapping her cheerfully on the behind, he left the room.

Men! It's not that they're brutish, boorish, shallow and insensitive – though I dare say many are. It's just that they're so damned blind. So incredibly stupid. Men in myth and fiction at least. In real life we are keen, clever and entirely without fault of course.

Creusa's wedding gifts arrived, a gold coronet of leaves and a gorgeously embroidered and scented robe – all smeared by Medea with deadly poison. Creusa could not wait to try them on in front of a mirror of polished bronze. Within minutes the venom burned through her skin and entered her bloodstream. Her howls of pain summoned her father Creon, who held the dying girl in his arms, wailing and sobbing. But when he tried to lay her body down, he found that the poison gown was stuck to him and he too died in agony.

Now Medea prepared to kill her sons.*

It might seem that what Medea was about to do is the most terrible of her catalogue of gruesome crimes; but in *Medea*, Euripides puts in her mouth a great speech in which she prevaricates over whether or not to do the deed. It stands as one of the great soliloquies in drama. From it Medea emerges sympathetically as a tragic and wholly human dramatic hero.†

The infanticide is something she agonises over. At first she decides she cannot and must not do it. Then she pictures what the children's fate will be if she does not. Less kindly hands than hers will take their lives.

Medea
I have determined to do the deed at once,
to kill my children and leave this land,
and not to falter or give my children
over to let a hand more hostile murder them.
They must die and since they must
I, who brought them into the world, will kill them.
But arm yourself, my heart. Why hesitate
to do these tragic, yet necessary, evils?
Come, unhappy hand of mine, take the sword
take it, move to the dismal turning point of life.
Do not be a coward. Do not think of your children –
how much you love them, how you gave them birth.
For this one short day forget your children,
and mourn tomorrow. For even if you kill them
still you loved them very much. I am an unhappy woman.

---

* The eldest of the three, Thessalus, was away being tutored by Chiron and survived. He would return from Chiron's cave to rule over Iolcos and Greater Aeolia, which we now call Thessaly in his honour.
† It seems that almost all the actresses who play the part win Tony or Olivier Awards these days.

In an astonishing *coup de théâtre* Medea appears above the stage in a chariot drawn by dragons, sent by her grandfather Helios, god of the sun. She has the bodies of her children with her, fearing that if she leaves them in Corinth they will not be given proper burial. Jason, having been told what has happened to his sons, calls up to her. Their exchange of blame and curses is magnificent. Jason's final plea to her falls on deaf ears:

Jason
In the name of the gods
let me touch the soft skin of my children.

Medea
That will not happen. Your words are thrown
    into the empty air.
(*She flies off toward Athens*)*

In Athens we will meet Medea again.†

A broken Jason lived on in Corinth until his old friend and fellow Argonaut Peleus, brother of Telamon, persuaded him to return to Iolcos and overthrow Acastus. This they managed and Jason was finally installed as king. His reign did not last long, however. He fell asleep one afternoon under the stern of his beloved *Argo* and a rotten and poorly attached beam fell on him and killed him instantly.

Forward on the prow, the figurehead muttered to itself. 'I warned him when the sternpost was sheared off by the Clashing Rocks all those years ago. "Mend it well," I said. "Mend it well, or one day you'll regret it." Mortals, there's no helping them.'

---

* Translation by C. A. E. Luschnig.
† See the story of Theseus (page 353). It is Medea's presence in Athens, as we shall see, that makes it impossible for Theseus to have been an Argonaut.

Atalanta

BORN TO BE WILD

Many Greek heroes were the mongrel offspring of humans, minor deities, demigods and even full Olympians. Some were born to prophetic curses that caused them to be outcast and raised by foster parents or even foster animals. A great many others would find their divine lineage a curse. Their heroism, perhaps, derived from their ability to bring their mix of the human and the divine to bear against the grinding pressures of fate. Well of course it did. That's where all heroism comes from. I use the word 'hero' shorn of gender. Hero was a reasonably common female first name in the ancient world* and I hope we can agree that a division into heroes and heroines would be clumsy and unnecessary.

The great hero Atalanta had a most royal pedigree: her mother was CLYMENE of the royal Minyad clan† and her father, depending on whether you believe Ovid or Apollodorus as a source, was called either IASUS or SCHOENEUS‡. Whatever his name, he was an Arcadian king and the kind of ruler who had no use for female offspring. When his firstborn by Clymene proved to be a girl, he had the child taken

---

* As in the lovers HERO and LEANDER, whose tragic tale is recounted in the first volume of *Mythos* (page 359) – and the daughter of Leonato in Shakespeare's *Much Ado About Nothing*.

† Minyas was the founder king of Orchomenos in Boeotia, the great rival city state of Thebes. Heracles defeated Minyas' descendant Erginos and was given the hand of Megara in marriage as a reward.

‡ Pronounced 'Skeenius' to rhyme with 'genius'.

273

from the palace and exposed on a mountainside to die. He was neither the first nor the last royal father to consign an infant to such a fate, as we shall see.

The baby was abondoned in a high cranny on Mount Parthenion where she would soon surely die. Indeed, only half an hour after the palace guard laid her down a bear, attracted by the cries or perhaps the unfamiliar human scent, lumbered up to investigate. As luck would have it – or MOROS, the deep fate that determines all – this was a she-bear, a she-bear, moreover, who had lost her newborn cub to wolves not twenty-four hours earlier. A maternal instinct still drove the bear, and instead of eating the infant she suckled her.

And so the human baby girl grew to be a shy, wild and swift forest creature. Whether she thought herself a bear or knew her difference at first we cannot know. She might have remained one of those legendary wild children of the woods adopted by animals and unsocialised by her own species – an ancient Greek Kaspar Hauser or Victor of Aveyron, a female Tarzan or Mowgli – were it not that, one day, she was seen and taken by a group of hunters. Luckily for her, they were well-disposed and kindly. They named her Atalanta* and taught her the secrets of trapping and killing, of shooting with arrows, spears and slings, coursing, hunting, tracking and all the arts of venery and the chase. She quickly equalled and surpassed their skill, combining as she did human subtlety with the ferocity and speed of the bear that brought her up. Her supreme swiftness and unmatched ability as a huntress made Atalanta a natural devotee of the goddess of Chastity and the Chase, Artemis, to whom she committed herself, heart and soul.

---

* The name means, so far as I can tell, 'equal in weight' – which is a strange thing to call someone. But perhaps she got the name because the men who found her believed her to be a man's equal.

One day she found herself cornered by two centaurs, the half-human, half-horse hybrids famed for the accuracy and the speed of draw of their archery. Atalanta loosed two arrows that found their mark before either centaur had managed even to raise his bow. Her reputation spread and soon everyone in the Mediterranean world had heard stories of the beautiful girl, dedicated to Artemis, who ran faster and shot straighter than any man.

And when Artemis cursed a neighbouring kingdom with a monstrous boar that ravaged the people and their crops and livestock, it was to be Atalanta, the goddess's most faithful servant and adherent, who would lift that curse.

THE CALYDONIAN BOAR

Somehow the citizenry and rulers of the city state of Calydon, part of the kingdom of Aetolia, now called Thessaly, had become lax in their devotions to the goddess Artemis. This was still a time when it was foolish to neglect any jealous deity, least of all the chaste huntress of the moon. As punishment for so insulting a slight to her honour and dignity, Artemis sent to Calydon a monstrous boar* with razor-sharp tusks the size of tree branches and an insatiable appetite for goats, sheep, cows, horses and infant humans. It trampled down the crops, ravaged the vineyards and barns and, like Robert Browning's rats in Hamelin, bit the babies in their cradles and drank the soup from the cooks' own ladles. And much worse. The people in the countryside fled in terror to within the city walls and soon famine threatened.

---

* The same that had done for King Ancaeus of Samos before he had a chance to taste his wine.

Oeneus, the King of Calydon – in his excessive worship of Dionysus* over the other Olympians – had been the one most directly responsible for Artemis's wrath, and so he took it upon himself to be the one to devise the means to rid the land of the rampaging boar. He sent out word out to all Greece and Asia Minor.

'The Calydonian Hunt will gather in one month. Let only the bravest and best hunters come forward. The reward for whosoever makes the killing thrust will be the right to keep the trophies of the chase: the beast's tusks and pelt. But, more importantly, eternal glory and honour in the annals of history will be theirs as the conqueror of the Calydonian Boar and as the greatest hero of the age.'

Many of those who answered Oeneus's call were former Argonauts – including Jason himself† – bored by the return to the placid dullness of domestic life after the camaraderie and excitement of the quest for the Golden Fleece. The band of hunters would be led by Oeneus's son Prince Meleager, himself a distinguished member of the *Argo*'s crew.

Though he did not know it, Meleager lived under a strange curse, and it is worth going back to the time of his birth to hear about it. I have said that Meleager was the son of Oeneus, but it seems likely that Ares, the god of war, had some part in his paternity too. As we have already heard, this is a feature of the heroes of the age. It is certain, though, that his mother was Oeneus's queen ALTHAEA, who came from a most distinguished royal line herself, sometimes known, on account of its patriarch THESTIOS, as the THESTIADES. She had four brothers, an obscure sister called HYPERMNESTRA,

---

* His name means 'Man of Wine'.

† It's not entirely clear when in Jason's busy life this adventure took place. It is usually assumed to be between the return of the Argo and the flight from Iolcos after the death of Pelias.

whose name surely is due for a revival,* and another called Leda, whose experience with Zeus in the form of a swan was to inspire many artists in ages yet unborn. Her story is for another time. Our attention for now is on Althaea, who lay with Oeneus (or possibly Ares) and nine months later gave birth to a boy, Meleager.

It was a difficult labour and the effort sent Althaea into a deep sleep. The baby lay babbling in its cot before the fire. The mother slept on.

Into this peaceful scene crept the three Fates, the Moirai. This baby, who could well be a son of Ares, might have an important future and it was for the Fates to tell it in their usual manner.

Clotho spun the thread of Meleager's life and declared the boy would be noble. Lachesis measured it by drawing it out from Clotho's spindle. She foretold that Meleager would be accounted brave by all who knew him. Atropos snipped the length of the yarn and announced that for all her sisters' prognostications she knew that the child would only live as long as the central log in the fireplace remained unconsumed by fire.

'What can you mean?' asked Lachesis and Clotho.

'When that log burns up and is no more,' said Atropos, 'so will Meleager, son of Ares, Oeneus and Althaea, be no more!'

All three gave a cackle of delight and vanished into the night air chanting:

Meleager's life will end in a flash
When his log of fate is turned to ash

Althaea opened her eyes wide. Could she really have heard that right, or was it some mad dream? She got out of bed and

---

* It means, according to Robert Graves, 'excessive wooing'.

went to the fire. There was indeed a great log in the centre of the hearth. Flames were flickering around it, but it had not yet fully caught light. In her fevered imagination it resembled, in size and form, a newborn baby. Her own infant Meleager! She pulled the log out and dropped it hastily into a copper vat of water that stood warming by the fire. The flames went out with a sizzle. The baby gurgled happily in its cradle.

What should she do now? She wrapped the log in a swaddling blanket and hurried down to one of the unvisited and unused basement rooms in the palace, a room with an earthen floor where she could bury the log deep. Her son might have died in five minutes if she had done nothing. Now he might live for eternity!

So we have a picture of the Calydonian palace of King Oeneus and Queen Althaea, outside the walls of which rampages a marauding boar. Their heir, the tall, strong, noble and brave Prince Meleager – now fully grown – lives with them, of course, as do his six sisters – GORGE, MELANIPPE, EURYMEDE, Deianira*, MOTHONE and PERIMEDE – and his uncles, Althaea's four brothers, the Thestiades – TOXEUS, EVIPPUS, PLEXIPPUS and EURYPYLUS. The Thestiades are fine huntsmen, but fully aware that in order to corner and catch a prey as huge and monstrous as the Calydonian Boar they will need every member of the great hunting party that has answered Oeneus's summons.

But – what can this be? – the uncles burst out laughing when a tall woman, dressed in animal skins, a hunting bow over her shoulder and hounds at her feet, enters the palace and hurls a spear into the wall to stake her claim to join the hunting party.

---

* The Deianira who was to go on and play such a fateful role in the life and death of Heracles.

Meleager has taken one look at this slim, fierce, tanned, toned and beautiful girl and fallen instantly in love.*

'If she wants to join us, I have no objection.'

Meleager's uncles hoot with derision.

'Girls can't throw,' jeers Toxeus.

'Girls can't run in a straight line without bumping into trees or tripping over,' snorts Evippus.

'Girls can't shoot arrows without the bowstring snapping back and stinging them in the face,' smirks Plexippus.

'Girls don't have the stomach to kill,' sneers Eurypylus.

'Let us see,' says Atalanta, and at the sound of her dark, throbbing, yet commanding voice Meleager falls even more deeply in love.

She has gone to the window. 'Those three trees. Which of us can put an arrow in each trunk first?'

The uncles join her at the window and follow her gaze to a distant line of three aspens, shaking in the breeze.

'You may give the signal,' Atalanta tells Meleager.

Meleager raises an arm and drops it. 'Fire at will!' he cries.

The Thestiades scramble to pluck arrows from their quivers and draw back their bows but –

'Wheep, wheep, wheep!'

Three arrows fly in an instant from Atalanta's bow and now she is standing with her back to the window, her arms folded and a mocking smile playing on her face. Meleager and the uncles look over her shoulder and towards the trees. In each of the aspen trunks is embedded an arrow, perfectly centred.

In his hectic rush to draw at speed, Plexippus has fumbled his bow, which falls with a clatter to the floor. He does not take kindly to being made to look like a clumsy child.

---

* But Meleager is married already, to a very beautiful girl called CLEOPATRA (no relation to the one we know) the daughter of Prince IDAS and Princess MARPESSA.

'Ah, but strength,' he growls. 'I'll grant you may have a reasonable eye and quick hands, but this boar is fierce and strong. A mere woman could never hope –'

No one will ever discover what he is going to say next. Speech and breath are robbed of him as he finds himself quite unexpectedly lifted off his feet. Atalanta has picked him up and raised him above her head as if he were no heavier than a kitten.

'Where shall I throw him?' she enquires of the others. 'Out of the window or into the fire?'

Hastily they concede her right to join them in the hunt. But there is now disgruntlement in the ranks of the hunting party. The proud brothers cannot know, as we do, that Artemis not only sent the boar to Calydon, but also sent her most fanatical votary, Atalanta, to represent her in the hunt. Artemis intends, through Atalanta, to sow as much mischief in the ranks of the hunters as she can. How much Atalanta is a knowing proxy for the goddess and how much an unconscious vessel for her will has never quite been decided.

The smitten Meleager got nowhere with this wonderful girl who was, in the words of Edith Hamilton, 'too boyish to be a maiden, too maidenly to be a boy.' As a devoted follower of Artemis, Atalanta had, as a matter of course, turned her back on men and on love. Nonetheless, she welcomed Meleager as a companion, and for a young man so deeply in love, the thrilling propinquity of the beautiful huntress was better than nothing.

The classical sources name at least fifty members of the hunting party that gathers around Meleager and the four Thestiades. As with the manifest of the *Argo* there is much confusion and inconsistency in the sources and perhaps a deal of wishful thinking on the part of later grand Greek families who wanted to claim descent from these heroes.

Aside from Jason, the throng of former Argonauts present at the hunt includes Meleager's cousins, the heavenly twins Castor and Pollux; bold Pirithous, King of the Lapiths; wise Nestor of Pylos and the indefatigable brothers Peleus and Telamon; hospitable Admetus, the friend of Heracles and sometime lover of Apollo; and Asclepius, unrivalled master of the medical arts. Even the great Theseus is there, drawn as much by his bond with Pirithous as by the addiction to extreme peril that unites them all. Such a muster of heroes will not be seen in the world again until the Trojan War.

They are all men, save for Atalanta.

THE CALYDONIAN HUNT

Oeneus held nine nights of feasting and revelry to welcome and thank the brave heroes, huntsmen and warriors who had answered his call. On the morning of the tenth day they gathered outside the palace, hounds streaming at their feet, pages buckling armour, grooms tightening girths, stewards offering up cups of hot wine. The cheers of the citizens safe within the walls of Calydon grew to a great roar of gratitude, encouragement, admiration and pride as the party made its way out through the main gate. Carts loaded with spare javelins, axes, maces and arrows brought up the rear of the train as it headed into the deserted and despoiled countryside.

No boar this gigantic had ever been seen or even rumoured of, let alone tracked down and killed. As the hunting party proceeded they witnessed ever fouler scenes of horror. Every field of corn was trampled, every vineyard uprooted, every chicken, cat, dog, calf, goat and sheep lay with its throat torn open and innards exposed to the sun – whether the poor creatures had been massacred for food or fun, the shocked huntsmen did not know. A hundred wild boars of natural size could never have created such destruction.

Meleager and his uncles had formed a plan. Some miles to the north there stood a ruined barn. If the party were to spread themselves into a line, shouting, stamping their feet and shaking burning torches, they could slowly funnel the boar in that direction and use nets, fire and clamour finally to trap it in the angle of the two remaining walls of the barn. That would be their killing ground.

'It will be like a stage and the pig will be our doomed hero,' said Meleager.

The uncles and senior huntsmen nodded their assent.

It took all morning and much of the afternoon to encircle the boar and flush it from cover. They made as much noise as they could – a great hullaballoo and smashing of spears onto shields – but no one there felt that the boar, forced though it was in the direction of the barn, was in any way frightened. From time to time it would turn, break cover and charge at one part of the line, scaring everyone in it half to death, and then canter back towards the barn, tusks down, squealing out what seemed like a laugh of triumph and derision.

'Whenever it does that, it is vital that the line holds!' commanded Oeneus.

'Simple for him to say, up on a horse and well behind the line,' Atalanta said to herself. She watched with disdain as the king swigged from a horn of wine. Meleager, by her side, seemed to guess what she was thinking.

'The old man is no warrior, but he is a fine administrator,' he said. 'He has brought this region peace and prosperity.'

'Until he forgot the great goddess Artemis,' said Atalanta.

'Well, yes ... Look, up ahead! It's working, the plan is working!'

Sure enough, the boar seemed to be edging in fits and starts slowly backwards towards the ruined barn. They could hear its trotters scrape and slide as they met the stone flags of its floor. The front row of hounds, growing in confidence, thrust their snarling heads at it, teeth bared and slavering. It was a sound and sight to put the fear of Hades into anyone, but in the boar it seemed merely to awaken it to its situation. With sudden and unimagined speed it rushed forward with its head down. It jerked up under the jaw of the lead hound and its left tusk went straight through the throat and out of the dog's skull.

Down went the boar's head again. And up, ripping open the sides of the second hound.

The third, fourth and all the other hounds in the pack needed no further invitation to set up a great howl of fright and flee in panic to hide, quivering, between the legs of their masters.

The hunters now braced themselves to face the boar. Flesh and fur hung from the points of the boar's tusks and blood soaked its bristles. Its eyes, everyone swore afterwards, burned like bright coals. The fierce orange and red light of them was trained in turn on every man, and the one woman, who crowded in on it.

'Now, now is the time!' cried Meleager, throwing a hunting net over the boar.

It was half enmeshed but angered enough to roll over and thrash its feet and jerk its head to free itself. This was the first time it had shown any vulnerability and the sight pricked the courage of the hunters. With great whoops and hollers, one hero after another hurled himself with axe, sword, spear and dagger at the enraged beast. Its instinct was to gore at groin and belly. Gonads and guts were torn open to the air. Blood was everywhere. Piteous were the screams of the brave heroes who threw themselves to their deaths.

None were more fearless than PELAGON, HYLEUS, HIPPASUS and ENAESIMUS, the first to engage and be instantly ripped to pieces for their troubles. Peleus flung a javelin from his cover in a thicket only for it to find and fatally wound EURYTION, King of Phthia, one of the most loyal of the Argonauts.

It was, in both the literal as well as the more common sense, a shambles.

Already disheartened by the sight of so many good men killed, the huntsmen saw the accidental death of Eurytion as an ill omen and began to think of turning tail. The boar, sensing victory, raised its head, sniffed the air and charged at Nestor, King of Pylos, who even in his middle age was reputed to be the wisest man in the known world. Certainly he was wise enough to know that wailing and screaming would achieve nothing and so he stood still and raised his eyes to the heavens.

Atalanta stepped forward from behind him and called out, 'Drop down, Nestor! Down – *now*!'

Nestor threw himself to the ground at the same time as an arrow flew from Atalanta's bow, passed through the place where Nestor's heart had been but a moment earlier, and pierced the throat of the charging boar.

ALCON, a hot-headed son of both King Hippocoön of Amykles and Ares, the god of war, rose to his feet and waved his spear. Facing his comrades he yelled, 'For shame, brothers. This is no work for a woman. Let's show the world what a man can do!' He turned back in time to see the boar, Atalanta's arrow dangling from its neck, lowering its head for a charge. By the time Alcon had set his spear, the beast was on him. Both tusks entered his stomach. Now the boar raised its head and performed a kind of gruesome dance, pulling

Alcon round and round, the tusks tearing open more and more of his guts until all the poor young man's bowels and innards had fallen out to make a red and slimy circle on the stone floor of the barn.

Only Meleager stood firm as the monstrous animal tossed Alcon's corpse from its tusks and scraped at the ground ready for another charge. As the boar hurtled forward, Meleager slid down onto his left side; lying back, he took aim with his right arm. The boar saw the movement and gave a roar of fury. Meleager launched his javelin sideways and upwards – straight into the boar's open mouth. The tip of the spear pierced the upper skull, bursting its way out again coated in gore and brain matter. The great beast shuddered and fell dead to the ground, slipping and skidding on the blood and entrails of its victims.

Oeneus clambered down half drunk from his horse and embraced his son.

'Meleager, my boy. What honour you have done our house! Yours is the kill, yours the trophy. Come, skin the creature, take its tusks, then bring it back to the palace and we will feast and toast your triumph in wine!'

Meleager turned to face the surviving huntsmen who even now were cupping and drinking the blood that gushed from the boar's wounds. 'The hide and tusks are to go to Atalanta!' he declared. 'It was she who struck the first blow. Without her true aim the monster would still be at large and we would be carrion for the crows and foxes. The trophies are hers.'

Meleager's uncles came forward. The Thestiades had not been conspicuously in the forefront of the hunt, but their sense of family honour and male pride now spurred them on.

'That witch is an outsider,' said Toxeus.

'A deranged virgin who took one lucky shot,' said Eurypylus.

'The honour of the kill must go to the house of Thestios,' said Evippus.

'A woman's place is the hearth, harem or home, not the hunt,' said Plexippus.

'I tell you, the prize is Atalanta's,' said Meleager. 'It is my decision to make, not yours.'

Plexippus approached the body of the boar. He took out a knife and began to gouge his way to the root of the tusk.

'Leave it!' shouted Meleager.

Toxeus raised his bow.* 'Stand aside, nephew. If you do not present the trophy to the family, the family will take the trophy.'

With a roar of anger Meleager flicked a knife from his belt. It flew straight into Toxeus's eye.

Before Toxeus was dead on the ground, Meleager had thrust a sword into the side of Plexippus and slit the throat of Eurypylus. Only Evippus was now left alive.

At the sight of the blood-maddened fire in Meleager's eyes, Evippus dropped the sword he had been struggling to draw. 'Spare me, dear nephew!' he pleaded. 'Think of your mother. My sister. You cannot deprive her of four –'

Meleager, crazed by his love for Atalanta and crazed by the killing, had no time for mercy. He brought up his knee into the older man's groin. Evippus doubled up in pain, as Meleager took his head and twisted it once, twice, three times before the sound of the neck cracking assured him that the last of his uncles was dead.

Atalanta sighed in sorrow and turned away.

The women, children, priests, cowards, merchants and

---

* Toxeus actually means 'bowman', as in toxophily.

286

older men from the city and the palace were streaming out to view the body of the boar. Queen Althaea arrived in time to see her son Meleager standing in dazed triumph over the bodies of her four brothers.

Demented with sorrow and raging for revenge, Althaea ran back to the palace. Down to the cellars she went until she came at last to the deserted chamber in whose floor she had buried the log on the day her son was born. Meleager would live, Atropos and her fellow Moirai had proclaimed, for as long as that log was not consumed by fire. But Althaea was now inexorable: after killing her beloved brothers, Meleager had forfeited the right to live one moment longer.

She scrabbled at the earth and brought out the log, still wrapped in what was left of the woollen blanket she had swaddled it in all those years ago.

Meleager's life will end in a flash
When his log of fate is turned to ash

Althaea hurried into the kitchens, where a great open fire roared all day and all night. She looked up and saw that across the opening in the floor of the feasting room above a great spit had been suspended directly over the flames. On this the skinned and gutted carcass of the boar would be transfixed and slowly roasted for the evening's banquet.

Still engulfed by her fury, Althaea unwrapped the log and hurled it into the heart of the fire.

The instant she saw the old log spark and bloom into flames Althaea regretted what she had done. She tried to find a way to pull it out, but the heat was too intense. She could not reclaim the log without burning up herself.

But perhaps, she told herself, she had only dreamed the whispered conversation between the three Fates all those years ago. She had long convinced herself that this was probably so. The proclamations of the Moirai were not for mortal ears. They would never have talked to each other if there had been a chance of being overheard. It had all been imagination.

Surely!

She stroked her cheek with the tattered blanket.

Surely?

Althaea turned and ran outside, drawn by a sense of deep and terrible foreboding towards the shouts of horror that came from the ruined barn where lay the corpses of the Calydonian Boar and so many heroes, including her brothers.

She arrived in time to see her son Meleager running, jumping and screaming in pain, his voice sounding horribly like the squealing of the monstrous boar.

'I'm burning! I'm burning!' he screeched. 'Help me, mother! Help me!'

Everyone pulled back in confusion and apprehension to see this brave young man so suddenly overtaken by madness. No flames leapt from him, yet he howled and writhed back and forth, falling to the ground and rolling over and over as if he were being consumed by living, scorching flame. Finally his screams turned to sobs, his sobs to a great shuddering sigh and he fell silent, quite dead. His body, as the soul left it, blackened, charred and disintegrated into grey ashes that were whipped away by the wind, leaving behind nothing but a memory of the proud and handsome Meleager's mortal remains.

With a grief-stricken wail Althaea ran blindly into the woods.

They found her some hours later, suspended from the branch of a tree, remnants of an old blanket clutched in her hands. Before she hanged herself she had torn out her own cheeks in the wild throes of her anguish.

This whole sorry train of events came about, you may recall, because King Oeneus had failed properly to worship Artemis. Her punishment was first to send a boar that ravaged the countryside and nearly brought ruin to Oeneus's kingdom, then to despatch Atalanta to sow discord amongst his family and the warriors who gathered to his aid. The hunt itself resulted in the deaths of dozens of fine heroes before the outbreak of enmities that caused the slaughter of Oeneus's brothers-in-law, the uncanny seizure and death of his son Meleager and the frightful suicide of his wife Althaea. But Artemis didn't stop there. She transformed the Meleagrids – Meleager's grieving sisters Melanippe, Eurymede, Mothone and Perimede – into guinea fowl, who clucked and mourned their brother for eternity.*

Two other daughters of Althaea and Oeneus were spared by Artemis, however. They were Gorge and Deianira, whom Moros, fate, had marked out for important contributions to the heroic years to come.†

Atalanta, her task complete, left the bitter and blighted kingdom of Calydon, never to return.

THE FOOT RACE

Atalanta's triumphant role in the Calydonian Boar Hunt caused her name to be sounded far and wide. It came to the ears of her father King Schoeneus. He had cruelly left her to die exposed on a mountainside, but now he was only too keen to welcome her back to his palace. He may have been

---

* To this day there are species of guinea fowl and turkey that bear the scientific name meleagrididae.
† See under Heracles for the fate of Deianira. Her sister Gorge had a child by her own father, Oeneus, who grew up to feature in the Trojan War.

the first cruel, abusive and unfit parent to reclaim a child once they became famous or rich, but he would certainly not be the last.

'My darling child,' he said, spreading his arms wide to show the breadth of his kingdom, 'this will all be yours.'

'Really?' said Atalanta.

'Well, your husband's, naturally,' said Schoeneus.

Atalanta shook her head. 'I will never marry.'

'But consider! You are my only child. If you do not marry and have children, the kingdom will go to outsiders.'

Atalanta's devotion to Artemis and her lifelong objection to marriage had not altered. 'I will only a marry a man,' she said, 'who can . . .'

She considered. She was a superb shot with a bow, but it was conceivable that the man might live who was better. It was the same with her skill with javelin, discus and on horseback. What was there that no man could ever best her at? Ah! She had it.

'I will only a marry man who can run faster than me.'

'Very well. So let it be.'

Atalanta was safe. Her speed could never be matched.*

'Oh, and any suitor who takes the challenge and fails must die,' she added.

Schoeneus grunted his assent and arranged for the word to be put out.

Great was Atalanta's fame and beauty, great the value of Schoeneus's kingdom and great the conviction of many fine, fit and fast young fellows that no woman could ever best them. Many made the journey to Arcadia: all were defeated and all were killed. The crowds loved it.

In amongst the spectators one day was a young man called

---

* And never was, until Achilles . . .

HIPPOMENES. He watched a prince from Thessaly run against Atalanta, lose and be taken off to be beheaded. The crowd cheered as his head rolled in the dust but all Hippomenes could think of was Atalanta. Her impossible swiftness. Those long striding legs. The hair streaming behind. The stern frown on that beautiful face.

He was in love and he meant to win her. But how could he do it? He was no runner – the prince who had just lost his head was much faster, and had been nowhere in sight when Atalanta crossed the finish line.

Hippomenes made his way to a temple of Aphrodite, knelt before the statue of the goddess and prayed his heart out.

The statue seemed to move and he heard a voice whisper in his ear. 'Look behind the altar and take the things you see. Use them to win the race.'

Hippomenes opened his eyes. Fragrant incense was burning strongly. Had wreaths of its smoke snaked into his head and made him imagine Aphrodite's voice? He was alone in the temple; surely there was no harm in looking behind the altar.

Something gleamed in the shadows. He reached out a hand and pulled out one, two, *three* golden apples.

'Thank you, Aphrodite, thank you!' he whispered.

The following day Atalanta looked at the next young man foolish enough to challenge her to a race, the next young lamb to the slaughter.

'What a pity,' she thought to himself, 'he's rather good-looking. A young Apollo. But he's stupid enough to have a satchel slung over his shoulder. Doesn't he know how much that will slow him down? Ah well . . .' she crouched and waited for the starting signal.

Hippomenes set off after her as fast as he could. His running style was poor at best, but hampered by the bag of apples swinging from his shoulder it was preposterous enough to cause the crowd to hoot with laughter. They howled even louder when he started fumbling with the bag.

'He's decided to have his lunch, now!'

Hippomenes took out one of the apples and rolled it along the ground ahead of him. It shot along the track and overtook Atalanta, who sprinted after it and picked it up.

How beautiful, she thought, turning it round in her hand. A golden apple! Like the apples Gaia gave Zeus and Hera as a wedding gift. The apples in the Garden of the Hesperides. Or perhaps this one came from Aphrodite's sacred apple tree in Cyprus? She glanced up to see Hippomenes flailing past her. 'I'll soon reel *him* in,' she muttered to herself, shooting off again.

Indeed, it wasn't long before she had passed him. She was just feeling the heft of the apple in her hand when *another* one rolled past her. Once again she stopped to pick it up; once again Hippomenes overtook her; once again she regained her position ahead of him with ease.

The third apple Hippomenes deliberately rolled at an angle, so that as it shot past Atalanta it veered off the track. Atalanta saw it flash by and took off in hot pursuit. The damned thing was stuck in an acacia bush. Its thorns scratched her and caught in her hair as she plucked it out. She now had three golden apples. How marvellous. But there was that damned boy racing past her again. She turned and streaked after him.

It was too late! Unbelievable, but true. The crowd roared as the exhausted Hippomenes crossed the line arms aloft and staggered, doubled up, hands on hips, sobbing and panting from the exertion.

Atalanta came through in a creditable but shocked second place.

She was too honourable to go back on her word and she

and Hippomenes were soon married. You can say it was the work of Aphrodite, you can say it was love – it amounts to the same thing – but Atalanta found herself growing fonder and fonder of Hippomenes until it could safely be said that she loved him with an ardour equal to his for her. They had a son, PARTHENOPAEUS, who grew up to be one of the Seven against Thebes.* Their married life, though, was to end strangely.

It seems that Hippomenes neglected to thank Aphrodite properly for her aid in winning Atalanta. As a punishment, she visited great lust upon the couple while they were visiting a temple sacred to the goddess CYBELE †. Unable to resist the urge, they made furious love on the floor of her temple. The outraged Cybele transformed the pair into lions. This might not seem so terrible a punishment, lions being kings of the jungle and high up the food chain; but to the Greeks it was the worst fate that could befall lovers, for they believed that lions and lionesses were unable to mate with each other. Lion cubs, they thought, came exclusively from the union of lions and leopards. And so Atalanta and Hippomenes were doomed to live out their lives drawing Cybele's chariot, closely harnessed to each other but eternally denied the pleasure of sex.

---

* See the story of Oedipus (page 323). Parthenopaeus was described by most sources as long-haired, fast-running and outstandingly beautiful, like his mother. He figures prominently as a heroic figure in Statius's *Thebiad*.
† Cybele was a Phrygian deity associated with both Artemis and Gaia.

OEDIPUS

THE ORACLE SPEAKS

The Greeks believed that the first city state, or *polis*, to appear in the world was Thebes in Boeotia, the first *polis* or city state.* The family of its founder hero Cadmus could claim amongst its members the only Olympian god with mortal blood in his veins. It was notorious for internecine dynastic wars, curses and homicides that for catastrophic generational ruin matched even those of Tantalus and the doomed house of Atreus. If they weren't casseroling their children they were sacrificing them; while those who made it to adulthood, if they weren't committing incest with their parents were murdering them.†

To be biblical, Cadmus and HARMONIA begat Semele, who exploded and begat Dionysus, her son by Zeus. Cadmus and Harmonia also begat Agave, Autonoë and Ino. Agave begat PENTHEUS, who was torn to pieces by all three of the sisters, his mother included – a fate arranged by the god Dionysus as punishment for the women's failure to honour his mother, their sister Semele.‡ Ino, as we saw in the preamble to the story of Jason, begat Learchus and Melicertes, tried to

---

* The foundation of Thebes, as befits its precedence, is recounted in the first volume of *Mythos* (page 224).
† The story of Tantalus is treated in *Mythos* (page 261): the fate of House of Atreus belongs to the story of the Trojan War.
‡ See the first volume of *Mythos* (page 230).

get Phrixus and Helle sacrificed and was finally transformed into Leucothea, the white goddess of the sea.

As well as their four daughters, Cadmus and Harmonia also begat a son, POLYDORUS, who begat LABDACUS, who begat LAIUS,* who – as if the enmity of Ares and Dionysus was not enough to blight the fortunes of the house of Cadmus – attracted a new curse.†

Without going into too much detail, when Laius was still a baby, his father Labdacus had been overthrown by the twins AMPHION and ZETHUS.‡ His life in peril, the infant Laius had been smuggled out of Thebes by Cadmean loyalists keen to ensure that the royal line could one day be restored.

Laius grew up as the guest of King Pelops of Pisa§. It seems he fell in love with Pelops's illegitimate son CHRYSIPPUS, taught him chariot driving and took him to the Nemean Games, where the youth competed in the races.

Instead of returning him safely home to Pelops, Laius brought Chrysippus with him when he went on from the games to Thebes to reclaim his throne. Chrysippus, who did not consent to this abduction and was ashamed of his public position as a kept lover, committed suicide.¶ When news of

---

* Pronounced *Lie-us*.

† The curse of Ares had lain on the royal house of Thebes ever since Cadmus slew the Ismenian water dragon. See the first volume of *Mythos* (pages 220 and 244).

‡ They were responsible for finishing the construction of Thebes' walls and its acropolis, the Cadmeia. See the first volume of *Mythos* (page 225).

§ As previously pointed out, not the Italian Pisa, but a city state in the Peloponnese (which hadn't yet earned that name from Pelops), the large peninsula to the south west of Greece joined to the mainland by the Isthmus of Corinth. It was inherited by Pelops when he won the hand of Hippodamia in marriage. See the story of Perseus (page 14).

¶ Another version of the story maintains that Chrysippus was killed by his half-brothers Atreus and THYESTES out of jealousy at their father's love for him. Euripides wrote a play about the life and fate of Chrysippus that is sadly lost to us.

this reached Pelops he cursed Laius and his line for ever.

Whether as a result of the curse or slack sperm motility, or both, Laius – who had reclaimed the throne that was his birthright and married a Theban noblewoman called JOCASTA – found that he was unable to father a child. Not for the first time we follow a king without an heir as he visits the Delphic oracle for advice.

The son of Laius and Jocasta shall kill his father.

Well, that would never do. The prophecy that had told Acrisius of Argos he would be killed by his grandson was bad enough, but this . . . Acrisius had indeed died at the hand of his grandson, the hero Perseus, even if it was an accident; but Acrisius, Laius thought to himself, had been a fool. *He* would have found a surer way to beat the oracle than throwing the infant in a wooden chest and casting him into the sea. *He* would have had the brat's head chopped off and there would have been an end to it. Nonetheless, perhaps it might be safer to stay away from the marriage bed.

But Laius was a man, wine was wine and Jocasta was beautiful. The morning following a great feast, he barely remembered having spent a night of passion with her; but when, nine months later, she presented him with a baby son, he began to understand Acrisius's dilemma. To kill his own son would be to invite the certain fury of . . . the Furies. He sat on his throne and pulled on his beard. At last he sent for his most trusted servant, Antimedes.

'Take this baby and expose it on the highest point of Mount Cithaeron.'

'Yes, my lord.'

'And, Antimedes, just to be sure, stake him to the hillside. I don't want him crawling away, you understand?'

Antimedes bowed and did as he was told, piercing the

infant's ankles with iron staples and shackling them to a peg that he drove deep into the ground.

It was not long before a shepherd called PHORBAS came on the scene, attracted by the loud wails.

'Oh my good gods,' he cried, smashing the fetters with a rock and cradling the bawling infant in his arms. 'Who can have done such a terrible thing?'

The baby screamed and screamed.

'Shush, now, little one. It's no good me keeping you. Plain country people don't treat babies this way. Only a great and powerful ruler can have done a thing so cruel. No, I daren't be found with you.'

It happened that Phorbas had a friend from Corinth staying with him, another herdsman. This friend, Straton by name, was happy enough to take the abandoned foundling home with him.

Back in Corinth, Straton presented the baby to his king and queen, POLYBUS and MEROPE. Long childless themselves, they adopted the infant and brought him up as their own son. On account of the scars from the shackles that had staked him to the ground, they called him Oedipus, which means 'swollen foot'.

So Oedipus grew up far away from Thebes, wholly ignorant of his true origins. His life might have turned out like that of any attractive, intelligent, proud princeling – especially one so much indulged by loving parents – were it not for the spite of a drinking companion who had always been jealous of his popularity and casual air of superiority. One evening the sight of beautiful young women queuing up for Oedipus's attentions maddened the young man past enduring.

'They only go for you because they think you're a prince,' he blurted out, deep in wine.

'Well,' said Oedipus with a smile, 'I know it's unfair, but

as it happens I *am* a prince, and there isn't much I can do about it.'

'You may think you are,' jeered the friend. 'But you're not.'

'Excuse me?'

'You're a peasant orphan bastard, nothing more.'

The others in the group tried to silence him, but the drink and malice had taken hold.

'Queen Merope was always infertile, everyone knows that. Barren as the Libyan desert. You were adopted, mate. You're no more a royal prince than I am. Less probably. Ask your so-called parents how you got those scars on your feet.'

Other friends rushed to undo the damage.

'Don't listen, Oedipus. He doesn't know what he's saying. You can see how drunk he is.'

But Oedipus read the fear in their eyes plain enough. After a sleepless night he went to the king and queen for reassurance.

'Of course you're our son! What makes you think otherwise?'

'The scars on my ankles?'

'You were a breech birth. They had to pull you out of my womb with pincers.'

So outraged and indignant were Polybus and Merope that Oedipus believed them. *Almost* believed them. There was a certain way to settle the question once and for all. He made his way to the oracle at Delphi.

He did not know what he expected in reply to the simple, bald question, 'Who are my true parents?' but it was not the simple, bald answer he received.

Oedipus will kill his father and mate with his mother

That was all he could get out of the Pythia. As ever with oracles, all supplementary questions were met with silence.

Oedipus left Delphi in a daze, striking out on a road that took him in the exact opposite direction from Corinth. He must never see Polybus and Merope again. The risk of harming Polybus through some accident was too great. And as for the second part of the prophecy . . . the idea made him feel physically sick. He was very fond of his mother, but in *that way*?

One thing was certain, the greater the distance he put between himself and Corinth, the better.

WHERE THREE ROADS MEET

Oedipus was beginning to enjoy his wanderings. As a prince of Corinth he had become accustomed to being escorted everywhere by stewards, pages and bodyguards. He found life on the road as a free and unaccompanied traveller full of interest. He took pleasure in finding ways to make the small supply of coins in his purse go further. He slept in hedge-rows, offered himself up in each village and town he came to as a gardener, schoolteacher, minstrel, baker's assistant or whatever might be needed. He was good with his hands, fast on his feet and matchlessly quick with his wits. Mental arith-metic, languages, accounting, the memorising of long lines of poetry – they all came easily and quickly to his supremely agile brain.

One afternoon, in the countryside outside the small town of Daulis, he found himself at a place where three roads met. While he stood debating with himself which one to take, an opulent chariot sped towards him. The old man driving stood up in his seat and tried to force him out of the way.

'Move, peasant!' he shouted and struck down with a whip.

This was more than the proud Oedipus could bear. He

snatched at the whip and pulled, jerking the old man out of the chariot. Four armed men jumped down from the back and ran towards him, shouting. Oedipus wrested a sword from one and in the fight that followed killed three. The fourth ran away. When Oedipus stooped to examine the old man, he discovered that he had fatally broken his neck in the fall.

Oedipus covered the four corpses with earth and commended their spirits to the underworld. Uncoupling the horses from the chariot, he slapped their hindquarters and sent them skittering down the road.

Once again he debated which way he should take. In his head he named the choices 'Road One', 'Road Two' and 'Road Three', plucked a branch from an olive tree and picked off the leaves one by one, counting as he did so. 'One, two, three . . . one, two, three . . . one, two, three . . . one, *two*! So be it. I take Road Two.'

What might have happened had one more leaf – or one fewer – grown on that branch we can never know. Matters of immense import may depend on such issues, but we can never do more than guess the outcomes of the roads we do not take.

Oedipus walked cheerfully down Road Two and that was that. His fate was sealed.

THE RIDDLE OF THE SPHINX

The province of Boeotia through which Oedipus had been walking was a land of pleasant fields, gentle valleys and sparkling rivers. He found that the path he had chosen rose up towards a mountain pass. A voice called to him.

'Wouldn't go that way, if I were you.'

Oedipus turned to see an old man leaning on a stick.

'No? Why not?'

'That's Mount Phicium, is that.'

'So?'

'Haven't you heard tell of the Sphinx?'

'No. What is a "Sphinx"?'

'I'm a poor man.'

Oedipus sighed and dropped a coin into the man's outstretched palm.

'Thankee kindly, sir.' The old man wheezed and crinkled his eyes. 'Some say the Sphinx was sent by the Queen of Heaven herself as a punishment to King Laius. You've heard of him, at least?'

Oedipus had always paid attention in the schoolroom. He had been obliged to commit to memory endless lists of dull provincial kings, princes and tribal chiefs. 'Laius, King of Thebes. Son of Labdacus, son of Polydorus, son of Cadmus.'

'You've got him. Great-grandson of the sower of the dragon's teeth himself. Husband to Queen Jocasta and a mighty powerful king and lord.'

'So why would Hera wish to punish him?'

'Ah, well now. He raped Chrysippus of Pisa, so they say. The lad killed himself, at any rate.'

'I heard the story. But surely that was ages ago?'

'Twenty years or more. But what's that to the gods?'

'And so she sent this sphincter . . . ?'

'Ha! You're a funny one. *Sphinx*, I said. Terrible creature, head of a mortal woman, but the body of a lion and the wings of a bird. You don't want to mess with her. She stands at the top of the pass there, just where you was headed. She stops every traveller with a riddle. If they can't answer it right, she throws them down to their deaths on the rocks below. Nobody's answered the riddle yet. Trade nor traffic from the north can't get through to Thebes. You want to go there, you'd best go all the way round the mountain to avoid her.'

'I'm good at riddles,' said Oedipus.

The old man shook his head. 'See the buzzards circling in the air? They'll be picking the flesh from your broken bones.'

'Or from the sphincter's.'

'Sphinx, boy. That's a *Sphinx*, and don't you forget it.'

Oedipus left him cackling, wheezing and tutting, and walked on.

It was true that he was good at riddles. He had invented a whole new style of word game in which you rearranged the letters of one word to make another.* He had stumbled across the idea as a child when told the story of Python, the great snake that Gaia – Mother Earth – had sent up to guard the Omphalos, the navel stone of Greece at Pytho, now called Delphi.† Oedipus had excitedly pointed out to his mother that Typhon, another of Gaia's great monster sons, shared the same letters as Python.

'And Hera is the same as her mother Rhea!' he had cried.

'Very good, dear. But it doesn't *mean* anything.'‡

No, he supposed that it didn't. But it was fun. Conundrums, puzzles and codes continued to delight him and bore most other people. Now the prospect of a life-or-death riddle appealed to his intellectual vanity.

The mountain pass was narrowing as he ascended. The old man had been right about the buzzards, a full dozen wheeled above him, screeching in anticipation.

---

* The Greek for that is 'anagram'.

† Zeus's mother RHEA had fooled her husband Kronos into eating the stone, thinking it was the infant Zeus. When Kronos later vomited up the stone, Zeus threw it so that it landed at Pytho/Delphi. See the first volume of *Mythos* (page 97).

‡ And of course, in Greek letters Python and Typhon are *not* anagrams, but we'll pretend we don't know that.

'Halt!'

He looked up and saw a winged figure crouching on a ledge above him. It leapt down and landed softly on the path in front of him, opening and closing its wings.

A human face, the body of a lion, just as the old man had said.*

'Good morning, sir,' said Oedipus.

'Sir? *Sir?* Are you blind?'

'Forgive me. Hard to tell. I can't even be sure which is your face and which your arse.'

'Oh, I am going to enjoy watching you die,' said the Sphinx, her lion's fur bristling.

'You'll have quite a wait,' said Oedipus. 'I don't plan on doing that for years yet. Now, if you'll excuse me, I have to get through.'

'Not so fast! No one passes me unless they can answer my riddle.'

'Oh, I see. The riddle being why your mother didn't strangle you at birth? No?'

The Sphinx, who thought herself exceptionally fine-looking – as indeed she was – spat with rage. 'You will answer the riddle or die!' She indicated the sheer face of the cliff below her. Oedipus looked down. Hundreds of bleached human bones lay scattered on the rocks beneath.

'Ooh. Nasty. Right then, fire away. Haven't got all day. Have to be in Thebes before night.'

The Sphinx settled herself down and tried to compose herself. She had never met anyone quite like Oedipus before.

'Tell me this, traveller. What walks on four feet in the morning, two feet at noon and three in the evening?'

---

* The Sphinx is usually given as a child of Echidna and Typhon, though some sources suggest she was their grandchild – a daughter of Orthrus and Chimera.

'Hm . . . four feet in the morning, two at noon, three in the evening?'

'Just give me the answer to that,' purred the Sphinx, 'and you may freely pass.'

Oedipus sucked in through his teeth. 'Man, oh man,' he said, shaking his head, 'that's a teaser and no mistake.'

'Ha! You can't solve it, then?'

'But I did,' said Oedipus raising his eyebrows in surprise. 'Didn't you hear me?'

The Sphinx stared. 'What do you mean?'

'I just told you. "Man, oh man," I said. And "man" is the answer. When Man is born, in the morning of his existence, he crawls on all fours; in his prime, the noontime of his day, he goes upright on two legs; but in the evening of his life he has a third – a stick to help him on his way.'

'B-but . . . how . . . ?'

'It's called "intelligence". Now let me try one out on you. Let me see . . . What has the face of a hag, the body of a sow, the wings of a pigeon and the brains of a pea? No?'

The Sphinx reared up with a screech and before she had time to open her wings, fell backwards off the cliff's edge, claws thrashing the air, down onto the rocks below. With screams of delight, the buzzards swooped.

Oedipus passed on and began to make his own, more gentle, descent from the mountain.

The city of Thebes lay spread out in the valley below, threaded through by the waters of Lake Copais. As he went he encountered shepherds, goatherds and a body of soldiers who were all amazed to see someone coming down from the mountain pass. By the time he reached the gates of Thebes, the story of his defeat of the Sphinx had spread throughout the city. He was welcomed by an ecstatic populace, who carried him shoulder-high to the palace and the presence of their ruler, Creon.

'You have rid us of a quite terrible problem, young man,' said Creon. 'That creature not only choked off an important commercial route, her presence caused many to believe that Thebes lay under a curse. Other cities and kingdoms were refusing to trade with us. My sister, the queen, wishes to thank you personally.'

Queen Jocasta welcomed the hero with a sweet smile. Oedipus smiled back. She was older than him by some years, but remarkably beautiful.

'You are in mourning, majesty,' he said bowing low and holding her hand for a little longer than many might have thought suitable.

'My husband, the king,' Jocasta replied. 'He was ambushed and killed by a gang of robbers. My brother Creon has been ruling as regent ever since.'

'My sincere condolences, madam.'

What a *very* attractive woman, Oedipus thought to himself.

What a *very* attractive young man, Jocasta thought to herself.

LONG LIVE THE KING

Oedipus stayed on in the royal palace of Thebes, an honoured guest. He had quickly proved himself invaluable to Creon. His grasp of the intricacies of commerce, taxation and governance astounded the older man. Jocasta, meanwhile, adored his company. They played games together, sang songs and composed poetry.

One afternoon Oedipus approached Creon and asked if he might have a private word with him.

'It's your sister Jocasta,' he said. 'We've fallen in love. I know she is older than me, but –'

'My dear fellow!' Creon grasped him warmly by the hand. 'Do you think I'm blind? I saw from the first that there was something between you. Eros shot from his bow the moment you met. I couldn't be happier. And Oedipus . . . if you are to marry the queen, why, you must be crowned king.'

'Sir, I wouldn't for a moment wish to usurp your –'

'"Usurp" poppycock. And no "sirs", brother. A young king is just what the city needs. The people love you. You were sent by the gods, who can doubt it?'

And so, to widespread rejoicing, Oedipus married Jocasta and was crowned King of Thebes in a grand ceremony on the Cadmeia. The Thebans loved Oedipus. Aside from the great victory over the Sphinx, his arrival seemed to have brought the city luck.

In the opinion of Creon and the council of Theban elders, their new king was strikingly *modern*. Oedipus rarely conferred with priests. He was negligent in his attendance at the temples on all but the most important holy days. He was almost blasphemous in his casual approach to prayer and sacrifice. But he was remarkably energetic, efficient and effective. He drew up mathematical tables and charts connected to everything from taxation to population, he instituted laws on household and palace management, on justice and on trade.

The money from taxation and tariffs rolled in like never before, of which a proportion was expended on schools and gymnasia, *asclepia** and roads. Oedipus's name for this radically new style of government was *logarchy*, 'rule by reason'. Every Theban agreed that they had been ruled over by no wiser a king since the days of their great founder Cadmus.

---

* An *asclepion* was a cross between a health spa, a hospital and a temple to Asclepius.

King Oedipus and Queen Jocasta had four children: two boys, ETEOCLES and POLYNICES, and two girls, ANTIGONE and ISMENE. It was a happy family. With the city continuing to prosper and flourish so that it became the envy of the Greek world, onlookers predicted a long and successful reign.

And so it might have been, were it not for the outbreak of a terrible epidemic.

Rumours were heard of a family struck down with a disease that had made them vomit and flame with fever for a day before dying. Soon the sickness was smouldering through the streets of the poorer quarter of the city; then it burned like a wildfire through all of Thebes. Scarcely a household was unaffected.

The calm logic and reason that Oedipus espoused as the answer to all ills now looked insufficient. Frightened citizens crowded the temples and the air was soon filled with sacrificial smoke. Petitions reached the king, who turned to Creon.

'I have to admit that I am stumped,' said Oedipus. 'I try to tell the people that plagues are part of the natural order of things, and will naturally pass in time, but they insist on believing they betoken some kind of divine punishment or cosmic retribution.'

'Let me travel to the Delphic oracle and see if it offers any advice,' said Creon. 'What harm can it do?'

Oedipus was sceptical, but he consented. While Creon was away, Oedipus and Jocasta's own daughter Ismene fell ill and nearly died. She was still recovering when Creon returned, grim-faced.

'Delphi was crowded,' he said. 'I queued up as an ordinary citizen. When my turn came at last I asked the Pythia one question, "Why is Thebes suffering from plague?"'

'Not "How do we get rid of it?"' asked Oedipus.

'It amounts to the same thing, surely?' said Creon. 'Anyway, this was the Pythia's answer: *"Thebes will be relieved when the murderer of King Laius is named and found."*'

Jocasta gasped. 'But that's absurd. Laius was killed by a gang!'

Oedipus thought hard. 'If it was a gang, one of them must have dealt the fatal blow. The truth can always be uncovered if you go about it systematically. But let me first say this. Make it known that whoever dares house or protect the killer of Laius will be punished. As for the killer himself – my curse is on him. He will wish he'd never been born. He will be identified, hunted down and justice served on him without mercy. I'll see to it personally. So let it be proclaimed.'

'Very good,' said Creon. 'And there's always Tiresias. All the way home, I was thinking "Why on earth didn't we consult Tiresias?"'

'Surely he can't still be alive?' Oedipus had heard of the great Theban seer. Everyone had. 'He must be ancient.'

'He is not young, certainly, but he still has his wits. We can send for him.'

Messengers were despatched to Tiresias. Oedipus was curious to meet the prophet who had undergone so much at the hands of the gods. As a young man, Tiresias had aroused the wrath of Hera, who turned him into a woman. He served in her temple as a priestess for seven years before she restored him to male form. Then he had the misfortune to attract her ire again and this time she struck him blind. Out of pity Zeus gave him inner sight, the gift of prophecy.* For generations his wisdom and prophetic powers had been at the service of the Theban royal house, but now he lived in secluded retirement.

---

* See the first volume of *Mythos* for the full story (page 330).

Tiresias was not pleased to be hauled to the palace in the middle of the night and summoned before a man a quarter of his age. The interview did not go well. Oedipus expected all the deference due to a king and especially to the great ruler and Sphinx-slayer who had transformed the fortunes of Thebes and its people. Instead he was treated with grumpy insolence.

'I am blind,' said Tiresias, leaning on his long staff. 'But it is you who cannot see. Or perhaps you refuse to see. Those who curse are most accursed. Those who look out are those who most need to look in.'

'No doubt the unlettered and the credulous are fooled by your mystical drivel and portentous riddles,' said Oedipus, 'but I am not. Riddles just happen to be my speciality.'

'I am not talking in riddles,' said Tiresias, fixing his blind eyes on a spot just above Oedipus's head. 'I speak clearly. You want to find the polluter of Thebes, then look in the mirror.'

Oedipus could get no more out of him and sent him back to his villa in the country. 'And put him in the most uncomfortable cart you can find. Let his mad old bones have some sense shaken into them as he goes.'

'Damn such people,' Oedipus said to Jocasta when he reported on the interview later. 'The oracle at Delphi we know to be truthful. It is directed by Apollo and the ancient powers of Gaia herself, but this Tiresias is nothing but a fraud. Full of all that "You will not find the truth but the truth will find you", "Seek not to know, but know to seek", "You don't make mistakes, mistakes make you", rubbish. Anyone can do it, you just turn sentences upside down and inside out. Horse shit. Meaningless. He must think I'm an idiot.'

'Sh . . .' said Jocasta, 'take wine and calm yourself.'

'Ah,' said Oedipus wagging his finger, closing his eyes and

giving a fair imitation of Tiresias. 'Take wine, but do not let wine take you.'

Jocasta laughed. 'Anyway,' she said. 'I wouldn't set too much store even by the oracle at Delphi. It foretold that Laius would be killed by his son, not by a gang of robbers.'

'Yes, I meant to ask you again about the death of Laius,' said Oedipus. 'If he and his party were all killed, how can we find out anything about the gang responsible?'

'Oh, but they weren't *all* killed. Antimedes, one of Laius's servants, escaped. He ran back to Thebes to tell us what had happened.'

'And what exactly did he say?'

'He said it had been an ambush. There were more than a dozen of them, all armed with clubs and swords. They sprang out at a place where three roads met. They pulled Laius out of his chariot . . .'

Oedipus stared at her. 'Say that again.'

'They pulled him out of his chariot –'

'No. Before that. "Where three roads met"?'

'So Antimedes said.'

'Where is this Antimedes now?'

'He lives near Ismenos, I think.'

'And he's truthful?'

'My husband trusted him above all his servants.'

'He must be fetched.'

Oedipus was thinking furiously. An old man pulled from a chariot where three roads met. A coincidence, surely. After all, this Antimedes had described a murderous gang, bristling with weapons, not one unarmed young man. All the same, it was disturbing.

He paced the palace grounds and waited for the arrival of Antimedes. The plague continued to claim dozens of lives a day.

'I can't solve this without more information,' he said to himself. 'Without fresh facts, the brain just churns round and round, like a wheel stuck in mud.'

The next morning Oedipus was sitting with Jocasta when a page came forward.

'A messenger, sire.'

'News from Antimedes?'

'No, majesty, this man is from Corinth.'

'Can't it wait?'

'He says it is urgent, sire.'

'Oh well, send him in.'

'Corinth,' said Jocasta as the page withdrew. 'Isn't that where you grew up?'

'Yes. I haven't thought about the place for years. Now, sir. What brings you here?'

A weather-beaten and sunburnt old man had entered and was bowing low. 'Great majesty.'

'Yes, yes,' said Oedipus, peering at him with some surprise. 'You look exhausted.'

'I came by foot, sire.'

'I don't know who chose you as a messenger, but it was unkind to send someone so past their prime of life on such a long journey. I hope you will stay with us and rest before returning.'

'You are considerate and kind, sire,' said the messenger. 'As for the journey, I myself begged to be the one chosen to come to you.'

'Oh?'

'I wanted to look with my own eyes on the face of the famous King Oedipus.'

Oedipus, never impervious to flattery, smiled. 'As the queen will tell you, I'm just an ordinary man,' he said.

'Never that, my dear,' said Jocasta. She smiled at the

messenger. 'Your news is urgent, we are told. Rest your legs and tell us.'

'I will stand, majesty,' said the messenger, declining the offered stool, 'for the news I bear is heavy. You father, sire, King Polybus . . .'

'What of him?'

'His life's course is run.'

'Dead?'

'It must come to us all, sire. His life was long and filled with blessings.'

'How did he die?'

'In his bed, sire. Queen Merope held his hand as he breathed his last. He was well beyond his eightieth year. It was his time.'

'Ha!' said Oedipus, clapping his hands. 'So much for oracles. Don't look shocked,' he added quickly. 'I am filled with sorrow to hear of the death of my father. He was a fine man and a wise king.'

Jocasta pressed his hand and murmured her sympathy.

'May I hope, majesty,' said the messenger, 'that you will return to Corinth with me for the funeral ceremony? And that you will take up the throne? Queen Merope yearns for it.'

'How is my mother?'

'Full of grief for the loss of her husband, and for the loss of her son, too. The young man who walked out one day and never returned.'

'I have written to her many times,' said Oedipus. 'But there are deep and secret reasons why I may never set foot in Corinth again.'

'The people long for you, majesty.'

'Surely there is no reason why you cannot reign in Thebes *and* Corinth?' said Jocasta. 'Double kingdoms have been known. Look at Argolis. It would be a wonder and a glory for you to reign over two great cities.'

'Not while my mother is alive,' said Oedipus.

Jocasta's look of puzzlement provoked an explanation. 'Since we were talking earlier about oracles, you should know this. When I was young, I visited Delphi and was told that it was my destiny to kill my father and . . . share a bed with my mother. The part about killing my father is obviously untrue, but I cannot risk returning to Corinth and somehow fulfilling the second part of the prophecy. Can you imagine anything so vile?'

'But you are always telling me that reason is a greater guide to action than prophecy.'

'I know, I know, and reason tells me it's all nonsense; but even if the probability of it coming true is unimaginably low, the crime itself is so unimaginably monstrous that it is worth doing anything to avoid it.'

'But sire, sire!' The messenger astonished them both by jumping up and down, clapping his hands and beaming with joy. 'Forgive me, but I have wonderful news that will relieve your mind. You are safe, quite safe from such a crime. For Merope is not your mother!'

'Not my mother?' Oedipus stared. His mind rushed back to the drunken oaf whose jeers all those years ago had pricked him on his way to Delphi: *You're no more a royal prince than I am . . . You were adopted, mate.*

'No, sire,' said the messenger. 'I can explain. Who better? There's a good reason why I wanted to be the one to bring you news of King Polybus's death, why I wanted to look upon your features. You see, I was the one who found you.'

'Who *found* me? Explain yourself.'

'My name is Straton, sire, and in earlier times I was a herdsman. Many years ago I was visiting Phorbas, a shepherd I knew who tended flocks on Mount Cithaeron, on the border with Attica. One afternoon Phorbas happened on a terrible sight. A baby left on the mountain to die.'

Jocasta gave a moan.

'Aye, majesty. Well you might cry out. For this poor child had been staked to the hillside. Shackled. Pierced through the ankles . . .'

Jocasta clutched at her husband's arm. 'Don't listen to this, Oedipus. Don't listen! Go away, sir. Leave us. This story is nothing. How dare you tell such disgusting lies?'

Oedipus pushed Jocasta away. 'Are you mad? It's what I've waited all my life to know. Go on . . .'

Jocasta, with a wild cry, ran from the room. Oedipus paid no attention, but grabbed Straton by his tunic. 'This baby, what happened to it?'

'Phorbas gave him to me to look after. When it was time for me to return to Corinth, I took him with me. King Polybus and Queen Merope heard about it and asked that they might have him. I gladly gave him . . . you . . .'

'Me? That baby was me?'

'None other, sire. The gods put you into my hands and guided you to Corinth. The wounds on your ankles healed and you grew up to be a fine boy, a noble prince. I was always so proud of you, so very proud.'

'But who were my real parents?' Oedipus's hands twisted Straton's tunic until the old man almost choked.

'I never knew, sire! No one knows. They cannot have been good people, for they staked you to a mountainside and left you to die.'

'What about this friend of yours? Could he be my father?'

'Phorbas? No, sir. Oh no. He's a good man. Whoever had you shackled and left to die was unworthy to be called a parent. You deserved better and the gods made sure you were given better. They led Phorbas to you and Phorbas to me. Now come back home to Corinth with me, my boy, and rule as our king.'

Oedipus let go of him. It was true that he could now safely return to Corinth. He need never have left. But he had to know who he was. Who had left him to die so cruel a death? Why had he been unwanted?

Oedipus clapped his hands and summoned his page.

'Take this fine old gentleman through to the kitchens and feed him well. Find him a chamber in which he can rest.' He turned back to Straton. 'I will send for you again when I have thought this thing through, sir.'

The page bowed. 'And I was to tell you, sire, that Antimedes of Ismenos has arrived and awaits your pleasure.'

Damn. Oedipus wasn't sure he wanted to see Antimedes now. He was far more concerned with getting to the truth of his birth and abandonment on Mount Cithaeron. Still, Antimedes might have information that would bring them all closer to discovering who killed Laius. With the plague still ravaging Thebes, he could not in all decency ignore that opportunity. Besides, he was Oedipus. He could follow ten complex lines of investigation at once, if he put his mind to it.

'Send him in.'

Why had Jocasta run off moaning like that? The image of a baby having its ankles pierced with iron staples must have upset her. Women feel things like that. Ah well.

Ah, this must be Antimedes now, Oedipus said to himself. Shifty-looking individual. Won't meet my eyes. He's afraid of something.

'Stand before me, Antimedes, and tell me the truth of what happened the day Laius was killed.'

'I've told it a hundred times before,' grumbled Antimedes,

staring down at the floor. 'There will be a report in your archives, won't there?'

'Any more of that sulky manner and I'll have you flogged, for all your white hairs,' snapped Oedipus. 'I want to hear the story from you. Look me in the eye and tell me what happened. If you lie, I shall know. And the deaths of hundreds of Thebans will be upon your conscience.'

Antimedes stared. 'How can that be?'

'The oracle has told us that the disease scourging our people has been sent by the gods because the killer of Laius lives amongst us and pollutes our kingdom.'

'Well, that is indeed the truth of the matter,' said Antimedes, gazing steadily at Oedipus. 'The killer is here in Thebes.'

'He is?' Oedipus's eyes shone with excitement.

'The killer of Laius is in this very room.'

'Ah!' Oedipus became grave. 'It is as well that you are honest. Tell me all truthfully and it may be that your only punishment will be exile. How did you come to kill your king?'

Antimedes gave a thin smile. 'I'll tell you exactly what happened, my lord king,' he said, and something in the way he said the last three words struck Oedipus as offensive. 'We were travelling, King Laius, his three bodyguards and me. Near Daulis we came to a place where three roads meet . . . There was some clod of a vagrant standing there, right in our way.'

'But you were ambushed by a gang, surely?' Oedipus's heart felt as if it had been seized by an icy hand and his whole body began to tremble.

'You wanted the truth, I'm now telling it. A lone traveller it was, a young man who looked as though he'd been on the road many a month. Laius ordered him out of the way. The man snatched at his whip and pulled him out of the chariot, like a fisherman landing a fish. The bodyguards, they sprang out . . . But why am I telling you this? You already know.'

In his agony of soul Oedipus wanted to hear it all. 'Go on,' he said.

'You wrenched the sword out of the hand of one of them and killed all three.'

'And you ran away . . .'

Antimedes bowed his head. 'And I ran away. But what business did you have to kill the king after that?'

'I didn't! That is . . . he was dead when he hit the ground. His neck broke. I never meant for him to die. He struck first, with his whip.'

'If you say so,' said Antimedes. 'Well, I made my way to Thebes and yes, I did tell them it was a gang that set upon us. Maybe I was ashamed to have run away. Ashamed that we could all have been set upon by one unarmed man.'

Oedipus was the man who had killed Laius. Oedipus had proclaimed a curse upon the killer of Laius. A curse upon himself.

'And then?'

'Nothing more to say. I left Thebes. I didn't want to serve under Creon. My loyalty was always to Laius and Jocasta. When I heard a young man had come to rule in Laius' place – you – I thought perhaps you were his son found at last, but then I heard you married the queen and knew that couldn't be.'

'His son?' said Oedipus. 'But Laius and Jocasta had no children.'

'Ah, she told you that did she? They had one son, but they couldn't keep it.'

'What are you saying?' Oedipus shook Antimedes by the shoulder. 'What are you saying?'

'I might as well tell it all,' said Antimedes. 'I'm not long for this life and I don't want to face the Judges of the Underworld with an unclean soul. The oracle warned Laius that any son of his would kill him; so when a boy was born to Jocasta, he gave the child to me and bid me peg him to the hillside on Mount Cithaeron and . . . Oh, by the gods!' It was Antimedes' turn to stare. 'Never say it. No, no –'

Loud screams came from another part of the palace. The moment Straton had told his story of taking the baby Oedipus from Mount Cithaeron to Corinth, Jocasta had understood the terrible truth and taken her own life. When Oedipus followed the screams to her bedchamber, he saw her body hanging from the ceiling and his daughters weeping beneath it. He sent them from the room.

It was all clear. He was the killer of Laius who had brought the plague to Thebes. That would have been terrible enough on its own. Now he knew that the whole truth was deeper, darker and more unbearable still. Laius had been his father. He had taken his mother Jocasta to be his wife, and had four children by her. He had loudly and publicly hunted for the truth and boasted that he would find it but – as blind Tiresias had warned him – he had not been able to see. He was a pollutant. A contaminant. He was the disease.

He wanted to kill himself, but how could he? Suppose he met his mother-wife Jocasta in the underworld? And the father that he had killed? He could not face that. Not yet, at least. Not until he had been punished for his unspeakable crime.

He reached up, pulled the long gold brooch pins from Jocasta's dress and thrust them into his own eyes.

THE AFTERMYTH

If the preceding scene sounds like something from a drama, that is because I have freely (too freely, some may think) drawn the narrative from Sophocles' play *Oedipus the King*,* probably the best known of all the classical Greek tragedies. As with almost every myth, there are variant storylines, but the version that has come down through Sophocles is the most often told and retold.

Creon took over the throne and blind Oedipus tapped his way† into self-banishment and exile, his faithful daughter Antigone by his side. Two more plays, *Oedipus at Colonus* and *Antigone,* constitute what is known as Sophocles' 'Theban Cycle' telling the story of the further episodes in the life of Oedipus and his family. In *Oedipus at Colonus*, the blind king is looked after by Theseus and dies in Athens, bestowing the place of his death upon the Athenian people as a blessing which will grant them victory in any future wars with Thebes.

Sophocles' two great rivals, Aeschylus and Euripides,‡ found themselves equally unable to resist dramatising this beguiling and perplexing story. Aeschylus wrote his own Theban Cycle consisting of three separate trilogies: the

---

* *Oedipus Tyrannos* in its original Greek, but often confusingly given the Latin title *Oedipus Rex.* I was a perfectly dreadful Oedipus in a production (the W. B. Yeats translation) at the Edinburgh Fringe in 1979. The unhappy citizens of Edinburgh still talk about it in hushed, disbelieving tones. One of Laurence Olivier's most celebrated feats was his double bill as Oedipus and as Mr Puff in Sheridan's *The Critic.* They say Olivier's scream as Oedipus when he suddenly realises the truth about himself – the cascade of truths – was one of the great moments in theatrical history. They don't say that of my performance.

† As in the third state of man in the Sphinx's riddle . . .

‡ Literally rivals, since their plays were submitted in competition, only the prize-winning texts going into production.

Laius and *Oedipus* are lost, but the *Seven Against Thebes* (which chronicles the struggle between Oedipus's sons Eteocles and Polynices for the throne of Thebes after their father's death) is extant, if rarely performed, being generally considered dramatically underpowered and overladen with stodgy dialogue.*

The prodigiously profuse, prolific and productive Euripides wrote an *Oedipus* that is lost† while his *Phoenician Women* treats the same episode that Aeschylus covers in the *Seven against Thebes*. It has been inferred that in the *Oedipus* of Euripides, Jocasta does not commit suicide and Oedipus is blinded not by himself, but by vengeful Thebans loyal to the memory of Laius.

In other versions of the myth, Oedipus marries Jocasta but has no children by her. After he discovers the truth about himself he divorces her and marries EURYGANEIA (who may have been Jocasta's sister) and it is by her that he has his four children. In this telling Eteocles, Polynices, Antigone and Ismene are clean of the taint of incest.

However they were conceived, the main lines of the story tell us that, after Oedipus went into exile, his sons Eteocles and Polynices assume the throne of Thebes, each ruling in

---

* There was also a fourth work by Aeschylus, a comic companion piece or 'satyr' play, called *Sphinx*. They are sometimes collectively referred to as Aeschylus's *Oedipodea*.

† I sometimes dream that a great find will restore thousands of the great lost works of antiquity to us. Many perished in the catastrophic fire (or fires) at the Library of Alexandria in Egypt, but who knows? – maybe one day a huge repository of manuscripts will be uncovered. We have eighteen or nineteen plays by Euripides, for example, yet he is known to have written almost a hundred. Only seven of Aeschylus's eighty remain, while just seven plays of Sophocles have come down to us out of a hundred and twenty known titles. Almost every character you come across when reading the Greek myths had a play about them written by one, other or all three of the great Athenian masters. The loss of so many of their works might be regarded as the greatest Greek tragedy of them all.

alternate years. Naturally, brothers being brothers, it all goes wrong. Eteocles refuses to give up the throne when it is his brother's turn to take over. In a huff, Polynices storms off to Argos to raise an army led by seven champions, the so-called Seven against Thebes, but they perish during a botched assault on the city walls. Polynices and Eteocles kill each other in battle and Creon now takes over as king in his own right, ruling that the body of Polynices, whom he considers to have been the guiltier of the pair, be denied proper burial. Antigone, distraught at the idea of her brother's soul being denied rest, attempts to cover the corpse but is caught in the act. Creon sentences her to death for her disobedience and has her sealed up in a cave. Although he changes his mind at the last minute and commands her to be set free, it is too late. She has hanged herself.

By the end of Sophocles' dramatisation of this myth, Antigone and her fiancé HAEMON (Creon's own son) have both committed suicide. At the news of this so too does Creon's wife, EURYDICE. The curse on the Theban royal house was relentless and the Greeks seemed endlessly to be fascinated by it.

Sigmund Freud notably saw in the Oedipus myth a playing out of his theory that infant sons long for a close and exclusive relationship with their mothers, including an (unconscious) sexual one, and hate their fathers for coming between this perfect mother–son union. It is an oft-noted irony that, of all men in history, Oedipus was the one with the least claim to an Oedipus Complex. He left Corinth because the idea of sex with his mother Merope (as he thought) was so repugnant. Not only was his attraction to Jocasta adult (and the incestuous element wholly unwitting), but it came after the killing of his father Laius, which itself was accidental and entirely unconnected to any infant sexual jealousy. None of which put Freud off his stride.

Aside from the encounter with the Sphinx, there is little in Oedipus to connect him to the common run of Greek heroic figures. He strikes us today as a modern tragic hero and political animal; it is hard to picture him shaking hands with Heracles or joining the crew of the *Argo*. Many scholars and thinkers, most notably Friedrich Nietzsche in his book *The Birth of Tragedy*, have seen in Oedipus a character who works out on stage the tension in Athenians (and all of us) between the reasoning, mathematically literate citizen and the transgressive blood criminal; between the thinking and the instinctual being; between the superego and the id; between the Apollonian and the Dionysian impulses that contend within us. Oedipus is a detective who employs all the fields of enquiry of which the Athenians were so proud – logic, numbers, rhetoric, order and discovery – only to reveal a truth that is disordered, shameful, transgressive and bestial.

THESEUS

THE CHOSEN ONE

It's the archetype of fiction for children, young adults and – let's be honest – pretend grown-ups like us too. A mysterious absent father. A doting mother who encourages you to believe that you are special. The Chosen One. 'You're a wizard, Harry!' that kind of thing.

It goes like this.

You grow up in the city state of Troezen in the backwaters of the northeastern Peloponnese. Your mother is Aethra, daughter of the local king, Pittheus.* You are a member of a royal house, yet you are treated differently because you have no father.

Who is – or was – he?

Your mother is exasperatingly playful on the subject. 'Perhaps he is a great king.'

'Greater than grandfather Pittheus?'

'Maybe. But perhaps he is a god.'

'My father a god?'

'You never know.'

'Well, I am faster and stronger than any of the other boys. Cleverer too. Handsomer.'

'You're not good at everything, Theseus.'

'I am! What aren't I good at?'

'Modesty.'

---

* The same Aethra to whom Bellerophon had once been engaged.

329

'Poo! Honesty is more important.'

'Let's just say immodesty is rather unattractive. Your father really wouldn't approve.'

'Which father? The king or the god?'

And so the teasing and the gentle bickering would go on as you grow from boisterous toddler to proud child.

One great and happy day your cousin Heracles comes to stay at the palace. He is related to your mother through an important ancestor called Pelops.* You have worshipped him from the first moment you heard stories of his extraordinary adventures. The monsters he has slain, the tasks he has performed. His strength. His courage. When he arrives he slings a lion skin down in front of the fire. The pelt of the Thespian Lion, the first of his great conquests.† All the other palace children scream and run away. You are only six but you run up and seize the lion by its mane. You roll round and round on the floor with it, roaring and roaring. You try to strangle it. A laughing Heracles plucks you up.

'Here's a young fellow after my own heart. What's your name, copper-top?'

'Theseus please.'

'Well, Theseus Please. Plan to grow up a hero?'

'Oh yes, cousin, yes indeed.'

And he laughs and puts you down on the lion skin and from that moment on you know that it is your destiny, even though you are not entirely sure what the word means, to be a hero.

On your twelfth birthday your mother takes your hand and leads you out of Troezen and up a path that leads to a

---

* In Euripides *Heracleidae* or 'Children of Heracles', it is given that Aethra was the daughter of Pelops's son Pittheus, making him the common grandfather of Heracles and Theseus. Hence my occasional use of the word 'cousin' when talking of the two heroes.

† See the story of Heracles (page 59).

promontory with a view over the whole city and surrounding countryside. She indicates a great rock.

'Theseus, if you can roll that rock away I will tell you all about your father.'

You leap at the rock. You push it with arms stretched out, you turn round and strain against it with your back. You heave, you yell, you swarm all over the rock, but at last you fall exhausted to the ground. The great boulder has not budged by so much as the breadth of your little finger.

'Come on, little Sisyphus, we'll try again next year,' says your mother.

And each birthday from then on you go together to the rock.

'I do believe,' your mother says some years later, 'that you are growing the outlines of something approaching a beard, Theseus.'

'It will give me strength,' you say. 'This is the year.'

But it is not the year. Nor is the next. You grow impatient. No one can match you in a foot race, even if you give them a half *stadion* start. No one can throw a javelin or discus further. Troezen seems too small for your ambitions. You are not quite sure what they are, but you know that somehow you will shake the world.

You are almost weary as you trudge up the hill with your mother this particular birthday. The rock is a fake test. It will never move.

But you are wrong.

UNDER THE ROCK

Theseus did not feel that he was stronger this birthday than last. The palace guards joked with him that he was now tall enough to be one of their number if he chose. His beard sometimes needed trimming. It was darker than his hair, which was an unusual russety kind of red. He had hated that when he was young, but he was used to it by now. A girl he liked had told him it was attractive.

Otherwise he was the same old Theseus.

But this time the rock shifted! It really moved. Theseus could have sworn it was not the same rock, but that was nonsense. Perhaps he was not the same Theseus. He braced, dug in his feet and pushed further. With almost comical ease the rock turned one whole revolution towards the edge of the path, then another.

'Shall I let it roll down the hill?'

'No, you can leave it just where it is.' His mother was smiling. 'It's now exactly where it was before your father rolled it to the place it has stood for the last eighteen years.'

'But what does it all mean?'

'Have a dig in the ground and see if you can find anything.'

The grass was white where the boulder had rested on it all those years. Theseus scrabbled at the earth until his fingers found something and he came up with a pair of sandals, one of which was a little perished or had perhaps been chewed by beetles.

'Great,' he said. 'Just what I wanted for my birthday. Some old leather sandals.'

'Keep digging,' his mother said, smiling.

He dug deeper and his fingers closed around something cold and metallic. He pulled up a sword, which gleamed like silver.

'Whose is this?'

'It was your father's, but now it's yours.'

'Who was he?'

'Sit down on the bank and I will tell you.' Aethra patted the grass. 'Your father was and is King AEGEUS of Athens.'

'Athens!'

'He married twice, but neither union was blessed with children. He wanted a son and so he visited the oracle at Delphi. You know how strange her pronouncements can be. This was one of the strangest of all.

Aegeus must not loosen the bulging mouth of the wineskin until he has reached the heights of Athens, or he will die of grief.

'What does that mean?'

'Exactly. Now Aegeus happened to be a close friend of my father, good King Pittheus.'

'Grandfather?'

'Your grandpapa, exactly. So Aegeus went out of his way to stop by here in Troezen while travelling back from Delphi to see if perhaps Pittheus might be able to interpret the words of the oracle for him.'

'And could he?'

'Well now, Theseus, here you have to admire your grandfather's cunning. He did understand the prophecy. He understood it perfectly. "The bulging mouth of the wineskin" meant, so far as he could see, Aegeus's . . . manhood, let us say. So the prophecy was saying to Aegeus, "Don't . . . er . . . conjoin with any woman until you return to Athens."'

'*Conjoin?* That's a new one.'

'Shush. Now, Pittheus thought it might be rather wonderful for me, his daughter, to carry a child by a king of such a great city as Athens. It would allow the baby – you as it turned out – to be king of a united Athens and Troezen. So grandfather pretended he thought the prophecy meant that Aegeus should abstain from drinking wine until he got home to Athens. He then called for me and told me to show Aegeus round the palace and gardens. One thing led to another. We found ourselves in my bedchambers and . . .'

333

'. . . I was conceived,' said a stunned Theseus.

'Yes, but there's more,' sad Aethra, crimson with embarrassment. She had always known this day would come and had rehearsed her telling Theseus the story of his birth many times, but now that the day had come the words seemed to stick in her throat.

'More?'

'That night, after Aegeus, your father, had . . . had . . .'

'. . . had loosened his bulging wineskin?'

'Yes, that. He rolled off and fell asleep. I couldn't sleep, though. I went to the spring, the one down there dedicated to Poseidon, to cleanse myself and think. My father had sent me to sleep with a stranger so that he could play at politics. I was angry, but I had found to my surprise I liked Aegeus. He was kindly, manly and . . . exciting.'

'Mother, please . . .'

'But when I washed myself in the waters of the spring, who do you think arose from the pool?'

'Who?'

'The god Poseidon.'

'What?'

'And he . . . he took me too.'

'He . . . he . . . he . . . ?'

'It's not funny, Theseus . . .'

'I'm not laughing, mother. Believe me, I am not laughing. I'm just trying to understand. Don't tell me Poseidon loosened *his* bulging wineskin?'

'I swear to you, it's all true. The very same night that I slept with Aegeus, Poseidon took me too.'

'So which one is my father?'

'Both, I am quite sure of it. I returned to Aegeus's bed, and when he awoke in the morning he embraced me and apologised. He was married, you see, so he could hardly take me back to Athens with him. We left the bedchamber before anyone else was awake and he brought me up to this place. He buried his sword and his sandals just there, and rolled the rock over the place. "If our union of last night bears fruit and a boy child is born to you, let him move the rock when he is man enough and tell him who he is. Then he may come to Athens and claim his birthright."'

As you can easily imagine, Theseus was thunderstruck by the news. His mother's teasing over the years had convinced him that the idea that his mysterious father was a king or god was nothing but childish fantasy.

'So grandpapa knew the prophecy meant that Aegeus, my father, would have a son the next time he . . . he had sex? And he decided you should be the mother?'

'That's right.'

'But the prophecy said Aegeus should not loosen his bulging wineskin – where do these oracles get their metaphors from? – before he got to Athens, or he would die of grief.'

'Well, yes . . .'

'But he did loosen it before he got to Athens. Has he since died of grief?'

'Well, no, he hasn't,' Aethra conceded.

'Oracles!'

They talked and talked until the evening star had risen.

Mother and son wound their way home, Theseus swishing the sword at the long grass. When they arrived at the palace, Aethra sought for them an immediate interview with King Pittheus.

'So, my boy. Now you know your history. A son of Troezen and a son of Athens. Think what this will mean for the Peloponnese! We can unite our fleets and rule Attica. Corinth will be furious. And Sparta! Ha, won't they spit with envy! Now, what to do first? We'll equip a ship for you as soon as possible to sail over to Piraeus – tomorrow! why not? – and you can get yourself up to the Athenian court and make yourself known to old Aegeus. He'll be so tickled! You know he married Jason's widow, don't you – Medea of Colchis? Terrifying woman by all accounts *. A sorceress and murderer of her own close kin. I'll hunt out a present for you, a little treasure of some kind you can give them both with my regards. Oh, that was a good night's work. What a good night's work that was.'

Pittheus embraced his daughter and punched his grandson playfully on the arm.

Theseus had other ideas. He went to his room and wrapped his few possessions in a handkerchief. A Prince of Troezen arriving by ship, holding some jewelled trinket and waving a silver sword with a 'Hello, daddy, it's me!' – how heroic was that? Not heroic at all. Would Heracles have presented himself like that, like an spoiled princeling? Never. Theseus knew that when he entered Athens he should enter as a hero – and he thought he had an idea how that could be achieved.

There were only two ways to get to Athens from Troezen. By sea, across the waters of the Saronic Gulf, or by foot, walking around its coastline. The latter was a long and arduous journey, but more than that, it was notoriously dangerous. Some of the most brutal and merciless outlaws, robbers and murderers in all of Greece lay in wait there. Naturally it was the route any self-respecting hero would take. If Theseus arrived in Athens having rid the highway of its legendary brigands, now that *would* be something . . .

Theseus put on his father's old sandals, buckled the sword

---

* How Medea acquired such a dreadful reputation, and how she came to be in Athens, you will recall, is told in the story of Jason (pages 234 and 239).

to his belt, wrapped his few other possessions and slipped out.

A few moments later he was back. He scribbled a note to his mother and grandfather and left it on the bed.

'Didn't like the idea of a sea voyage. Thought I'd go on foot. Love, Theseus.'

THE LABOURS OF THESEUS

1. PERIPHETES

Theseus had hardly been travelling more than an hour before he found his path blocked by a lumbering, shuffling one-eyed giant wielding an enormous club. Theseus knew exactly who this must be: PERIPHETES, a.k.a. CORYNETES, the 'club man'.

'Oh dear, oh dear,' wheezed the Cyclops. 'A nice soft head for Crusher, my club. He's made of bronze, you know. My father is a smith. The smith of smiths my father is.'

'Yes, we all know you claim to be a son of Hephaestus,' said Theseus, affecting boredom. 'People have fallen for your story because you are ugly and lame. But I cannot believe that an Olympian god would ever have so stupid a child.'

'Oh, stupid am I?'

'Incredibly so. Claiming that your club is bronze. Who sold it to you? Anyone can see that it's oak.'

'I made him myself!' hooted Periphetes in outrage. 'He is not oak! Would an oaken club be so heavy?'

'You say it's heavy, but I can see you swinging it from one hand to the other as easily as if it were made of feathers.'

'That's because I'm strong, cretin! You try. I bet you can't even hold it.'

'Oh my, yes, it is heavy,' said Theseus, taking it. His hand dropped down almost to the ground, as if unable to take the weight. 'And I can feel the cold hardness of the bronze.'

'See!'

'Nice . . . balance . . . to it!' said Theseus suddenly lifting it high and sweeping it round. On the word 'balance' it met Periphetes' thigh-bone with a satisfying crunch. The giant fell with a howl of pain.

'I . . . think . . . I . . . like . . . this . . . club!' said Theseus, crashing it down on Periphetes' skull with six splintering blows.

In the rocks to the side of the road Theseus found the robber's hideout. A hoard of gold, silver and stolen valuables had been laid neatly and carefully on the ground in a perfect semicircle around a towering shrine of crushed skulls. Theseus unearthed a leather bag and filled it with the treasure. He felt he had to keep the club too. Heracles always carried a club, so should he.

2. SINIS

Further north, the road swung east along the Isthmus of Corinth. As Theseus walked, enjoying the sun on his face and the sea glittering to his right, he encountered plenty of friendly travellers. To those in need he gave coins and precious objects from his satchel.

Perhaps the talk of terrifying brigands on this road is exaggerated, he thought to himself. And just as he had decided that this must be the case, he came to a rise in the ground where he saw a man standing between two trees.

'What's in that bag, boy?'

'That is my affair,' said Theseus.

'Oh! Oh, it's "your affair", is it? Well, well. I have a special way of dealing with snotty little runts of the litter like you. See these two trees?'

Theseus knew at once this must be SINIS PITYOCAMPTES,

Sinis the Pine Bender. Stories of this strange and terrible man were told all around the Peloponnese. He would tie travellers between two pine trees that, with his great strength, he could bend down. After tormenting his victims for a while, Sinis would release his hold on the trees which would would straighten up, pulling the poor travellers apart. A cruel, horrible death. A cruel horrible man.

'I'll put down my club,' said Theseus. 'I'll put down my sword and I'll put down my satchel. Because I want to kneel before your greatness.'

'How's that?'

'I've been travelling four days on this road and I hear nothing but tales of the marvellous Sinis Pityocamptes.'

'Yes, well, that's fine, but don't go weird on me.'

'Oh gods, I am not worthy to meet so fine a man, so pure a hero.' Theseus prostrated himself on the grass.

'Look, just come here, will you!'

'I cannot move, I am awestruck. Sinis the Great. Sinis the Marvellous. Sinis the Magnificent. Bender of Pines. Mender of Men.'

'You're soft in the head, you are,' said Sinis, advancing. 'Come on, get up.'

But somehow, in the ensuing confusion Theseus and Sinis managed to swap positions. Now Sinis was spread-eagled out on the ground, with Theseus above him, pinning him down.

'Come, great Sinis. It is not fair that you have given so much pleasure to so many, but received none yourself.'

'Let me go!'

'No, my lord,' said Theseus, dragging Sinis by his wrist through the grass, like a child pulling a toy cart. 'You have done such kindness to so many strangers without any thought for yourself. Now, if I attach your arm to this tree and pull it down like so . . .'

Sinis sobbed, blubbed and begged as Theseus set to work.

'Your modesty does you nothing but credit, Sinis,' he said, reaching for a second pine, 'but surely it is only right the world should have not one of you, but two.'

'I beg you, I beg you. There is treasure buried beneath those bushes. Take it, take it all.'

Theseus now held both pine trees firmly in his grip. 'You squeal and gibber like a pig, and I note that you wet yourself like a frightened child,' he said, suddenly very stern. 'But what mercy did you ever show your terrified victims?'

'I'm sorry, truly sorry.'

Theseus thought for a while. 'Hm. I can see that you truly are. I'll just go and see if you are telling the truth about your treasure and if you are I'll spare you.'

'Yes, yes! But don't let go, don't . . .'

'Let's see, your treasure if over here, you say?'

Theseus stepped back, releasing his hold. The pines whipped apart, tearing Sinis in two as they shot upright, releasing a shower of needles from their shivering branches.

'Oops. Clumsy me,' said Theseus.

Theseus only left the place after he had unearthed the treasure and chopped down both the trees with his sword. He lit a fire of pinewood and sent the sweet-smelling smoke in gratitude up to the gods.

3. THE CROMMYONIAN SOW

Theseus resumed his journey along the Isthmus road as it hugged the coast. Before long he was approaching the village of Crommyon, midway between Corinth and the city of Megara. He was already nearer Athens than Troezen. Increasingly travellers hurrying south, or farmers labouring nervously in the fields, paused briefly to warn Theseus of a fearsome creature ravaging the land, which they called the CROMMYONIAN SOW.

From the stories he was told, Theseus wasn't sure whether the Crommyonian Sow was a real snorting, squealing, snuffling, living pig, or a malicious and murderous old woman going by the name of PHAEA. Some swore they had seen a grey hag transform herself into a pig. Others maintained that Phaea was simply the pig's keeper.

Theseus never saw any grey old hag, but he did encounter a large and aggressive wild pig. The great bronze club was more than a match for it and it was not long before the gods were treated to something even more delicious than fragrant pine smoke – the aroma of freshly roast bacon.*

4. SCIRON

Further along the coast road, between Megara and Eleusis, there lurked a notorious outlaw called SCIRON or Sceiron. He had been there so long that the cliffs over the bay at that point were known as the Scironian Rocks. Far below them, in the blue waters of the Saronic Gulf, a giant turtle swam about in impatient circles. Sciron and the turtle had an interesting and disturbing relationship. Sciron's modus operandi was to force travellers to wash his feet, right on the cliff's edge. The unwitting victims would have their backs to the sea and, when they knelt down to start washing, he would give a great kick and they would tumble down into the waters below, where the greedy turtle was waiting for them, jaws open.

---

* Some say that the Crommyonian Sow was the mother of the Calydonian Boar. See the story of Atalanta (page 271).

'No, no, no, no, no!' said Theseus, after Sciron had leapt out from behind a tree and, at swordpoint, told him to wash his feet. 'They're disgusting. I'm not touching those.'

'Would you rather be run through with a sword?' said Sciron.

'Well, no,' conceded Theseus. 'But where's the bowl of hot water? Where are the scented oils? Where's the goatskin flannel? If I'm going to clean your feet, I may as well do it properly.'

With a sigh of impatience, Sciron – his sword pointing at Theseus all the time – showed him where he kept all the implements and artefacts necessary for the perfect footbath. Theseus insisted on boiling water in a copper bowl that he found.

'After all,' he said cheerfully, 'if a thing's worth doing, it's worth doing properly.'

'Now go over yonder,' growled Sciron, when Theseus at last pronounced that he was satisfied. 'I'll sit on this stool, you squat down there.'

'It's very close to the edge,' said Theseus doubtfully.

'I like to look out to sea when I'm having my feet washed. No more talking, let's just get on, shall we?'

Theseus carried the bowl of steaming water carefully towards the spot. He could feel Sciron's swordpoint in the small of his back, urging him on.

'Right, so . . . here?'

'Closer to the edge.'

'Here?'

'Closer still.'

'Goodness, that's steep – whoah!'

Theseus tripped and stumbled forward. Free of the swordpoint against his skin, he turned in an instant and hurled the scalding contents of the bowl into Sciron's face. The outlaw gave one short scream from the pain and shock, then – after a sudden shove from Theseus – he gave a second longer scream as he tottered wildly on the cliff edge before tumbling down into the blue, blue sea.

Theseus looked down and saw the creamy wake of a giant turtle closing in on the thrashing form.

5. CERCYON AND THE BIRTH OF WRESTLING

At the temple of Demeter and Kore* at Eleusis, Theseus paused to offer sacrifices and prayers of thanks for his survival thus far. When he set out again on his journey, the coastline began to curl sharply south. For the worthy and indigent there were still plenty of gifts in his satchel, but his mind was now more occupied with how his father would react when they met than with the threat of brigands and outlaws.

Theseus was just thinking of finding a place to bivouac and sleep for the night when two tall thin men appeared on either side, seemingly out of nowhere, with their knives pointed at his throat. A third figure then stepped out in front of him. Theseus had never seen someone so big. He would have dwarfed even Periphetes, the first of his adversaries on this journey. Theseus knew perfectly ordinary people who were shorter than this man was broad.

'Who gave you permission to enter my kingdom?' the giant roared.

'Excuse me?'

'I am Cercyon, king of this realm. You enter without permission.'

'Well, how very wrong of me. Please accept my apologies.'

---

* *Kore*, meaning the 'maiden', was the embodiment of Persephone when she rose up from the underworld in the spring and summer months as per her mother Demeter's arrangement with Hades.

'I offer strangers a fight without weapons. If you win, this kingdom is yours.'

'And if I lose?'

'Then you die.'

Theseus looked round. 'Not much of a kingdom, is it? I mean, compared with Corinth, say.'

'Do you accept the challenge?'

'Oh yes, I accept.'

'Then remove your sword and your clothes.'

'Excuse me?'

'This is a fight without weapons. Only arms and fists, and legs and feet. Pure fighting.'

Theseus looked at the giant, who had cast off his cloak and other articles of clothing and now stood naked before him. Maybe this was all some elaborate courting ritual. Being embraced by such a huge musclebound man in an act of love was as horrible a prospect as being embraced by him in an act of combat. The tall thin guards with their knives at his throat were not going to go away, and with no other options open to him, Theseus laid down his sword and club with a sigh and stepped out of his tunic.

'I can crush bones in one hug,' said Cercyon.

'Really?' said Theseus. 'Your mother must be very proud of you. Tell me . . .' he added, leaping nimbly to one side as Cercyon came forward in a rush, 'if I win, will your men really submit to me?'

'If you win,' chuckled Cercyon, beckoning Theseus forward, 'they will serve you to the end of their days and you will be their king. Come to me, come to me!'

Theseus ducked between Cercyon's legs and felt the giant's balls brushing the top of his head. 'Revolting,' he said to himself. 'But they do present a good target.'

'Will you keep still!' exclaimed Cercyon, infuriated by

Theseus's starts and sideways jumps. 'You don't fight like a man, you dance like a girl.'

Slowly Cercyon began to tire. He was too strong for Theseus to allow himself to engage, for it would only take one great bear-hug and his ribs would crack. But the giant's lunges and swipes were slowing. Every time he made a move, Theseus found a way to turn his strength against him, tiring him further. The next time he ducked between Cercyon's legs, he leapt onto the giant's scrotum and hung there, twisting it round and round.

Cercyon howled in agony. 'Stop it! You can't do that, it's cheating!'

With one last vicious tug, Theseus dropped to the ground.

'I'll get you, I'll get you!' thundered Cercyon.

He's lost his temper, Theseus thought to himself. I've got him now.

Cercyon stamped and lurched forwards, blind to anything but revenge. Theseus nipped at his ankles, snapped at his balls, jumped on his toes, laughed and teased and raced around him until Cercyon was more like an enraged bull than any kind of artful fighter.

At last Theseus lured him to a row of jagged rocks and tripped him. Cercyon fell face down on the sharp rocks and Theseus jumped up and down on him like a child bouncing on a bed. The giant's blood spurted up in a fountain and fell in crimson drops as Cercyon shuddered and gave up his last breath.*

---

* The Athenians believed that Theseus invented wrestling. His use of wit, technique and skill to turn Cercyon's brute strength against him exemplified everything ancient Athens valued. The specific art he developed, what we might call 'mixed martial arts' was called by the Greeks *pankration* . . . 'all strength'. If you recall, Heracles had picked up some of the technique and employed it on Antaeus during his Eleventh Labour.

Theseus turned to see the two thin guards kneeling on the ground in front of him.

'Sire!'

'Majesty!'

'Oh, stop it,' said Theseus, panting from his exertions. 'Go away. You're free. Quick, go! Before I do to you what I did to your king.'

As he watched them scampering down the hillside, Theseus donned his tunic and gathered up his possessions.*

6. PROCRUSTES, THE STRETCHER

Theseus's last adversary appeared before him in a valley of Mount Korydallos. Unlike the others, he did not leap out from behind a rock or a tree. He did not bar Theseus's way and he did not threaten him with swords, clubs or knives. Instead he stood in the doorway of a pleasantly appointed stone house and welcomed him with a smile and an offer of hospitality.

'Hello, stranger! You look as though you have travelled a few leagues.'

'That I have,' said Theseus.

'You will surely be in need of refreshment and a bed for the night.'

'I was thinking of making straight for Athens this evening.'

'Oh, it's a good twelve miles. You'll never make it before

---

* Other interpretations of this confrontation would have it that the story was reverse-engineered to fit the myth of Theseus' youthful Labours, and that it actually had its origins in a later and more routine political takeover. This reading has it that Cercyon was a real king and that Theseus wrested, rather than wrestled, his realm – Eleusis – from him in later days, when Theseus was by that time a king himself.

nightfall. And there are thieves and murderers waiting out there, I can assure you. Believe me, much better to stay here and make the final leg of your journey when you're fresh. We offer cheap, clean lodging at an affordable price.'

'Sold,' said Theseus, thrusting out his hand. 'Theseus of Troezen.'

'PROCRUSTES of Erineus. Make yourself welcome under our roof.'

There was something in the smiling and the bowing that Theseus did not quite like, but he said nothing and entered the small house. A middle-aged woman was busy wiping down the wooden table with mint leaves. She welcomed him with a bobbing curtsy and a beaming smile.

'A guest, my dear,' said Procrustes, ducking his head to avoid the lintel as he entered, for he was a tall man.

Procrustes' wife bobbed again. She smiled quite as much as her husband and Theseus found the nature of the smile quite as off-putting.

'Do you have water somewhere that I might wash myself?' he asked.

'Wash yourself? Why would you do that?' Procrustes asked, amazed.

'Never you mind, Procrustes. If the young gentleman wants to wash, then let him. Strangers have strange ways and there's an end to it. There's a pond out the back where the ducks swim,' she added to Theseus. 'Might that serve your needs?'

'Perfectly,' said Theseus and he made his way out.

He saw the pond but did not make for it: instead he doubled round to the window at the back under which he crouched, listening.

'Oh, he's perfect, my dear,' the wife was saying. 'Did you see that bulging satchel he's carrying? There'll be silver and gold in there enough.'

'He's neither tall nor short,' Procrustes put in thoughtfully. 'When I take him to be fitted to the bed, should he be stretched out, do you think?'

'Oh, I love it when you manacle them and stretch them out, Procrustes. The screams, the screams!'

'Ah, but there's fun to be had when they're too tall for the bed, too. Chopping off their feet . . . They scream plenty then too.'

'Stretch him, Procrustes, rack him! It lasts longer.'

'I believe you're right, my dear. I'll go to the room now and make the bed long. What's he doing, anyway? Who ever heard of a man washing himself? He's not making a sound, neither.'

Theseus quickly picked up a stone and threw it into the pond. It landed with a splash and a chorus of angry quacking.

'He's frightening the ducks, at any rate.'

'Maybe he's from Sparta,' suggested his wife. 'You hear strange things of Spartans.'

'He said he was from Troezen.'

'They're strange too.'

'We'll hear stranger things of him soon enough,' said Procrustes as he left the room.

Theseus came back by way of the pond and was suitably dripping when he came back into the house.

'You'll have a cup of wine by the fire,' said the woman. 'That water must be making you chilly.'

'How kind.'

'All right and tight for you,' said Procrustes, coming back in, with a wink. 'Just been making sure your room is comfortable.'

'That's so thoughtful of you,' said Theseus. 'They say the gods reward hospitality.'

'Well, it's the least we can do,' said Procrustes. 'It's a rough road from Eleusis to Athens. You can meet some nasty customers on the way.'

'I've certainly encountered plenty of interesting and un- usual people on my journey.'

'No one who wanted to harm you?' said the woman with motherly concern.

'I found most of them to be as polite and friendly as you are,' said Theseus, with a broad smile.

'Enough chat, my dear,' said Procrustes. 'This gentleman will be wanting to see his room. Make sure the bed fits, that kind of thing.'

'A bed?' said Theseus. 'Goodness me, I've become used to sleeping out in the open. What luxury a bed will be.'

'Come along then and I'll show you.'

It was a pleasant room into which Procrustes ushered his guest. He had gone to the trouble of setting a vase of flowers on the table. The frame of the bed itself seemed to be of bronze. Theseus saw that there were rings built in all around the sides that seemed to be decorative, but could easily serve as manacles or cuffs.

'How charming,' said Theseus, surveying the room. 'Irises. My favourites.'

'Now, if you'll just lie out on the bed, I'll see if it fits.'

'No, no,' said Theseus. Quick as a flash he executed one of his wrestling moves, which deposited Procrustes face down on the bed. While he was still stunned, Theseus grasped his hands and quickly fixed them to the restraints, then he did the same to Procrustes' ankles. Procrustes swore loudly, but Theseus shushed him.

'What a remarkable bed this is,' he said walking round it slowly. 'There's a handle here, I wonder what it does?'

He picked up the crank and fitted it to the mechanism at

the end of the bed. When he turned the handle, the bed shortened in length.

'Language, Procrustes, please! I see you have an axe here. Perhaps that is to fit your guests properly to the bed? I wonder if it works.'

Theseus lopped off Procrustes' protruding feet at the ankles. The screams were terrible, so Theseus silenced them by chopping off his head too. The body quivered and jerked for a few seconds, blood spouting from each end.

As he was detaching Procrustes and rolling him off the bed, he heard the wife coming down the passageway.

'Oh, you haven't started without me, have you, my love? I heard the screams, but I had bread in the oven and I –'

She stopped and stared at the sight that met her: Theseus standing cheerfully, axe in hand, her husband dead on the floor and blood everywhere.

'No, you're not too late,' said Theseus. 'Why don't you lie down and let me fit you to the bed? No, no, don't struggle. It's much easier if you lie still and let me attach you to these clever manacles ... like so. Dear me, you are far too short for this bed, you know. Far too short. Let me make you a better fit.'

The woman spat and screamed curses but Theseus took no notice as he turned the handle.

'You see, now I can stretch you. They say that is very good for the muscles.'

He cranked until he could hear the woman's shoulders creak as her arms were slowly pulled from the shoulder sockets.

'Still not quite a fit . . .'

Now her hips began to click and snap.

'You were right about the screams,' said Theseus. 'Just as well you have no neighbours.'

She died in terrible agony, but Theseus thought of the agony of the many travellers who had had the misfortune to accept hospitality from the couple. He found plenty of stolen jewellery and, behind the duckpond, a macabre midden of bones. More than two hundred had screamed their last in this evil place.

Theseus threw lit rushes into the windows of the house and crossed the road to lie down in the field opposite and watch it burn down – Procrustes, wife, bed and all. As the embers died, he curled up and thought to himself how the best beds were to be found in nature, in the hedgerows and under the wise all-seeing stars. In the morning he should stop off at the River Cephissus and cleanse himself. That, he felt, was important.

THE WICKED STEPMOTHER

The figure that strode through the morning market in the Athenian agora attracted attention right away.* He was tall, he was handsome, yet despite his youth he was fierce of demeanour and confident in his bearing. The lithe tread and broad shoulders spoke of a warrior or athlete. Such figures were not rare in Athens, but neither were they an everyday sight.

It was the club he carried that started the rumours flying. Theseus stopped off at a stall to buy a melon; a small boy saw the club and, intrigued, touched it.

'Is that . . . is that . . . bronze?' he asked.

Theseus nodded gravely. 'That is what the man I took it from claimed and I have every reason to believe him.'

---

* We even know the day of Theseus's arrival in Athens. It was, according to Plutarch, the eighth day of the month of Hecatombaion, somewhere around July and August in our calendar. It was the month in the Attic calendar when each year a hundred cattle were ritually sacrificed to the gods.

The stallholder leaned forward. 'I heard that Periphetes the bandit was killed. He carried a club like this, they say.'

'Periphetes Corynetes!' went the cry.

'Is this the man we've heard tell of?'

'The one who tore Sinis apart with his own pine trees?'

'The lone traveller who outfought Cercyon . . .'

'. . . and slew the Crommyonian Sow . . .'

'. . . and lopped off the legs of Procrustes the Stretcher . . .'

'. . . and fed Sciron the cliff-killer to the tortoise . . .'

Theseus found himself being lifted bodily and carried to the palace by a cheering crowd. Here was the nameless hero of the Isthmian Road, the Saviour of the Saronic Coast! His name is Theseus and he is a Prince of Troezen. Hurrah for Troezen! Hurrah for Theseus!

Theseus had deliberately set out to make a name for himself and he had succeeded. That is why he chose the footpath of greatest danger over the sea-lane of greater safety. But he was not entirely vain, and he had enough sense to understand that fame and hero-worship cut two ways. They may embolden and excite the populace, but they aggravate and alarm the powerful. He had no wish to alienate his father before they had even met. With smiles and friendly back-slapping, he managed to extricate himself from the cheering crowd.

'Thank you, friends,' he said, safely back at street level. 'Thank you, but I am just a man like any other, and it is as a humble citizen that I beg an audience with your king.'

Such modesty of course served only to increase the adoration of the Athenian citizenry. They understood and respected such humility and allowed him to enter the palace alone and unencumbered by an entourage of admirers.

King Aegeus received Theseus in the throne room. Seated beside him was his third wife, Medea. Everyone had heard of Medea and the part she played in ensuring the success of the quest for the Golden Fleece. Stories abounded of her powers as an enchantress and of her implacable will. Her passion as a lover, wife and mother had driven her, they said, to do the most unspeakable things. Child murder, blood murder – there was nothing of which she was not capable, but looking at her you saw only beauty and simple sweetness. Theseus bowed before both.

'So this is the young man of whom we have heard tell, eh? A Prince of Troezen no less, grandson of my old friend Pittheus. Rid us of our infestation of bandits, did he?' Aegeus did not, of course, recognise his son. If there was something in the russet of Theseus's hair that matched his own sparse and greying thatch, it did not cause much comment. The Grecian mainland, Macedonia in particular, was filled with men and women of varying degrees of sandy, ginger, copper and red hair.

Theseus bowed again.

'That's a lot of killing, young man,' said Medea, with a smile and flash of her green eyes. 'I hope you have done something to purge your soul of so much blood?'

'Yes, majesty,' said Theseus. 'I saw the PHYTALIDES who have a temple beside the River Cephissus and begged for atonement. They purified me.'*

'That was very clever of you – very *proper* of you,' Medea emended her words, but Theseus caught the spark of enmity. Aegeus too, he had to confess to himself, seemed far from pleased to see him.

'Yes, well, I'm sure we're very grateful,' said the king. 'Please make yourself at home here in the palace. I'm sure we

---

* According to Plutarch and Pausanias, they were the sons of PHYTALUS ('butterfly', perhaps?) who had once shown great kindness to Demeter. In recompense, the goddess granted his descendants the power to expiate those who broke the laws of hospitality.

can find something for you to do in the . . . er . . . the army, or somewhere . . . there are many ways a good man may be of service to us.'

Aegeus's throne was, in truth, far from secure. Being childless (as he and the world thought) his brother PALLAS's fifty sons – yes, *fifty** – all expected a share in the throne when he was gone. Their aggressive impatience at his refusal to abdicate or die caused Aegeus many sleepless nights. Medea and Aegeus had a son, Medus, whom she hoped would rule Athens after Aegeus's death.

Medea looked at the young man now standing before her with such false modesty and fake charm. She was not fooled for an instant. She looked again more closely and her heart leapt in her breast. She saw the hair, but more than that she noticed a look, a cast of features that she knew from Aegeus. Rumours had abounded of his visit – when was it? Yes, seventeen or eighteen years ago – to the Delphic oracle and thence to Troezen and his friend Pittheus, who had a daughter, Aethra. Yes, this bold youth was the bastard of that union, Medea was certain of it. The searching gaze he was giving Aegeus only confirmed her conviction. Well, she would put an end to this threat. Nothing would come between her and the plans she had for Medus to inherit the throne.

'Actually, I can think of something he might do for us, if he – excuse me, Theseus was it? What an unusual name – if Theseus might consider . . .' She leaned across and whispered into Aegeus's ear. He nodded brightly.

'Yes, yes. The queen, as always, is wise. You seek adventure, young man? You would like to help Athens?'

Theseus nodded eagerly.

'The villagers over near Marathon have been complaining

---

* Known as the Palliantidae.

about some terrifying bull that is rampaging around the plain. Terrible – from Crete originally, they tell me. It's making trade and civil congress in the region all but impossible. If what they say about you and that sow in Crommyon is true . . . you don't think . . . ?'

'Say no more, sire,' said Theseus. With his most respectful bow he left on his mission.

'What a good idea, Medea, m'dear,' said Aegeus. 'I didn't like the cut of that young man. And such popularity is dangerous. Did you hear how the crowd cheered him?'

'A dangerous youth, for certain.'

'Well, we've seen the last of him. That bull breathes fire from its nostrils. It's untameable. I should know.'

'I am not so sure,' said Medea. 'I shall make a fire and look into the flames. There's something about that boy . . .'

THE MARATHONIAN BULL

The news that Aegeus had sent Theseus to kill the bull at Marathon sent shockwaves throughout Attica. For the king had sent a young man on the very same mission before, with disastrous consequences. He had received Prince ANDROGEUS, a son of King Minos of Crete, as a guest, and foolishly sent him on the same errand, to rid Athens of a terrible bull that was devastating the countryside. The bull had promptly killed Androgeus, and as a punishment for such an egregious sin against the laws of hospitality, Minos had invaded Attica and threatened to raze the city to the ground unless . . . Well, we will come to that soon enough. For the moment, everyone wondered how Aegeus could be making the identical same disastrous mistake, for it was the identical same disastrous bull.

We first encountered this prodigiously significant beast when it was known as the Cretan Bull, the very one Heracles had been ordered to capture for his Seventh Labour.* After he let it go, you will recall, it fled from Mycenae and eventually ended up in Marathon, where it had been terrorising the inhabitants ever since.

Theseus went to Marathon and once more demonstrated the difference between his brand of heroism and that of Heracles who, if you remember, had planted himself on the ground and let the bull come at him, seizing it by the horns and using his sheer physical strength to subdue it. Theseus approached the problem in his own way. He watched the bull for some time. He saw no flames jetting from its nostrils, but he did see enormous strength and a terrible primal savagery in its furious snorting, bellowing and pawing of the ground. The ravaged countryside, gored livestock and flattened buildings all told him of the animal's formidable power and instinct to kill.

'But he's really no more frightening than Cercyon, whom I wrestled to the ground and dashed on the rocks,' he said to himself.

Sure enough, employing that same subtle art of turning the strength of an adversary against him, Theseus wore the bull out. Theseus was too lithe, nimble and quick for it. Each time the bull came at him, Theseus jumped into the air and the baffled animal found itself charging through vacant space beneath him.†

---

* See the story of Heracles (page 77). But don't think too hard about timelines and the relative ages of Theseus and Heracles or we'll all go mad.

† Here again Theseus invented an art, that of bull-leaping. It may sound comical, but plenty of archaeological evidence has been uncovered showing this mixture of sport and entertainment. It can be considered a forerunner of modern bullfighting. Both techniques rely on finesse and timing and aim to tire the bull out rather than engage with it fairly. So different from dear, honest Heracles.

'You don't breathe fire,' said Theseus, leaping over him for the tenth time, 'but your breath is hot.'

At last the great beast was too tired to resist any further. Theseus harnessed him and ploughed the Plain of Marathon.* The ploughing demonstrated his mastery of the beast and proved to the delighted inhabitants that they could now grow crops and farm their land in safety.

Theseus returned in triumph to Athens with the bull, which he sacrificed to Apollo in the agora.

THE QUEEN OF POISONS

Aegeus's plan could not have backfired more spectacularly. Far from ridding himself of this threat to his peace and security, he had propelled Theseus to even greater heights of popularity and acclaim. All Athens thrilled at the procession through the streets as Theseus led the great bull, once so ferocious, but now as placid and docile as a castrated ox, and made the noble and modest sacrifice to Apollo. The people had never seen such a hero. Aegeus was bound to throw a feast in his honour and it was while he was moodily dressing for this that Medea entered his chamber.

'This young man bodes nothing but ill for us, my husband.'

'I am aware of it.'

'See here . . .' Medea showed him a small crystal phial. 'In there is a quantity of wolf's bane . . .'

---

* The same Plain of Marathon saw the soldiers of Athens win their startling victory against the Medes and Persians in 490 BC. Pheidippides was said to have run the 25 or so miles from Marathon to Athens to break the news of the victory, shouting the word 'nenikekamen!' – 'we won!' – before expiring the ground of exhaustion at having run the first 'marathon'.

'The queen of poisons, they call it, do they not?'

'It has many names,' said Medea coldly. 'Blue rocket, devil's helmet, leopard's fire, aconite.* It is enough to know that it kills. I drop the contents into the popinjay prince's cup and lo! we are rid of the problem. It will seem as though he has had a fit, a storm in the mind, and we shall put it about so. Hades was greedy for so great a soul to come to the Underworld, we will say, and he sent Thanatos, Lord of Death, to bring Theseus to his eternal rest in paradise.'

'You're a clever little thing,' said Aegeus, chucking her under the chin.

'Don't ever do that again.'

'No, Medea, m'dear.'

He did not see Medea slip the poison into Theseus's cup at table, but a sign from her showed that she had managed to do so. She did not go quite so far as to tap the side of her nose and wink, but the slow and meaningful nod she gave Aegeus assured him that all was ready.

'So now, my people,' said Aegeus rising with a cup in his hand. 'I offer a toast to our guest, this prince of Troezen, this slayer of bandits and tamer of bulls, our new friend and protector. Let us drink to the health of *Lord* Theseus, for so I now name him.'

Enthusiastic murmurs of assent ran round the hall as the guests drank to Theseus, who sat modestly nodding his thanks.

'And now our guest must reply,' said Medea.

'Oh, now, well . . .' Theseus rose to his feet, grasping a goblet in nervous hands. 'I am not much of a fellow for talking. I know the art of speech-making is prized here in Athens

---

* It sprang from where Cerberus's drool hit the ground when Heracles took him to the Upper World.

and I hope some day to learn. For the most part I let my sword do the talking . . .' he opened his cloak slightly and put a hand to the hilt of his sword. A murmur of sympathetic and admiring laughter ran round the hall. 'But I drink to –'

'*No!*'

To the astonishment of all present King Aegeus suddenly leaned forward and violently struck the cup from Theseus's hands.

'That sword,' he said, pointing to Theseus's side. 'I buried that very sword in the ground for my son to find.'

'And these rotten old sandals,' said Theseus with a laugh, pulling one of them from his foot. 'How I cursed them when I was on the road.'

Father and son fell into each others' arms. It was a moment before Aegeus called Medea to mind.

'And as for you, sorceress, witch and –'

But she had gone. She left Athens never to return. Some swore that they saw her flying across the sky in a chariot drawn by dragons, her son Medus by her side.*

THE STORY OF THE TRIBUTE

Aegeus's next act was to announce that he would one day soon abdicate his throne in favour of Theseus, news received with much joy by the people of Athens. Aegeus was not unpopular, but it was widely accepted that he had been a

---

* Just as Perseus's son Perses gave us Persia and the Persians, so Medus went on to give us the Medes. Medes and Persians in turn, went on to attempt to get their revenge on Theseus's city of Athens many, many generations later when they launched an invasion under Darius the Great and then Xerxes. One man's Mede, as Dorothy Parker observed, is another man's Persian. As for Medea, little more of her is heard, which is a pity. There was a tradition that had her in the Meadows of Asphodel marrying Achilles in the afterlife.

weak ruler. Fifty strong and angry men contested Theseus's right to rule, however – the Pallantidae, the fifty sons of Aegeus's dead brother Pallas. They declared outright war on their unwanted cousin. It is axiomatic in the world of Greek mythology that a hero never knows rest and it was with a good grace and healthy vigour that Theseus prosecuted his war against the fifty.

In two groups, each led by twenty-five of the brothers, the enemy planned a surprise pincer attack on Athens. But Theseus had spies in their camp. Informed of their plans by a herald named LEUS, he ambushed each army in turn, massacring every single one of the Pallantidae.

Theseus felt he now had time to enjoy the peace and prosperity that had at last come to Athens. Yet he noticed that far from looking happy, the citizenry was going about the town with sullen, downcast looks. He was still popular, he knew that. But he could not account for what he saw in the people's eyes. He went to Aegeus.

'I don't understand it, father. The Pallantidae are no longer a threat. That witch Medea no longer exerts her malign influence over you and the city . . . trade is booming. Yet there's a look in everyone's eyes. A look of fear, of . . . the only word I can think of is . . . *dread*.'

Aegeus nodded. 'Yes. Dread is the right word.'

'But why?'

'It's the tributes, you see. The time has come round again for the tributes.'

'Tributes?'

'Has no one told you? Well, you've been a little occupied since you got here, haven't you? I suppose what with those fifty nephews of mine . . . and the Marathonian Bull, of course. Well, it concerns that damned bull, as a matter of fact . . . Oh dear.'

'What about it, father? It's been dead this year or more.'

'We have to go back quite a few years. King Minos sent his son to stay with me. To take part in some games and learn a little Athenian town polish, you know. Manners and style. The Cretans are . . . well, you know what Cretans are like.'

Theseus did not know what Cretans were like, but he knew that the rest of Greece held them equally in awe, fear and contempt.

'So he came to us. Androgeus, his name was. Stupid boy, I thought him, not very interesting, and so boastful about his attributes as a fighter and athlete. I should never have encouraged him. It was wrong of me . . .'

'What happened?'

'He died, while a guest. His father Minos . . . er . . . didn't take it well. He sailed a fleet here which overwhelmed our navy. Troops poured out from their damned ships and before long he had us where he wanted us.'

'But he didn't occupy Athens?'

'Said it wasn't worth it. "No Cretan would want to live in such a place," he said. Cheek. He threatened to burn the whole city to the ground unless . . .'

'Unless?'

'Well, this is where we come to it. Every year we must send seven maidens and seven youths in a ship to Crete to feed their . . . their . . .' Aegeus dried up at this point and gestured helplessly.

'Feed their what? Their army? Their sexual appetites? Their curiosity? What?'

'I suppose I shall have to tell you a story within a story now. What do you know of Daedalus?'

'Never heard of it . . .'

'Daedalus is not an *it*, he's a *him*.'

'Never heard of him, then.'

'Really? Have you heard of ASTERION and Pasiphae, or the Bull from the Sea?'

'Father, you talk in riddles.'

Aegeus sighed. 'I had better call for wine. You should know these stories.'

THE BULL FROM THE SEA

Crete is, in many respects (said Aegeus to Theseus, once wine had been brought and they had settled themselves back on couches), a blessed spot. The fruit and vegetables they grow there are bigger, juicier and tastier than from any other lands. The fish they catch on their coastline is the best in the Mediterranean. They are a proud people, a fierce people. For many years King Minos, in his palace at Knossos, has ruled them sternly but fairly. They have prospered under him. But there is a dark secret at the heart of Knossos.

For many years Minos has been lucky to have in his court the most gifted inventor, the most skilled artificer outside the Olympian forges of Hephaestus. His name is Daedalus and he is capable of fashioning moving objects out of metal, bronze, wood, ivory and gemstones. He has mastered the art of tightly coiling leaves of steel into powerful springs, which control wheels and chains to form intricate and marvellous mechanisms that mark the passage of the hours with great precision and accuracy, or control the levels of watercourses. There is nothing this cunning man cannot contrive in his workshop. There are moving statues there, men and women animated by his skill, boxes that play music and devices that can awaken him in the morning. Even if only half the stories of what Daedalus can achieve are true then you can be certain that no more cunning and clever an inventor, architect and craftsman has ever walked this earth.

They say he is descended from CECROPS, the first King of Attica and ancestor of all Athenians, Cecrops who judged in favour of Athena when she and Poseidon vied for control of the new town he was building. That is why we call the city Athens and bask in the wisdom and warmth of the great goddess's protection. I only mention this because although he works for Minos, our enemy, I think of Daedalus as Athenian, as one of us. After all, I would hate to think of a Cretan being so clever. As a matter of fact, Daedalus was expelled from Athens. He had a nephew named PERDIX who served as his apprentice and was, they say, even more ingenious and gifted than his brilliant uncle. Before he even reached the age of twenty, Perdix had invented the saw (inspired, they say, by the serrations on the backbone of a fish), compasses for architectural planning and geometry, and the potter's wheel too. Who knows what he would have gone on to devise had his jealous uncle not thrown him off the Acropolis, where he fell to his death. The goddess Athena turned him into a partridge. If you've ever wondered why partridges* always skim low and never soar into the air and even build their nests on the ground, it is because they recall their terrifying plummet from the heights of Athens.

Yes, yes, you are right, Theseus, this is all a little far from the point, but I must tell this story in my own way. Minos has a wife, Pasiphae – she and Daedalus are very close. Some even suggest that they . . . Well, let us say Minos is a difficult husband and no one would blame Pasiphae for looking else-where. She is a proud woman, daughter of the sun god Helios, no less, and imbued with great powers. She is the

---

* The zoological name for the genus is still *perdix,* the Latin for partridge.

sister of Circe and Aeëtes and an aunt, therefore, of Medea. There's a story that she became so annoyed by Minos's unfaithfulness to her that she secretly added a potion to his wine which caused him, in the act of love-making, to ejaculate only snakes and scorpions, which was most painful for all concerned. But what she did next took everyone by surprise.

One day Poseidon sent a white bull from the sea. Oh no, I am still not quite in the right order of things.

You know the story of Europa?* Who does not. How Zeus in the form of a bull† carried the girl off from Tyre right under the eyes of Cadmus and her other brothers. They went to Greece to get her back, and in the course of his adventures Cadmus founded Thebes, of course, and his brothers all established dynasties too, Phoenicia, Cilicia and so on, but they never found their sister, who had landed with Zeus on Crete. Well, Europa bore the god a son, Minos, who ruled the island and became, after his death, one of the Judges of the Underworld. His son ASTERION ruled Crete and his son, MINOS II, the current Minos, took over. But Minos had brothers who objected to his claim. Minos, though, insisted that the gods always intended him to be king, and to prove it he offered up a prayer to Poseidon.

'Send a bull from the sea, my lord Poseidon,' he cried, 'so that my brothers may know Crete is mine. I will sacrifice the bull in your name and venerate you always.'

Sure enough, the most beautiful white bull emerged from the waves. So beautiful, in fact, that there were two disastrous outcomes. Firstly, Minos decided it was far too handsome an animal to kill, so he sacrificed a lesser beast

---

* See *Mythos*, Vol. I.
† That bull ascended to the heavens as the constellation Taurus.

from his own herd, which very much enraged Poseidon. And secondly, the bull's astonishing beauty attracted Pasiphae. She couldn't take her eyes off it. She wanted it. She wanted it on her, around her and in her – I'm sorry, Theseus, it's true. I'm telling the story as it is known. There are those who say it was the angry Poseidon who crazed her with this lust – part of his punishment of Minos for failing to sacrifice the bull, but however it came about, Pasiphae became frenzied in her desire for the animal.

The bull was, of course, a bull and so had no sense of how to respond to a woman's advances. In the froth and frenzy of her erotic passion the lovestruck Pasiphae went to her friend, and perhaps ex-lover, Daedalus and asked if he could help her have her way with the bull. Without so much as a second thought Daedalus, excited perhaps by the intellectual challenge, set about manufacturing an artificial heifer. He made it from wood and brass, but he stretched a real cow's hide over the frame. Pasiphae fitted herself inside, the correct part of her presented to the correct opening. The whole contraption was wheeled to the meadow where the bull was grazing. I know, my boy, it *is* gross, but I am telling you the story as the world knows it.

Astonishingly, the depraved plan worked. Pasiphae screamed in a delirium of joy as the bull entered her. Never had she known such carnal ecstasy. Yes, laugh, mock and snort with derision as much as you like, but this is what happened, Theseus.

Still not satisfied that Minos had suffered enough for his disrespect, Poseidon now sent the bull mad. Its untameable terrorizing of the island caused Eurystheus to choose it as the seventh task he set for Heracles, who came to Crete, subdued it and took it to Mycenae. This was of course the bull that escaped from Mycenae, crossed into mainland Greece

1. The Pythia at Delphi.

2. Hylas and
the nymphs.

3. The Clashing Rocks.

4. Jason taming the Khalkotauroi.

5. Medea.

6. Medea tames the Colchis Dragon.

7. Jason finds the Golden Fleece.

8. The Calydonian Hunt.

9. The Foot Race.

10. Oedipus answers the riddle of the Sphinx.

11. The Labours of Theseus.

12. Theseus and the Marathonian Bull.

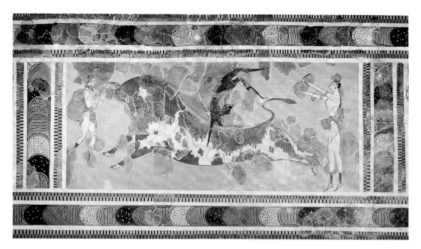

13. The art of bull-leaping.

14. The Tribute.

15. The Cretan Labyrinth.

16. The Minotaur.

17. The Fall of Icarus.

18. Ariadne, abandoned.

19. Theseus in Athens' Syntagma Square.

and tore up the plain of Marathon until you, my splendid boy, tamed it and brought it to Athens, finally, to be sacrificed. Quite a bull, wasn't it?

But its story and the curse of it is not over, for what happened on Crete next was even more dreadful. In due course Pasiphae, the bull's seed inside her, gave birth. What emerged was – as might be expected and thoroughly deserved – a monstrous aberration, half human and half bull. Minos was disgusted but neither he nor Pasiphae had the heart or stomach to kill the abomination. Instead, Minos commissioned Daedalus to construct a building in which this creature – which they named Asterion after Minos's father, but which the world called the MINOTAUR – could be safely housed and from which it could never escape.

The building Daedalus designed, which he named the Labyrinth, was an annex to his great Palace of Knossos, but so elaborate and complex was its maze-like design of passageways, blank walls, false doors, dead ends and apparently identical corridors, galleries and alcoves that a person could be lost in its interior for a lifetime. Any can enter, but none can ever find their way out. Indeed, the cunning of the labyrinth is that its design leads inevitably to the central chamber that lies in its very heart. It is a stone room where Asterion the Minotaur lives out his wretched, monstrous life. High above is a grating, which lets in some sunlight, and allows food to be thrown down to him. As he grew from infant-calf to man-bull (I should say that his lower half is human and his upper half is bull, complete with a full set of horns) it became clear that his favourite food was flesh. Human flesh for preference. A certain number of thieves, bandits and murderers are likely to be sentenced to death on Crete in the normal course of events and their carcasses go some way to satisfying the Minotaur, but every year he has a special treat. And this, Theseus, is where your father comes into the story – to his everlasting shame and dishonour.

Minos and Pasiphae's elder son Androgeus came to stay with me as a guest, as I told you, here at this palace in Athens. It happened to be around the time the bull that was the Minotaur's father had escaped from Mycenae and was now terrorizing Marathon. Androgeus was a tediously vain and boastful youth, endlessly going on about how superior to Athenians Cretan men were at running and wrestling and so on. One evening I snapped, and said 'Well, if you're so damned brave and athletic why don't you prove it by ridding Marathon of that damned bull?'

He was brave enough, or foolish enough, to go and of course he was killed. The bull gored him, ripped out his insides then tossed him a full *stadion*'s length across the plain, so they say. Minos was told, wrongly I assure you, that I sent Androgeus deliberately to his death because I was annoyed at how easily he beat our home-grown Athenian athletes in the games, but that is nonsense. It was the boy's boasting that provoked me.

Well, in his grief and rage Minos raised a fleet and laid siege to Athens. We were totally unprepared. An oracle told us we would die of famine and plague unless we yielded and agreed to his peace terms.

And this is where we have got to. Minos's terms.

He would generously forgo burning Athens to the ground if we agreed every year to send seven girls and seven youths by ship to Crete for them to be . . . there's no nice way of saying this . . . for them to be fed to the Minotaur. In return for this tribute, Athens retains its independence and freedom from attack.

Yes, I agree, it is a disgrace and certainly, you are right, it shames us all – but what else can we do?

TO CRETE

'I'll tell you what we can do,' said Theseus rising angrily from his couch. 'We can act less like frightened goats and more like true Athenians!'*

'That's all very well for you to say, you weren't there when Minos's fleet stood in Piraeus harbour . . .'

But Theseus was not interested in the past, only the future. It is one of the distinguishing features of heroes that makes them appealing and unappealing at one and the same time.

'How are these fourteen sacrificial lambs chosen?'

'I am proud to say,' said Aegeus, summoning up what dignity and regal authority he could, 'that like the true Athenians they are, they volunteer. Hundreds offer themselves willingly every year. We draw lots to choose the final seven for each group.'

'One of the seven youths will be me,' said Theseus. 'And we shall select the other thirteen not by lots, but by holding games. I want only the most fit, fleet, cunning and clever to accompany me to Crete and end this nonsense . . .'

'But Theseus, my boy – consider!' wailed Aegeus. 'The conditions lay down that the fourteen must arrive on Crete unarmed. What hope can you have when you will be under guard from the moment you make landfall? What will it matter how fast, strong or smart you are? Why throw your life away? The system has worked for the past five years. It is not . . . ideal, and I readily admit that it reflects little credit on us, but defeat is defeat and . . .'

Not another word would Theseus hear. He left the room

---

* This was an especially cutting remark for Aegeus's name means 'goatlike'.

and set to work right away on devising the games and tests that would select the cream of Athenian youth for the journey to Crete.

Aegeus sighed. He loved his son dearly but he was beginning to wonder if, all those years ago, he had been wrong to let Pittheus persuade him to loosen his bulging wineskin . . . maybe this is what the oracle had meant about it all ending with grief.

On a fine spring morning on the sixth day of the month of Mounichion,* Aegeus sat nervously on his throne, which had been carried in a litter to the harbour wall at Piraeus. A small ship, enough for a crew of five and fourteen passengers, was being provisioned. The king, under a flapping canopy, busied himself issuing commands for the loading of some extra cargo.

'There's no harm in offering Minos gifts,' he told Theseus. 'He may have softened his heart. If he knows that my own son . . . my own son . . .'

Theseus put a hand on his father's shoulder. 'Cheer up. The gods favour boldness. We will all be back before you know it.' He turned and jumped up onto the gunwales of the ship to address those gathered on the quayside to see them off. The families of the thirteen young people hand-picked by Theseus from all those who offered themselves were at the front, easily identifiable by their pale, drawn faces and the black mourning cloaks they wore.

'People of Athens!' cried Theseus. 'Be of good cheer. We young people go with glad hearts and will return to gladden yours.'

The thirteen behind him, all dressed like Theseus in sacrificial white and garlanded with flowers, raised their arms in

---

* A spring month.

salute and cheered. The anxious and stricken families on the quay did their best to cheer back.

'Hoist sails and ho for Crete!'

As black sailcloth was unfurled from the yards, Aegeus came bustling up to his son. 'Now listen,' he said. 'I have given the captain instructions. I will be standing on the top of the Acropolis every day to watch for your return. If the ship returns empty, if disaster has struck and you have failed . . .'

'. . . never happen . . .'

'. . . then he is to fly the black sails, but if the gods have been pleased to spare you and the ship returns in triumph . . .'

'. . . which is a certainty . . .'

'. . . he is to hoist white sails. So that I will know. You understand?'

The earnestness of the king's demeanour amused Theseus. 'Don't you worry yourself, father. It will be white sails all the way home. Now, grab an olive branch to wave and try to look happy. We are ready to sail.'

'May the gods bless you and watch over you always, Theseus my son.'

Prayers to Poseidon were offered up, petals and grains of corn were tossed into the waters and the ship sailed.

THE DUNGEONS OF KNOSSOS

Aegeus had been right to suppose that the moment the party from Athens made landfall in Crete they would be taken prisoner. On the way over, Theseus had tried to imagine ways in which they could overpower any guards set over them and make a fight of it, but no stratagem suggested itself to. Their ship had been met in open water and steered into harbour by an aggressive Minoan fleet before they had even sighted the island.

A small knot of jeering Cretans accompanied them from the docks at Heraklion to the palace dungeon where they were to spend the night. A group of children ran alongside hurling stones and insults as they approached the great gates of Knossos.*

'The bull man awaits!'

'He will grind your bones!'

'You'll wet yourselves! You always do!'

'He loves the taste of Athenians . . .'

'He'll fuck you first, then eat you!'

One of the young men started to whimper.

'Sh!' said Theseus. 'They want to see you afraid. Don't give them that satisfaction. Let's sing . . .'

In a voice more admirable for its strength than its musicality Theseus began to sing. It was the old anthem of Attica, the song that told the story of Cecrops and the founding kings of Athens. How Pallas Athena gave the people olive trees and contested with Poseidon over who should be the city's guardian.

Slowly and with gathering confidence the other thirteen joined in. The jeering children were unsure how to cope with this and fell away disappointed. A guard snarled at them to

---

* The Greek poet Bacchylides tells in one of his lyrics, his 'dithyrambs', that when the ship arrived Minos tried it on with one of the Athenian girls, Eriboia, and that Theseus defended her. Minos claimed that as a son of Zeus (in this version he is the first Minos, issue of Europa and Zeus) he had the right. Theseus countered that he was a son of Poseidon. Minos tested him by throwing a golden ring into the sea and telling Theseus to fetch it back. Theseus dived in and was taken by a dolphin to Poseidon's palace where Nereids gave him the ring and all kinds of gifts besides. He then emerged from the sea and presented the ring and other treasures to an astonished Minos. All this is charming but it seems odd that Minos would then imprison Theseus with the others as if nothing had happened. He would surely be wary that Theseus might be the first Athenian to prove himself a match for the beast and the labyrinth itself.

be quiet, but they only sang louder and more lustily. The gates opened and their voices echoed off the ramparts.

Into the palace they trooped, tramping their feet in time to their singing. They were stopped at the head of a stairway that led down to the dungeons, but still they sang. The stairhead was protected by a locked iron gate. As the lead guard took out a large key and fitted it to the lock, a door opened in the gallery above and Theseus glanced up. A girl appeared in the doorway, perhaps drawn by the unexpected sound of singing. She looked down and straight into his eyes. Instantly Theseus felt a surge of heat shoot through his whole body. The girl quickly closed the door.

Theseus found he could no longer sing. In a daze he let himself be led along with the others, the ship's crew included, to a large round cell under the palace. By the light of torches in brackets set around the wall, he saw a long table covered in dishes of the most colourful and appealing food. Some of the Athenians cried out in surprised delight as they fell on the feast, but Theseus felt no such pleasure. Naturally the Minotaur would prefer to gorge on well-fed flesh.

The captain of the guard banged his spear on the ground. 'Stop. Girls on the left, boys on the right. His majesty will inspect you.'

The door to the cell opened and the royal party came in. King Minos entered clutching the hand of a young girl whose eyes were cast down. When she looked up, Theseus saw that it was the same girl he had seen in the doorway. Their eyes met again.

'I shall examine the young men, Ariadne,' Minos was saying to her. 'Why don't you and your mother inspect the maidens?'

Queen Pasiphae stepped out from the shadows and took her daughter's arm. So this was the woman who mated with a bull and gave birth to the Minotaur. She seemed ordinary and disappointingly domestic to Theseus's eyes, which were only for her beautiful daughter. Ariadne! What a perfectly delightful name.

Theseus lined up with the other six youths. The maidens were ranged opposite so Theseus could only see Ariadne's back as she walked with her mother down the line, appraising the Athenian girls.

'Well, they *look* like virgins,' he heard Pasiphae saying in a sceptical voice, 'but how can one tell?' Ariadne said nothing. Theseus would have loved to know what her voice sounded like.

Meanwhile Minos stalked down the line looking the young men up and down with a critical eye. When he arrived at Theseus he prodded him with his ivory sceptre. Theseus restrained an enraged desire to throw a punch right at his arrogant, smirking face.

'Red hair, eh?' Minos said. 'Well-muscled too. Asterion will like that. Very good. Now this is how it works,' he raised his voice and turned to address both groups. 'Over the next two weeks you will be given all the food and drink you require. Starting tomorrow a youth will be selected and taken into the labyrinth. The next day it will be a girl. A youth the day after, and so on until the two weeks are over and the last of you has been taken. The ship's crew will then be released to sail back to Athens under safe passage with the news that the tribute is paid and your kingdom safe for another year. Understood?'

Silence. Theseus looked towards Ariadne who seemed to be examining the stone flags of the cell floor.

'No snivelling, no sobbing, I admire that,' said Minos. 'Keep your heads high and meet your fate proudly and doubtless you will be rewarded in the afterlife. That is all. Come, Pasiphae, Ariadne.'

At the last minute Ariadne glanced up towards Theseus

and again his eyes locked with hers for the briefest instant. The briefest instant that contained an entire lifetime of joy, love and explosive bliss.

The door clanged shut and the young people turned expectant faces on Theseus. They were thrilled to see that he was smiling.

'You have a plan?' they enquired of him.

Theseus was jerked from his trance. 'Plan? Well now . . . plan . . .'

He looked about him. Something would occur to him, surely? After the feelings that had swept over him when he looked into the eyes of Ariadne it was impossible to believe that his life and the lives of his companions were going to end. Surely Eros had been at work with his bow? Surely the tumult in his heart was in her heart too? It couldn't be for nothing. It had to mean something.

'You all sleep. By morning I shall have my plan.'

'But what will it be?'

'Sleep. Just sleep. All will be clear.'

The plenteous good food and strong wine had tired them out and it was not long before Theseus was the only one left awake and standing.

Silence descended and Theseus found himself sliding to the floor and nodding off too, but HYPNOS never fully took his mind and he was quickly jerked awake by a sound. Someone was coming along the passageway. He stood upright and stepped over to the door.

Two murmuring voices grew louder. He could distinguish an older man, who seemed distressed or anguished in some way and the lower murmur of a female voice.

The handle of the cell door turned and through the grille he saw to his unnameable joy the face of Ariadne. She opened the door and came in, followed by an old man who nervously closed the door behind him. Theseus approached her.

'Why are you here?'

She looked steadily into his eyes. 'You have to ask?'

It seemed natural to take her face in his hands and cover her in kisses.

The kisses were returned.

'Ariadne!' he breathed.

'What is your name?' she asked.

'Theseus.'

'Theseus?' Her eyes rounded in wonder. 'Son of Aegeus?'

'The same.'

'Of course . . .' she fell into his arms.

The old man tapped her impatiently on the shoulder. 'Ariadne!' he whispered. 'The guards may come at any moment.'

She broke off. 'You're right of course, we must hurry. Come with me, Theseus. We'll leave the island together.'

Theseus stopped. 'I do not leave without my companions,' he said.

'But . . .'

'I have come not to be spirited away, but to kill the Minotaur and free my people of the burden that has been placed upon them.'

She gazed deep into his eyes again. 'Yes,' she said at length. 'We wondered if you might say that.' She indicated the old man by her side. 'This is Daedalus. He built the labyrinth where the creature lives.'

The old man nodded at Theseus. 'Once inside its endless maze of corridors you will never find your way out,' he said.

'Is there not a key?' said Theseus. 'I have heard that if you take the first right and second left, or some such set sequence, then you can always solve a maze.'

'This has no such cheap solution,' said Daedalus testily. 'There is one way – Ariadne, tell him.'

376

'The corridors that lead from here through the labyrinth are dark,' she said. 'They take you inevitably to the centre. But to escape you will need this ball of thread. From the point where the guard leaves you, attach the end to the doorway and unroll it as you go further in. That way you will always be able to follow it out.'

'Suppose I am the last chosen for the Minotaur,' said Theseus. 'I cannot let thirteen good young Athenians die. I must be chosen first.'

'Don't you worry about that. I shall bribe the captain of the guard and you will be chosen tomorrow morning, I promise. I can give you no weapon though. You must tackle Asterion on your own.'

'I fought his father without weapons and won,' said Theseus, thinking back to the Marathonian Bull.

'When you kill him, kill him quickly and mercifully. He is a monstrous mistake, but he is my brother. My half-brother at least.'

Theseus smiled into her eyes. 'I love you, Ariadne.'

'I love you, Theseus.'

'When I have killed him, I shall return and release my companions. You will sail with me back to Athens and we shall rule together as king and queen. Now leave, both of you, before we are discovered.'

'One last kiss,' said Ariadne.

'One last mmmnn . . .' said Theseus.

THE BULL MAN

Fully awake though he remained, the next few hours passed like a fevered dream for Theseus. He had met the woman with whom he was destined to share his life. The gods were good.

He had no way of calculating the passage of the hours. The sea-captain was the first of the Athenians to wake. He came over to Theseus and they looked down at the sleeping young people. They lay on the floor, arms encircling one another – the very flower of Athenian youth.

'They say the monster kills quick,' said the captain. 'In with the horns and up with its head, slicing through to the lung and heart. There are worse deaths.'

'It is the Minotaur who dies today.'

'My lord?'

'Let us suppose I am chosen first, but that I return here the way I came. Are you ready to prepare the others for a fight?'

'We have no weapons.'

'I'll see what I can do about that.'

'It is good of you to plant the seed of hope but – great Zeus, what was that?' The captain broke off and stared about him, a look of terror on his face.

A sound like none that they had ever heard came to their ears from deep within the palace. It had begun as a deep, mournful bellow and was swelling now into a great roar of rage.

Theseus put a hand on the sea-captain's shoulder. 'Our friend the Minotaur has woken up and is calling for his breakfast.'

As he spoke the door opened and four soldiers marched in followed by an overweight and self-satisfied-looking captain of the guard.

'Up! Get up, the pack of you!' he barked, strutting round and kicking the prisoners awake. 'Let's see . . . who shall we pick, eh?' The young Athenians shrank back and tried to look invisible. 'You!' The captain stabbed his forefinger at Theseus. 'Yes, you. Follow me.'

The other Athenians covered their natural feelings of

relief at being spared by offering far from convincing cries of shocked distress.

'No, no! Not Prince Theseus!'

One even dared to call out 'Take me! Take me instead!'

Theseus quietened them. 'Brave friends,' he said. 'I go willingly and gladly to meet my fate. Fear not, we shall meet again and laugh at the memory.'

The captain of the guard pushed him towards the door. Theseus pressed the ball of thread into his armpit and trusted that the unnatural way his arm hung could be put down to fear.

As they marched away down a dark corridor, the captain gave him a long sideways look. 'What you do to upset the Princess Ariadne, then? She begged me to make sure the tall one with copper hair be taken to the labyrinth first. What you say to her?''

'I can't imagine.'

'Must have said something.'

'Perhaps it's the way I looked at her.'

'Well you're going to pay the price, sure enough.'

They approached a giant bronze gate into which was set a smaller door which the captain opened.

'In you go, mate. If you can find your way back to this door, why then . . . but no one ever has and no one ever will.' He gave Theseus a push through. 'Give the bull man my regards.'

The door closed behind him and Theseus was in darkness. It was not total darkness; far above at roof level were gratings that let in enough moonlight to pick out the damp edges and corners of the passageway in which he found himself.

He stood for a while, allowing his eyes to accustom themselves to these new conditions. A lick of light showed him the small door he had come through. He tried its handle. It was unlocked!

'Oh no you don't, mate,' came the sneering voice of the captain of the guard. 'I'm staying here till I know you've gone.' Theseus felt the door being pushed closed against him. Never mind, there was a stud on his side around which he could wind the end of his thread.

He turned now and walked away from the door, playing out the thread behind him as he went.

It was like no other experience he had known. At first he felt the floor rising, then he turned a corner and it sloped downwards. He started in shock as he made out the shape of a man creeping stealthily towards him. He laughed when he d that it was his own reflection in a panel of polished bronze. This happened four more times as he went on. Corners and blind recesses baffled him. He was sure at one point that he had come full circle and yet he could tell from the smell and the continuing downward slope that this could not be so.

He became aware of distant sounds that grew in volume the further he pressed on: snuffling and stamping, baying, grunting and growling. There was a forlorn quality to the way the growls and grunts were being pushed out that reminded Theseus of something. He was on the verge of placing it when he stepped on something that crunched under his feet. He stooped to pick up a human rib bone, and then another and another.

'Asterion, O Asterion!' he called. 'I'm coming for you . . .'

He leaned against a wall and looked down a long corridor from which came more light than he had seen for the past half hour. A high roof, open to the sky, poured moonlight down into what he believed must be the heart of the labyrinth. He had made so many turns; he had ascended and descended more than he could recall and had almost collided with dozens of mirrors and dead ends. Seemingly he had doubled back and redoubled his course multiple times, looping round and up and along the same passageways, but – if the clue he was leaving, the thread, was to be believed – this was an illusion. The genius of the design seemed to lie as much in the appearance of complexity as in its reality. The labyrinth induced panic and eroded self-belief.

As Theseus approached the central room, a smell of rotting flesh, shit and urine met his nostrils. He laid the almost depleted ball of thread down and left it on the ground, coughing at the putrid stench. The stone floor was level here and he could be confident that his lifeline would not roll away.

He was delighted to find himself completely unafraid, yet puzzled to feel his heart beating thunderously in his chest nonetheless. Could he be frightened and not aware of it? A shuffling, growling and stamping came from up ahead. So much bright silver light poured down from the open roof high above that Theseus had to open and close his eyes wide to see properly.

He was in the Minotaur's lair. He was treading on bones, clods of manure and damp straw which Theseus guessed had been dropped in from the roof above. Silence but for the thudding of his own heart and the alternate crunching and slushing of his footsteps. But now a new noise, a scraping of horn against stone. Something in the corner was moving. A form arose in the corner and emerged from the shadows. Red eyes burned as they looked towards the mortal man who had dared approach.

'Hello there . . .' said Theseus. He had meant his words to be loud and clear, but they came out as a whisper.

The great head was raised and the Minotaur let loose a mighty bellow. The roar echoed off the stone and down the four corridors that ran from this central chamber. Theseus stepped in from the head of his corridor.

'No, no,' he said, 'you can't threaten me with that. Any bull in a field can roar.'

Theseus's eyes were able to pick out more and more detail. The Minotaur was standing upright now on its two human legs. The head was huge, the horns sharply pointed. The neck widened onto human shoulders, the chest below was matted with fur-like hair or hair-like fur that patched the whole body. A great pizzle swung between the legs, almost reaching the two hoofs that banged and scraped on the stone flags. The creature stopped roaring and looked sideways at Theseus. A long string of drool fell from its chops.

'You're a sight, aren't you?' said Theseus. 'Does no one ever wash this place down?'

They both raised their heads at the same time to look at the square of light above.

Theseus laughed at the comical synchronization. 'I really believe you understood me.'

The Minotaur growled, snorted and grunted.

Theseus realised with a stab of astonishment what it was that had struck him earlier as so strange about the creature's voice. It mimicked the rhythms of human speech. He was unaccountably certain that the Minotaur was trying to speak, but that the bovine vocal cords with which he had been born were incapable of fashioning the right sounds.

'You're trying to speak, aren't you?'

The hoarse cry that came from the bull's head was surely an affirmation.

'You poor thing. Asterion, that is your name? Asterion, listen to me. I know the way out of this maze. Why don't you come with me? We will sail for Athens. I will make sure you have a field to yourself.'

Something like a howl emerged and the animal's great dewlaps shook.

'No? What then?'

The Minotaur stood tall and screamed.

'Shush now. Try to help me understand,' said Theseus, quite unfazed. 'Surely anything is better than a fight? There can only be one outcome. I will kill you. I wouldn't want that. Now that I've met you I find that I like you.'

Now the Minotaur strained to make a new noise. It summoned all its breath and focussed it into a whine that sounded in Theseus's ears like 'Hill he! Hill he!'

Then he understood. 'Kill me? You're saying kill me?'

The Minotaur dropped his great head in a form of assent.

'Kill you? Don't ask me that.'

The Minotaur reared up. *'Hill he! hill he!'*

Theseus rose to his full height too. 'Let it be a duel at least,' he said. 'You kill me . . . kill *me!*' So saying he aimed a kick at a heap of dung. Thick pieces flew up into the Minotaur's face. 'Come on, then!'

The creature gave a roar of outrage as flecks of his own faeces stung his eyes. He stamped his hoofs, shook his head and lunged at Theseus.

Theseus stepped left and then right, goading the Minotaur to come at him. It shook its head one way and the other in confusion.

'Yah! Yah! Come on now,' shouted Theseus, backing towards a wall.

It made up its mind, lowered its horns and charged. Theseus leapt aside at the last moment and the Minotaur crashed headfirst into the stone wall. The left-hand horn snapped with a great crack and hung down loose. Theseus rolled forward in a somersault, wrenched the horn free and before the dazed creature had time to know what was happening, he thrust the sharp point deep into the folds of its throat and pulled viciously across, severing the windpipe.

The eruption of blood covered Theseus from head to foot. The creature stamped about in a jerking dance as more and more blood jetted out from its neck in a fountain. Its hoofs slipped on the blood-wet stones and it fell, shuddering to the ground.

Theseus knelt beside it and talked gently into its ear. 'I send you to your eternal rest with all speed and respect, Asterion. The world will know that you died a brave and noble death.'

The act of slashing the creature's neck must have loosed the tight vocal cords that moments earlier had denied it the power of speech. Now, despite the blood bubbling from the open gash in its throat, it managed to speak. Theseus heard as clearly as from an orator on the Acropolis the words '*Thank you*' before the creature's ghost departed its monstrous body.

'Farewell, bull man,' breathed Theseus. 'Farewell, Asterion, son of Pasiphae, son of the Bull from the Sea, the Cretan Bull, the Marathonian Bull. Farewell brother of the beautiful Ariadne. Farewell, farewell.'

ABANDONMENT AND FLIGHT

Theseus followed the thread out of the labyrinth. When he emerged through the door inset in the great gate he saw opposite him the captain of the guard asleep in a chair. He crept up to break the man's neck and take his keys, but found that he had been dead for some time and that the great iron ring at his belt had already been stripped of its keys. Making his way towards the dungeon where his fellow Athenians were imprisoned, he found Ariadne standing outside. Her eyes were shining as she waved keys in front of Theseus's face.

'I knew you'd make it,' she said.

Theseus embraced her. She could not but recoil.

'You're *covered* in blood!'

'I'll wash it off when we're clear of here.'

'Was it horrible?'

'I gave him a quick death. Did you dispatch the captain of the guard?'

'The pig had it coming,' said Ariadne. 'The things he tried to do to me when I was little. Now, let's free your friends.'

The pair of them, along with the shipmates and the joyful thirteen Athenians stole silently out of the palace by a side gate and made their way to the harbour, where they holed the bottoms of the Cretan ships at anchor before boarding their own vessel and setting sail.

The day was taking over morning as they slipped into the open sea. The six youths and seven girls, Theseus and the crew added oar power to the sails and soon the landmass of Crete was out of sight. Although they had scuttled the Cretan fleet in Heraklion harbour there was still the risk of a patrolling warship, so they did not stop until they reached the island of Naxos where they dropped anchor and waded ashore to spend the night.

Theseus, now cleaned of the caked blood of the Minotaur at last lay with Ariadne. They made love three times in the moonlight before falling asleep in each other's arms.

A most terrible dream came to Theseus while he slept. It began as a shouting in his ears.

'Leave! Leave the island now. Go! Take your Athenians, but leave Ariadne, who is promised to me. Leave or you all die. You all *die.*'

Theseus tried to resist but the outline of a figure formed out of the mists of the dreams and came towards him. A young man with vine leaves in his hair approached. He was at once both beautiful and terrible to look upon.

'Three choices. Stay here with Ariadne and you die. Take Ariadne with you and you and all your companions die. Leave with your people and you live. My ships are coming. Nothing can stop them. Go, go, go!'

Theseus knew the young man to be the god Dionysus. He sat up, sweating and breathless. Ariadne lay peacefully asleep beside him.

Leaving her he went down to the beach to think. The sea-captain had also been unable to sleep and joined him. They paced up and down the sand in silence for a while.

'I had a dream,' said Theseus at last. 'Just a dream, but it worries me.'

'The god Dionysus?'

Theseus stared. 'Don't tell me you had it too?'

They silently woke the others.

'We don't have a choice,' the sea-captain said to Theseus time and again. 'We have to leave her.'

When they were far out to sea Theseus looked back and thought he could see the desolate figure of Ariadne standing on the shore in the moonlight. Approaching the island from the other side they could already see the fleet of Dionysus. Theseus mourned the loss of the girl he had fallen in love with, but he knew that the safety of the young people in his charge overrode everything. He had to sacrifice his own happiness. He had to sacrifice her.

That, at least, is the Athenian explanation of the abandonment of Ariadne on Naxos. Other versions maintain that Theseus left her on the island because he had no more use for her. She had served her purpose and could be dispensed with. In some Cretan tellings, Dionysus duly arrived in force on Naxos, married Ariadne (raising her wedding diadem to the heavens as the constellation Corona Borealis), had at least twelve children by her and rewarded her after her death by rescuing her from Hades, along with his own mother Semele, and they all lived happily ever after on Olympus.

It is hard for us to like a Theseus who could coldheartedly abandon the girl who had been so instrumental in saving him and his companions, and doubtless that is why the Athenian version of the story lays emphasis on the hard choice that faced him and even goes so far as to suggest that Ariadne was already in some way engaged to Dionysus when she first met Theseus, thus throwing all the blame on her. The Athenians didn't like to hear anything that showed their favourite hero in a bad light.

On their way back to Athens, a gloomy and contemplative Theseus was shaken on the shoulders by the sea-captain. 'Look up, sir, look up!'

Theseus saw that the entire ship's complement was staring up at the sun.

'What is it?' he said, squinting up in the direction of their gaze. 'What am I supposed the be looking at?'

And then he saw it. Two of them, flying in the sky above. An older and a younger man. They had wide white wings. The younger man swooped up and then down. Even from their distance it was clear that he was enjoying himself.

FATHER AND SON

Minos was awakened and told the terrible news. They had looked down through the high grating and seen the Minotaur slain in his chamber. The captain of his guard was dead too. The Athenians were gone and the great Minoan fleet was crippled. What is more Princess Ariadne could not be found. Perhaps she had been taken prisoner, perhaps . . .

Minos knew who to blame. If the Minotaur was dead and

his killer had escaped it could only mean that Daedalus had somehow betrayed the secret of the labyrinth. Minos ordered that the inventor and his son Icarus should be imprisoned in his tower room at the top of the palace, a twenty-four-hour guard posted outside. There they could await a sentence of death.

Icarus stood at the windows of their prison and looked out at the sea.

'I suppose if we jump out far enough we might miss the rocks and land in the water?' he said.

Daedalus did not reply. He was busy. The tower in which they had been imprisoned was filled with roosting birds, their shit and their feathers.

'What are you doing, dad?'

'Pass me those candle stumps.'

'Making something?'

'Sh! Don't bother me.'

He always shushed him like that when he was working on something important. Icarus laid himself full length on the floor and went to sleep.

He had no idea how much time had passed when his father shook him awake excitedly. 'Up, Icarus, up! Put these on.'

'What are they?'

'Wings, boy, wings!'

Icarus rose groggily to his feet and allowed Daedalus to fit leather straps around him. He looked round to see what was happening and why his back and shoulders tickled.

'Stand back and give yourself space and try to spread them.'

'You've really done it this time, dad.'

Daedalus was fitting his own set. 'Stop giggling and give me a hand here.'

Slowly he instructed Icarus in their use.

'But dad, are you saying we have to jump out the window and trust them to keep us in the air?'

'I have spent a lifetime studying birds. The air is not empty space to them, it is as solid as the earth is to us, or water to a fish. It holds them up and it will hold us up. Have faith.'

He adjusted the leather straps on his son's wings so that they sat square and straight and took him by the shoulders. 'Now listen to me, Icarus. We are flying over the sea to Athens, where I am sure Theseus will welcome us. But take care as you go. Fly too low and the waves will soak your wings and drag you under. Fly too close to the sun and the heat of its rays will melt the candle wax that is holding the feathers together, you understand?'

'Sure,' said Icarus bouncing up and down with excitement. 'Not too low, not too high.'

'Now, shall I go first?'

'Don't worry, dad,' cried Icarus rushing to the window, 'I've got this. Whoooooooo!'

He jumped and heard his father's voice calling behind him.

'Spread your wings! Spread them! Present them to the air.'

He did as he was told and immediately felt the rush of the air press against the wings and hold him up. He was flying! His wings held in the wind and he knew that they would keep him there. His father was right, the air was a solid thing. He accustomed himself to using his arms to steer this way and that. The smallest movement from him was all that was needed to control his flight. Below him crawled the wrinkled sea, hugging the shoreline of Crete, the only home he had ever known. His father appeared in front of him, his own wings spread out.

'The pillars of warm air rising from the cliffs below are holding us up for the moment,' he shouted. 'Once we're over open sea we can beat and glide, beat and glide.'

'Like the gulls?'

'Just like the gulls. Follow me, Athens is this way. And remember . . .'

'I know – not too high, not too low,' laughed Icarus.

'And don't forget it.'

'*Whoah*!' Icarus cried out in sudden surprise as a seagull flew right in his path. He gathered himself together and dived after his father.

From far below Theseus looked up and saw Icarus swooping and soaring, plunging and looping.

Icarus was some way from Daedalus now, out of earshot, when he spotted the beak-prowed Athenian ship far below. Haha! he thought to himself, I'll give them the shock of their lives. But first some height.

Up and up he flew, gaining height for his planned dive-bombing. He was so high now he could hardly see Theseus's ship below, so high that . . . so high that it was hot. He cried out in alarm as feathers began to fall from his wings. The wax was melting! He rolled over to point his head down and dive down as far from the sun as possible, but it was too late. The feathers were falling like snow all about him and he started to plummet. The air, now cold and hard, banged against him. He heard his father cry out. There was nothing he could do. The sea was rushing up towards him. Perhaps if he narrowed his shoulders he might be able to plunge below the surface and come up safe.

Daedalus looked down in impotent despair. He knew that from such a height the sea would be like a bed of granite. He watched the body break on the waves and knew that his son's bones would be smashed to pieces and the life gone from him.

'Oh Icarus, Icarus, my beloved boy. Why couldn't you listen? Why did you have to fly so close to the sun?'

Tragic laments like this, with changes of name, have been

heard from generations of fathers ever since. It is the destiny of children of spirit to soar too close to the sun and fall, no matter how many times they are warned of the danger. Some will make it, but many do not.*

Daedalus dived down and rescued the broken body of his son, which he buried on a nearby island, called to this day Icaria. They say that a partridge witnessed the burial and flapped its wings, mewing with triumph. Perdix enjoyed the tragic justice of Daedalus's son falling to his death, just as he had been pushed by Daedalus to his. The grieving father wandered the Mediterranean, finding employment at last in the court of King COCALUS of Camicus, in southern Sicily.

The rage of Minos on finding that his birds had, quite literally, flown, was ungovernable. His daughter lost, his reputation as a mighty and unconquerable king severely dented, humiliated by the escape of Daedalus, he vowed that he would have his revenge. Accordingly, he scoured the Greek world for the inventor, taking with him a spiral sea-shell. At each kingdom, island or province he visited, Minos announced that he would reward with gold anyone who could successfully pass a thread through the shell's complex helical chambers. He believed that Daedalus was the only man alive clever enough to hit upon a way of doing it.

After years of searching, at last Minos arrived in Camicus. King Cocalus accepted Minos's challenge and took the shell to Daedalus, who quickly solved the problem by tying one

---

* The story of Daedalus and Icarus has long been a favourite with artists. The combined brilliance of Pieter Breugel the Elder and W. H. Auden has given us the latter's poem 'Musée des Beaux Arts', one of his finest. Sculptures and paintings on the subject abound. My favourite use of the myth is in the relief representation of the falling Icarus on the wall outside the bankruptcy court of Amsterdam. Rembrandt might well have looked up at it during the proceedings against him and been reminded of the perils of soaring ambition. So far as I know he never painted an Icarus picture himself but scores, hundreds, of artists and sculptors have.

end of the thread to an ant, which he coaxed through the shell with drops of honey. King Cocalus triumphantly presented Minos with the threaded seashell and demanded the reward.

Minos drew himself up to his full height. 'Only Daedalus the artificer, Daedalus the inventor, Daedalus the traitor can have done this,' he declared. 'Give him up to me or I will leave this instant for Crete and return with a fleet to crush you and conquer your kingdom.' Minos may have been bested by Theseus, but he was still the ruler of a great naval power.

'Let me go to my council chamber and consult,' said King Cocalus.

By this he meant, 'let me ask my daughters.' He knew that his girls adored Daedalus, who had entertained them when they were growing up by teaching them all kinds of clever tricks. He gathered the girls together and told them about the threat.

'Tell Minos,' said the eldest daughter, 'that you will offer Daedalus up in chains tomorrow. But tonight, let him bathe, eat, drink, listen to music and be royally feasted as befits so great a king.'

Cocalus, as he always did, obeyed his daughters and relayed the message.

Minos bowed at the honour done to him.

It so happened that the restless and ever inventive Daedalus had designed and installed a heating system for the palace, consisting of a network of pipes which carried hot water from a central boiler, the first of its kind in the world.

Minos got into his bath that evening, but he never got out. Down in the hypocaust, the sisters heated the water until it boiled. It burst from the pipes in the bathroom and scalded Minos to an agonising death.

THESEUS, THE KING

We left Theseus on board ship with his thirteen compatriots, staring up at Daedalus and Icarus in flight. What with his gnawing guilt at the abandonment of Ariadne and feelings of astonishment and dismay at the sight of Icarus falling to his death, Theseus's mind was fully occupied as the ship sailed homeward towards Athens.

So wrapped in thought were he and the sea-captain that even as the ship came within sight of Piraeus harbour something very important slipped both their minds. They entirely forgot their promise to pull down the black sails and hoist white ones to let Aegeus know that they were sailing back in triumph.

The king had stood every day on the cliffs waiting for a sight of the ship. Now he saw on the horizon the familiar outline of an Athenian vessel. It was beyond question the ship of his son Theseus, but what colour were the sails? The ship was so far away. Against the white of the sky the sails looked black, but perhaps because they were in silhouette . . . no . . . that was too much to hope for. The closer the ship sailed, the clearer it was that its sails were as black as death. His brave, foolish, newly found son was dead.

That prophecy from the oracle:

Aegeus must not loosen the bulging mouth of the wineskin until he has reached the heights of Athens, or he will die of grief.

Aegeus finally understood what it had meant. He should have gone straight from Delphi to Athens all those years ago. Instead he had gone to Troezen where he had somehow found himself in bed with Aethra. He had loosened his bulging wineskin. He had fathered Theseus, who had given him a brief time of joy, but now – it was true, the oracles were always right – he found himself overcome by mortal grief.

With a cry of despair Aegeus threw himself to his death in the sea below, the sea that ever since has been called, in his honour, the Aegean.

It is hard to know for sure what kind of a king Theseus was. Later, the Athenians, who wrote most of the history that has come down to us, so revered their Founder King that, if we are to believe them, he was the inventor, not only, as we have discovered, of wrestling and bull-leaping, but of democracy, justice and all good government too, as well as being a paragon of intelligence, wit, insight and wisdom – qualities that the Athenians (much to the contempt of their neighbours) believed uniquely exemplified their character and culture. It is generally accepted that he merged the smaller regional and provincial units (known as demes) of Attica under the rule of the central Athenian polis or city state,* a system that served as the model for Ancient Greek administrative government up to the historical period.

What is certainly clear is that Theseus was very much a human being, with all the weaknesses, strengths and inconsistencies that the condition confers upon us. Much of what followed in his life after the Minotaur was a result of one of the great male friendships in Greek myth, that between Theseus and Pirithous.† As with the later bromance of Achilles and

---

* He federated Megara (a region, not to be confused with Heracles' first wife), for example, and installed Cercyon's son Hippothoon on the throne of Eleusis, which extended the reach of Athens as far as Corinth.

† Usually pronounced 'Pirry-*tho*-us' with an unvoiced 'th', as in 'thistle' – think, 'Pirry-throw-us' without the R.

Patroclus, there is a suggestion in some Greek sources that there may have been a sexual element in the relationship, but if there was it had no effect on the womanizing and philandering propensities of either man.

Pirithous, King of the Lapiths, was a son of Dia and Zeus. Dia had been the wife of Ixion. It seems hypocritical that Zeus might bind Ixion to a wheel of fire for attempting to seduce Hera and then set about ravishing the man's wife, but Zeus was never anything if not Zeus. In the form of a stallion he had his way with Dia who bore Pirithous, who in adulthood earned a reputation for being a fine warrior and, perhaps unsurprisingly, horseman.*

Hearing of the equally excellent reputation of Athens' new king and wanting to test it, Pirithous raided Marathon, coming away with a herd of Theseus's most prized cattle.† Outraged, Theseus made his way to Larissa, the capital of the Lapith kingdom, and tracked Pirithous down, meaning if not to kill him, at least to teach him a very severe lesson. But the moment they met they decided that they liked each other and instead of fighting swore eternal friendship.

The bond was soon tested, for Pirithous was not without challengers to his throne in Thessaly. The centaurs, half-man half-horse, felt that as descendants of Ixion they had a greater right to rule than Pirithous.‡ They had been given Mount Pelion as a base, but they took this as an insult and demanded

---

* The Lapiths were credited with inventing the bit for greater control of the horse's mouth.

† Issue, some say, of the Marathonian Bull who fathered them before Theseus tamed him and took him to Athens to be sacrificed. The Marathonian Bull that had been the Cretan Bull that fathered the Minotaur, of course. The baleful influence of that animal seems to have no end.

‡ They were children of Ixion and Nephele, the cloud goddess in the shape of Hera that was created by Zeus to prove Ixion's wickedness. The same Nephele who went on to send down the Golden Ram to rescue Phrixus.

more. It all came to a head during the wedding of Pirithous and his bride, Hippodamia*. Out of diplomatic necessity Pirithous had made sure that the centaurs were invited, but as milk drinkers they were unused to the wine which flowed during the feast. Its effect caused them to start behaving abominably.† One of them, EURYTION, tried to rape the bride Hippodamia herself while the rest of the centaurs pushed themselves on all the women and boys present. Pirithous and Theseus, an honoured guest at the wedding, fought back.

A rather touching side story in this otherwise grim and frenzied fight (sometimes called the *Centauromachy* or 'Battle of the Centaurs'‡) involves the sad end of a Lapith called Caeneus. He had been born a woman, Caenis. She was spotted one day by Poseidon who liked what he saw and took it. Entirely delighted by the experience, the grateful god offered Caenis any wish. She had taken no pleasure at all in the violation and asked that she might be turned into a man and thus avoid any indignity of that kind in the future. Poseidon, perhaps abashed, not only granted this wish but also bestowed invulnerable skin upon her – now *him*. Caeneus was present at the wedding of Pirithous and Hippodamia and fought the centaurs alongside Pirithous and Theseus. One of the centaurs, Latreus, mocked him for having once been a woman. Caeneus struck Latreus but was himself, due to his invulnerability, unharmed by a furious volley of counterstrikes. The other centaurs, discovering that their arrows and spears were bouncing off Caeneus's

---

* Her name means 'tamer of horses'. Horses gallop all the way through the story of Pirithous.

† Similar to its effect on the centaurs including, fatefully, Nessus, who drank wine in Pholus's cave during Heracles' Fourth Labour.

‡ 'War' rather than 'battle' really, but battle sounds better in English somehow. The accidental rhyme in 'War of the Centaurs' or 'Centaur War' seems inelegant.

impenetrable hide, resorted to heaping stones over him and hammering him into the ground with pine trees until he died by suffocation in the earth.

Despite the loss of Caeneus, Pirithous and his Lapiths finally prevailed. The surviving centaurs galloped away, defeated and dejected. Among the surviving centaurs who galloped away, defeated and dejected, was Nessus, who was fated to be Heracles' bane.*

Peace having now descended on Thessaly, Pirithous was able to help his friend Theseus acquire a wife. They chose the Amazon warrior ANTIOPE, sister of Hippolyta, whose war belt had been fatally wrested from her by Heracles during his Labours.† Although Antiope was forcibly abducted it is generally believed that after Theseus installed her as his queen and wife in Athens she grew to love him. She bore him a son, Hippolytus, whom they named in honour of her sister, the great Amazonian queen.

The Amazons had other ideas. Marriage to a man was a betrayal of everything these proud, misandrous warrior women stood for.‡ They combined forces in a sustained attack on Athens known as the Attic War. The Amazons were defeated at the final battle on the Areopagus, the Hill of Ares.§ During that fight Antiope was badly wounded. A fellow Amazon called MOLPADIA, although fighting on the opposite side, put her out of her agony with a swift arrow through the neck. Theseus, seeing this, killed Molpadia. Her

---

* See the story of Heracles (page 127).

† In some versions (including Shakespeare's *A Midsummer Night's Dream*) Theseus is married to Hippolyta herself. In these tellings Theseus accompanies Heracles on the Ninth Labour, and instead of Heracles killing Hippolyta, he gives her to Theseus.

‡ For more on the Amazonian lifestyle see Heracles' Ninth Labour (page 88).

§ Sited just below the heights of the Acropolis, the Areopagus was the meeting place of the Athenian Council of Elders, and later the site of the court where serious crimes were tried. John Milton invoked it in his great polemic against censorship, the *Areopagitica*.

tomb, like so many mythic sites, was visited by the traveller Pausanias, whose observations often form a pleasing bridge between myth, legend and something close to history.

The Attic war, like Heracles' ravaging of Hippolyta and her band during the Ninth Labour, is part of the wider Amazonomachy, yet another -*machy*, yet another taming of the wild in which the Greeks characterised themselves as ridding the world of the more barbarous, monstrous and uncivilised elements that threatened, like encroaching swarms, their sense of harmony and the potential graces of ordered civilisation.*

This 'war with the Amazons', together with the CENTAUROMACHY (the battle between the Lapiths and centaurs at Pirithous's wedding), the TITANOMACHY (the war of the Olympian gods against their Titan forebears)† and the GIGANTOMACHY (the war of the gods against the giants, in which Heracles fought so valiantly),‡ formed some of the favourite subjects of Greek painting and sculpture.§ Collectively their themes are best understood in symbolic terms, as representations of the way the Greeks characterised themselves as the champions of order and civilization against the chaotic hordes of barbarism and the monstrous. Which also makes them narrative playings-out of the struggle to tame

---

* The German classicist Bruno Snell puts it very well: 'For the Greeks, the Titanomachy and the battle against the giants remained symbols of the victory which their own world had won over a strange universe; along with the battles against the Amazons and Centaurs they continue to signalize the Greek conquest of everything barbarous, of all monstrosity and grossness.'
† See the first volume of *Mythos* (page 43).
‡ See the story of Heracles (page 124).
§ For example, the Parthenon in Athens prominently featured sculptures depicting the Gigantomachy, the Amazonomachy and the Centauromachy. Examples of the latter can still be seen to this day, as can the Centauromachy that once adorned another of the most important buildings of classical Greece, the temple of Zeus at Olympia.

the savage instincts, the dark and dangerous elements of human nature.

The Amazons defeated, a kind of midlife crisis overtook Pirithous and Theseus. They decided to choose new brides for themselves. Their choices were wild and calamitous.

His new friend helped Theseus abduct the young Helen of Sparta,* while for himself Pirithous decided it would be amusing to have Persephone, Queen of the Underworld for a wife. When he proposed the insane idea of descending into the realm of the dead and snatching Persephone from under the very nose of her husband Hades, Theseus the hero, Theseus the wise, Theseus the clever, Theseus the great king and counsellor nodded his head vigorously.

'Why not? Sounds like fun.'

The pair went to the spot that Orpheus had chosen for his descent, Tainaron on the southern tip of the Peloponnese, also called Cape Matapan, and boldly made their way down through the caves, passageways and galleries into the kingdom of the dead. Whether Pirithous imagined that his rough soldierly charm would win Persephone over or whether they planned to take her by force of arms is not known. The expedition was predictably disastrous. An unamused Hades cast them into stone chairs, their naked buttocks stuck to the seats, their legs bound by living snakes. There they would have stayed until the crack of doom had not Heracles, as we have seen, happened past them on his way to parley with Hades for the loan of Cerberus.† In order to release Theseus, Heracles had to jerk him quite violently from his seat. Theseus was pulled free but his buttocks were left behind. It was as if they had been superglued to the stone of the chair. Athenian

---

* This story is better told another time . . .

† See Heracles' Twelfth Labour (page 112).

representations of the older, post-Hades Theseus, portray him as apygous, essentially arseless.*

Theseus returned to the upper world to discover that Helen had been rescued by her brothers, the twins Castor and Polydeuces, also known as the Dioscuri.†

Chastened, he chose a new bride for himself. His eye fell on PHAEDRA, the younger sister of Ariadne. Perhaps she reminded Theseus of his first love, perhaps he felt an alliance with her might repair the old wrong of leaving Ariadne on Naxos, perhaps it was nothing more than a political move. The motives of Theseus seem always the hardest to read of any of the heroes.

Minos, the old enemy of Athens was dead, of course, boiled alive in Sicily. His son DEUCALION had inherited the throne and – presumably because he knew that Athens was now stronger than Crete and also saw the value of an alliance – approved and even helped arrange the marriage, all thoughts of Theseus's abandonment of his sister Ariadne and slaughtering of his half-brother the Minotaur put aside.

Phaedra and Theseus had two sons together, ACAMAS and DEMOPHON, who would grow up to feature in a touching and honourable cameo in the Trojan War.

Meanwhile, what of Hippolytus, Theseus's son by Antiope? He had been sent to Theseus's old home of Troezen. He grew into a handsome, athletic young man, whose greatest passion was hunting. His devotion to Artemis, the goddess of the chase and the chaste, was equalled by his contempt for Aphrodite and the distractions of love. No man or

---

* Think Mick Jagger.

† The twins not only returned Helen to Sparta, but they forcibly took Theseus's mother Aethra along with her to act as her nurse and companion. This position she held into extreme old age. Her grandsons Acamas and Demophon would finally rescue her during the fall of Troy. But that too is a story for another time.

woman interested him. Aphrodite, of course, did not take kindly to being ignored and the revenge she prepared for this insolent young man's neglect of her altars and practices was terrible indeed.

When his father Theseus and step-mother Phaedra visited Troezen, Hippolytus welcomed them dutifully. Theseus and Hippolytus hit it off at once. Greek myth is full of fathers who kill sons and sons who kill fathers so the mutual bond of affection and admiration that blossomed between these two seems especially remarkable. During the visit they spent all day and every day in each other's company. Hippolytus barely noticed Phaedra. She, however, noticed him. She slowly became obsessed and one night visited him and declared her love.* With a touch more horror and visible disgust than was wise or tactful, Hippolytus rejected her advances. As with Stheneboea and Bellerophon and Potiphar's wife and Joseph, the scorned and humiliated Phaedra cried rape to Theseus who cursed his son and called on his father Poseidon to punish him. As Hippolytus was driving his chariot along the shore one morning the god sent one of his great bulls from the sea which maddened the horses. The boy was trampled to death. Phaedra, on hearing this, took her own life.

The goddess Artemis appeared to Theseus and explained that his son had been innocent all along and that the tragedy had been the result of spurned love and Aphrodite's resentment.

Exiled from his kingdoms of Athens and Troezen for his role, however unwitting, in the deaths of his son and wife, wretched, bitter, desolated and drained of all passion and

---

* The versions by Euripides in *Hippolytus* (the surviving play of two that he wrote on the story) and in *Phaedra* by the Roman playwright Seneca both alter this a little. She never speaks of her love, but commits suicide and leaves a note implicating Hippolytus.

purpose, Theseus came to a bathetic and pathetic end. A guest of King Lycomedes of Skyros, Theseus was pushed by his host over a cliff to his death. The cause of the argument between them is lost to us.

Cimon, a historical king of Athens many many years later, invaded Skyros and brought Theseus's body back to the city that he done so much to make great. Lycomedes achieved greater fame for the part he was to play in the upbringing of Achilles.

A fine statue of a naked Theseus stands proudly today in Athens' central place of assembly, the city's hub, Syntagma Square. Even today he is a focus of Athenian identity and pride. The ship he brought back from his adventures in the Labyrinth of Crete remained moored in the harbour at Piraeus, a visitor attraction right up to the days of historical ancient Athens, the time of Socrates and Aristotle. Its continuous presence there for such a long time caused the Ship of Theseus to become a subject of intriguing philosophical speculation. Over hundreds of years, its rigging, its planks, its hull, deck, keel, prow, stern and all its timbers had been replaced so that not one atom of the original remained. Could one call it the same ship? Am I the same person I was fifty years ago? Every molecule and cell of my body has been replaced many times over.*

It is appropriate that Theseus should be linked in this way with the Athens of logic, philosophy and open enquiry for he was the hero who more than any other embodied the qualities Athenians most prized. Like Heracles, Perseus and Bellerophon before him, he helped cleanse the world of

---

* The Grandfather's Axe, its blade and handle regularly replaced, presents a similar ontological conundrum in the field of study known as the Metaphysics of Identity.

dangerous monsters, but the way he did so employed wit, intelligence and fresh ways of thinking. He was fallible and flawed, as the all the heroes were, but he stood for something great in us all. Long may he stand in Syntagma Square and long may he stand high in our regard.

ENVOI

The heroes cleansed our world of chthonic terrors – earth-born monsters that endangered mankind and threatened to choke the rise of civilisation. So long as dragons, giants, centaurs and mutant beasts infested the air, earth and seas we could never spread out with confidence and transform the wild world into a place of safety for humanity.

In time, even the benevolent minor deities would find themselves elbowed out by the burgeoning and newly confident human race. The nymphs, dryads, fauns, satyrs and sprites of the mountains, streams, meadows and oceans could not compete with our need and greed for land to quarry, farm and build upon. The rise of a spirit of rational enquiry and scientific understanding pushed the immortals further from us. The world was being reshaped as a home fit for mortal beings only. Today, of course, some of the rarer and more vulnerable mortal creatures that have shared the world with us are undergoing the same threats to their natural territories that caused the end of the nymphs and woodland spirits. Habitat loss and species extinction have all happened before.

The days of the gods themselves were numbered too. Prometheus's gift of fire, as Zeus had feared, would one day allow us to do even without the Olympians.

But not yet.

Heracles, without knowing it, had started the clock on a countdown to a cataclysmic event in our history. The installation of Tyndareus in Sparta and Atreus in Mycenae and the

sparing of the life of Priam after the destruction of old Troy*
– these would prove to be sticks of kindling that would one
day burst into the greatest conflagration the world had yet
seen.

Not yet. Zeus and the Olympians were not finished with
us yet.

---

* See the story of Heracles (pages 122, 124 and 133).

THE RAGES OF HERACLES

I was reading not long ago about the strange and sad case of Chris Benoit, a World Wrestling Entertainment star who strangled his wife and son in 2007. An inexplicable and terrible crime that has been put down variously to 'roid-rage' (the psychotic effects of synthetic and natural testosterone, nandrolone, anastrozole and other hormones and steroids used by wrestlers*) or the effects of traumatic brain injury similar to those experienced by some NFL players, as highlighted in the Peter Landesman/Will Smith film, *Concussion*. It seems Benoit specialised in a move called the 'diving headbutt' which may have caused serious trauma to his brain.

The similarity between Heracles' murder of Megara and his children and the Benoit case struck me at once. Two musclebound men, boiling over with an excess of testosterone, have a moment of rage or delusion and spend the rest of their lives regretting it. In Benoit's case not a long rest of life: he hanged himself two days after the murders.

I don't believe all myths must be founded in some historical truth, but I do think it interesting that when the collective unconscious of the Greeks imagined and gave life, character and narrative to a mythical strong man, they included in him a terrible and inexplicable tendency to explode in destructive psychotic rages† – I'm thinking not only of the savage

---

* The Benoit case has resulted in a much stricter regime of testing and a zero-tolerance of drug taking in the WWE, I am told.

† Perhaps comic book fans will also want to draw a comparison with Bruce Banner, the Incredible Hulk.

murder of his family, but the massacre of the centaurs in the cave of Pholus and the killing of Iphitus too.

Of course plenty of musclemen are gentle, kind and sweet-natured (André the Giant springs to mind) but I do not think it is outside the realms of possibility that the Greeks had heard of a real strongman who had a tendency to be overcome by savage fits of violence followed by periods of agonised remorse.

AFTERWORD

Timelines in myth are often confusing and inconsistent, especially when it comes to the heroes. According to Euripides, for example, Heracles kills his first wife Megara *after* his Twelfth Labour, whereas in most tellings of the myth the Labours are set for him specifically as a punishment for that crime. In Shakespeare, and other versions, Theseus is seen to have gone on to marry Hippolyta, Queen of the Amazons, who has surely been killed by Heracles during his Ninth Labour? Some heroes are listed as Argonauts and participants in the Calydonian Hunt after they have been killed or before they could possibly have been born.

Myth is not history. Variant tellings and narrative lines are inevitable. I have tried where possible to give some overarching shape to the stories of the heroes whose lives and deaths I have told here, but chronological incongruities are bound to make themselves manifest. Apollodorus's *Bibliotheca* (Library) is a major source for all Greek myth, though he is often at variance with Hesiod and Homer. Apollonius Rhodius wrote the *Argonautica,* from which most of the details of Jason's great voyage in search of the Golden Fleece are derived. The Roman writers Hyginus and Ovid embroider and elaborate in their way, and the travellers and geographers Pausanias and Strabo in theirs.

The heroes, however, more than the gods, nymphs or other mortals, live on in the works of the three great Athenian tragedians, EURIPIDES, AESCHYLUS and SOPHOCLES. They embellish and alter the myths, it is true, but as playwrights their interest lay in dramatic truth and a focus on characters in crisis.

Sophocles' Theban Cycle is the source for the most commonly told versions of the tragic story of Oedipus and his family. Euripides enters the hearth and home of Jason, Theseus and Heracles, and concentrates on the women in their lives. Aeschylus comes into his own later, outside the parameters of this volume. I have plundered a great deal from all three of these great contemporaries and rivals.

As with *Mythos,* I have tried to tell the stories without offering explanations or interpretations. Myth is ripe for interpretation and I hope you often find yourself putting the book down and speculating on what the Greeks meant (or thought they meant) by Chrysaor and Pegasus bursting from the severed neck of Medusa, or how they distinguished between the Harpies, the birds from the Isle of Ares and the Stymphalian birds. Myths are not crossword puzzles or allegories with single meanings and answers. Fate, necessity, cause and blame are endlessly mixed in these stories as they are in our lives. They were no more soluble to the Greeks than they are to us.

There are those who like to think that many myths are pearls built up around grains of fact. In the past, even in antiquity, mythographers regularly attempted to trace almost all mythic stories back to some actual, historical truth. This is sometimes called Euhemerism or the historical theory of mythology. It is true that archaeology has shown that a Troy really existed, and a Mycenae. Bronze Age and Minoan wall paintings in Crete show bull-leaping and a maze-like structure that suggests the reality of the Labyrinth. Centaurs and Amazons are seen as Greek explanations for the arrival from the east of horses and their archer riders. Another good example of Euhemerism is the idea that the Chimera defeated by Bellerophon was in fact the pirate ship of Cheimarrhus with its lion's figurehead for a prow and serpent for a sternpost. There are plenty of opportunities for that kind of interpretation as well as for more metaphysical and psychological speculation too.

Carl Jung described myths as the product of our 'collective unconscious'. Joseph Campbell put it another way and called them 'public dreams'.* Oneiromancy, the interpretation of dreams, is free, fun and harmless, but difficult to prove in the real world. Some explanations of the 'meaning' of myths may convince you, some may not. It is an open field in which anyone can till and harvest.

Scholars and mythographers are interested in what is known as 'double determination', the tendency of poets, playwrights and other authors to attribute agency and causality to both the inner person and an outer influence, a god or an oracle, for example. If Athena 'whispers in your ear', is it just a poetical way of saying that a clever thought has struck you, or did the goddess really speak? If someone falls in love, is it always the work of Aphrodite or Eros? When we are intoxicated or frenzied are we driven by Dionysus? Did Heracles suffer from a hallucination and seizure or did Hera send a delusional fit to him? Did Apollo send plague arrows into Troy or was it simply that disease broke out in the city? When an oracle tells a king that a son or grandson will kill him, is that perhaps an external expression of the internal fear of patricidal overthrow that many rulers suffer from? Authors will say to this day that the Muse has abandoned them when what they really mean is that they are suffering from writer's block. The further along the timeline of Greek myth we go from the founding of Olympus to the end of the

---

* And dreams, 'private myths'.

411

Trojan War, and humanity begins to take centre stage from the immortals, the more difficult it is to be sure. Greeks of the historical age would still write of Ares giving them courage or Apollo inspiring them when it is clear that they did not mean it literally.

It is possible to tell many of the stories – the torments and Labours of Heracles, for example – with almost no reference to the gods. When the sources write that Apollo gave the young hero bows and arrows, is that not a way of saying Heracles grew up to be a talented archer? Athena needn't have taught the *Argo*'s helmsmen Ancaeuss and Tiphys how to manage rigging and sails, surely it is enough to believe that they were wise and handy in their use of them? Nor need she have manifested herself and given Heracles a rattle when he tried to rid the Stymphalian Marshes of those smelly birds – maybe he was smart enough to think of it himself?

Let's face it, even today we cannot understand or explain much of what drives us. Take love, for example. To say 'she fell in love' is to describe a mystery. One might as well say 'Eros pierced her heart with his arrow' as 'gametes fizzed, hormones seethed, psychological affinities and sexual connections were made' . . . the gods in Greek myth represent human motives and drives that are still mysterious to us. Might as well call them a god as an impulse or a complex. To personify them is a rather smart way – not of managing them perhaps, but of giving shape, dimensions and character to the uncontrollable and unfathomable forces that control us. Do 'superego' and 'id' reveal any more about our inner selves than Apollo and Dionysus? Evolutionary behaviouralism and ethology may tell us more about who and how we are as scientific fact, but the poetic concentration of our traits into the personalities of gods, demons and monsters are easier for some of us dull-witted ones to hold in our heads than the abstractions of science. Myth can be a kind of human algebra which makes it easier to manipulate truths about ourselves. Symbols and rituals are not toys and games to be dispensed with on our arrival at adulthood, they are tools we will always need. They complement our scientific impulse, they do not stand in opposition to it.

As with the interpretation of myths, double determination – the attribution of inner and outer influence – is as much a matter of preference as anything else. Some love to see the gods appear, interfere and direct, others are happier following humans doing their thing with the minimum of divine intervention.

The Muses whisper in my ear and tell me I am done.

LIST OF CHARACTERS

OLYMPIAN GODS

APHRODITE Goddess of love. Offspring of *Ouranos*'s blood and seed. Wife of *Hephaestus*. Mother (by *Ares*) of *Eros* and *Phobos*. Inflicts dreadful punishments on those who neglect her, such as *Atalanta* and *Hippomenes*, *Hippolytus*, and *Medea*. Lover (and lifesaver) of *Butes*, by whom she has *Eryx*.

CHILDREN OF KRONOS AND RHEA

DEMETER Goddess of fertility and the harvest. Mother (by *Zeus*) of *Persephone*, whose absence in the underworld she mourns for six months each year. Worshipped in the Eleusinian Mysteries.

HADES* God of the underworld. Also known as *Plouton*. Abductor and husband of *Persephone*. Master of *Cerberus*; lends him to *Heracles*. Possessor of hood of invisibility and Chair of Forgetfulness. Abettor of *Perseus*. Grants *Orpheus* the chance to bring *Eurydice* back from the dead. Imprisons *Pirithous* and *Theseus* for attempting to kidnap *Persephone*.

HERA Queen of the Gods. Wife of *Zeus*. Mother (by *Zeus*) of *Ares*, *Eileithyia*, *Hebe* and *Hephaestus*. Breastfeeding accident gives rise to Milky Way. Possessor of malevolent gadflies and ferocious giant crab. Persecutor of *Heracles*; later his mother-in-law. Her honour defended by *Heracles* during the

---

* Hades spent all of his time in the underworld, so technically he is often not regarded as one of the twelve Olympians.

Gigantomachy. Enemy of *Neleus* and *Pelias*. Abettor of *Jason* in his quest for the Golden Fleece. Sender of the *Sphinx* to punish Thebes in fulfilment of *Pelops's* curse on *Laius*.

POSEIDON God of the sea. Inventor (and god) of horses. Father of *Antaeus* (by *Gaia*), *Bellerophon* (by Eurynome), *Chrysaor* and *Pegasus* (by *Medusa*), *Eurytus and Cteatus* (by Molione), the *golden ram* (by *Theophane*), *Neleus* and *Pelias* (by Tyro), *Theseus* (by *Aethra*), and possibly of *Cercyon, Procrustes, Sciron* and *Sinis*. Grandfather of *Aegyptus, Cepheus* and *Phineus*, and of *Hippolytus* and *Nestor*. Persecutor of *Andromeda*. Abettor of *Bellerophon* and *Heracles*. Builds Troy's walls with *Apollo*; then sends sea monster to devour *Hesione* when *Laomedon* reneges on payment. Sends *Minos II* the *Cretan Bull*; then sends *Pasiphae* mad with lust for it. Grants *Caenis* gender reassignment. Fulfils *Theseus's* curse on *Hippolytus*.

ZEUS King of the Gods. Overthrower of *Kronos*. Liberator of his siblings from *Kronos's* captivity. Husband of *Hera*. Father of OLYMPIAN GODS. Father of the immortals *Eileithyia* and *Hebe* (by *Hera*), *Persephone* (by *Demeter*) and the *Muses* (by Mnemosyne). Father of the mortals *Aeacus* (by Aegina), *Amphion and Zethus* (by Antiope), Dardanus and Harmonia (by the *Pleiad* Electra), the *Dioscuros* Polydeuces and *Helen* (by *Leda*), *Heracles* (by *Alcmene*), *Minos I* and *Rhadamanthus* (by *Europa*), *Perseus* (by *Danaë*) and *Pirithous* (by Dia). Creator of *Nephele*. Punisher of *Asclepius, Atlas* and *Prometheus*. Wielder of thunderbolts. Possessor of the oracle at Dodona.

CHILDREN OF ZEUS

APOLLO Archer god and god of harmony. Son of *Zeus* and the TITANESS Leto. Half-brother of *Zeus's* plethora of progeny. Twin of *Artemis*. Father of *Aristaeus* and *Idmon* (by Cyrene), *Asclepius* (by Coronis), *Hymen* (by the Muse *Urania*), *Linus* and

Orpheus (by the *Muse* Calliope) and *Lycomedes* (by Parthenope). Grandfather of *Eurytus*. Slayer of *Python* and establisher of the *Pythia*'s oracle at Delphi. Slayer of the *Cyclopes* in revenge for *Zeus*'s smiting of *Asclepius*. Servant and lover of *Admetus*. Devises plan with the *Moirai* to grant *Admetus* immortality. Abettor of *Heracles* and *Orpheus*. Builds Troy's walls with *Poseidon*; then infects the city with plague when *Laomedon* reneges on payment.

ARES God of war. Son of *Zeus* and *Hera*. Brother of *Hephaestus*. Half-brother of *Zeus*'s plethora of progeny. Father of *Eros* and *Phobos* (by *Aphrodite*); of the Amazons, notably *Antiope* and *Hippolyta* (by the nymph Harmonia); and of *Alcon*, *Diomedes* and *Eurytion*. Perhaps father (by *Althaea*) of *Meleager*. Forebear of the Thracians. Possessor of man-eating metal birds. Along with *Dionysus*, a curser of the house of *Cadmus*.

ARTEMIS Goddess of chastity and the chase. Daughter of *Zeus* and the TITANESS Leto. Twin of *Apollo*. Half-sister of *Zeus*'s plethora of progeny. Mistress of the *Cerynaeian Hind*; lends her to *Heracles*. Venerated by *Atalanta* and *Hippolytus*. Sensitive to slights: sends snakes to ruin the wedding night of *Admetus* and *Alcestis*; sends the *Calydonian Boar* and *Atalanta* to punish Calydon and the family of *Oeneus*, and transforms most of the *Meleagrids* into guinea fowl.

ATHENA Goddess of wisdom. Daughter of *Zeus* and the *Oceanid* Metis. Half-sister of *Zeus*'s plethora of progeny. Patron of Athens. Abettor of *Bellerophon*, *Heracles*, *Jason* and *Perseus*. Possessor of Aegis (see *Medusa*). Imprisons the GIANT *Enceladus* under Mount Vesuvius.

DIONYSUS God of dissipation and disorder. Son of *Zeus* and the mortal *Semele*. Half-brother of *Zeus*'s plethora of progeny. Suckled by his aunt *Ino*. Along with *Ares*, a curser of the house of *Cadmus*. Drives his aunts *Agave*, *Autonoë* and *Ino* mad. Transforms *Ino* and his cousin *Melicertes* into sea deities.

Causes *Agave* and *Autonoë* to help tear apart his cousin *Pentheus*. Orders *Theseus* to surrender *Ariadne* so that they can marry and produce numerous offspring. Restores *Ariadne* and *Semele* to life so that they can all live together on Olympus.

HEPHAESTUS Smith god. Son of *Zeus* and *Hera*. Brother of *Ares*. Half-brother of *Zeus*'s plethora of progeny. Possibly the father of *Cercyon* and *Periphetes*. Cast out of Olympus as an infant by *Hera* and lamed. Abettor of *Heracles*. Creator of marvels including a golden breastplate and bronze rattle for *Heracles*, the *Khalkotauroi* for *Aeëtes*, and (some believe) *Talos*.

HERMES Messenger of the gods and arch-psychopomp. Son of *Zeus* and the *Pleiad* Maia. Half-brother of *Zeus*'s plethora of progeny. Father of *Abderus* and *Autolycus*. Abettor of *Heracles* and *Perseus*. Possessor of *caduceus* (winged staff), *petasus* (winged helmet), *talaria* (winged sandals).

PRIMORDIAL BEINGS

GODS

EREBUS The darkness. Son of Chaos. Father of *Moros*. Father (by *Nyx*) of *Charon*, *Hypnos*, *Thanatos* and the *Hesperides*.

GAIA The earth. Daughter of Chaos. Mother of *Ouranos* and Pontus. Mother (by *Ouranos*) of the *Cyclopes* and the first generation of TITANS. Mother (by *Ouranos*'s blood and seed) of the *Furies* and the GIANTS. Mother (by Pontus) of *Charybdis*, *Nereus* and *Phorcys and Ceto*. Mother (by *Poseidon*) of *Antaeus*. Mother (by *Tartarus*) of *Echidna* and *Typhon*. Creator of the *harpe* sickle used to castrate *Ouranos*.

NYX Night. Daughter of Chaos. Mother (by *Erebus*) of *Charon*, *Hypnos*, *Thanatos* and the *Hesperides*.

OURANOS The sky. Son of *Gaia*. Father (by *Gaia*) of the *Cyclopes* and the first generation of TITANS. Castrated by *Kronos*. Progenitor from his blood and seed of Aphrodite and (by *Gaia*) the *Furies* and the GIANTS.

TARTARUS The hidden deeps. Son of Chaos. Father (by *Gaia*) of *Echidna* and *Typhon*.

TITANS (CHILDREN OF GAIA AND OURANOS)

KRONOS King of the Gods. Father (by *Rhea*) and consumer of OLYMPIAN GODS. Castrator of *Ouranos*. Overthrown by *Zeus*.

OCEANUS God of the sea ('the River of Ocean'). Father (by *Tethys*) of the *Oceanids* and of *Achelous* and *Nilus*. Grandfather of the *Nereids*, the numberless progeny of the *Oceanids*, and of *Atlas*, *Prometheus* and *Zeus*.

RHEA Wife of *Kronos*. Mother of OLYMPIAN GODS. Conceals the existence of *Zeus* from *Kronos* so that he can overthrow his father and free his siblings.

TETHYS Goddess of the sea. Mother (by *Oceanus*) of the *Oceanids* and of *Achelous* and *Nilus*. Grandmother of the *Nereids* and of *Atlas*, *Geryon*, *Prometheus* and *Zeus*.

TITANS (LATER GENERATIONS)

ACHELOUS River god. Son of *Oceanus* and *Tethys*. Brother of *Nilus* and the *Oceanids*. Father (by the *Muse* Melpomene) of the *Sirens*. Wrestles *Heracles* for *Deianira*'s hand, and loses. Gives *Heracles* the Horn of Plenty.

ATLAS Supporter of the heavens. Son of Iapetus and Clymene. Brother of *Prometheus*. Father of the *Pleiades*. Outwitted by *Heracles*.

HECATE Goddess of witchcraft and enchantments. Daughter of Perses and Asteria. Thought by some to be mother of *Scylla*. Venerated by *Medea*.

HELIOS God of the sun. Son of Hyperion and Theia. Brother

of *Selene*. Father of *Aeëtes*, *Circe* and *Pasiphae* (by the *Oceanid* Perseis), and *Augeas*. Grandfather (with *Gaia*) of *Theophane*. Possessor of Ocean-going cup and herd of magnificent cattle. Abettor of *Heracles*. Theft of his cattle by *Alcyoneus* sparks the Gigantomachy.

NILUS God of the River Nile. Son of *Oceanus* and *Tethys*. Brother of *Achelous* and the *Oceanids*. Forebear of *Andromeda*, *Cadmus*, *Minos* and *Perseus*.

PROMETHEUS Creator and friend of humans. Son of Iapetus and Clymene. Brother of *Atlas*. Stealer of the divine fire. Freed from eternal punishment by *Heracles*. Accepted back onto Olympus by *Zeus*. Fights on the side of the OLYMPIAN GODS during the Gigantomachy.

SELENE Goddess of the moon. Daughter of Hyperion and Theia. Sister of *Helios*.

GIANTS (Offspring of Gaia and Ouranos)

ALCYONEUS Brother of *Porphyrion*. Theft of *Helios*'s cattle sparks the Gigantomachy. Attempts to rape *Hera*. Buried by *Heracles* under Mount Vesuvius.

ENCELADUS Most powerful of all the giants. Survives the Gigantomachy. Imprisoned by *Athena* under Mount Etna.

EURYMEDON King of the Giants. Attempt to rape *Hera* during the Gigantomachy thwarted by *Heracles*. Stunned by *Zeus*'s thunderbolt and slain by *Heracles*.

PORPHYRION Brother of *Alcyoneus*. Attempt to rape *Hera* during the Gigantomachy thwarted by *Heracles*. Stunned by *Zeus*'s thunderbolt and slain by *Heracles*.

OTHER CHILDREN OF GAIA

CYCLOPES *Arges*, *Brontes* and *Steropes*. One-eyed giants. Sons of *Ouranos* and *Gaia*. Brothers of the *Furies*, the GIANTS and the first generation of TITANS. Servants of *Hephaestus*. Forgers of the thunderbolts of *Zeus*. Slain by Apollo in revenge for the smiting of *Asclepius*.

FURIES *Alecto*, *Megaera* and *Tisiphone*. Daughters of *Gaia* and *Ouranos*'s blood and seed. Sisters of the *Cyclopes*, the GIANTS and the first generation of TITANS. Remorseless goddesses of retribution, especially against those guilty of blood crimes. Also known as the *Erinyes* or *Eumenides*.

NEREUS Shape-shifting 'Old man of the Sea'. Son of *Gaia* and Pontus. Brother of *Charybdis* and *Phorcys and Ceto*. Father (by the *Oceanid* Doris) of the *Nereids*. Wrestling partner of *Heracles*.

PHORCYS AND CETO Gods of the sea. Children of *Gaia* and Pontus. Siblings of *Charybdis* and *Nereus*. Parents of the *Gorgons* and the *Graeae*.

PYTHON Giant serpentine guardian of the Omphalos at Delphi. Slain by *Apollo*, who establishes the oracle of the *Pythia* in atonement. Offspring of Erebus and Nyx

CHARON Ferryman of the underworld, who transports dead souls across the River Styx. Charmed by the music of *Orpheus*.

HESPERIDES The three nymphs of the evening. Keen gardeners; producers of immortality-bestowing apples.

HYPNOS Sleep. Father of *Morpheus*.

MOIRAI The three Fates: *Clotho*, who spins the thread of life; *Lachesis*, who measures its length; and *Atropos*, who cuts it. Agree with *Apollo* not to cut the thread of *Admetus*'s life if another volunteers to die in his place. Foretell *Meleager*'s life will be the duration of a flaming brand.

MOROS Doom or Destiny. All-powerful, all-knowing controller of the cosmos. Most feared entity in creation, even by immortals.

MORPHEUS God of dreams. Son of *Hypnos*.

THANATOS Death. Servant of *Hades* and psychopomp. Wrestles *Heracles* for the soul of *Alcestis* (and loses).

ARISTAEUS Minor god of rustic matters. Son of *Apollo* and
Cyrene. Immortal brother of *Idmon*, and half-brother of
Apollo's other progeny. Husband of *Autonoë*. Father of
Actaeon. Tragically besotted with *Eurydice*.

CHIRON Greatest and wisest of centaurs. Son of *Kronos* and the
Oceanid Phylira. Grandfather of *Peleus* and *Telamon*. Healer.
Tutor of heroes, including Achilles, *Asclepius, Jason* and
Thessalus. Tends to *Pegasus*'s *Chimera* burns. Possible victim of
Lernaean Hydra blood. Catasterized as Sagittarius.

CYBELE Phrygian mother goddess, often associated by the
Greeks with *Gaia*, Rhea (the mother, by *Kronos*, of OLYMPIAN
GODS) or *Artemis*. Punisher of *Atalanta* and *Hippomenes*.

EILEITHYIA Goddess of childbirth. Daughter of *Zeus* and
Hera. Half-sister of *Zeus*'s plethora of progeny. Fails to prevent
birth of *Heracles*.

EROS Youthful god of sexual desire. Son of *Ares* and *Aphrodite*.
Brother of *Phobos*. Leader of the Erotes. Possessor of
devastating bow and arrows.

GLAUCUS Former fisherman turned god of distressed seamen.
Prophecies prevent the Argonauts from turning back after
they abandoned *Heracles* and *Polyphemus*. In later traditions,
member of a tragically romantic love triangle with *Circe* and
Scylla.

GRAEAE *Dino, Enyo* and *Pemphredo*. Also known as the *Phorcides*.
Daughters of *Phorcys and Ceto*. Sisters of the *Gorgons*. Cousins
of *Iris* and the *Hesperides*. Joint possessors of a single eye and
tooth, information of value to *Perseus*, and seemingly not
much else.

HEBE Cupbearer of *Hera* and goddess of youth. Daughter of
Zeus and *Hera*. Half-sister of *Zeus*'s plethora of progeny, not
least *Heracles*; his wife after his apotheosis.

HYMEN Also known as *Hymenaios*. Youthful god of wedding ceremonies; one of *Eros*'s retinue of Erotes. Son of *Apollo* and the muse *Urania*. Half-brother of *Apollo*'s other progeny. Cousin of the *Sirens*. Spoils his half-brother *Orpheus*'s wedding to *Eurydice*.

IRIS Goddess of the rainbow and messenger of the gods. Daughter of the sea god Thaumas and the *Oceanid* Electra. Sister of the *Harpies*. Cousin of the *Gorgons* and the *Graeae*. Protects her sisters from attack by *Calais and Zetes*.

MUSES Nine daughters of *Zeus* and the TITANESS Mnemosyne (Memory). Goddesses of poetry, song and dance, and learning. Half-sisters of *Zeus*'s plethora of progeny. They include: *Calliope*, Muse of epic poetry, and mother (by *Apollo*) of *Linus* and *Orpheus*; *Melpomene*, Muse of tragedy, and mother (by *Achelous*) of the *Sirens*; *Terpsichore*, Muse of dance; *Thalia*, Muse of comedy; and *Urania*, Muse of astronomy, and mother (by *Apollo*) of *Hymen*.

NEPHELE Cloud goddess and goddess of *xenia*. Created by *Zeus* to decoy *Ixion* from *Hera*. Forebear (with *Ixion*) of the centaurs. Wife of *Athamas*. Mother of *Phrixus* and *Helle*. Sends *golden ram* to rescue them from *Ino*'s murderous plot.

NEREIDS Sea nymphs. Daughters of *Nereus* and the *Oceanid* Doris. Cousins of *Poseidon*, and share his palace. Givers of gifts and hospitality, some say, to *Theseus*.

OCEANIDS Sea nymphs. Daughters of *Oceanus* and *Tethys*. Sisters of *Achelous* and *Nilus*. Cousins of *Poseidon*. They include: *Callirrhoë*, mother (by *Chrysaor*) of *Geryon*; *Doris*, mother (by *Nereus*) of the *Nereids*; *Electra*, mother (by Thaumas) of *Iris* and the *Harpies*; *Idyia*, mother (by her nephew *Aeëtes*) of *Absyrtus*, *Chalciope* and *Medea*; *Metis*, mother (by *Zeus*) of *Athena*; *Perseis*, mother (by *Helios*) of *Aeëtes*, *Circe* and *Pasiphae*; *Pleione*, mother (by *Atlas*) of the *Pleiades*.

PERSEPHONE Also known as *Kore*. Queen of the Underworld and goddess of spring. Daughter of *Zeus* and *Demeter*. Half-sister of *Zeus*'s plethora of progeny. Abducted and married by *Hades*, with whom she spends six months of every year. Persuades him to allow *Orpheus* the chance to bring *Eurydice* back from the dead. Target of unsuccessful kidnapping plot by *Pirithous* and *Theseus*. Worshipped in the Eleusinian Mysteries.

PHOBOS Terror. Son of *Ares* and *Aphrodite*. Brother of *Eros*. Likely to be present at encounters between ordinary mortals and the heroes, gods and monsters of this book.

PLEIADES Seven heavenly daughters of *Atlas* and the *Oceanid* Pleione. They include: *Electra*, mother (by *Zeus*) of Dardanus and Harmonia; *Maia*, mother (by *Zeus*) of *Hermes*; *Merope*, mother (by *Sisyphus*) of *Glaucus* of Corinth; *Sterope*, mother (by *Oenomaus*) of *Hippodamia*. *Taygeta*, ancestor (with *Zeus*) of *Tyndareus*.

MONSTERS

PRIMORDIAL MONSTERS

CHARYBDIS Monstrous creator of an inescapable whirlpool. Daughter of *Gaia* and Pontus. Sister of *Nereus* and *Phorcys and Ceto*. Believed by some to have been the mother of *Scylla*, from whom she is generally inseparable in myth. Avoided by *Jason*.*

ECHIDNA Daughter of *Gaia* and *Tartarus*. Sister of *Typhon*. Half woman, half water snake.

GORGONS *Stheno* and *Euryale*. Daughters of *Phorcys and Ceto*. Sisters of the *Graeae*. Cousins of *Iris* and the *Harpies*. Companions of *Medusa*. Possessors of boar-like tusks, brass claws and snaky hair.

---

* But not by Odysseus on a later occasion.

HARPIES *Aello* and *Ocypete*. Daughters of the sea god Thaumas and the *Oceanid* Electra. Sisters of *Iris*. Cousins of the *Gorgons* and the *Graeae*. Ravenous birdwomen sent by *Zeus* to torment *Phineus* of Salmydessus. Driven away by *Calais and Zetes* during the quest for the Golden Fleece. Protected by *Iris*.

TYPHON Giant serpentine son of *Gaia* and *Tartarus*. Brother of *Echidna*. First and worst of all monsters.

OFFSPRING OF TYPHON AND ECHIDNA

CAUCASIAN EAGLE Sent by *Zeus* to tear out *Prometheus*'s liver. Slain by *Heracles*.

CERBERUS Tricephalic canine guardian of the gates of hell. Borrowed by *Heracles*. Charmed by *Orpheus*.

CHIMERA Fire-breathing snaky-tailed lion–goat hybrid. Slain by *Bellerophon*.

COLCHIAN DRAGON Sleepless guardian of the Golden Fleece. Mesmerized by *Medea*.

CROMMYONIAN SOW Also known as *Phaea*. Said by some to be the mother of the *Calydonian Boar*. Slain and eaten by *Theseus*.

LADON Hundred-headed draconian guardian of the Apples of the *Hesperides*. Slain by *Heracles*.*

LERNAEAN HYDRA Polycephalic self-regenerative venomous-blooded serpentine guardian of the gates of hell. Slain by *Heracles* with the assistance of *Iolaus*. Blood involved in the deaths of the GIANTS and of *Eurytion, Geryon, Nessus, Pholus* and *Heracles*.

NEMEAN LION Slain, skinned and worn by *Heracles*.

ORTHRUS Bicephalic canine guardian of *Geryon*'s cattle. Slain by *Heracles*.

SCYLLA Six-headed sea monster. Believed by some to have been the daughter of *Charybdis* or *Hecate*. In later traditions,

---

* In some but not all versions of Heracles' Eleventh Labour.

member of a tragically romantic love triangle with *Circe* and the sea god *Glaucus*. Generally inseparable in myth from *Charybdis*. Avoided by *Jason*.*

SPHINX Woman's-headed lion-bodied bird-winged monster with limited sense of humour. Sent by *Hera* to punish Thebes in fulfilment of *Pelops*'s curse on *Laius* and his line. Fatally outsmarted by *Oedipus*.

OTHER MONSTERS AND CREATURES

ANTAEUS North African half-giant and wrestling aficionado. Son of *Gaia* and *Poseidon*. Half-brother of Gaia's and Poseidon's respective progenies Slain by *Heracles*.

CALYDONIAN BOAR Giant baby-eating bane of Aetolia. Said by some to be offspring of the *Crommyonian Sow*. Sent by *Artemis* to punish the family of *Oeneus* for neglecting her worship in favour of *Dionysus*. Hunted by heroes including *Admetus*, *Asclepius*, the *Dioscuri*, *Jason*, *Nestor*, *Peleus*, *Pirithous*, *Telamon*, *Theseus* and the *Thestiades*. Slayer of *Alcon*, Enaesimus, Hippasus, Hyleus and Pelagon. Slain by *Atalanta* and *Meleager*.

CERYNEIAN HIND Golden-horned, brass-footed deer. Sacred to *Artemis*. Briefly captured by *Heracles*.

CETUS Sea dragon. Sent by *Poseidon* to punish Ethiopia and devour *Andromeda*. Slain by *Perseus*.

CHRYSAOR Golden youth. Offspring of *Medusa* (by *Poseidon*). Brother of *Pegasus*; half-brother of the rest of Poseidon's progeny. Father (by the *Oceanid* Callirrhoë) of *Geryon*.

CRETAN BULL Also known as the Marathonian Bull, or the Bull from the Sea. Creature of *Poseidon* sent in answer to the prayers of *Minos II*. Father (by *Pasiphae*) of the *Minotaur*. Tamed by *Heracles*, brought to mainland Greece and released. Tamed and sacrificed by *Theseus*. Athenian tribute to the

---

* But not by Odysseus on a later occasion.

Minotaur compensation for *Aegeus*'s role in the bull's slaying of (his half-uncle) *Androgeus*.

ERYMANTHIAN BOAR Giant suidian terror of Arcadia. Popular with pot painters. Captured by *Heracles*.

EURYTION Giant son of *Ares*. Herdsman of *Geryon*. Slain by *Heracles*.

EURYTION Thessalian centaur. His drunken overtures to *Pirithous*'s wife at their wedding responsible for the Centauromachy.

GERYON Three-bodied vicious-tempered cattle-breeder of Erytheia. Son of *Chrysaor* and the *Oceanid* Callirrhoë. Master of *Eurytion* and *Orthrus*. Slain by *Heracles*.

GOLDEN RAM Bearer of the Golden Fleece. Offspring of *Poseidon* and *Theophane*. Half-brother of *Poseidon*'s other progeny, including *Pelias*. Sent by *Nephele* to rescue *Phrixus* and *Helle* from *Ino*'s murderous plot. Bears *Phrixus* to Colchis. Sacrificed by *Phrixus* to *Zeus*, who catasterizes him as Aries. His Golden Fleece sacred to *Hera*, but presented to *Aeëtes*. Stolen and returned to Greece by *Jason* and *Medea* with the assistance of the Argonauts *Acastus, Ancaeus, Argus, Augeas, Butes, Calais and Zetes*, the *Dioscuri, Euphemus, Eurytion, Heracles, Hylas, Idmon, Meleager, Nestor, Orpheus, Peleus, Philoctetes*, the *Phrixides, Pirithous, Polyphemus, Telamon* and *Tiphys*.

KHALKOTAUROI Two fire-breathing bronze-hoofed bulls. Created by *Hephaestus*. Kept by *Aeëtes*. Tamed and yoked by *Jason*.

MARES OF DIOMEDES *Dinos, Lampon, Podargos* and *Xanthus*. Insane anthropophagous fire-breathing equines. Devour *Abderus*. Fed their owner *Diomedes* by *Heracles*, who tames them. Ancestors of Bucephalus.

MEDUSA Gorgon. Daughter of *Poseidon*. Possessor of snaky hair and petrifying stare. Slain by *Perseus*. Progenitor of *Chrysaor* and *Pegasus*. Posthumous petrifier of *Cetus, Phineus* and *Polydectes*. Head transformed into the Aegis of *Athena*.

MINOTAUR True name *Asterion*. Takes after both his parents: the *Cretan Bull* and *Pasiphae*. Half-brother of *Androgeus*, *Ariadne*, *Deucalion* and *Phaedra*. Imprisoned in the labyrinth of *Daedalus*. Recipient of the Athenian tribute demanded by his stepfather *Minos II* for the slaying of his half-brother *Androgeus* by his father the *Cretan Bull*. Unsurprising identity issues resolved (terminally) by *Theseus*.

NESSUS Arcadian centaur. Survivor of the massacre by *Heracles* at *Pholus*'s cave. Later killed by *Heracles* when he molests *Deianira*. Posthumously obtains his revenge thanks to his shirt.

PEGASUS Winged white horse. Offspring of *Medusa* (by *Poseidon*). Brother of *Chrysaor*; half-brother of the rest of Poseidon's progeny, including *Bellerophon*. Aids *Bellerophon* in slaying the *Chimera* and in subduing the Amazons, the Solymi and *Cheimarrhus*. Healed by *Chiron* of his *Chimera* burns. Tries (and fails) to carry *Bellerophon* up to Olympus. Catasterized.

PHAEA Terrorizer of travellers on the Isthmus. Alter ego, or keeper, of the *Crommyonian Sow*.

PHOLUS Arcadian centaur. Friend and host of *Heracles*. Accidentally poisoned with *Lernaean Hydra* blood.

SIRENS Birdwomen whose enchanting song lures sailors to their doom. Daughters of *Achelous* and the *Muse* Melpomene. Cousins of *Hymen*, *Linus* and *Orpheus*. Out-sung by *Orpheus* to give the Argonauts safe passage.

TALOS Giant bronze automaton. Created by *Daedalus* or *Hephaestus*, or the offspring of the Meliae nymphs. Guardian of Crete. Encountered by the Argonauts. Mesmerized by *Medea*. Destroyed by *Pirithous*.

MORTALS

MEN

ABDERUS Son of *Hermes*. Page and lover of *Heracles*. Devoured by the *Mares of Diomedes*. City of Abdera founded by *Heracles* in his honour.

ABSYRTUS Son of *Aeëtes* and *Idyia*. Brother of *Chalciope* and *Medea*. Dismembered by *Medea* to delay *Aeëtes* pursuit of the Argonauts.

ACAMAS AND DEMOPHON Sons of *Theseus* and *Phaedra*. Rescuers of *Aethra* during the fall of Troy.

ACASTUS Son of *Pelias*. Brother of the *Peliades*. Possibly one of the Argonauts. Holds magnificent funeral games to honour *Pelias*. Succeeds to the throne of Iolcos after turning its people against *Jason* and *Medea*. Tricked by his wife Astydameia into trying to murder *Peleus*. Overthrown by *Jason* (at *Peleus*'s instigation).

ACRISIUS King of Argos. Brother of *Proetus*. Father of *Danaë*. Distant cousin of *Aegyptus*, *Cepheus* and *Phineus*. Accidentally slain by his grandson *Perseus*.

ADMETUS King of Pherae. Son of *Pheres*. Famed for his hospitality and kindness to strangers. Master and lover of *Apollo*. Husband of *Alcestis*. Their wedding night spoiled by *Artemis*'s snakes in their bed. Accepts *Alcestis*'s offer to die on his behalf and fulfil *Apollo*'s scheme to make him immortal, until *Heracles* brings her back from death. Hunter of the *Calydonian Boar*.

AEACUS King of Aegina. Son of *Zeus* and Aegina. Half-brother of *Zeus*'s plethora of progeny. Husband of *Chiron*'s daughter. Father of *Peleus* and *Telamon*. With his half-brothers *Minos I* and *Rhadamanthus*, one of the three Judges of the Underworld. Charmed by the music of *Orpheus*.

AEËTES King of Colchis. Son of *Helios* and the *Oceanid* Perseis. Brother of *Circe* and *Pasiphae*. Husband of (his aunt) the *Oceanid* Idyia. Father of *Absyrtus, Chalciope* and *Medea*. Distrustful grandfather of the *Phrixides*. Custodian of the Golden Fleece. Owner of the *Colchian Dragon* and the *Khalkotauroi*. Sets *Jason* tasks to fulfil in order to acquire it.

AEGYPTUS Grandson of Libya and *Poseidon*. Brother of *Cepheus* and *Phineus*. Father of *Busiris*.

AEGEUS King of Athens. Husband of *Medea*. Father (by *Aethra*) of *Theseus*, and (by *Medea*) of *Medus*. Uncle of the *Pallantidae*. Employs the *Cretan Bull* to rid him of *Androgeus*. Tries the same with *Theseus*, then *Medea*'s poison, before recognizing his son. Sends *Theseus* as part of the tribute demanded by *Minos II* for his role in the death of *Androgeus*. Fatal victim of filial forgetfulness. Site of his death named 'Aegean Sea' after him.

AESON Rightful king of Iolcos. Son of *Cretheus* and *Tyro*. Brother of *Pheres*; half-brother of *Neleus* and *Pelias*. Husband of *Alcimede*. Father of *Jason* and *Promachus*. Deposed and imprisoned (with *Alcimede*) by *Pelias*. Entrusts *Jason* to *Chiron*. Either murdered by *Pelias*, or driven to murder-suicide with *Alcimede* and *Promachus* by *Pelias*, while *Jason* absent on the quest for the Golden Fleece.

ALCINOUS King of the Phaeacians. Husband (and uncle) of *Arete*. Kind-hearted and protective host of *Jason, Medea* and the Argonauts.

ALCON Spartan prince. Son of *Ares* and Hippocöon of Amykles. Slain (messily) by the *Calydonian Boar*.

AMPHION AND ZETHUS Usurper kings of Thebes. Twin sons of *Zeus* and Antiope (sister-in-law of *Polydorus*). Half-brothers of *Zeus*'s plethora of progeny. Assist *Cadmus* in constructing the walls and citadel of Thebes. Overthrow their kinsman *Labdacus* and rule in his place.

AMPHITRYON Grandson of *Perseus* and *Andromeda*. Husband of

Alcmene. Exiled to Thebes for killing his uncle/father-in-law Electryon. Father of *Iphicles* and Laonome.

ANCAEUS King of Samos. Son of Lycurgus of Arcadia. Brother of *Iasus*. Possible uncle of *Atalanta*. Joins the Argonaut. Succeeds *Tiphys* as helmsman of the *Argo*. Navigates the Wandering Rocks.

ANDROGEUS Cretan prince. Son of *Minos II* and *Pasiphae*. Brother of *Ariadne*, *Deucalion* and *Phaedra*. Half-brother of the *Minotaur*. While guest of *Aegeus*, slain by (his half-uncle) the *Cretan Bull*. Athenian tribute to the *Minotaur* compensation for his death.

ANTIMEDES Trusted servant and facilitator of *Laius*. At his command exposes the infant *Oedipus*. Later discloses to *Oedipus* vital clues as to his true identity.

ARGUS Prince of Argos and shipwright. Joins the Argonauts. Aided by *Athena* in constructing the *Argo* (named in his honour).

ASCLEPIUS Master of healing. Son of *Apollo* and Coronis. Half-brother of *Apollo*'s other progeny. Kinsman of *Caenis* and *Polyphemus*. Raised by *Chiron*. Temporarily slain by *Zeus* for his *hubris* in resurrecting the dead. Hunter of the *Calydonian Boar*. Later immortalized. Catasterized as Ophiuchus.

ATHAMAS King of Boeotia. Grandson of Hellen. Brother of *Cretheus*, *Salmoneus* and *Sisyphus*. Husband of *Nephele*, *Ino* and Themisto. Father of *Phrixus* and *Helle* (by *Nephele*); of Learchus and *Melicertes* (by *Ino*); and of *Schoeneus* (by Themisto). Tricked by *Ino* into attempting to sacrifice *Phrixus* and *Helle*. Kills Learchus and drives *Ino* and *Melicertes* to suicide.

ATREUS Son of *Pelops* and *Hippodamia*. Brother of *Nicippe*, *Pittheus* and Thyestes; half-brother (and, some think, murderer) of *Chrysippus*. Installed as King of Mycenae by *Hyllus* and the Heraclides. Father of Agamemnon and Menelaus. Scion and forebear of much-cursed houses.

AUGEAS King of Elis. Son of *Helios*. Father of *Phyleus*. Uncle of *Eurytus and Cteatus*. Kinsman of *Tiphys*. Possessor of immortal cattle and filthy stables. Tricks *Heracles*; later slain by him in revenge. One of the Argonauts.

AUTOLYCUS Light-fingered son of *Hermes*. Father of Eumolus (musical supply teacher of *Heracles*). Grandfather of Odysseus.

BELLEROPHON 'The slayer of monsters'. Son of *Eurynome* and either *Glaucus* of Corinth or *Poseidon*. (Half-)brother of *Deliades*, whom he fatally mistakes for a boar. Possible half-brother of *Poseidon*'s other progeny, including *Pegasus*, whom he tames with *Athena*'s golden bridle. Cousin of *Jason*. Briefly betrothed to *Aethra*. Fitted up by *Proetus* and *Stheneboea*. Slayer of the *Chimera*. Subduer of the Amazons, Solymi and *Cheimarrhus*. Repelled from Xanthus by its womenfolk's buttocks. Settles differences with *Iobates*, receiving the hand of *Philonoë* and the succession to his kingdom. Crippled by *Zeus* for his *hubris* in trying to enter *Olympus*.

BUSIRIS King of Egypt. Son of *Aegyptus*. Cousin of *Heracles*. Enthusiastic practitioner of human sacrifice. Slain by Heracles and his capital renamed Thebes.

BUTES Sicilian king and expert apiarist. One of the Argonauts. Goes overboard in his admiration for the *Sirens*. Rescued by *Aphrodite*, who becomes his lover. Father (by *Aphrodite*) of *Eryx*.

CADMUS Often known as 'the First Hero'. Founder king of Thebes. Grandson of *Poseidon* and Libya and of *Nilus* and *Nephele*. Brother of *Europa*. Husband of Harmonia. Father of *Agave, Autonoë, Ino, Polydorus* and *Semele*. Forebear of a much-cursed house.

CAENEUS Lapith hero. Formerly *Caenis*, until granted gender reassignment (and invulnerable skin) by *Poseidon*. Buried alive by centaurs at *Pirithous*'s wedding.

CALAIS AND ZETES Also known as the *Boreads*. Quasi-immortal flying sons of Boreas (the North Wind) and

Orithyia, daughter of Erechtheus. Brothers-in-law of *Phineus* of Salmydessus. Join the Argonauts. Free *Phineus* from the *Harpies*. Slain by *Heracles* in revenge for abandoning him during the quest for the Golden Fleece.

CECROPS Founder king of Attica. Responsible for giving Athens its name and its divine protector, *Athena*.

CEPHEUS King of Ethiopia. Grandson of Libya and *Poseidon*. Brother of *Aegyptus* and *Phineus*. Husband of *Cassiopeia*. Father of *Andromeda*.

CERCYON Big-boned King of Eleusis and wrestling aficionado. Son of *Hephaestus* or *Poseidon*. As such, half-brother possibly of *Periphetes* or of *Poseidon's* other progeny, including *Procrustes*, *Sciron* and *Sinis*. Slain by (his half-brother?) *Theseus* and his kingdom wrested from him; later returned to his son Hippothoön.

CEYX King of Trachis. Husband of Alcyone. Father of *Hylas*. Friend and host of *Heracles*.

CHEIMARRHUS Fearsome Lycian pirate. Subdued by *Bellerophon*. Thought by Euhemerists to be the *Chimera*.

CHRYSIPPUS Illegitimate son of *Pelops*. Half-brother of *Atreus*, *Nicippe*, *Pittheus* and Thyestes. Groomed by *Laius*; then kills himself from shame (or, as some think, is murdered by *Atreus* and Thyestes). *Pelops* curses *Laius* and his line in revenge for his death.

COCALUS King of Kamikos in Sicily. Patron and protector of *Daedalus*. Daughters responsible for unfortunate bath-time incident involving *Minos II*.

CREON King of Corinth. Probably a descendant of *Sisyphus*. Father of *Creusa*. Provides sanctuary to *Jason* and *Medea*. Arranges marriage between *Jason* and *Creusa*. Agonizingly poisoned by *Medea*.

CREON Ruler of Thebes. Grandson of *Pentheus*. Brother of *Jocasta*; brother-in-law of *Laius* and *Oedipus*. Husband of

Eurydice. Father of Haemon. Scion of a much-cursed house. Father of *Megara*; father-in-law of *Heracles*. Provides sanctuary to *Amphitryon* and *Alcmene*. Regent following *Laius*'s death; resigns in favour of *Oedipus*. Resumes regency after *Oedipus* vacates the throne. Becomes king in own right after deaths of *Eteocles* and *Polynices*. Sentences *Antigone* to death for defying his laws. Eurydice and Haemon commit suicide in protest at his actions.

CRETHEUS King of Iolcos. Grandson of Hellen. Brother of *Athamas*, *Salmoneus* and *Sisyphus*. Husband of *Tyro* and *Sidero*. Father (by *Tyro*) of *Aeson* and *Pheres*.

CYZICUS King of the Dolionians. Husband of *Clite*. Accidentally slain by *Jason* in night-time battle with the Argonauts.

DAEDALUS Inventor, artificer and architect of genius. Descendant of *Cecrops*. Uncle, master and murderer of *Perdix*. Takes refuge in Crete, where employed by *Minos II*. Facilitator of the coupling between *Pasiphae* and the *Cretan Bull*. Creator of the labyrinth of Knossos and (some believe) *Talos*. Originator of manned flight. Takes refuge in Sicily, where employed by *Cocalus*. His bathroom designs to die for.

DELIADES Also known as *Alcimenes* or *Peiren*. Son of *Glaucus* of Corinth and *Eurynome*. (Half-brother) of *Bellerophon*; mistaken by him for a boar and accidentally slain.

DEUCALION King of Crete. Son of *Minos II* and *Pasiphae*. Brother of *Androgeus*, *Ariadne* and *Phaedra*. Half-brother of the *Minotaur*. Forwards marriage of *Ariadne* and *Theseus*.

DICTYS Fisherman. Brother of *Polydectes*. Husband of *Danaë*. Foster father of *Perseus*.

DIOMEDES King of Thrace. Son of *Ares*. Fed to his own *Mares* by *Heracles*.

DIOSCURI The twin 'boys of Zeus': *Castor* (son of *Leda* and

Tyndareus) and *Polydeuces* or *Pollux* (son of *Leda* and *Zeus*). Brothers of Clytemnestra and *Helen*. Half-brothers of *Zeus*'s plethora of progeny. Cousins of *Deianira* and *Meleager*. *Heracles*' combat training conducted by *Castor*. Join the Argonauts; *Polydeuces* their champion boxer. Hunters of the *Calydonian Boar*. Rescue *Helen* from the unwanted attentions of *Pirithous* and *Theseus*; provide her with *Aethra* as companion. Jointly catasterized as Gemini.

ERYX Sicilian king and boxing champion. Son of *Butes* and *Aphrodite*. Knocked dead by *Heracles*.

ETEOCLES Joint king of Thebes. Son of *Oedipus* and *Jocasta*. Brother of *Antigone*, Ismene and *Polynices*. Scion of a much-cursed house. Incapable of ruling in tandem with *Polynices*. Kill each other in battle.

EUPHEMUS Son of *Poseidon*. Grandson of the GIANT Tityus. Able to walk on water. Joins the Argonauts. Becomes relief helmsman after the death of *Tiphys*.

EURYSTHEUS King of Argolis. Son of *Sthenelus* and *Nicippe*. Cousin of *Heracles*. Commands him to perform Labours to expiate his murder of *Megara*. Slain by *Hyllus*.

EURYTION King of Phthia. One of the Argonauts. Hunter of the *Calydonian Boar*. Accidentally slain by his son-in-law *Peleus*, who coincidentally inherits his kingdom.

EURYTUS King of Oechalia. Grandson of *Apollo*. Father of *Iole* and *Iphitus*. Archery tutor of *Heracles*. Refuses to let *Heracles* marry *Iole*. Refuses his offer of expiation for slaying *Iphitus* and stealing cattle. Eventually slain by *Heracles* in revenge for these slights.

EURYTUS AND CTEATUS Also known as the *Molionides*. Conjoined twins. Sons of *Poseidon* and Molione. Half-brothers of *Poseidon*'s other progeny. Nephews of *Augeas*. Slayers of *Iphicles*. Split in two by *Heracles*.

GANYMEDE Cupbearer and beloved of *Zeus*. Son of *Tros*.
Brother of *Ilos*. Uncle of *Laomedon*. Abducted by *Zeus*.
Immortalized. Catasterized as Aquarius.

GLAUCUS King of Corinth. Son of *Sisyphus* and the *Pleiad*
Merope. Husband of *Eurynome*. Possible father of *Bellerophon*.
After being eaten by his own chariot horses returned as a
ghost known as 'the Horse-Scarer'.

HERACLES 'Hera's glory'. Named *Alcides* at birth. Son of *Zeus*
and *Alcmene*. *Zeus*'s favourite human son. Half-twin of *Iphicles*.
Half-brother of Laonome and of *Zeus*'s plethora of progeny.
Cousin of *Busiris*, *Eurystheus* and *Theseus*. Brother-in-law of
Polyphemus. Persecuted by *Hera*; later her son in law. Favoured
by *Apollo*, *Athena*, *Hephaestus*, *Hermes* and *Poseidon*. Married to
Megara (whom he kills), *Deianira* (who kills him), and his
half-sister *Hebe* (with whom he spends half eternity). Father
of numberless *Heraclides*, including *Hyllus* (by Deianira). Lover
of *Abderus*, *Hippolyta*, *Hylas*, *Iolaus* and *Omphale*. Infant
herpetocide. Performs Labours for *Eurystheus* to expiate his
murder of *Megara*. Joins the Argonauts. Abandoned by them
when searching for *Hylas*. Wrestles *Thanatos* for the soul of
Alcestis. Liberator of *Prometheus*. Temporary supporter of the
heavens. Rescuer of *Theseus* from the underworld. Threatens
the *Pythia* with violence. Serves *Omphale* to expiate his murder
of *Iphitus*, learning the joys of cross-dressing. Founder of the
Olympic Games. Victor of the Gigantomachy. Wins Horn of
Plenty from *Achelous*. Bane of Amazons, centaurs, Gegeneis,
GIANTS, the OFFSPRING OF TYPHON AND ECHIDNA,
Antaeus, the Cithaeronian Lion, *Eurytion* and *Geryon*, and the
Trojan Sea Monster. Tamer of *Cerberus*, the *Ceryneian Hind*,
the *Cretan Bull*, the *Erymanthian Boar* and the *Mares of Diomedes*.
Sacker of Troy. Slayer of *Augeas*, *Busiris*, *Calais and Zetes*,
Diomedes, *Eurytus*, *Eurytus and Cteatus*, *Eryx*, *Hippocoön*,
Hippolyta, *Iphitus*, *Laomedon*, *Linus* and *Neleus*. Fatally wounded

by *Nessus*'s shirt soaked in *Lernaean Hydra* blood. Immolated by *Philoctetes*. Immortalized and catasterized by *Zeus*.

HIPPOCOÖN King of Sparta. Brother of *Tyndareus*, whom he ousted from the throne. Slain by *Heracles* for aiding *Neleus* against him.

HIPPOLYTUS Son of *Theseus* and *Antiope*. Half-brother of *Acamas and Demophon*. Grandson of *Poseidon*. Punished by *Aphrodite* for his devotion to *Artemis*, by having his stepmother *Phaedra* driven mad by desire for him. Killed by the bull sent by *Poseidon* in answer to *Theseus*'s curse.

HIPPOMENES Megaran prince. Son of Megareus, grandson of *Poseidon*. Aided by *Aphrodite* to outsmart *Atalanta* and win her hand. Father (by *Atalanta*) of Parthenopaeus. With *Atalanta*, punished by *Aphrodite* for ingratitude, then transformed into a lion by *Cybele* for involuntarily profaning her temple.

HYLAS Son of *Ceyx*. Page and lover of *Heracles*. Joins the Argonauts. Surrenders to the attractions of water nymphs.

HYLLUS Son of *Heracles* and *Deianira*. Witnesses deaths of his parents. Leader of the Heraclides. Slayer of *Eurystheus*. Installs *Atreus* as King of Mycenae.

IASUS Arcadian king. Son of Lycurgus. Brother of *Ancaeus*. Possibly husband of *Clymene* and father of *Atalanta*, whom he exposes as an infant.

ICARUS Son of *Daedalus*. Pioneer of aviation. Flies too close to the sun.

IDMON Seer of Argos. Son of *Apollo* and Cyrene. Mortal brother of *Aristaeus*, and half-brother of *Apollo*'s other progeny. Joins the Argonauts, despite prophesying his own demise on their quest. Gored to death by wild boar.

IOBATES King of Lycia. Father of *Philonoë* and *Stheneboea*. Sets Bellerophon deadly tasks. Settles differences with him by offering the hand of *Philonoë* and the succession to his kingdom.

IOLAUS Son of *Iphicles*. Nephew, page and lover of *Heracles*. Devises plan to defeat the *Lernaean Hydra*. Witnesses the death of *Heracles* from *Lernaean Hydra* blood.

IPHICLES Son of *Amphitryon* and *Alcmene*. Half-twin of *Heracles*. Brother of Laonome. Brother-in-law of *Polyphemus*. Father of *Iolaus*. Slain by *Eurytus and Cteatus*.

IPHITUS Son of *Eurytus*. Brother of *Iole*. Slain by *Heracles* while his guest.

IXION King of the Lapiths. Husband of Dia. Stepfather of *Pirithous*. Condemned to eternal torment in Tartarus for attempting to ravish *Hera*. Forebear (with *Nephele*) of the centaurs.

JASON 'The healer'. Rightful heir to the throne of Iolcos. Son of *Aeson* and *Alcimede*. Brother of *Promachus*. (Half-)nephew of *Neleus* and *Pelias*. Cousin of *Bellerophon*, *Hellen*, *Phrixus* and *Schoeneus*. Kinsman of *Atalanta* and the *Phrixides*. Father (by *Medea*) of Mermerus, Pheres and *Thessalus*. Raised by *Chiron*. Favoured by *Athena* and *Hera*. By *Pelias* set the task of recovering the Golden Fleece. Leads the Argonauts. Lover of *Hypsipyle* (whom he abandons). Father of Euneus and Thoas (by *Hypsipyle*). Slayer of *Cyzicus*. With the aid of *Medea*'s magic, tames the *Khalkotauroi*, defeats the Spartoi, overpowers the *Colchian Dragon* and take the Golden Fleece. Evades *Aeëtes*, the *Sirens*, *Scylla* and *Charybdis*, the Wandering Rocks and *Talos* to return in triumph to Iolcos. Holds *Pelias* responsible for the deaths of *Aeson*, *Alcimede* and *Promachus* in his absence. Held responsible (with *Medea*) by the Iolcians for the death of *Pelias*. Takes refuge with *Medea* in Corinth. Planned wedding to *Creusa* spoiled by *Medea* murdering his bride, his father-in-law *Glaucus*, and their sons Mermerus and Pheres. Hunter of the *Calydonian Boar*. Reclaims throne of Iolcos from *Acastus*. Slain in a shipyard accident involving the *Argo*.

LABDACUS King of Thebes. Son of *Polydorus* and Nicteis.

Cousin of *Dionysus* and *Pentheus*. Father of *Laius*. Scion of a much-cursed house. Overthrown by his kinsmen *Amphion and Zethus*.

LAIUS King of Thebes with poor impulse control. Son of *Labdacus*. Cousin of *Creon* and *Jocasta*. Husband of *Jocasta*. Father of *Oedipus*. Scion and forebear of a much-cursed house. After his father overthrown by *Amphion and Zethus*, raised in exile by *Pelops*. Repays that trust by grooming *Chrysippus*. Cursed by *Pelops* for role in *Chrysippus*'s death, causing *Hera* to send the *Sphinx* to Thebes. Reclaims throne. Exposes the infant *Oedipus* to avoid an oracle of the *Pythia*. Victim of unfortunate road rage incident.

LAOMEDON King of Troy. Son of Ilos. Grandson of *Tros*. Tricks *Apollo* and *Poseidon* out of payment for building Troy's walls; then *Heracles* when rescues *Hesione* from *Poseidon*'s sea monster. Later slain by *Heracles* in revenge.

LICHAS Servant of *Heracles*. Helps him put on the shirt of *Nessus*. Slain by *Heracles* for his pains.

LINUS Son of the *Muse* Calliope and *Apollo* (or possibly *Oeagrus*). Brother of *Orpheus*; half-brother of *Apollo*'s other progeny; possibly stepbrother of Marsyas. Cousin of the *Sirens*. Short-tempered music teacher, slain by his pupil *Heracles*.

LYCOMEDES King of Skyros. Son of *Apollo* and Parthenope. Half-brother of *Apollo*'s other progeny. Host of the exiled *Theseus*, then slayer of him in a clifftop quarrel.

MEDUS Son of *Aegeus* and *Medea*. Half-brother of *Theseus*. Accompanies his mother when she flees Athens after failing to secure the succession of the Athenian throne in her favour. Gives his name to the Medes.

MELEAGER Son of *Althaea* and *Oeneus* (or *Ares*). Brother of *Deianira* and the other *Meleagrids*. Nephew of the *Thestiades*. Cousin of the *Dioscuri*. Neglectful husband of Cleopatra. Cursed with a life the duration of a flaming brand. One of the Argonauts. Smitten by *Atalanta*. Leads the hunt for the *Calydonian Boar*. Awards *Atalanta* the trophy for slaying the boar; then slays the *Thestiades* for protesting; and is slain by *Althaea* in revenge, fulfilling his natal prophecy. Posthumous matchmaker between *Deianira* and *Heracles*.

MELICERTES Son of *Athamas* and *Ino*. Half-brother of *Helle*, *Phrixus* and *Schoeneus*. Cousin of *Jason*. Killed during his mother's suicide. Transformed by his cousin *Dionysus* into the dolphin-riding deity *Palaemon*.

MINOS I King of Crete. Son of *Zeus* and *Europa*. Half-brother of *Zeus*'s plethora of progeny. Grandfather of *Minos II*. With his brother *Rhadamanthus* and half-brother *Aeacus*, one of the three Judges of the Underworld. Charmed by the music of *Orpheus*.

MINOS II King of Crete. Grandson of *Minos I*. Husband of *Pasiphae*. Father of *Androgeus*, *Ariadne*, *Deucalion* and *Phaedra*. Defies *Poseidon* by not sacrificing the *Cretan Bull*. Demands Athenian tribute for the *Minotaur* in compensation for *Aegeus*'s role in the *Cretan Bull*'s slaying of *Androgeus*. Patron, then persecutor, of *Daedalus*; boiled alive in a bath designed by him.

NELEUS King of Pylos. Son of *Poseidon* and *Tyro*. Brother of *Pelias*; half-brother of *Aeson* and *Pheres*, and of Poseidon's other progeny. Father of twelve sons, including *Nestor*. (Half-) uncle of *Jason*. With *Pelias* earns *Hera*'s enmity for slaying their stepmother *Sidero*. Aids *Pelias* in seizing Iolcos from *Aeson*. Refuses to purify *Heracles* for the slaying of *Iphitus*; later slain by *Heracles* in revenge.

NESTOR Youngest son of *Neleus*. Nephew of *Pelias*. Grandson of *Poseidon*. Inherits throne of Pylos after *Heracles* slays his father and eleven elder brothers. One of the wisest and longest-lived of kings. Joins the Argonauts. Advises *Jason* to take the long way home from Colchis. Hunter of the *Calydonian Boar*. Counsellor of the Greeks during the Trojan War.

OEAGRUS King of Thrace. Thought by some to be father of *Linus*, Marsyas and *Orpheus*.

OEDIPUS 'The swollen footed'. King of Thebes. Son of *Laius* (whom unwittingly murders) and *Jocasta* (whom unwittingly marries). Father of *Antigone*, *Eteocles*, Ismene and *Polynices*. Scion and forebear of a much-cursed house. Exposed as an infant by *Antimedes* at the command of *Laius*. Rescued by *Phorbas* and *Straton*. Fostered by *Polybus* and *Merope*, who raise him as their own son. Flees Corinth thinking to escape the *Pythia*'s prophecy. Fatally outwits the *Sphinx*, earning first a hero's welcome then a royal one in Thebes. Blinds and exiles himself after discovering his unnatural, prophesied crimes.

OENEUS King of Calydon. Husband of *Althaea*. Father of *Deianira* and the other *Meleagrids*, and probably of *Meleager*. His neglect of *Artemis* in favour of *Dionysus* punished by the *Calydonian Boar*.

OENOMAUS King of Pisa. Thought by some to be son of *Ares*. Husband of the *Pleiad* Sterope. Father of *Hippodamia*. Slain by *Pelops* in chariot race to win *Hippodamia*'s hand in marriage.

ORPHEUS 'The obscure'. Greatest of all musicians. Son of the *Muse* Calliope and *Apollo* (or possibly *Oeagrus*). Brother of *Linus*; half-brother of *Apollo*'s other progeny; possibly stepbrother of Marsyas. Husband of *Eurydice*. Favoured by Apollo with music lessons, a golden lyre and strings braided from the god's golden hair. Charms denizens of the underworld with his music. Fails in quest to bring *Eurydice* back to life. Joins the Argonauts. Out-sings his cousins the *Sirens*. Torn apart by the women of Thrace. Severed head serves as an oracle on Lesbos. Finally reunited in death with *Eurydice*. His golden lyre catasterized.

PALLANTIDAE The fifty sons of Pallas, brother of *Aegeus*. Cousins of *Medus* and *Theseus*, and rivals with them for the throne of Athens. Slain in battle by *Theseus*.

PELEUS Thessalian king. Son of *Aeacus* and *Chiron*'s daughter. Brother of *Telamon*. Comrade of *Heracles*. One of the Argonauts. Hunter of the *Calydonian Boar*; accidentally slays his then father-in-law *Eurytion*, whose kingdom coincidentally he inherits. Falsely accused by *Acastus*'s wife of dishonouring her. Reciprocates by persuading *Jason* to reclaim Iolcos from *Acastus*. Slayer of Amazons. Sacker of Troy. Father (by the *Nereid* Thetis) of Achilles.

PELIAS Usurper king of Iolcos. Son of *Poseidon* and *Tyro*. Brother of *Neleus*; half-brother of *Aeson* and *Pheres*, and of Poseidon's other progeny (including the *golden ram*). Father of *Acastus* and the *Peliades*. Uncle of *Nestor*; (half-)uncle of *Jason*. With *Neleus* earns *Hera*'s enmity for slaying their stepmother *Sidero*. Promises his daughter *Alcestis* to whomever harnesses a boar and a lion to a chariot. Seizes throne of Iolcos from *Aeson*. Sets *Jason* the task of recovering the Golden Fleece. Either murders, or drives to murder-suicide, *Aeson*, *Alcimede* and *Promachus* in Jason's absence. Slain by the *Peliades* in unfortunate kitchen mishap instigated by *Medea*.

PELOPS Son of Tantalus, King of Lydia, and Dione. Made a gods' dinner of by his father; then resurrected by *Zeus*.* Winner, in a chariot race, of the hand of *Hippodamia* and her father *Oenomaus*'s kingdom of Pisa. Father of *Atreus*, *Nicippe*, *Pittheus* and Thyestes (by *Hippodamia*), and *Chrysippus*. Fosters *Laius*; then curses him and his house for the death of *Chrysippus*, causing *Hera* to send the *Sphinx* to Thebes. Southern Greece known as his 'island' (*Peloponnesos*) because ruled by his progeny. Scion and forebear of much-cursed houses.

PENTHEUS King of Thebes. Son of *Agave* and *Echion* (one of the founding lords of Thebes†). Nephew of *Autonoë*, *Ino*,

---

* It was Zeus's punishment for this appalling crime that immortalized Tantalus's name. See the first volume of *Mythos* (page 263).

† See the first volume of *Mythos* (page 224).

Polydorus and *Semele*. Cousin of *Dionysus* and *Labdacus*. Grandfather of *Creon* and *Jocasta*. Scion of a much-cursed house. Torn apart by followers of *Dionysus* (including *Agave* and *Autonoë*) for failing to honour the god.

PERDIX Ingenious inventor of craftsmen's essential tools. Murdered out of jealousy by his master and uncle *Daedalus*. His spirit transformed into a partridge by *Athena*.

PERIPHETES Also known as *Corynetes*. One-eyed giant. Self-proclaimed son of *Hephaestus*. As such, possibly half-brother of *Cercyon*. No relation of the *Cyclopes*. Robber of travellers on the Isthmus. Slain by *Theseus*.

PERSEUS 'The destroyer'. Son of *Zeus* and *Danaë*. Half-brother of *Zeus*'s plethora of progeny. Saviour and husband of *Andromeda*. Father of Alcaeus, Electryon and Perses. Great-grandfather of *Heracles*. Slayer of *Acrisius, Cetus, Medusa, Phineus* and *Polydectes*. Founder king of Mycenae. Catasterized.

PHERES Former King of Pherae. Son of *Cretheus* and *Tyro*. Brother of *Aeson*; half-brother of *Neleus* and *Pelias*. Father of *Admetus*. Refuses to die so that his son becomes immortal.

PHILOCTETES Comrade of *Heracles*. One of the Argonauts. Immolates *Heracles* to end his torment from the *Lernaean Hydra*'s blood. Inherits his bow and Hydra-venom-tipped arrows.

PHINEUS Blind seer and King of Salmydessus. Brother-in-law of *Calais and Zetes*. Tormented by the *Harpies* as punishment by *Zeus* for abusing his prophetic powers. Freed from them by *Calais and Zetes*. Advises the Argonauts how to navigate the Clashing Rocks.

PHINEUS Grandson of Libya and *Poseidon*. Brother of *Aegyptus* and *Cepheus*. Slain by *Perseus*.

PHORBAS Theban shepherd. Rescues the infant *Oedipus* from exposure. Passes him to *Straton* for safekeeping.

PHRIXIDES *Argos, Cytoros, Melos* and *Phrontis*. Sons of *Phrixus* and *Chalciope*. Kinsmen of *Jason*. Flee Colchis after their grandfather *Aeëtes* threatens to kill them. Join forces with the Argonauts.

PHRIXUS Son of *Athamas* and *Nephele*. Twin brother of *Helle*. Half-brother of *Melicertes* and *Schoeneus*. Cousin of *Jason*. Rescued from his stepmother *Ino*'s murderous plot by the *golden ram*. Takes sanctuary with *Aeëtes*, to whom he presents the Golden Fleece. Husband of *Chalciope*. Father of the *Phrixides*, who implicate *Aeëtes* in his death.

PHYLEUS Son of *Augeas*. Exiled to Dulichium for admiring *Heracles*. Installed as King of Elis *by Heracles* after the latter slew *Augeas*.

PIRITHOUS King of the Lapiths. Son of *Zeus* and Dia. Stepson of *Ixion*. Half-brother of *Zeus*'s plethora of progeny. Cousin of the centaurs. One of the Argonauts. Destroyer of *Talos*. Hunter of the *Calydonian Boar*. Wedding to Hippodamia spoiled by centaurs. Bosom friend and bad influence on *Theseus*. Together, succeed in abducting *Antiope* and *Helen*; fail in abducting *Persephone*. *Heracles* unable to free from the underworld. Ultimate fate uncertain.

PITTHEUS King of Troezen. Son of *Pelops* and *Hippodamia*. Brother of *Atreus*, *Nicippe* and Thyestes; half-brother of *Chrysippus*. Scion of a much-cursed house. Father of *Aethra*. Grandfather of *Theseus*, and possibly of *Sciron* or *Sinis*.

POLYBUS King of Corinth. Childless husband of *Merope*. Together they foster *Oedipus* and raise him as if their own son. Dies of old age.

POLYDECTES King of Seriphos. Brother of *Dictys*. Enamoured of *Danaë*. Slain by *Perseus*.

POLYDORUS King of Thebes. Son of *Cadmus* and Harmonia. Brother of *Agave*, *Autonoë*, *Ino* and *Semele*. Uncle of *Dionysus*. Scion of a much-cursed house. Husband of Nycteis (aunt of

Amphion and Zethus). Father of *Labdacus*. Grandfather of *Laius*.

POLYIDUS Seer of Corinth. Reveals *Bellerophon*'s feelings for *Pegasus*.

POLYNICES Joint king of Thebes. Son of *Oedipus* and *Jocasta*. Brother of *Antigone*, *Eteocles* and Ismene. Scion of a much-cursed house. Incapable of ruling in tandem with *Eteocles*. Kill each other in battle. *Antigone* sentenced to death for trying to bury him.

POLYPHEMUS Son of the Lapith chieftain Elatus. Brother of *Caenis*. Husband of Laonome. Brother-in-law of *Heracles* and *Iphicles*. Kinsman of *Asclepius*. One of the Argonauts. Abandoned by them when searching for *Hylas*. Founds the city of Cius. Dies while trying to rejoin his former comrades.

PRIAM King of Troy. Youngest son of *Laomedon*. Brother of *Hesione*. Spared during *Heracles'* sack of Troy.

PROCRUSTES Possibly the son of *Poseidon* or the father of *Sinis*. Possible half-brother of the rest of *Poseidon*'s progeny, including *Cercyon* and *Sciron*. Robber of travellers on the Isthmus. Unlicensed practitioner of extreme osteopathy. Terminally cut down to size by (his half-brother?) *Theseus*.

PROETUS King of Mycenae. Brother of *Acrisius*. Husband of *Stheneboea*. Unwitting accomplice to her attempted revenge on *Bellerophon*.

PROMACHUS Son of *Aeson* and *Alcimede*. Brother of *Jason*. Born while his parents imprisoned by *Pelias*. Deemed too young to join the Argonauts. Either murdered by *Pelias*, or driven to murder-suicide with *Alcimede* and *Aeson* by *Pelias*, while *Jason* absent on the quest for the Golden Fleece.

RHADAMANTHUS King of Aegean islands. Son of *Zeus* and *Europa*. Half-brother of *Zeus*'s plethora of progeny. Second husband of *Alcmene*. With his brother *Minos I* and half-brother *Aeacus*, one of the three Judges of the Underworld. Charmed by the music of *Orpheus*.

SALMONEUS King of Elis. Grandson of *Hellen*. Brother of
Athamas, *Cretheus* and *Sisyphus*. Father of *Tyro*. Thunderstruck
by *Zeus* for his *hubris*.

SCHOENEUS Arcadian king. Son of *Athamas* and Themisto.
Half-brother of *Helle*, *Melicertes* and *Phrixus*. Cousin of *Jason*.
Probably husband of *Clymene* and father of *Atalanta*, whom he
exposes as an infant, then acknowledges once she is famous.

SCIRON Possibly the son of *Poseidon*, or the grandson of *Pittheus*.
Possible half-brother of *Poseidon*'s other progeny, including
Cercyon and *Procrustes*. Robber of travellers on the Isthmus and
psychopathic foot fetishist. Enjoys symbiotic relationship
with giant anthropophagous turtle. Slain by (his half-brother?
cousin?) *Theseus*.

SINIS PITYOCAMPTES Possibly the son of *Poseidon* or *Procrustes*,
or the grandson of *Pittheus*. Possible half-brother of *Poseidon*'s
other progeny, including *Cercyon*. Robber of travellers on the
Isthmus. Hoist on his own bent pinewood petard by (his
half-brother?) *Theseus*.

SISYPHUS King of Corinth. Grandson of *Hellen*. Brother of
Athamas, *Cretheus* and *Salmoneus*. Husband of the *Pleiad*
Merope. Father of *Glaucus* of Corinth; grandfather of
Bellerophon. Probably a forebear of *Creon* of Corinth.
Condemned to eternal torment in Tartarus.

STHENELUS King of Mycenae. Grandson of *Perseus* and
Andromeda. Husband of *Nicippe*. Father of *Eurystheus*. Uncle
of *Heracles*.

STRATON Corinthian shepherd. Receives the infant *Oedipus*
from *Phorbas*. Hands him to *Polybus* and *Merope* for fostering.
Later discloses to *Oedipus* vital clues as to his true identity.

TELAMON King of Salamis. Son of *Aeacus* and *Chiron*'s
daughter. Brother of *Peleus*. Comrade of *Heracles*. One of the
Argonauts. Feuds with *Calais and Zetes*. Hunter of the

Calydonian Boar. Slayer of Amazons. Sacker of Troy. Husband of Periboea and *Hesione.* Father of Ajax (by Periboea) and Teucer (by *Hesione*).

THESEUS 'The founder'. King of Athens. Son of *Aethra* and *Aegeus* and *Poseidon.* Stepson of *Medea.* Half-brother of *Poseidon*'s progeny and of *Medus.* Cousin of the *Pallantidae.* Kinsman of *Atreus* and *Heracles.* Husband of *Antiope* and *Phaedra.* Father of *Hippolytus* (by *Antiope*) and *Acamas and Demophon* (by *Phaedra*). Slayer of *Cercyon, Molpadia,* the *Pallantidae, Periphetes, Procrustes, Sciron* and *Sinis.* Expert and ruthless livestock wrangler: slaughterer (and eater) of the *Crommyonian Sow*; tamer (and sacrificer) of the *Cretan Bull*; slayer of the *Minotaur*; hunter of the *Calydonian Boar*; bane of centaurs. Smitten by *Ariadne*; then abandons her at the command of *Dionysus.* Shameful filial forgetfulness causes death of *Aegeus.* Bosom friend of *Pirithous.* Together, succeed in abducting *Antiope* and *Helen*; fail in abducting *Persephone.* Rescued from the underworld by *Heracles.* Exiled for his role in the deaths of *Hippolytus* and *Phaedra.* Killed by *Lycomedes* in a clifftop quarrel. Inventor of the *pankration* and bull-leaping; proficient in deep-sea diving. Unifier of Attica, laying the foundations of Athens's historical greatness.

THESSALUS Son of *Jason* and *Medea.* Brother of Mermerus and Pheres. Tutored by *Chiron.* Escapes maternal bloodbath that claims his brothers. Becomes ruler of Thessaly, the region named in his honour.

THESTIADES *Eurypylus, Evippus, Plexippus* and *Toxeus.* Sons of Thestios. Brothers of *Althaea,* Hypermnestra and *Leda.* Uncles of *Deianira* and *Meleager.* Hunters of the *Calydonian Boar.* Slain by *Meleager* for their hopelessly regressive sexual politics.

TIPHYS Son of Hagnias of Thespiae. Kinsman of *Augeas.* Joins the Argonauts. Helmsman of the *Argo* (succeeded by *Ancaeus*). Inventor of the sliding rowing seat. Navigates the Clashing Rocks. Succumbs to fever.

TIRESIAS Aged seer of Thebes. Father of *Historis*. Gender temporarily reassigned by *Hera*, then permanently blinded by her. Bestowed with gift of prophecy by *Zeus*. Foretells fates of *Heracles* and *Oedipus*.

TROS Founder king of Troy. Son of Dardanus. Grandson of *Zeus* and the *Pleiad* Electra. Father of *Ganymede* and Ilos. Grandfather of *Laomedon*. Recipient of magical horses from *Zeus*.

TYNDAREUS King of Sparta. Brother of *Hippocoön*. Husband of *Leda*. Father of the *Dioscuros* Castor and Clytemnestra. Ousted from his throne by *Hippocoön*; later restored to it by *Heracles*.

WOMEN

ADMETE Teenage daughter of *Eurystheus* with a passion for Amazons.

AETHRA Daughter of *Pittheus*. Briefly betrothed to *Bellerophon*. Mother of *Theseus* (by *Aegeus* and *Poseidon*). Carried off the *Dioscuri* in revenge for *Theseus*'s abduction of *Helen*. Freed after long service to *Helen* by *Acamas and Demophon*.

AGAVE Daughter of *Cadmus* and Harmonia. Sister of *Autonoë*, *Ino*, *Polydorus* and *Semele*. Aunt of *Dionysus*. Scion of a much-cursed house. Wife of Echion (one of the founding lords of Thebes). Mother of *Pentheus*. Driven mad by *Dionysus*; unwittingly helps tear apart *Pentheus*.

ALCESTIS Daughter of *Pelias*. Sister of *Acastus* and the *Peliades*. Abets her sisters in mistakenly casseroling their father. Wife of *Admetus*. Their wedding night spoiled by *Artemis*'s snakes in their bed. Willingly dies to fulfil *Apollo*'s scheme to make *Admetus* immortal. Brought back from death by *Heracles*.

ALCIMEDE Also known as *Polymede*. Granddaughter of Minyas.

Cousin of *Atalanta*. Wife of *Aeson*. Mother of *Jason* and
Promachus. Imprisoned with *Aeson* by *Pelias*. Either murdered
by *Pelias*, or driven to murder-suicide with *Aeson* and
Promachus by *Pelias*, while *Jason* absent on the quest for the
Golden Fleece.

ALCMENE Granddaughter of *Perseus* and *Andromeda*. Wife of
Amphitryon, accidental slayer of her father Electryon. Later
wife of *Rhadamanthus*. Mother of *Heracles* (by *Zeus*), and of
Iphicles and Laonome (by *Amphitryon*).

ALTHAEA Daughter of Thestios. Sister of Hypermnestra, *Leda*
and the *Thestiades*. Wife of *Oeneus*. Mother of *Meleager* (perhaps
by *Ares*) and of *Deianira* and the other *Meleagrids*. Attempts to
forestall the future foretold for *Meleager* by the *Fates*. Ends up
fulfilling the prophecy when she kills *Meleager* in revenge for
his slaying the *Thestiades*, then hangs herself out of grief.

ANDROMEDA Daughter of *Cepheus* and *Cassiopeia*. Offering to
Cetus. Rescued and married by *Perseus*. Mother of Alcaeus,
Electryon and Perses. Great-grandmother of *Heracles*.
Catasterized.

ANTIGONE Daughter of *Oedipus* and *Jocasta*. Sister of *Eteocles*,
Ismene and *Polynices*. Scion of a much-cursed house.
Accompanies *Oedipus* into exile. After his death returns to
Thebes. Sentenced to death by *Creon* for trying to bury
Polynices after he is killed fighting *Eteocles*. Hangs herself,
causing her fiancé Haemon (son of Creon) to commit suicide.

ANTIOPE Amazon princess. Daughter of *Ares*. Sister of
Hippolyta. Abducted by *Theseus* and *Pirithous*. Becomes
former's wife and mother of his son *Hippolytus*. Slain by
Amazons for betraying their way of life.

ARETE Wife (and niece) of *Alcinous*. Kind-hearted and
protective host of *Jason*, *Medea* and the Argonauts.

ARIADNE *Daughter* of *Minos II* and *Pasiphae*. Sister of *Androgeus*,
Deucalion and *Phaedra*. Half-sister of the *Minotaur*. Provides

Theseus with the key to the labyrinth. Surrendered by him to *Dionysus*. Married to *Dionysus*, mother of his children. Restored to life by him and brought to live with her mother-in-law *Semele* on Olympus. Her wedding diadem catasterized as the Corona Borealis.

ATALANTA 'The coequal'. Daughter of *Clymene* and *Schoeneus* (or possibly *Iasus*). Cousin of *Alcimede*. Possibly niece of *Ancaeus* and kinsman of *Jason*. Exposed as an infant. Fostered by a she-bear; later raised by hunters. Votary (and devastating tool) of *Artemis*. Too much of a girl, in *Jason*'s view, to be an Argonaut. Too amazing, in *Meleager*'s view, not to be a *Calydonian Boar* hunter. Awarded the trophy for slaying the boar, with fatal consequences for the *Thestiades* and *Meleager*. Resists *Schoeneus*'s efforts to marry her off, before being outsmarted by *Hippomenes*. Mother (by *Hippomenes*) of Parthenopaeus. With *Hippomenes*, punished by *Aphrodite* for ingratitude, then transformed into a lioness by *Cybele* for involuntarily profaning her temple.

AUTONOË Daughter of *Cadmus* and Harmonia. Sister of *Agave*, *Ino*, *Polydorus* and *Semele*. Aunt of *Dionysus* and *Pentheus*. Scion of a much-cursed house. Wife of *Aristaeus*. Mother of Actaeon. Driven mad by *Dionysus*; helps unwittingly tear apart *Pentheus*.

CAENIS Daughter of the Lapith chieftain Elatus. Sister of *Polyphemus*. Kinswoman of *Asclepius*. Violated by *Poseidon*. Transformed by him at her request into *Caeneus*.

CASSIOPEIA Wife of *Cepheus*. Boastful mother of *Andromeda*. Catasterized.

CHALCIOPE Daughter of *Aeëtes* and *Idyia*. Sister of *Absyrtus* and *Medea*. Wife of *Phrixus*. Mother of the *Phrixides*.

CIRCE Enchantress with a penchant for making pets out of passing sailors. Daughter of *Helios* and the *Oceanid* Perseis. Sister of *Aeëtes* and *Pasiphae*. Curses *Medea* for murdering

Absyrtus. In later traditions, member of a tragically romantic love triangle with the sea god *Glaucus* and *Scylla*.

CLITE Wife of *Cyzicus*. Hangs herself in grief after *Cyzicus* is accidentally killed by *Jason* in night-time battle with the Argonauts.

CLYMENE Daughter of Minyas. Wife of *Schoeneus* (or possibly *Iasus*). Mother of *Atalanta*, whom she allows her husband to expose as an infant.

CREUSA Daughter of *Creon* of Corinth. Attracts the amorous attentions of *Jason*, who wishes to marry her. Attracts the murderous attentions of *Medea*, who agonizingly poisons her.

DANAË Daughter of *Acrisius*. Mother (by *Zeus*) of *Perseus*. Wife of *Dictys*.

DEIANIRA Daughter of *Oeneus* and *Althaea*. Sister of the other *Meleagrids* and *Meleager*. Niece of the *Thestiades*. Cousin of the *Dioscuri*. Saved from the attentions of *Achelous* by *Heracles*, whom she marries. Mother of five of his Heraclides, including *Hyllus*. Molested by *Nessus*. Out of jealousy of *Iole*, accidentally kills *Heracles* by making him wear *Nessus*'s shirt without washing the *Lernaean Hydra* blood out first. Kills herself with *Heracles*'s sword.

ERIBOIA Athenian maiden. One of the tribute sent by *Aegeus* to the *Minotaur*. Defended from *Minos*'s lust by *Theseus*.

EUROPA Granddaughter of *Poseidon* and Libya and of *Nilus* and *Nephele*. Sister of *Cadmus*. Mother (by *Zeus*) of *Minos I* and *Rhadamanthus*.

EURYDICE Beloved wife of *Orpheus*. Killed while trying to avoid the attentions of *Aristaeus*. *Orpheus* fails in his attempt to bring her back from the dead. Finally reunited with him after his death.

EURYNOME Daughter of King Nisus of Megara. Favoured by *Athena*. Fancied by Hesiod. Wife of *Glaucus* of Corinth. Mother of *Bellerophon* and *Deliades*.

GALANTHIS Friend and attendant of *Alcmene*. Turned into a weasel by *Hera*.

HELEN Daughter of *Zeus* and *Leda*. Sister of the *Dioscuros* Polydeuces. Half-sister of the *Dioscuros* Castor and Clytemnestra, and of *Zeus*'s plethora of progeny. Abducted by *Pirithous* and *Theseus*. Rescued by the *Dioscuri*, who carry off *Aethra* to be her long-serving companion. Grows up to be a real man-killer.

HELLE Daughter of *Athamas* and *Nephele*. Twin sister of *Phrixus*. Half-sister of *Melicertes* and *Schoeneus*. Cousin of *Jason*. Rescued from her stepmother *Ino*'s murderous plot by the *golden ram*. Tumbles from his back and drowns in the strait named the *Hellespont* after her.

HESIONE Daughter of *Laomedon*. Sister of *Priam*. Offering to the Trojan Sea Monster. Rescued by *Heracles*. Spared during *Heracles*' sack of Troy and given to *Telamon*. Mother (by *Telamon*) of Teucer.

HIPPODAMIA Daughter of *Oenomaus* and the *Pleiad* Sterope. First prize in chariot race won by *Pelops*. Mother of *Atreus*, *Nicippe*, *Pittheus* and Thyestes. Forebear of a much-cursed house.

HIPPOLYTA Queen of the Amazons. Daughter of *Ares*. Sister of *Antiope*. Possessor of marvellous jewelled girdle. Lover of *Heracles* and slain by him.

HISTORIS Friend and attendant of *Alcmene*. Daughter of *Tiresias*.

HYPSIPYLE Queen of Lemnos. Thought by some to be granddaughter of *Dionysus* and *Ariadne*. Lover of *Jason*, and mother of his sons Euneus and Thoas. After discovery she had spared her father from the massacre of Lemnian menfolk, fled the island with her sons. Captured by pirates and sold into slavery.

INO Daughter of *Cadmus* and Harmonia. Sister of *Agave*, *Autonoë*, *Polydorus* and *Semele*. Scion of a much-cursed house.

Suckler of her infant nephew *Dionysus*. Wife of *Athamas*. Mother of Learchus and *Melicertes*. Attempts to murder her stepchildren *Phrixus* and *Helle*. Commits suicide. Transformed by *Dionysus* into the sea goddess *Leucothea*.

Io   First mortal woman beloved by *Zeus*. Transformed by him into a cow. Persecuted by the gadfly of *Hera*. Gives name to the Bosporus (Cow-Crossing).

IOLE   Daughter of *Eurytus*. Sister of *Iphitus*. First prize in an archery contest. Forbidden from marrying *Heracles*. Later enslaved by *Heracles*, igniting *Deianira*'s fatal jealousy.

JOCASTA   Granddaughter of *Pentheus*. Sister of *Creon*. Scion and forebear of a much-cursed house. Wife of *Laius* and (unwittingly) *Oedipus*. Mother (by *Laius*) of *Oedipus*, and (by *Oedipus*) of *Antigone*, *Eteocles*, Ismene and *Polyneices*.

LEDA   Daughter of Thestios. Sister of *Althaea*, Hypermnestra and the *Thestiades*. Wife of *Tyndareus*. Mother (by *Tyndareus*) of the *Dioscuros* Castor and Clytemnestra, and (by *Zeus*) of the *Dioscuros* Polydeuces and *Helen*.

MEDEA   Enchantress. Daughter of *Aeëtes* and *Idyia*. Granddaughter of *Helios*. Sister of *Absyrtus* and *Chalciope*. Mother (by *Jason*) of Mermerus, Pheres and *Thessalus*. Wife of *Aegeus*; mother (by him) of *Medus*; stepmother of *Theseus*. Devotee of *Hecate*. As punishment for neglecting *Aphrodite* struck with desire for *Jason*. Magically aids *Jason* to tame the *Khalkotauroi*, defeat the Spartoi, overpower the *Colchian Dragon* and take the Golden Fleece. Dismembers *Absyrtus* to delay *Aeëtes*' of the Argonauts. Cursed by *Circe*. Mesmerizes *Talos*. Tricks the *Peliades* into killing *Pelias*. Takes refuge with *Jason* in Corinth. In jealous rage kills *Creon* of Corinth, *Creusa*, Mermerus and Pheres. Escapes retribution in *Helios*'s chariot. Takes refuge in Athens. Fails to secure the Athenian succession on *Medus*. Makes her escape in *Helios*'s chariot again. Believed to have returned to Colchis.

MEGARA Daughter of *Creon* of Thebes. Wife of *Heracles*. Killed, along with her children, by him in fit of delusive rage. His Labours expiation for this crime.

MELEAGRIDS *Deianira, Eurymede, Gorge, Melanippe, Mothone* and *Perimede*. Daughters of *Oeneus* and *Althaea*. Sisters of *Meleager*. Except for *Deianira* and Gorge, transformed into guinea fowl by *Artemis*.

MEROPE Queen of Corinth. Childless wife of *Polybus*. Together they foster *Oedipus* and raise him as if their own son. After *Polybus*'s death, sends *Straton* to offer *Oedipus* the throne of Corinth.

MOLPADIA Amazon. Merciful slayer of *Antiope*. Mercilessly slain by *Theseus*.

NICIPPE Daughter of *Pelops* and *Hippodamia*. Sister of *Atreus*, *Pittheus* and Thyestes; half-sister of *Chrysippus*. Scion of a much-cursed house. Wife of *Sthenelus*. Mother of *Eurystheus*.

OMPHALE Queen of Lydia. Widow of the mountain god Tmolus. Served by *Heracles* in expiation of his murder of *Iphitus*. Cross-dresser with, and lover of, *Heracles*.

PASIPHAE Daughter of *Helios* and the *Oceanid* Perseis. Sister of *Aeëtes* and *Circe*. Wife of *Minos II*. Mother by him of *Androgeus*, *Ariadne, Deucalion* and *Phaedra*. Enamoured of the *Cretan Bull*. Mother by him of the *Minotaur*.

PELIADES *Alcestis, Alcimede, Antinoë, Asteropeia, Evadne, Hippothoë, Medusa, Pelopia* and *Pisidice*. Gullible but doting daughters of *Pelias*. Tricked by *Medea* into casseroling their father.

PHAEDRA *Daughter* of *Minos II* and *Pasiphae*. Sister of *Androgeus*, *Ariadne* and *Deucalion*. Half-sister of the *Minotaur*. Wife of *Theseus*. Mother of *Acamas and Demophon*. Driven mad (by *Aphrodite*) with desire for her stepson *Hippolytus*; then madder with revenge when rejected. Kills herself after actions lead to death of *Hippolytus*.

PHILONOË Daughter of *Iobates*. Sister of *Stheneboea*. Develops crush on *Bellerophon*; later his wife.

PYTHIA Also known as the *Sibyl*. Priestess and oracle of Apollo at Delphi: riddling but always right in the end. Consulted by *Acrisius, Aegeus, Creon, Heracles, Laius, Oedipus, Oenomaus, Perseus*. Falsified by *Ino* and *Pelias*.

SEMELE Daughter of *Cadmus* and Harmonia. Sister of *Agave, Autonoë* and *Ino*. Mother (by *Zeus*) of *Dionysus*. Scion of a much-cursed house. Slain (explosively) by *Zeus*. Restored to life by *Dionysus* and brought to live with her daughter-in-law *Ariadne* on Olympus.

SIDERO Second wife of *Cretheus*. Stepmother of *Neleus* and *Pelias* and of *Aeson* and *Pheres*. Killed by *Neleus* and *Pelias* for mistreating their mother *Tyro*.

STHENEBOEA Also known as *Anteia*. Daughter of *Iobates*. Sister of *Philonoë*. Wife of *Proetus*. Seeks revenge on *Bellerophon* for rejecting her advances. Kills herself out of fear of exposure after plot fails.

THEOPHANE Daughter of Bisaltes. Granddaughter of *Gaia* and *Helios*. Mother (by *Poseidon*) of the *golden ram*.

TYRO Daughter of *Salmoneus*. Wife of her uncles *Cretheus* and *Sisyphus*. Mother of *Neleus* and *Pelias* (by *Poseidon*), and of *Aeson* and *Pheres* (by *Cretheus*).

ACKNOWLEDGEMENTS

I have first to thank Tim Carroll, the Artistic Director of the Shaw Festival Theatre in Niagara-on-the-Lake, Ontario, Canada. We first became friends in 2013 when he directed me in a production of *Twelfth Night* in London and New York. Aside from being a distinguished and acclaimed theatre director, Tim Carroll is a man who reads Homer in the original Greek for pleasure. He was naturally the first person I thought of as a collaborator when I hit upon the idea of presenting on stage *Mythos*, the book on Greek myths I had written in 2017. We met and talked and somehow out of our discussions came the notion of not one show, but three. The first would cover the same ground as *Mythos* (the primordial deities and Titans, the birth of the gods, the creation of mankind and some of the earlier myths in which gods and mortals mingle), the second would be dedicated to the Heroes (the book you have now in your hand, on your screen or in your ears) and the third would follow the story of the Trojan War and its aftermath.

We presented the *Mythos* trilogy at the Shaw Theatre in Niagara-on-the-Lake in the early summer of 2018. The heroes who featured in the second show were Perseus, Heracles and Theseus. For this book I have added Bellerophon, Jason, Atalanta, Orpheus and Oedipus.

I owe Tim a huge amount: his instinctive, intelligent and imaginative grasp of story-telling, chronology and point-of-view taught me a great deal about theatrical narrative. Much of what I learnt from him has found its way, one way or another, into the book. Naturally he cannot be held accountable for infelicities, but you may take it on trust that his benign influence has helped the book enormously and for that and for his friendship, wisdom, wit and breathtaking cacolalia, I thank him.

Other thanks go to all at Michael Joseph, the imprint of Penguin Random House that publishes my books, and most especially Managing Director Louise Moore and editor Jillian Taylor. Without their warmth and passion, enthusiasm and encouragement, diligence and support this book could never have been come into being. Particularly deserving of thanks and acknowledgement is the brilliant and wise Kit Shepherd, copy-editor of this book and its predecessor. His knowledge and fearsome eye for narrative inconsistency have been of immeasurable value. If there are chronological, source or historical errors here, they exist because I have chosen to ignore or override his suggestions for the sake of my own wild preferences.

A special word of thanks to Roy McMillan, the director, actor, producer and sound engineer who makes the recording of audiobooks so pleasurable. His deep knowledge, patience and surefire instincts are beyond price.

Anthony Goff of David Higham Associates brings authors and publishers together in amity and mutual respect like no other literary agent and I always benefit from his wisdom and experience.

Nothing can happen in my life without the wonderful work of Jo Crocker who knows me better than I know myself.

And of course I owe all things always to my beloved husband and hero of heroes, Elliott.

PICTURE CREDITS

SECTION ONE

1. *Olympus.* Iliad Room, Palazzo Pitti (fresco), Luigi Sabatelli. De Agostini Picture Library / Bridgeman.

2. *Prometheus Bound*, Peter Paul Rubens, c.1611–18. Philadelphia Museum of Art, Pennsylvania, PA, USA / Purchased with the W. P. Wilstach Fund, 1950 / Alamy.

3. *Danaë*, 1907–8, Gustav Klimt. Galerie Wurthle, Vienna, Austria / Bridgeman.

4. *Danaë and Baby Perseus being Rescued by Corsali in Serifo Island*, Jacques Berger, 1806. De Agostini Picture Library / Bridgeman.

5. *Perseus*, Jacques-Clément Wagrez, 1879. Peter Horree / Alamy.

6. *Medusa*, painted on a leather jousting shield, Caravaggio, c.1596–98. Galleria degli Uffizi, Florence, Tuscany, Italy / Bridgeman.

7. *Perseus and Andromeda*, Carle van Loo, seventeenth century. State Hermitage, St Petersburg / Alamy.

8. *Young boy portrayed as Heracles choking the snakes* (marble), Roman, (second century AD). Musei Capitolini, Rome, Italy / Heritage Image Partnership / Alamy.

9. *The Origin of the Milky Way*, 1575, Jacopo Tintoretto. National Gallery / Alamy.

10. *Heracles and the Nemean Lion*, Pieter Paul Rubens. Historic Collection / Alamy.

11. Athenian Attic black-figure amphora with Heracles carrying the Erymanthean Boar, c.510 BC. J. Paul Getty Museum, Los Angeles, USA / Alamy.

12. *Amazonomachy*, first century BC, clay with polychrome remains. Campana collection, Italy / Alamy.

13. *Heracles*, Attic *Kylix* in the style of Douris, c.480 BC. Vulci, Papal Government – Vincenzo Campanari excavations, 1835–1837 / Vatican Museums.

14. *The Garden of the Hesperides*, c.1892. Frederic Leighton. Lady Lever Art Gallery / Alamy.

15. *Zeus Striking the Rebelling Giants (the Fall of Giants)* in The Hall of Jupiter, 1530-33 (fresco). Perino del Vaga. Villa del Principe, Italy / Ghigo Roli / Bridgeman.

16. *Winged horse Pegasus, ridden by Greek mythological hero Bellerophon.* Official symbol of the Parachute Regiment / Alamy.

17. *Orpheus before Pluto (Hades) and Persephone*, Francois Perrier, seventeenth century. Louvre, Paris, France / Bridgeman.

18. *Orpheus and Eurydice*, Enrico Scuri, nineteenth century. De Agostini Picture Library / A. Dagli Orti / Bridgeman.

SECTION TWO

1. *Priestess of Delphi*, John Collier, 1891. Art Gallery of South Australia, Adelaide / Alamy.

2. *Hylas and the Nymphs*, 1896, John William Waterhouse. Manchester Art Gallery, UK / Alamy.

3. *Jason and the Argonauts Sail Through the Symplegades* (Clashing Rocks). Engraving depicting Jason and the Argonauts from 'Tableaux du temple des muses' (1655). Almay.

4. *Jason Taming the Bulls of Aeëtes*, 1742, Jean Francois de Troy. The Henry Barber Trust, The Barber Institute of Fine Arts, University of Birmingham, UK / Bridgeman.

5. *Medea*, Anthony Frederick Augustus Sandys, nineteenth century. Birmingham Museums and Art Gallery, UK / Bridgeman.

6. *Medea Putting the Dragon guarding the Golden Fleece to Sleep*, Spanish School, nineteenth century. Private Collection / © Look and Learn / Bridgeman.

7. *And plunged them deep within the locks of gold* (pen and ink on paper), Maxwell Ashby Armfield, Illustration for 'Life & Death of Jason' by William Morris. Private Collection / Bridgeman.

8. *The Calydonian Boar Hunt*, 1617, Peter Paul Rubens. Kunsthistorisches Museum, Vienna / Alamy.

9. *Atalanta and Hippomenes*, c.1612, Guido Reni. Prado, Madrid, Spain / Bridgeman.

10. *Oedipus and the Sphinx*, 1864, Gustave Moreau. Metropolitan Museum of Art, New York, USA / Alamy.

11. Red-figured *Kylix*, depicting the deeds of the hero Theseus, made in Athens. Dated fifth century BC. British Museum / Alamy.

12. *Theseus Taming the Bull of Marathon*, 1745, Charles-André van Loo. Los Angeles County Museum of Art / Alamy.

13. *The Toreador Fresco*, Knossos Palace, Crete, c.1500 BC (fresco) / National Archaeological Museum, Athens, Greece / Bridgeman.

14. *The Tribute to the Minotaur*, woodcut engraving from the original painting by Auguste Gendron, 1882. Glasshouse Images / Alamy.

15. *The Legend of Theseus with a Detail of the Cretan Labyrinth* (engraving), sixteenth century. Private Collection / Bridgeman.

16. Attic bilingual eye-cup with black-figure interior depicting running minotaur and inscription reading 'the boy is beautiful'. Werner Forman Archive / Bridgeman.

17. *Landscape with Fall of Icarus*, Carlo Saraceni, 1606–7. Museo di Capodimonte, Naples, Campania, Italy / Mondadori Portfolio/Electa/Sergio Anelli / Bridgeman.

18. *Ariadne in Naxos*, 1925–26 (tempera on handwoven linen), Joseph Southall. Birmingham Museums and Art Gallery, UK / Bridgeman.

19. Statue of Theseus, Athens. © Sotiris Tsagariolos / Alamy.

INDEX

Abdera (city), 87

Abderus, son of Hermes, 86–7

Abraham, 189n

Absyrtus, 233, 234, 241, 246, 251

Acamas, 400

Acastus, 265–6, 270

Achelous, river god, 127–8

Achilles, 205, 265, 402

Acrisius, king of *Argos*, 9, 10–11, 41–2

Actaeon, 59n

Admete, daughter of Eurystheus, 88, 94

Admetus, king of Pherae, 79–86, 281

Adonis, 256n

Aeacus, 174

Aeaea (island), 254–5

Aeëtes, king of Colchis: and the Golden Fleece, 190, 202, 231; receives Jason and the Argonauts, 232–7; sets Jason tasks to win the Fleece, 240–5; pursues Jason and the Argonauts, 250–1

Aegean Sea, 394

Aegeus, king of Athens: and the birth of Theseus, 332–5; receives Theseus in Athens, 353–6; sends Theseus to kill the Marathonian Bull, 356–8; recognizes Theseus as his son,

360; and the Athenian tribute to King Minos, 360–71; casts himself into the sea, 393–4

Aegis (shield), 24, 31

Aegyptus, 36–7, 103

Aello, 219n

Aeolia, 192–3

Aeolus, 208

Aeschylus: *Seven Against Thebes*, 323; lost plays of, 322–3, 323n

Aeson (father of Jason), 192, 199, 207, 263

Aethra (mother of Theseus), 147, 329–36, 400n

Agamemnon, 123

Agave, 186, 297

Aia (city), 232, 234

Ajax, 205

Alcestis, 79, 83–6, 264

Alcides *see* Heracles

Alcimede (mother of Jason), 192, 207, 263

Alcimede (one of the Peliades), 264

Alcinous, king of the Phaeacians, 258–60

Alcmene: impregnated by Zeus, 48–50; gives birth to Heracles (Alcides) and Iphicles, 53–4; consults Tiresias, 56–7

Alcon, 284–5

Alcyone, 128

Alcyoneus, 124, 125–6

Deucalion, king of Crete, 400
Dictys, 12–13, 18–19, 39–40
Dike (Justice), 105n
Dino (one of the Graeae), 28–9
Dinos (horse), 86
Diomedes, king of Thrace, 78, 87
Dionysus: born of Semele and
    Zeus, 186, 297; and the
    Thracian women, 180;
    transforms Ino into Leucothea,
    191; and Ariadne, 386–7
Dioscuri (Castor and Polydeuces),
    59n, 205, 400
Dodona, oracle of, 20–1, 203
Dolionians, 212–13
Doris (Oceanid), 101n
Dulichium, 75

Echidna, 3, 96, 100, 113, 154, 172,
    190n, 407
Eileithyia, goddess of childbirth,
    51, 51n, 53–4
Electryon, 48
Eleusinian Mysteries, 113–14
Elis, kingdom of, 74–5, 122, 123
Elysian Fields, 172n
Enaesimus, 284
Enceladus (giant), 127
Enyo (one of the Graeae), 28–30
Eos, 81
Erebus, god of darkness, 100
Erginos, king of Orchomenos,
    60, 273n
Eridanus (river), 101
Erinyes see Furies
Eros, god of desire, 239, 240
Erotes, 169
Erymanthus, Mount, 71
Erytheia, 94–5

Eryx, 256n
Eteocles, 310, 323–4
Ethiopia, 35
Etna, Mount, 257
Euhemerism, 410
Euinos (river), 129
Eumolpus, 58, 114
Euneus, 210, 212
Euphemus, 206, 225, 249, 261
Euripides: *Alcestis*, 83n; *The
    Bacchae*, 186n; *Heracleidae*, 330n;
    Hippolytus, 401n; *Medea*, 269–
    70; *Phoenician Women*, 323; lost
    plays of, 298n, 323, 323n
Europa, 50, 365
Euryale, a Gorgon, 17, 25, 33
Eurydice (wife of Creon, king of
    Thebes), 324
Eurydice (wife of Orpheus),
    168–70, 175, 177–9
Euryganeia, 323
Eurymede, 278, 289
Eurymedon, king of the giants, 126
Eurynome, 139, 142, 146
Eurypylus, 278–9, 286
Eurystheus, king of Mycenae:
    birth, 52–3; and the Labours of
    Heracles, 62–3, 64–5, 66–7, 69,
    71, 77, 87, 94, 98–100, 112; leaps
    into a stone jar for fear, 73, 117;
    defeated and killed by the
    Heraclides, 133
Eurytion (centaur), 396
Eurytion (giant), 95, 97
Euryton, king of Phthia, 284
Eurytus (one of the Molionides),
    122
Eurytus, king of Oechalia, 58,
    118–19, 121, 130

Heracles: sails on the *Argo*, 205, 210, 213, 214–17; kills Eryx, son of Butes, 256n; inspires the young Theseus, 330; birth, and named as Alcides, 54; strangles snakes in his cot, 55; name changed from Alcides to Heracles, 57; childhood and education, 57–8; slays his tutor Linus, 58; slays a lion on Mount Cithaeron, 59–60; defends Thebes from King Erginos of Orchomenos, 60, 273n; kills his own wife and children, 61; seeks to expiate blood crime, 61–3; First Labour: the Nemean Lion, 64–6; Second Labour: the Lernaean Hydra, 66–9; Third Labour: the Ceryneian Hind, 69–71; Fourth Labour: the Erymanthian Boar, 71–3; Fifth Labour: the Augean Stables, 74–6; Sixth Labour: the Stymphalian Birds, 76; Seventh Labour: the Cretan Bull, 77–8; Eighth Labour: the Mares of Diomedes, 78–9, 86–7; saves Alcestis from death, 84–6; Ninth Labour: the girdle of Hippolyta, 88–94; Tenth Labour: the cattle of Geryon, 94–100; Eleventh Labour: the golden apples of the Hesperides, 100–12; kills Antaeus in wrestling match, 102–3; rescues Prometheus from the rock, 104–5; Twelfth Labour: Cerberus, 112–18; kills

Iphitus, son of Eurytus, 119; consults the oracle at Delphi for expiation, 120; enslaved to Queen Omphale of Lydia, 121; exacts vengeance on Laomedon of Troy, 122; takes revenge on Augeas of Elis, 122–3; establishes Olympic Games, 123; attacks kingdom of Pylos, 123; kills Hippocoön and installs Tyndareus as king of Sparta, 123–4; saves the Olympians from the giants, 125–7; marries Deianira, 127–8; defeats Achelous and receives the horn of plenty, 128; kills Eurytus and takes Iole as slave, 130; poisoned by the Hydra poison, 131; death on his funeral pyre, 131–2; achieves immortality and divine status, 133; heroic status and characteristics, 134–5; rages of, 407–408

Heraclides (sons of Heracles), 133

Heraklion, 262

Hercules (constellation), 133

Hermes: assists Perseus in his search for Medusa, 21–6; takes Heracles to feed on Hera's milk, 56; presents Heracles with a sword, 59; assists Heracles in the underworld, 114–18, 116

herms (hermai), 40n

Herodotus, 121n

Hesiod (poet), 139n, 409

Hesione, daughter of Laomedon, 93–4, 122